ROUTLEDGE LIBRARY EDITIONS:
DEVELOPMENT

MONEY AND FINANCE IN AFRICA

AF695028

MONEY AND FINANCE IN AFRICA

The Experience of Ghana, Morocco, Nigeria, the Rhodesias and Nyasaland, the Sudan, and Tunisia. From the Establishment of Their Central Banks Until 1962

ERIN E. JUCKER-FLEETWOOD

Volume 33

Routledge
Taylor & Francis Group
LONDON AND NEW YORK

First published in 1964

This edition first published in 2011
by Routledge
2 Park Square, Milton Park, Abingdon, Oxon, OX14 4RN

Simultaneously published in the USA and Canada
by Routledge
711 Third Avenue, New York, NY 10017

Routledge is an imprint of the Taylor & Francis Group, an informa business

First issued in paperback 2013

© 1964 George Allen & Unwin Ltd

All rights reserved. No part of this book may be reprinted or reproduced or utilised in any form or by any electronic, mechanical, or other means, now known or hereafter invented, including photocopying and recording, or in any information storage or retrieval system, without permission in writing from the publishers.

British Library Cataloguing in Publication Data
A catalogue record for this book is available from the British Library

ISBN 13: 978-0-415-58414-2 (Set)
ISBN 13: 978-0-415-59571-1 (hardback Volume 33)
ISBN 13: 978-0-415-84961-6 (paperback Volume 33)

Publisher's Note
The publisher has gone to great lengths to ensure the quality of this reprint but points out that some imperfections in the original copies may be apparent.

Disclaimer
The publisher has made every effort to trace copyright holders and welcomes correspondence from those they have been unable to contact.

MONEY AND FINANCE IN AFRICA

The Experience of Ghana, Morocco
Nigeria, the Rhodesias and Nyasaland
the Sudan, and Tunisia
From the Establishment of Their Central Banks
Until 1962

BY

ERIN E. JUCKER-FLEETWOOD

London

GEORGE ALLEN & UNWIN LTD

RUSKIN HOUSE · MUSEUM STREET

First published in 1964

This Book is copyright under the Berne Convention. Apart from any fair dealing for the purpose of private study, research, criticism or review, as permitted under the Copyright Act, 1956, *no portion may be reproduced by any process without written permission. Inquiry should be made to the publisher.*

© *George Allen and Unwin Ltd*, 1964

To my children
Peter and Karin Fleetwood

PREFACE

This book is a study of the monetary and financial problems of emerging countries in Africa. In order to be able to investigate actual conditions and avoid unfounded generalities, it was necessary to choose, already in 1960, the countries to be examined. The prerequisite was that each had a Central Bank, an internal banking system and an independent financial structure. On this basis Ghana, Morocco, Nigeria, the Rhodesias and Nyasaland, the Sudan and Tunisia were selected in the hope that they would also represent the varied and often contrasting conditions of the continent of Africa.

Each of these countries has been visited by one or more of the Basle Centre staff at least once (except for the Rhodesias and Nyasaland). On these visits we have had the privilege of help from the Governors of the Central Banks and their staffs, the Ministries of Finance, the Commercial Banks, Development Banks and/or Corporations, the Central Bureaux of Statistics: also from innumerable public and private institutions and companies as well as a large number of officials and private persons. Without this generous assistance this book could never have been written. We stand, however, indebted to them for more than economic and financial information. Many of them went out of their way to demonstrate and explain the individuality of their countries; thus giving us the background knowledge, which no economist can afford to disregard. In the process, lasting and valued friendships were made.

The Author and her collaborators are also grateful for information from institutions and private companies with interests in Africa, but located in London, New York, Paris, Washington and Switzerland. Moreover, the staffs of the International Monetary Fund, the International Bank for Reconstruction and Development, the Economic Commission for Africa and the Organisation for Economic Co-operation and Development have encouraged the project.

The whole undertaking would not have been possible if it had not been for the financial support given by the Ford Foundation, New York. Furthermore, it was Mr Joseph E. Slater, of the Ford Foundation, who suggested that the monetary and financial specialization of the Basle Centre could usefully be applied to African problems, thus opening up a new and fascinating field of research. The Basle Centre has also received financial assistance for this project from several other sources, which prefer to remain anonymous. To all of them we offer our very real thanks.

The Author has had the collaboration of Monsieur Jean-Pierre Gern, now of Washington D.C., who specialized in Morocco and Tunisia and to some extent on Rhodesia. Moreover, Messrs Elyseo

J. Taylor, Kurt Spinnler, Kurt Dill and Frederic Probst have assisted with statistics and diagrams, while Miss Ursula Kremers has proved to be a secretary whose interest in the study put her on a par with the research assistants.

The Author's colleagues in the Basle Centre, Professor Gottfried Bombach of Basle University and Dr Walter S. Schiess, Treasurer to the Basle Centre, have always been ready to discuss and deal with any problems that have arisen in their own spheres. The late Per Jacobsson, Director of the Basle Centre and Chairman of the Board and Managing Director of the International Monetary Fund, acted as a benevolent godfather to the project.

While deeply grateful for all the help and assistance received, the Author wishes to stress that she alone has the responsibility for the analyses, interpretations and opinions expressed.

ERIN E. JUCKER-FLEETWOOD

Basle, October 1963.

NOTE ON STATISTICS

When this study was started in 1960 the countries Ghana, Morocco, Nigeria, the Rhodesias and Nyasaland, the Sudan and Tunisia were selected as its object partly because their statistics were comparatively good. During the intervening three years the countries themselves, the International Monetary Fund, the United Nations and the Economic Commission for Africa have greatly enlarged the scope and accuracy of the statistical information on Africa in general and these countries in particular. The new statistics have, where feasible, been substituted for the estimates made during the initial phases of the study.

In spite of the improvement in information it is inevitable that the statistics of the different countries are not always strictly comparable. As far as possible discrepancies have been indicated. The varying economic relevance should be clear from the text.

CONTENTS

TABLES

ILLUSTRATIONS AND GRAPHS

PART ONE

'Economic growth can be compared with the construction of a good house, with stability as its foundations. A good house can only be erected on solid foundations. Preparing the foundation, however, is not sufficient. There must be further initiative and activity and the necessary resources must be acquired to complete the building . . . for these efforts to be effective they have often to be supplemented by international assistance, technical and financial . . . monetary stability is often only the beginning of the efforts needed to achieve growth.'[1]

PER JACOBSSON
Vienna, 1961

[1] Address by the Managing Director of the International Monetary Fund. Summary Proceedings, International Monetary Fund, Sixteenth Annual Meeting 1961, Washington, 1962, pp. 30–1.

CHAPTER I

MONEY, FINANCE AND GROWTH

During the last fifteen years the theory of economic growth to hasten development has been one of the main topics of discussion. This theory has focused chiefly on certain central concepts such as balanced or unbalanced growth, the role played by the capital coefficient, the possibilities of the substitution of the factors of production and the parallel development of legal, social, educational and administrative sectors. Generally very little attention has been paid by the theoreticians to monetary and financial problems except some discussion of the role that a 'moderate' inflation might play as a means of encouraging or hindering economic growth. The numerous other aspects of the interrelation of the monetary and financial system with economic growth have been largely neglected. It is the purpose of this introductory chapter to stress some of these relations in an attempt to give a somewhat wider background to the study of monetary and financial problems in Africa.

It is important to state from the beginning that an essential condition for economic growth is the establishment of a workable monetary system including the basic fundamentals of a credit system. This is particularly obvious in countries which, until recently, have not developed a money economy so that the population in some sectors still uses mainly barter and money substitutes. While in such conditions some small degree of economic change is not impossible, it is necessarily restricted to specific local projects which need only the labour and raw materials available on the spot. While these may be of great importance to the local population, economic growth as envisaged today by the governments of the developing countries cannot possibly be based on a barter economy. It is only through the presence of money that the necessary transmutation can be brought about.

The first reason why a monetary system is needed is that the governments as well as individuals, need a flow of income and savings which can be used for any desired purpose. It is essential that there should be a free choice as to how income is to be spent and savings invested. The various attempts made to allow the payment of local taxes in natura have shown that the goods in which payments were made could not be mobilized for the purpose they were intended, and efforts have been made to replace these payments by systems of monetary taxation. It is evident that the free command of commodities and services of all kinds can only be achieved today by means of monetary demand.

A second reason why a monetary system is necessary is that it allows the formation of a price structure, where the individual prices normally correspond more or less to the supply and demand for the commodity in question. Where transport and communication are poor, market imperfections may lead to an important distortion of the price structure, but with the development of a monetary economy such conditions are gradually disappearing. The price structure in any given country is, as a matter of fact, used as a guidance for economic activity, whether this activity be along the lines of a planned economy or *laissez faire* or a judicious mixture of the two. Price movements are important both for the private and the public sectors, that is for the calculation of the cost of any single project or of a full-scale development plan. Even when a development plan has been based on an attempt to calculate estimated (shadow) or what may be called accounting prices, the actual prices prevailing at the time of departure have to be taken as the basis for the whole programme. It is therefore impossible for any rational economic activity to be carried on without regard to prevailing and relative prices and these are only obtained in a proper monetary system.

It is clear that the existence of money alone does not suffice to secure a free choice in spending and investment and the formation of general market prices. Modern economic development requires some additional facilities and these are to be found in the credit system.

One of the most important characteristics of the credit system is the flexibility it bestows on the payments structure, and in that way on the economy. There are here two aspects to this question. On the one hand, the credit system through banks and other financial institutions collects liquid funds currently not in use and places them through its lending activity at the disposal of persons, institutions and maybe governments in need of liquid funds to effect payments of different kinds. On the other hand, commercial banks are in a position to 'create credit'. Their capacity to do so is based on their experience of what proportion of reserves to commitments they can safely carry and there is thus a definite limit to the amount of credit that can be created. Such credit may be placed by the commercial banks at the disposal of the economy, over and above the amount representing the transfer of liquid funds.

The flexibility of the banking system makes it possible for the system to tackle the problem of financing seasonal needs, e.g. of crops (sometimes with the help of foreign funds) and of advancing prefinance as well as working capital for profitable, i.e. self-liquidating enterprises of all kinds. In fact, the transfer of liquid funds to prospective investors is, in most developing countries, the most important function of the commercial banks and other financial agencies and intermediaries. If the funds on current account are not invested in the country in which they have accumulated, but are left idle or are exported, the result is a depressive effect on the economy. However, the commercial banks and other intermediaries sometimes have difficulty in finding suitable investments in a country which is at the very start of economic development; a vicious circle may easily result. Such a circle may be broken by the creation of suitable domestic instruments of investment, Treasury Bills, government stock, etc. Measures of that kind are usually timed to coincide with an effort at economic expansion which, if successful, should create a demand for credit for suitable investment projects. The creation of new instruments usually marks the start of a domestic monetary policy, a step which seldom is taken before a central bank is established.

The establishment of a central bank is usually regarded as the outward symbol of attaining 'monetary independence'. In fact, it is more than a symbol. In a country which is of such a size and importance that it can confidently expect (at some future date) to have a domestic market significantly larger than the export sector of the economy, there seems to be a good case for the establishment of a central bank. The central bank should become the focal point of the domestic monetary system. It can attain this position by effectively contributing to the development of the monetary and credit system, by the control it establishes over monetary matters and by the roles it may fill as an adviser to the government in financial matters at least when these matters affect the monetary affairs of the country—as they usually do.

The contribution of the central banks to the formation of other financial intermediaries is, however, a task which has a wider impact than simply putting the monetary and credit system at the disposal of the economy. It is often assumed that the very existence of suitably chosen financial intermediaries can stimulate economic activity in spheres which previously had been deficient or lacking. Thus the creation of Development Banks is supposed to contribute actively to the starting of new industries, the establishment of Agricultural Banks to the reform of agriculture, the establishment of Savings Banks and Stock Exchanges to the accumulation of savings and the formation of risk capital. The assumption behind this argument is often correct provided that the institutions in question have an active, creative policy. Moreover, the institutions selected for establishment must correspond to the stage of growth reached by the economy, i.e.

they must be well timed and must harmonize with the future needs of the economy in question.

A deliberate policy of planning the establishment of monetary institutions is compatible both with a planned or a *laissez faire* economy or any mixture of the two. In practice most countries have a certain degree of planning; official development plans are usually drawn up to cover several years to come. These plans are essentially target plans; they attempt to channel the available resources in manpower, capital, raw materials and administrative features to the sector or sectors which are most in need of such resources, and where therefore, the return is highest in view of the desire to achieve fast economic growth.

In practice, some kind of balanced growth is usually aimed at, both in the relations between the sectors and within each sector. Not only is it economically necessary to develop, e.g. agriculture (to ensure home-grown food) parallel with industry, education and infrastructure, but it is usually the only politically feasible policy. Balanced growth implies maintaining over time a certain degree of expansion in each sector of the economy. The growth of the economy would then be similar to the growth of a crystal, the facet in question receiving continuously exactly the deposit needed for perfect formation. But in actual life this cannot generally be realized. In fact, advantage can be gained both from balanced and from unbalanced growth. Because minimum 'economic' investments are of a certain size, and because resources, human, technical as well as financial are limited, there is often one year an 'over-investment', maybe in infrastructure, while another year a preponderance of investment will occur in the field of either agriculture, commerce or industry. Thus, a zigzag pattern of investment will develop so that balance between the different sectors is not achieved every year. In practice, the unbalanced state of the economy will probably give an impetus to 'unplanned' investment in the private sphere, provided there are sufficient resources, both real and financial, at its disposal, i.e. that they have not all been appropriated by the government. Over a given period of say five or ten years sufficient investment in all sectors of the economy could be achieved so as to attain a reasonably balanced economic growth.

The encouragement of a large and vigorous private sector in both agriculture and industry is one of the guarantees of fast economic growth. The private investor cannot afford to start enterprises that do not promise to be profitable. Thus, he must make sure that efficient production is realized in the shortest possible time (and it is therefore essential that the legal and institutional framework should not act as a deterrent); and the most profitable production assures the fastest growth. Moreover, the private sector should be able to operate with units of enterprise which are not more than medium size, and thus give a variety to the structure of production, a variety which should help to induce (especially vertical) balance within the industrial sphere. This is the more important since medium sized and small industry can often be established relatively easily and can thus respond with 'induced' investment to the bottlenecks which even the best plans cannot eliminate. The private sector should be able to assist in the domestic production of goods and savings needed to satisfy the (multiplier) demand arising out of other investment projects. On the whole, such activities should contribute towards securing sufficient goods on the market. Failing the proper kind of domestic production, the demand for the goods in question might lead to increased imports and thus affect the balance of payments.

The other aim of the central bank in particular and of the financial authorities in general should be to maintain a stable value of the currency without hampering growth. This means that the internal purchasing power must be adequately controlled. If internal purchasing power is accumulated in any sector or sectors where it is not saved, there is the danger of pressure on the balance of payments, sometimes even leading to a crisis. Such a crisis would have been internally induced and would not be due, for instance, to external factors such as a fall in raw material prices. In either case the country can turn to the International Monetary Fund for financial assistance, while concrete measures are taken—but these measures have generally to be radical when there has been a period of financial laxity with an overdose of domestic purchasing power.

One of the purposes of preparing and approving a development plan is to obtain an idea of the financial costs as set out in the budget of the plan specifying the cost of each item of investment and the total of all these items. The total financial cost of the plan should evidently not exceed the internal and external resources which can reasonably be expected to become available during the period covered by the plan. One of the difficulties that the country may run into is that of a vicious circle. A developing country usually has to draw up a plan before it is able to know precisely what external resources may become available, partly because the availability may be dependent on the manner in which the plan has been constructed. The result is that the plans tend to be prepared larger in size than can ultimately be financed by the available internal and external resources. The frequently applied criterion that 50 per cent of the total planned investments can be obtained from abroad usually proves over-optimistic. Only too often the external resources have been and will probably continue to be collected on an ad hoc basis. Since the external resources are often those that cannot be collected in the amounts desired, it becomes important that no individual project should be started unless the available external finance needed for that particular project is already available. Otherwise 'free' foreign exchange needed to take care of any multiplier reaction resulting from the development plan, may have to be used for the financing of the projects in the plan. When such allocations have to be made on any considerable scale, the already slender reserves of the developing countries in question will be put under a strain which they cannot be expected to sustain.

The official external resources for the development plan are obtained chiefly by loans from the International Bank for Reconstruction and Development and loans or grants from the friendly governments of other countries or their agencies. Fairly considerable amounts of external finance have been obtained in recent years, but it may as well be stated here and now that the bulk of any country's development financing must be obtained from domestic savings. The total of foreign finance available is limited and it has to be distributed according to some criterion. Therefore, the projects which are to be financed by external resources must fulfil certain conditions of usefulness—and whenever the test of profitability can be applied, the projects should be expected to meet this test. The loan applications, after careful examination, are either granted or rejected. If large amounts are mentioned, conditions may be attached to the granting of the loan.

To secure semi-official and private loans or investments may be a much more difficult matter. Here, the legal security of foreign investments is bound to be a prime consideration. What are the prospects of private investments not being made subject to nationalization or current income as well as repayment on capital not being hindered by, for instance, measures of exchange control? Even the most sincere personal assurances of a Minister of Finance or the most emphatic statements by the Head of a State carry little weight when it is known that an important section of the politicians of the country in question have other ideas. It is, therefore, imperative that the developing countries realize that if they really want foreign capital they must whole-heartedly accept the conditions on which such capital can be obtained.

The internal resources consist of current domestic savings of which an important part often is the surplus in the current budget to which indirect taxes contribute by far the largest amount; there are also past and current savings of Marketing Boards or other national corporations; current voluntary private savings, often placed with Post Office Savings Banks; furthermore, in some countries as indicated above, resources which may be obtained from an expansion of credit without inflation; and finally, in countries with inflation, for a temporary period some forced savings, which, however, may add less to the available resources than supposed because of simultaneous flight of capital usually accompanying the inflation.

The total amount of resources that can be raised internally without inflation seems to vary between 5–10 per cent of the gross national product of the country in question. It is not easy to bring about an increase in the proportion of savings in any developing country. There are definite limits to what can be obtained without inflation from the credit system, either the central bank or the commercial bank, and if inflation is indulged a whole new set of disturbing problems arise. Therefore, great attention has to be given to fiscal, credit, price and cost policies; in fact, to the whole pattern of administration as it emerges in the new countries. Only the best husbandry will stretch the limited resources to the utmost.

However carefully the financing of the development plan has been considered and arranged, there are certain features that are likely to lead to inflationary pressure in the developing country. The investments connected with the development plan are likely to cause multiplier and accelerator effects, i.e. induced increases in consumption and investment. Their balance of payments effect can usually be approximately estimated on the basis of an overall model. When, therefore, allocating the available foreign exchange, irrespective of its origin, it is essential to earmark at least, and preferably more, than this amount, to cover the expected import demand. It is often possible when arranging foreign loans to obtain amounts exceeding the cost of the direct import of machinery and other capital goods designed to cover this contingency. The temptation to use this apparently 'free' foreign exchange for further investments must be resisted; otherwise the lack of goods on the domestic market may easily lead to unnecessary and irreversible price increases. However, even when the foreign exchange is available to meet the expected demand in the balance of payments, the time taken till the induced effects work themselves out and reach the balance of payments may cause a rise in prices, especially if there are market imperfections. Thus, bottlenecks caused by the increased activity may not be quickly overcome by increased supplies in the private sector and/or from imports, unless there are quickly mobilizable stocks to bridge the production and distribution period.

Up to the early 1960's it may be said that the main constraint on the African development plans was not the lack of finance; it was the lack of the right kinds of human and real resources. The result was that the actual expenditure lagged behind planned expenditure, sometimes very considerably. Nevertheless the price levels in many African countries showed a slight but not negligible increase. In future the rate at which expenditure can be effected is likely to be higher than in the past as there is an improved supply of qualified persons at all levels and both production and imports have been better co-ordinated with the development plans. The result will be that the lag between planned and actual expenditure will be shortened and may even disappear and the full effect will then be felt by the economy. The probability of price increasing pressures arising will be greatly increased and to moderate these pressures a very skilful policy on the part of the monetary and financial authorites will be required.

In these circumstances a main aim of the monetary authorities must be to ensure a stable internal and external value of the currency, which as a rule will amount to a stabilization of the country's general level of prices. This will assure confidence in the currency, provide a basis for economic calculations and enhance the country's credit-worthiness. Experience has shown that it provides the best basis for *sustained* economic growth.

Some of the main advantages secured by a policy of monetary stability and confidence are summarized in the following five points. They are all necessary to sustained economic growth and can only be secured when people have confidence in the internal and external value of the currency.

1. Developing countries need financial assistance from abroad in the form of foreign loans and grants both public, semi-public and private. There is a growing feeling among the richer countries that the assistance should be properly scrutinized so that waste is avoided, but in this context monetary stability becomes an important factor.

2. These countries need to promote internal savings, while the flow of genuine savings would shrink if inflation were allowed.

3. These countries cannot afford to price themselves out of the international market. If domestic prices rise without an alternation of the exchange rate, the country in question will suffer from the repressive influence of having an overvalued currency. The acceptance of a floating rate of exchange may eliminate this drawback but experience shows that the proper administration of a floating rate of exchange is no easy matter, since traders and others seem often to anticipate a recurrent depreciation in the value of the national currency.

4. Inflation, even a moderate one, will distort the price and cost structure on which the development plan has been based. Since it is impossible to foresee how individual prices, whether real or 'shadow', will change at a time of an inflationary rise, the cost accounting on which the plan has been based will be so deranged that distortions cannot be avoided. Even frequent revisions of the development plan are unlikely to be able to rectify the distortions caused by inflation because of the time needed for the completion of individual projects whose justification depends on the relative structure of original prices.

5. The social consequences of inflation may be disastrous in that speculative elements gain at the cost of the general public. Usually continuous inflation inhibits the formation of the strong middle class so greatly needed in modern societies and not least for the promotion of economic growth.

While there is general agreement that marked inflation will have a negative effect on sustained economic growth, reservations are sometimes made with respect to 'creeping' inflation, i.e. a price rise of 3–4 per cent p.a. Especially the politicians, though not necessarily the ministers of finance, who desire to mobilize additional credit facilities from commercial and central banks, would find it convenient to have a theoretical extenuation for a policy of monetary expansion beyond that needed to support justified economic expansion. However, any country with an active and successful economic development policy can expect price-increasing tendencies emanating from important 'frictional' factors. Unavoidable bottlenecks in production and distribution will enhance the difficulty of keeping the domestic market permanently supplied with goods and services, especially as their composition must be altered according to the changes in effective demand. The latter reflects the continuous changes in the wage structure. There will necessarily be a marked increase in the wage and salary bill—even if basic wages are maintained at levels justified by productivity—because of the promotion of newly qualified persons, not all necessarily in 'productive' employment. Though direct and indirect taxation can help to modify the resulting effective demand, there are definite limits to such a policy. If these price-increasing tendencies are then majored by a 'slightly' inflationary monetary and financial policy, they can easily become inconveniently large. In fact, in certain situations, the monetary authorities may well find that they have to curb credit expansion to counteract price increases emanating from frictional factors.

Naturally, these remarks do not apply to the developing countries where economic growth and development is sluggish. These countries are, however, usually characterized by a sufficiency, if not a plethora, of overall liquidity. The contribution of the monetary authorities there is to redirect already available funds into the most promising sectors. The success of their efforts depends upon that of the general economic and development policy of the government.

The innate advantage of monetary and, to some extent, financial policy is that they are flexible. Not only is the required policy radically different according to the two extreme situations contrasted above; these policies can be adjusted according to minor changes in the liquidity of the country concerned and thus keep it in line with the general monetary trends of the world. This applies, perhaps especially, in developing countries where the monetary and financial systems are still comparatively simple and the reactions to the absolute quantity of money (liquidity) made available by the monetary authority are decisive. By ever more refined techniques, specially adapted to the individual country concerned, this flexibility of monetary policy can be further enhanced. There is a more than latent danger, however, in that the scheme for financing the development plan may be established in a manner that decreases the freedom of action of the monetary authority by committing the latter to prearranged measures. When these measures, either in their extent or in their timing, prevent the monetary authority from exercising the full flexibility needed to control also the smaller fluctuations of the monetary situation, the edge of a valuable tool for maintaining monetary stability has been dulled.

The developing countries are not expected to achieve these difficult policies without support. The comprehension for their aims and difficulties has greatly increased among the industrialized countries. An almost bewildering variety of international and national institutions have been established for technical, commercial and financial assistance. The International Bank for Reconstruction and Development and its agencies as well as individual governments are mobilizing increasing financial assistance for the developing countries on terms that are compatible with their economic status. Moreover, it has been realized that the developing countries are dependent on the sales of their products to the industrial countries and that they will necessarily feel the impact of the policies in these countries. The leading industrial countries are pursuing expansionist policies which should increase the imports of raw materials and other goods and services of these countries and at the same time militate against a deflationary fall in prices. There is thus a chance of greater stability of prices on the world market, in any case much less risk of a fall in the general price level. The latter should receive further support when the proposed duty free imports into industrialized countries, not only of tropical produce but also of the manufactures of developing countries, become effective. The specific but thorny problem of the stabilization of raw material prices is also under constant review. As no overall solution has yet been found, a system of compensatory financing has been established by the International Monetary Fund to assist automatically countries subject to a loss of foreign exchange due to a fall in raw material prices. All these measures testify to the willingness of the industrialized countries not only to assist the developing countries but to enable them increasingly to participate to the fullest possible extent in international trade. Whether the developing countries will draw the maximum benefit from these facilities will depend in the last instance on the wisdom of their domestic policy for growth and development.

Modern economic growth and development requires the mobilization of the appropriate goods and services and a price system as a basis for calculation, their prerequisite being a system of money and credit. The latter has to be established and administered. In respect of both these activities the policy pursued by the monetary and financial authorities can contribute materially to the future growth of the country. The danger is inherent, however, that the advantages will be squandered by expecting too much from a system that cannot create goods and services. It can only facilitate their judicial distribution by maintaining the monetary rate of expansion needed to support genuine economic growth and activity. Any further monetary expansion (or unjustified contraction) will have negative effects on growth by distorting the domestic price system, inhibiting the accumulation of savings, discouraging foreign financial assistance, hampering export possibilities and retarding the development of a strong middle class. Thus the stability of the general level of prices should be maintained and the new central banks are becoming capable of applying flexibly the appropriate policies. In this policy they are supported by the Ministers of Finance who increasingly realize that the development plans should be financed through actually available present and future domestic and foreign resources, in order not to jeopardize their own countries' sustained economic growth, for the foundation of the latter is monetary and financial stability.

MAP OF AFRICA

CHAPTER II

THE AFRICAN CONTEXT

While a modern economic growth policy and especially a monetary and financial policy have certain general principles, to be successful they must both also take into consideration the characteristics of the individual country. The historical and social heritage, though given, is not static but interacts with the imported and therefore exogenous ideas and policies. The degree to which the traditional conceptions can fruitfully be adapted and integrated into the evolving society is liable to make the transition to new forms and institutions smoother. However, where their retention decreases the capacity of society to adapt to the conditions necessary for economic growth, their substitution by a suitable legal, social and institutional framework becomes advisable. While these aspects are mainly sociological and cannot be dealt with in detail in an economic discussion, sufficient attention must be given to them in order to be able to evaluate the viability of the policies adopted.

Though Africa is often regarded as one continent with one set of problems, the apparent similarities should not obscure the enormous diversity of the individual regions, countries and provinces. The continent is divided into Africa north and south of the Sahara. The former, now mainly Arab and Muslim, has for centuries been involved in the main trends of Mediterranean history. The individual countries were affected to a very different degree by the various waves of conquest leaving permanent differences in character and outlook. Africa south of the Sahara is populated mostly by a large variety of African negroid races and tribes. There has apparently not been any unifying common history till the European powers' penetration of Africa in the 19th century. The colonial area introduced western civilization and thus laid an essential, if fragmentary, basis for the present striving towards nationalism. The latter coupled with consciously desired economic growth and development is the first really unifying influence to which that part of Africa has been subjected.

Though the continent is thus separated by more than the Sahara, this inland sea has also acted, through the centuries, as a link between the two parts of the continent. Especially since the introduction of the camel in the first three centuries AD[1], there seems to have been a

[1] E. W. Bovill, *The Golden Trade of the Moors*, London, 1958, pp. 41 ff.

fairly intensive north-south trade between present day Libya and Kano, between Morocco and the former Ghana; east-west, there was trade with the African and Middle Eastern Arab states and the important kingdoms and empires of present day Nigeria.[1] Perhaps some sense of unity has remained from this history to help form the elite's acknowledgement of an African entity—as opposed to a political Pan-Africanism. There is a realization by the leaders of these countries that they are African, that they as such have a personality of their own, but a personality to be found and formed in the company of cousins closely related and with much the same problems, hopes and aspirations. Its existence has facilitated a certain practical and technical collaboration between countries north and south of the Sahara, a collaboration which has been achieved with or without the technical assistance of the Economic Commission for Africa and other similar organizations. Ever-increasing practical collaboration should help to lay a firm foundation for the harmonious political collaboration which Africa should be able to achieve. While the latter may take some considerable time to establish, it should be more fruitful than the hitherto abortive close political union of larger groups of states. These groups were, in fact, formally liquidated at the Addis Ababa conference of all thirty-two African states in May 1963. At the same time the Organization of African Unity was adopted. It commits all the governments to real political and other collaboration while fully respecting the sovereignty of each and all.

The important diversity found especially in Africa south of the Sahara is the reason why, at least for larger countries, a federative form of government is often the only viable solution. The boundaries of most states disregard ethnic, tribal and linguistic considerations. While the leaders of the nation desire its moulding into a unit,[2] the individual cannot be brought in one or even two generations from loyalty to family, village and tribe to that of loyalty to a nation of the size of 10–40 million people. Such a loyalty can, at best, be that of an elite. To run the country, communal, local and regional institutions are necessary and they have everywhere preceded the national unit.[3] The resulting organization may take the form of a federation of Nigeria's type, where the regional governments already represent sizable populations, or the retention of a high degree of autonomy by local tribal chiefs such as was found in the Sudan till the reform

[1] Michael Crowder, *A Short History of Nigeria*, New York 1962, pp. 19–56 and 78–107.

[2] Arnold Rivkin, 'The Politics of Nation Building: Problems and Preconditions,' *The Journal of International Affairs*, Vol. XVI, No 2, 1962.

[3] See e.g. Philip J. Harris, *Local Government in Southern Nigeria*, Cambridge 1957, and Ursula Hicks, *Development from Below: Local Government and Finance in Developing Countries of the Commonwealth*, Oxford, 1961.

of local government in 1960.[1] The purpose of the reform is here to create a democratic local and regional administration which allows for a measure of regional autonomy without undermining the unity of the nation and without incurring the expense and complications of federation in this vast and sparsely populated country. Such systems combine the traditional interests of the smaller unit with the new interests of the nation and have shown themselves as the best political system for the larger countries, at least during a transition period. Outright nationalistic organizations have so far only worked in smaller countries such as Ghana, Guinea and Tunisia or in relatively developed and homogeneous countries such as Egypt.

The need to achieve national unity has created a bias towards strong, one party governments in a large number of African states. Freedom is interpreted mainly externally as the nation's liberation from the colonial power and its supposedly 'restricting' legacy and not internally as the individual's political right to democracy. Only in Nigeria is there an effective party system, where the opposition party has a freedom of action comparable to that of a political party in present day Europe. The Federal government is a coalition which was formed in order to give the country a stable government. While as high a degree of political freedom as possible is an ideal for new countries, they are seldom, if only because of the still often high rate of illiteracy, capable of achieving both democracy and stable government. The latter is, in this formative period, probably the more necessary and does not exclude the gradual introduction, or reintroduction, of a more democratic form of government.

The need for stable government is heightened by the rootlessness and neurotic characteristics shown by some of the new intellectuals.[2] The shock impact of the new society and economy cannot be underrated especially when it is realized that the individual still often experiences the transition from bush to civilization within a few years. The customs and ideals of parents seem incompatible with the new ways, while these, in spite of the noble efforts of missionaries, seem to have little spiritual or moral content. With the concentration on production, trade, commerce and a high degree of efficiency, the new ways appear to be entirely materialistic and to give unlimited opportunities for status seeking, all in the name of a higher standard of living. Conspicuous consumption and investment have become the (essential) outward and visible signs of independence, success and prosperity. Evidently the philosophical, moral and in part religious

[1] *Sudan Almanac* 1960, Khartoum, pp. 110–11; and Henry Maddick, 'Decentralisation in the Sudan II and I', *Journal of Local Administration Overseas*, Vol. I, No 2, April 1962, pp. 71–83.

[2] See the modern African literature with its stress on the effects of the shock impact, e.g. Chinua Achebe, *No Longer at Ease*, London, 1960.

ideals which allowed the Western World to attain the standard it has, the positive content of liberalism with its demands for self-discipline, self-sacrifice and the tacit or explicit acknowledgement of a moral standard has not yet been passed on to the new countries in Africa. As the African elite are liberated from the immediate pressing practical tasks, they may realize the depth of the liberal philosophy.

Though hitherto uninterested in the philosophy of liberalism, the African, even the educated African, is hallmarked by a deep religiousness. It is a quality which is much more basic than the mere profession of a formal religion and involves the recognition of a daily spiritual experience—and it would be irreparably wrong if the modern heritage of a technocratic way of life should rob the African of his innate advantage. The African's sense of religion might temporarily allow him to mistake political fervour for something deeper, but he is quickly undeceived. In the same way, he does not really understand the western expert who might, perhaps, go to church on Sunday, but who does not carry the flame of a spiritual experience through his daily life. The religiousness of the African is usually equally fervent irrespective of the professed religion or religions. While the African religions are also practised, it is Islam that has been spreading through Africa. 'This dynamic, extremely plastic religious confession is propagated by Africans among people of colour. Thus, it has popular appeal as a fundamentally African religion. In addition, its dogma, which is fixed, is nevertheless susceptible to external influences, permitting local beliefs and other accretions to be baptized into the new religion.'[1] Moreover, it is often the religion of the political and business leaders of a community and adhesion to Islam is necessary to obtain a (better) job. The spread of Islam has affected all other religions including Christianity. The latter is divided not only among Roman catholics and protestants but also among the sects of the latter. It has thus hardly been a unifying element and has certainly not succeeded in transmitting an idea of puritanism[2] either directly or indirectly. While this strict and austere confession would probably hardly appeal to the people with the happy temperament of the Africans, the lack of it is to their disadvantage as it is also to the other developing countries. It has been

[1] William H. Lewis, 'Islam and Nationalism in Africa,' in *The Arab Middle East and Muslim Africa*, edited by Tibor Kerekes, Director of the Institute of Ethnic Studies, Georgetown University, Washington, D.C., New York, 1961, p. 69; and J. Spencer Trimingham, *Islam in West Africa*, Oxford, 1959.

[2] The Basler Mission which has been active in Ghana since 1835 (see Gustav Wanner, *Die Basler Handels-Gesellschaft A.G.* 1859–1959, Basel, 1959, p. 104 ff.) has as an exception succeeded in leaving 'signs of Puritanical outlook' in present-day Larteh where it opened a tiny school in 1853, and now has a large and important Mission. David W. Brokensha in *Christianity and Change*, Duquesne. University, Pittsburgh, 1961, p. 6.

shown that the idea of hard work, a modest way of living and a high rate of savings, which puritanism imposed as a moral duty, coincided with the important inventions and the rise of entrepreneurship in both Europe and the United States and that it thus gave the necessary foundations for the industrial revolution.[1]

These are the virtues of the middle class which in general are absent in almost all developing countries of Africa (see Table 1). The typical social structure of the developing countries is a small, often relatively wealthy aristocracy or elite and a large and heterogeneous mass living at—or just above—subsistence level. Trade and commerce are often in the hands of foreigners, who form their own social groups and who often remit the profits to their home countries. The further a country has progressed the larger is the group of skilled persons, that is the middle class.[2] The middle class in this context must be given the broadest definition and goes from the skilled worker and foremen, the garage owner, independent farmer and modern trader to the agronomist, doctor and lawyer. It has nothing to do with the (petit) rentier class a very few countries in Europe knew. It would be formed by persons who have a skill, live chiefly from their current income but have a certain degree of ownership in that a house, some land, some savings are in their possession. They normally form a stable social and political nexus and usually stand for ideals of personal property, ownership and therefore saving and change through evolution, instead of revolution.[3] This element of stability as well as the savings of the middle class are of prime importance. However, it is the skills possessed which are essential to a modern economy for it is characteristic of modern agriculture, industry, commerce and 'services' that they all require a very high proportion of persons with skills. It is not only the qualified agronomist, engineer, department store manager and doctor that are necessary. These are ineffective unless supported by several times their number of technicians of all kinds whether these be foremen, skilled workers of innumerable kinds, typists, nurses or radiologists. The list is quite unending and the unskilled worker has, in the developed economies, almost disappeared. The formation of a middle class is both the condition for and the result of economic growth. In Western countries, in the developed countries, the middle class was formed by the interdependent agricultural, industrial and social revolutions and is usually seen as the product of this development. In the developing countries the process must be reversed. Just as

[1] R. H. Tawney, *Religion and the Rise of Capitalism*, London, 1926. (The literature on this subject is considerable.)

[2] International Institute of Differing Civilizations, *Development of a Middle Class in Tropical and Subtropical Countries*, Brussels, 1956.

[3] Fritz Marbach, *Theorie des Mittelstandes*, Bern, 1942, pp. 423–5.

infrastructure and institutions are established for future needs and do not grow up organically in response to needs, so there must sometimes be a reversal in the manner in which social problems are approached. The conscious formation of a middle class must therefore become not merely the ideal but the active interest of the elites.

The African elite, whether political, commercial, technical or intellectual is still so relatively small compared to the total population

TABLE I

Distribution of the Active Population by Sectors

	Ghana	Morocco*	Nigeria†	Rhodesia	Sudan‡	Tunisia*
			Percentage			
Agriculture, forestry, fishing .	65	71	78	58	82	80
Mining and quarrying .	2	1	1	6	–	1
Manufacturing .	1	7	6	7		6
Construction . .	3	3	1	9	10	2
Commerce	10	4	6	4		5
Transport .	2	8	1	2		2
Services .	5	5	–	–	5	4
Unspecified occupations	12	1	7	14	3	–
	100	100	100	100	100	100

* Exclusive Europeans.
† African men.
‡ Males only.

SOURCES:

Ghana: Ministry of Finance, *Economic Survey* 1958, Accra, 1959, p. 21.

Morocco: Pierre Bertrand, *Dix années d'économie marocaine*, 1945–55. Insee, Paris, 1957, p. 11.

Nigeria: Federal Government Printer, *Economic Survey* 1959, Lagos, 1959, pp. 106–7.

Rhodesia: ILO, *African Labour Survey*, Geneva, 1958, pp. 666–7.

Sudan: Based on: Ministry for Social Affairs, Karol Jozef Krotki, 21 *Facts about the Sudanese* (First Population Census of Sudan 1955/56), Salzburg, 1958, p. 33.

Tunisia: FAO: *Projet FAO de Développement méditerranéen, Tunisie Rapport national*, Rome, 1959, p. II 40.

that it has an enormous responsibility for leadership.[1] Only a few are qualified for membership in the elite, but everyone of this privileged group by his or her very being is a potential example. The way of life this elite embraces, the outward and visible aims it upholds and encourages will help create the blueprint for the new broad middle class, which is already in formation.[2] The elite should encourage this evolution by example in, for instance, the choice of professions for their children as well as by exhortation and the creation of employment opportunities. It can also contribute by its own example; this should include the acceptance of manual labour. Because of real or misunderstood status considerations, the elite is often afraid of 'getting its hands dirty' and the engineer and agronomist will usually prefer a desk job in administration than the active practice of his profession. Moreover, the elite sometimes seems to acquire a vested interest in the *status quo* and the accusation is sometimes heard that the new leaders have much the same attitude to their fellow citizens as the representatives of the colonial powers had towards all Africans. Unfortunately there is some element of truth in this assertion. The elite tends to perpetuate strong tribal or absolutist social patterns and thus to reduce social mobility. The fact, however, that the first generation of the elite is usually largely trained in law, medicine and the humanities should force it to try to increase social mobility because of the pressing need for technocrats. Moreover, the restrictive tendencies of the elite, where this exists, should be a passing phase if only because of the political pressure to extend the benefits of education to the whole people.

Education is today the most desired commodity in Africa. It has become the 'indispensable key to personal and national progress' while 'it was in the classroom that the African acquired the linguistic and technical competence to confront the white man as an equal'.[3] Even as recently as a decade ago education was still regarded with mistrust by the majority and it was only a few far-sighted individuals who managed to secure a secondary or possibly, in a very few cases,

[1] Hugh H. Smythe and Mabel M. Smythe, *The New Nigerian Elite*, Stanford, 1960. Using the *Who's Who in Nigeria* a number of 956 leaders in a country of 35–40 million inhabitants was obtained. It is, however, unusual and encouraging to find that such essential occupations as businessmen, farmers and trade unionists were included. Such studies too often limit themselves to the academically qualified persons, which gives a very unrepresentative and, especially in new countries, incorrect picture.

[2] Richard F. Behrendt, 'The Emergence of New Elites and New Political Integration Form and Their Influence on Economic Development,' Reprint from *Transactions of the Fifth World Congress of Sociology*, Washington, 1962, Vol. II, pp. 3–32.

[3] Helen Kitchen (editor), *The Educated African: A Country-by-Country Survey of Educational Development in Africa*. Compiled by Ruth Sloan Associates, New York, 1962, pp. 3–4.

university education abroad. These pioneers would sometimes establish pilot schools in their own countries, the secondary school, Sadiqui College (established in Tunisia in the 1870's) being one of the first by half a century. The new schools and colleges normally had a general western humanitarian slant and the attempts of colonial administrators to introduce schooling with practical training. agricultural or technical, met with suspicion and sometimes even resistance.[1] This was due largely to the fact that the first job available to the educated African was that of Government clerk, a position for which a certificate of some kind was necessary. Social status was thereby acquired and the result was an over-valuation of both the desk job and the certificate.

While this attitude still exists among the population in general, the leaders recognize the necessity of practical as well as general education. Most independent governments hope to have sufficient schooling facilities to assure all children at least complete primary schooling by 1970, while some countries have already succeeded in having half the children (boys and girls) at school in the early 1960's. While attempting to give all children an education, those who can profit from secondary and graduate training are to have such facilities. Universities and Technical Colleges exist for higher levels, while a network of vocational and teacher training schools has also been established. These facilities are usually available equally to both boys and girls. Even in Muslim countries schooling at all levels is available for girls while the opposition to their education is decreasing. The educational system must, however, be built out considerably (especially in the secondary schools) before it can satisfy all needs and it is a very costly undertaking. Thus, in most countries fees have to be paid for part or all schooling (not in Ghana). They seldom cover the true cost, which would be prohibitive in view of the low incomes, and the difference is made up by government subsidy. Usually there is also a system of state scholarships. The enlargement and greater differentiation of the educational system has high priority as essential for economic development.[2]

Encouraging education is not entirely without its dangers. There is more than a possibility that the economic development will not keep pace with the production of educated persons. The speed with which the development plans are likely to create jobs could easily be slower

[1] V. L. Griffiths, *An Experiment in Education.* An account of the attempts to improve the lower stages of boys' education in the Moslem Anglo-Egyptian Sudan, 1930–50, London, 1953, p. 144. 'The real relevance of a curriculum to the needs of society was of comparatively minor importance compared with the teachers' and pupils' belief in the relevance of what they were doing.'

[2] Odd Aukrust, *Investeringer og økonomisk vekst,* Forhandlingerne ved det nordiske nationaløkonomiske møde. København 4–6. September, 1958. Copenhagen, 1959, pp. 50–69.

than the production of educated people. While a scarcity of engineers and technicians is usually ubiquitous there is often a surplus in other branches. In fact, the relative overproduction of persons seeking white collar jobs is a major social and political problem building up in developing countries. Both the unemployed clerk and the highly educated younger civil servant, who sees his way to promotion blocked by older, less well educated, but perhaps wiser men, are often forming vocal groups of dissatisfied persons. If the detailed tactics of developing countries' politics are carefully followed, it is possible to see how great an effort political leaders make to woo these dissatisfied intellectuals.

The intellectual has frequently loosened his own personal ties with the larger family which in traditional society assisted and/or absorbed the unemployed. While the educated person would normally not consider that he or she could expect help, the traditional system has usually survived so that the family makes claims on its educated member. Frequently, the large family assisted its brightest boys and girls to obtain education; this effort is regarded as an investment and help from the former recipient is automatically expected. Even highly placed civil servants give these demands as a reason for not being able to save.[1] In fact, the financial contributions to the family are a sort of extra-taxation of the successful, over and above any contribution they may make directly to the State. On the other hand, the operation of the large family means that there exists a kind of built-in social welfare system. Thanks to this, the governments can concentrate their available resources, financial and other, on productive investment and essential infrastructure instead of having to administer a costly social service which would only mean more consumption expenditure. By allocating a larger part of resources to investment in the first place, the country's total potential should be more quickly increased.

The fact that there is an important drain of population from the countryside to the cities shows that the large family ties are also loosening already at this level. The underemployed individual is no longer content to remain in his village but wanders to the city in search of a better life and, if possible, of employment. This influx gives rise to the shanty towns found on the outskirts of most large African cities and creates not only slum clearance problems for the city administrations but also social problems.[2] The new inhabitants are usually completely unfamiliar with city life. While the husband

[1] See Appendix II, esp. p. 305, for the effects of family ties on the banking system.

[2] See for instance: Peter Marris, *Family and Social Change in an African City, A Study of Rehousing in Lagos*, London, 1961; and Michael Banton, *West African City—A Study of Tribal Life in Freetown*. Published for the International African Institute, Oxford University Press, 1957.

at best has help from his place of employment, his wife has to learn the most rudimentary lessons pertaining to housekeeping and the education of children. The city administrations usually find they have to run classes in these subjects as well as supply special health centres. The problem created by this influx of people is of such dimensions that the new development plans not merely seek to modernize agriculture but to make living under rural conditions more attractive. This involves all kinds of measures from social status for the agricultural expert to small local factories. (It is usually hoped that private initiative will supply the local cinema). If these measures succeed, the African may eventually become a more permanent resident and abandon his practice of seasonal or periodic large-scale migration in search of paid employment. [1] In spite of the large-scale migration, most rural inhabitants of Western Africa, except the nomad tribes like the Fulani cattlebreeders, have some land of their own. The large-scale plantation, whether African or foreign run, is an exception. In Northern and Eastern Africa the plantation is an important institution and requires a corps of often landless labourers. In both areas larger farms and even sometimes plantations have recently been broken up to resettle landless rural inhabitants. The Republic of the Sudan has not only a large number of nomad tribes but also at Gezira and in the Managil a mixed form of land tenure whereby the whole cotton growing unit can be run as one plantation while the individual tenant farmer has a security of tenure which in practice makes his land his own.[2] The system seems to work well and combines the advantages of large-scale production with the sense of security land tenure gives.

Even this brief description of some of the most important characteristics of the African context gives a picture of rapid social and economic change. That change is too fast for both the individual and the nation, is often asserted. Other critics see the inhibiting effects of inertia and tradition. Inevitably, in a society in flux some sectors will change faster while others, perhaps more fundamental, will initially resist change. Only in retrospect will it be possible to judge whether the change was fast enough to allow economic growth and development not only to maintain the present standard of living as populations increase, but also to raise the standard of the individual.

[1] E. J. Taylor, 'Les marchés en développement au Mali,' *Revue économique et sociale*, No. II, June 1963, pp. 141–56. Also in Basle Centre Publication Series A No. 454.

[2] Arthur Gaitskell, *Gezira: A Story of Development in the Sudan*, London, 1959, pp. 83–95.

CHAPTER III

THE ECONOMIC BACKGROUND

Five of the six African countries with which this study is concerned were among the first to obtain their political independence in the new area of the history of Africa. They were all fortunate in that the obtention of sovereignty was relatively peaceful. In the case of Ghana, Nigeria and the Sudan a large measure of administrative responsibility had been transferred to the Africans well in advance of their formal acquisition of complete sovereignty. This enabled African officials to be trained and gave them the opportunity to accustom themselves gradually to the responsibility which autonomy entails. In Morocco and Tunisia other methods were followed but there were enough men who could take over the reins. Thus, the political structure of these countries promised to be relatively stable and there was no reason why the constructive development and economic growth of each country should not be able to proceed undisturbed by major political crisis.

The six countries also had finance ministries of their own and either already had or were very soon establishing their own central banks. This meant that these countries became distinct entities from the monetary and financial point of view with 'autonomous' policies in the process of being formulated. The existence of the ministries and central banks also assured that the most essential information on each individual country could be obtained either from the regular publications or through personal contacts.

The continent of Africa is still underpopulated compared to the other continents. It had a population of some 254 million people in 1960, which gives some eight inhabitants per square kilometre. Even if large areas offer very difficult conditions of life, the newly found mineral resources of all kinds promise, in combination with modern technology, a bounty which should help to alleviate the poverty of areas where the concentration of population is higher. The six countries represent 32 per cent of the population of Africa and 18 per cent of the surface area of that continent. They are therefore—with the exception of the Sudan—relatively densely populated. The rate of growth of population is, on an average, around 2 per cent per annum.[1] With rates of investment tending towards 10–15 per cent

[1] Morocco 3; Nigeria 1·9; Tunisia 1·5; Rhodesia and Nyasaland 2·6 per cent; Africa as a whole 2·2 per cent. U.N. *Demographic Yearbook* 1961, N.Y., 1961.

per annum it should be possible to equip the economies with the infrastructure, industry and the reform in agriculture and commerce necessary to sustain the growing population at increasingly higher standards of living. Thus, the economic development can, in Africa, be timed in such a way that it precedes the increase in population, thereby preventing the almost untractable type of problem which is so well-known from large parts of Asia.

TABLE II

Basic Economic Factors, 1960

	Area km2 million	*Population* million	*National Income** $ per capita	*Fixed Capital Formation* $ per capita *ca.* 1958	*Exports and Imports* % GNP	
Ghana	0·24	6·7	194	23	25	28
Morocco	0·44	11·6	150	20	21	24
Nigeria	0·88	*ca.* 37·0	*ca.* 81	*ca.* 8	15	22
Rhodesia	1·26	8·3	140	45	44	34
Sudan	2·50	11·5	56	6	17	18
Tunisia	0·14	4·2	176	15	—	—

* The large differences in national income per head, especially in Africa south of the Sahara, are partly due to a greater degree of monetization in some countries such as Ghana. The differences in the standards of living are apparently not as great as these figures would indicate.

SOURCES:

UN *Statistical Yearbook, 1960; Demographic Yearbook, 1962.*
Nigeria; *Digest of Statistics.*
Rhodesia and Nyasaland; *Monthly Digest of Statistics.*
UN *Economic Survey of Africa since 1950.*
UN *Economic Bulletin for Africa.*

The institutional, legal and social structures in these countries are almost amongst the most developed of the emerging countries in Africa. They have not yet, of course, found their definite forms and especially the social problems, caused by economic progress and migration of labour, both seasonal and more or less permanent to the towns, are very important. However, a certain degree of adaptation to the needs of the individual countries has taken place, while the best of the British and French inheritance has often been retained. The fact that in five of the countries there were either no important groups of expatriates or that a large number left at independence means that the population is now basically African. Thus the schizophrenic type of split between a poor and large indigenous and a rich and small foreign population has largely been avoided. The important and the rich people are indigenous, often having worked themselves up from very modest circumstances. The exception is Morocco, where the influence of the wealthy and ancient aristocracy is still important. Given the new and increasing educational facilities an always wider circle can benefit from the economic and social advance that is being made. A second, sometimes a third, generation is growing up, which will form the broad stratum of a middle class. Agronomists, doctors, engineers, foremen, minerologists, lawyers, teachers, skilled workers and many other professions are beginning to be represented. Traders are adapting themselves to the requirements of a modern monetized economy, while entrepreneurs, either spontaneously or through private and sometimes even state help, are increasing in number and importance.

In view of the comparatively low equipment of the essential infrastructure required for economic development shown in Table III—either overall or in certain sectors—it is not surprising that more or less explicit plans for economic development exist in all these countries. They all, on paper, put agricultural raw material and food production first, then attention is given to infrastructure and only in the third place does industrial production follow—primarily for the internal market. Thus the general structure of the plans, as they exist today, is appropriate even if their financial size usually exceeds the internal and external capital at present available. Over and above this are the problems of inter-African communication. All railway lines go to the coast, while adjoining countries have different gauges. The enormous distances and difficult terrain and climate make hard surface overland roads expensive to build and exorbitant to maintain. The important rivers have to be regulated if they are to carry really heavy traffic. Even intra-African air communications still leave much to be desired—especially across the continent—though this is probably the easiest way to secure regular and close communications for more valuable freight as well as persons. These problems are only just beginning to be tackled while the countries which have started airlines are finding the cost almost prohibitive.

All development plans, however, suffer from the defect that they have to concentrate on certain essentials. They cannot ensure the diversification a growing economy requires already at a very early stage—the secondary investment which supplies the tools required by the major projects and the increasing variety of goods demanded by the always larger number of people moving into better qualified and therefore better paid jobs—even under the assumption of stable wage rates. To meet this double secondary demand without undue strain on the balance of payments, the entrepreneurs and

TABLE III

Infrastructure

	Roads		*Rail Transport*		*Ports*		*Telephones*	*Per capita Consumption of Energy*	*Educational Expenditure*	*Health Expenditure*
		hard surface	ton-km		goods handled 1,000 m. tons		1,000	kg of coal equivalent	*% of Budget*	*% of Budget*
	km/km²	km/km²	1948	1959*	1948	1959	1959	1959	1958	1958
Ghana . .	0.1303[3]	0.103	207	315	1934	3430	24	87	14·5*	6·5*
Morocco .	0.040	0.013	1080	1598	6624	11839	129	135	16·0*	6·9*
Nigeria . .	0.0685[5]	0.007	1076[2]	2055[2]	2054	5723	37†	42	21·6	6·4
Rhodesia and Nyasaland .	0.0656[6]	n.a.	2868	6316	—	—	105	558	12·0‡	11·8‡
Sudan . .	n.a.	n.a.	607	1516	615	1695	21	n.a.	11·3	9·0
Tunisia . .	0.1247[7]	0.058	869	947	3977	5191	38	163	18·2[1]*	10·9[1]*

* Estimated figures.
† Including British Cameroons.
‡ Federal Government Budget 1962/63.
[1] 1959.
[2] 12 months beginning 1st April of year stated.
[3] 1/7/1957.
[4] 1/1/1957.
[5] 1958/59.
[6] 1955.
[7] 1/1/1959.

SOURCES: UN *Statistical Yearbook, 1960; Economic Bulletin for Africa*, June 1961 (UN); Bank of Rhodesia and Nyasaland *Annual Report*.

commercial people must have the opportunity of acquiring the know-how, the technical knowledge which makes it possible for them to go ahead and build up enterprises of all kinds on their own. This exchange has repeatedly been proved possible only if a relationship exists through international trade with countries more technically advanced than the country in question. Thus the greatest possible degree of freedom of trade and payments and legal security for the foreign trader and investor will bring not only capital but the new approach, the new methods and the new ideas.

The balances of trade of these countries reflect their often one-sided structure of production and show their dependence on their raw material exports for financing the major part of their imports. As is seen from diagram I, the main raw materials in question are: copper (Rhodesia), cocoa (Ghana), cotton, tobacco, lead zinc, palm

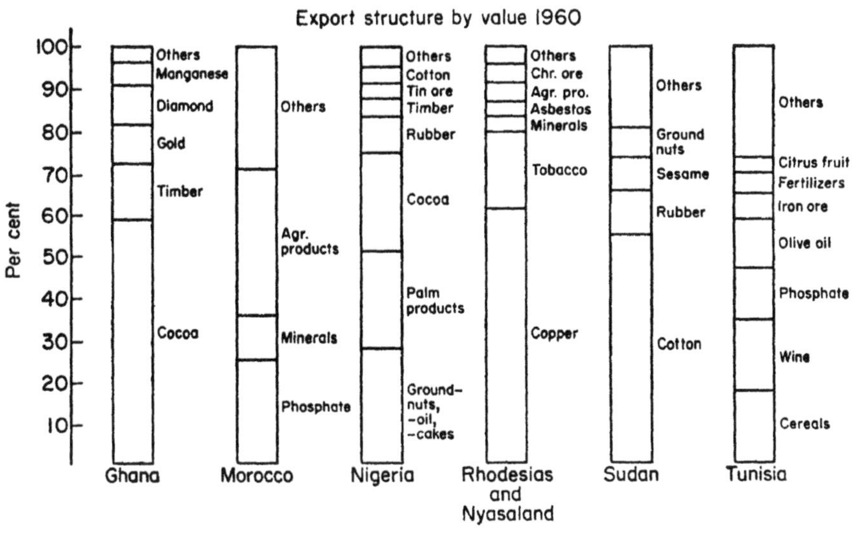

oil and in the future oil (Nigeria), cotton, gum arabic (Sudan), phosphates, grain, wine, vegetables and fish (Tunisia and Morocco). Of these, cocoa, gum arabic and copper have been good foreign exchange earners during several years; other raw materials have been less consistently valuable on the world market. As has been repeatedly pointed out by the annual reports of GATT, the terms of trade have, during the last few years been turning against the developing countries because of the relative change in prices between raw material and manufactures. African countries have suffered proportionally less than other developing countries because, on the whole, they have been able to increase their export earnings. Naturally, the countries concerned would like to be able to stabilize raw material prices. In spite of many proposals, no suitable plans have yet been developed for their stabilization. Flourishing economies in Europe, America and the often forgotten developing countries themselves, are the best guarantee for stable and high prices—and with the present world population increase, there would be no long term raw material surplus problem. The medium run problem is being investigated. The industrialized countries should at least co-operate by duty free imports of raw materials and by no internal luxury taxes on items such as cocoa, tea and coffee. However, when raw materials have inelastic demand curves or where structural changes in demand —nylon tending to replace cotton—take place, the long-term price changes should produce changes in production.

The structure of these countries' imports has changed radically with the inception of economic development programmes. Machinery, for instance, usually imported duty free or at much reduced rates, has become a major import. Due to the secondary demand generated by the economic development, especially consumer durables, though now subject to heavy duties, have also increased more than proportionately. As these are often incentive goods there are limits to how heavily they can be taxed. Moreover, a limitation on imports would only have the effect of increasing the monetary pressure in the country. The only realistic means of reducing the pressure of demand on the balance of trade, apart from financial and monetary measures, is by domestic production of consumer goods. The other growing item of imports is food. This is partly due to the neglect of domestic food production in favour of cash crops. A change in the structure of domestic agricultural production, using better methods and often hitherto unused land, could greatly ease this strain. So can the active development of sea and inland fishing and, where possible, poultry, swine and cattle. The processing of food of all kinds could create a new and important domestic industry and should, to some extent, be possible in smaller local industries. These would also help to solve the unemployment problem and to increase the standard of living of the rural population.

One of the main difficulties encountered is that the economy of these countries is basically trialistic and not dualistic as is usually maintained. There is a relatively small but important modern sector and a large but essentially static traditional sector. Between these two sectors there is normally a transitional sector about which very little is known. It consists of persons who have their roots in the traditional sector but who have responded to the incentives emanating from the modern sector. These are the small indigenous entrepreneurs with very little capital equipment and low credit rating. They have managed to turn a traditional occupation into a more profitable activity by the use of an acquired speciality and fairly modern mechanical equipment. Perhaps the many transport firms are the best example but the tailor with the sewing machine, the bicycle repair shop, the expanding baker and numerous smaller commercial enterprises all belong in this same category. The smaller real estate dealer and the smaller progressive farmer are also often borderline cases. The demarcations between the sectors are far from clear. Moreover, the size and importance of the transitional sector varies considerably from country to country. It seems to depend largely upon the degree of initiative shown by the population. But, on the other hand, the dynamism of the economic development of the country in question is of considerable importance. Where the money flows from the modern sector reach both the transitional and the traditional sectors, the transitional sector is more important and more dynamic. It serves both the new needs of the traditional sector and some of the unsatisfied needs of the modern sector. Its existence depends on an element of unbalanced growth which creates a response from the private sector. It can only come into being if resources, financial as well as real, are not all reserved for government purposes, whether for the current budget or for the development plan.

The transitional sector is of the greatest potential value to the country. It represents the natural response of the population to the new demands; it satisfies a large variety of needs while it simultaneously is a training ground for indigenous enterpreneurs. Some of the more successful enterprises enlarge and modernize till they have to be counted as part of the modern sector. The sons and daughters often improve the original enterprise or are able to acquire the education that puts them into the elite or the middle class. Naturally some enterprises are less successful; but even a minor success in the transitional stage is apt to encourage a member of the traditional sector to attempt some entrepreneurial activity. This is especially the case when there is an active demonstration effect so that the individual sees that a reward for effort is obtainable. As consumer, producer, creditor and saver the transitional sector is essentially dynamic. The larger this sector is, the greater the probability that the country's economic development will be fast.

In countries where the transitional sector is small or completely lacking there is probably both basic inertia and a lack of contact between the traditional and the modern sector. The effort needed in education, organization and investment to achieve economic growth and development will therefore have to be larger than in a country of similar size and structure where there is an important transitional sector.

This brief sketch of the economic background of the six countries shows how interdependent the several aspects are. Economic growth and development should therefore be pursued along a broad front with balanced growth as the objective. Sufficient resources should, however, be left free so that private enterprises can be established within both the modern and the transitional sectors, the latter especially responding to the element of unbalance in even the best development plan.

PART TWO

CHAPTER IV

CENTRAL BANKS IN AN AFRICAN CONTEXT

The creation of central banks in the newly emerging countries of the continent of Africa has been seen as the outward symbol of the attainment of monetary sovereignty. Actually, such a measure is only the first step in the long process of acquiring an independent monetary policy—to the extent that, in a world linked by the indispensable international trade and payments, any country can ever be considered autonomous. However, where the country in question is sufficiently important with respect to size, population and national wealth, the possession of a central bank competent within the unit of a politically independent area seems to be a feasible proposition.

While thus basically a positive attitude is taken to central banks in emerging countries of sufficient importance, the final judgement will have to be reserved till, in years to come, they themselves have proved their value.[1] This will depend largely upon the aims they set for themselves, legally and otherwise, how they are run and how they manage to collaborate with the Ministries of Finance as the representatives of the government on the one hand and with the whole gamut of financial intermediaries on the other.

The central banks have all to operate in countries where economic growth, understood as a higher per capita income, is a conscious aim. A carefully executed monetary policy, anchored within the framework of a well formulated financial and political policy, can help to assure the monetary stability essential for steady and balanced growth. This is conceded and recognized by the developing countries, but they also have specific aims to which they want their central banks to contribute.

As part of its contribution to development the central bank is expected to encourage and assist in the formation and the geographic spread of a large variety of financial intermediaries, imaginatively adapted to the many needs of a developing country. By putting in

[1] 'Central banking thus took more than a quarter of a century to mature in the most developed country in Africa, and it is safe to say that the latest recruits to central banking will require some little time before they can be said to exercise any overall control over the credit situation.' 'Central Banking in Africa,' *Barclays Bank Review*, Vol. XXXIII. No. 2, May 1958, p. 34.

correctly selected institutions ahead of time, it is believed that it will be possible to speed up the acceptance and the spread of a modern credit economy and that this will materially contribute to the rate of economic development. Actually, it is the provision of the economy, and especially of the domestic entrepreneur with bank credit which is supposed to be a major catalyst. Unfortunately, this problem proves to be delicate and fraught with misunderstandings—perhaps inevitably as a comprehension for the implications of bank credit and the limits to which it is subject is not inherent in developing countries. However, banks and other financial institutions could often contribute more than they actually do by a more imaginative and more flexible policy. The ways and means by which this can be effected are one of the more demanding aspects of monetary progress in developing countries.

Another specific demand made on the central bank is that it should insulate, as far as possible, the domestic economy from the fluctuations in the money supply caused by the balance of payments. 'Perhaps the most important and the most widely canvassed of its (the Currency Board's[1]) defects is the automatic link which the system is alleged to create between the money supply and the balance of payments. One of the objectives of the new Commonwealth central banks is to break this link and to ensure that the money supply is adjusted to domestic rather than external factors.'[2]

The economic, as opposed to the ideological, idea behind this demand is that a domestic economy cannot be created while the changes in the supply of money are adjusted exclusively by the state of the balance of payments. The resulting fluctuations in both credit and demand can, in fact, if they are extensive, submit the still small and struggling modern domestic sector to unnecessary restrictions. Thereby its dynamism could be affected and its growth retarded.

Protecting an already existing domestic sector against fluctuations in the money supply becomes progressively easier, the larger the domestic sector is. By then the effect of the money issued to purchase the cash crops has become a marginal—though still important—factor. The demand for goods engendered by the issue can also largely be satisfied by domestic production and should only marginally affect the balance of payments.

This state of affairs is, however, the final aim and the developing countries are in a dynamic transition period. The domestic economy is growing and should have, as far as possible, a steady flow of the

[1] The newer statutes of the currency boards make them more flexible. J. B. Loynes, 'From Currency Board to Central Bank,' *East African Economics Review*, December 1960, pp. 57–66, esp. pp. 64 ff.

[2] J. O. W. Olakanpo, 'Monetary Management in Dependent Economies,' *Economica*, November 1961, pp. 395–408, esp. p. 395.

right kinds of capital and credit. It is the aim of the new central banks actively to contribute to such a monetary system. They must naturally collaborate here with the government and especially the ministries of finance and economics as these two are usually the most concerned with the development plans. The central banks have, however, the difficult task of striking the correct balance between encouraging and facilitating the spread of credit and maintaining monetary equilibrium and the soundness of the currency.

The efficacy of the normal weapons at the disposal of the central bank is gradually improving, though there still is not the same degree of control as in financially mature countries. Foremost reliance is placed on liquidity ratios, which both as to absolute size and composition can be more or less stringent. They are sometimes supplemented or replaced by directional control of credit. Changes in bank rate are not very efficacious because the number and the amount of sensitive financial intermediaries and paper is still restricted. Moreover, the size of the credit superstructure compared to the total monetary economy or to the economy as a whole is small. Therefore, various means are tried to control different sectors, often by establishing specialized financial intermediaries. These are given preferential treatment in respect to capital, deposits and/or credit facilities. Because ordinary monetary policy is not as efficacious as might be desired, there is a tendency to try new means of enforcing it, some of which are effective. However, any measures which imply the use of tools, which restrict market freedom, should not be envisaged as a normal measure.

The use of ordinary central bank weapons is twice as effective if it has to operate in an economy where government finance is sound. Moreover, in several of the economies discussed here, marketing boards have in the past and may in the future to some extent stabilize raw material prices. Thereby the impact of the changes in world market prices is modified and an immediate effect is obtained on the money supply. A close collaboration between the central banks and the marketing boards is obviously needed and sometimes attempted so that their policies can be co-ordinated to the best possible advantage.

The problem of the positive contribution that can be made by the central bank to support the start of the development of a modern domestic sector is very complex. It is intimately linked with the efforts being made by private entrepreneurs and the government towards changing the composition of the national income. Essentially, it is a question of seeing that there is no disproportional limitation of suitable types of funds, whether short, medium or long term. The fundamental issue here, as seen from the central bank, is that it should be able to give the banking system a sufficiently flexible supply of credit so that when there is a real demand for funds, this demand can be satisfied. It is virtually a question of the distribution of the amount of credit available, not necessarily the enlargement of the total amount of credit. So far, there is no indication that total monetary stringency has retarded growth in any of the six countries under consideration. The apparent limitations, if any, have been due to a misunderstanding of the role that a modern commercial banking system can play when extending credit and to a lack of active saving, possibly reflecting a scarcity of viable investment projects.

Attention must here be given to the ways and means by which credit can safely be advanced to the domestic sector on the part of the banks. This task may be fairly complicated, especially where the domestic sector is composed of several branches with small or unimportant money flows between them and/or between them and the modern sector (or sectors).[1] Typical of this type of economy are Morocco and Tunisia. Secondly, the prospective entrepreneurs of developing countries must acquire a better understanding of the reasons for the conditions imposed by different sorts of banks. Not least should there be understanding for the fact that banks, to be effective, must have a corps of stable depositors as well as borrowers, i.e. that an increase in bank deposits, even on current account, greatly contributes to the efficiency of the banking system.

The policy of the central bank towards the modern domestic sector of the economy is mainly that it can actively encourage a more flexible and imaginative banking system. It can support it by supplying it with the funds needed within the limits imposed by the necessity to safeguard the currency externally and internally. The extent to which the fiduciary issue can be used to supplement available funds is a point that is always raised in respect to these questions. That the manner in which it is mobilized is of primary importance is often neglected. This[2] and other problems introduced here will be discussed more fully in the following.

Whatever specific steps are taken by the central bank in respect to any given problem, its main task is to maintain the overall external and internal stability of the currency.

This contribution from the side of the central bank becomes doubly important as the strains and stresses of capital expenditure for development plans and their secondary effects (whether multiplier or accelerator) come into being. Till the end of the 1960's such expenditure was usually within already available foreign exchange

[1] Jean-Pierre Gern, 'Les voies ouvertes à la politique monétaire dans un pays d'Afrique,' *Schweizerische Zeitschrift für Volkswirtschaft und Statistik*, No. 1, March 1963, pp. 2–29. Also in Basle Centre Series A, No. 44.

[2] Cp. p. 223.

reserves or contracted foreign credits and grants. From 1960 onwards the situation has changed radically as the momentum of expenditure has increased. While the governments still have the responsibility to see that the size of development plans is within the limits of possible foreign loans, a greater burden will fall on the central banks. With their monetary policy, they will have to supplement the ministries of finance in their efforts to contain the secondary demand engendered by the large-scale capital expenditure. The problems which will arise can be prevented or mitigated by well-planned monetary policy. However, they cannot on their own achieve everything. They are only effective if neither trade and investment policy nor the general political policy of the country in question counteracts them.

The monetary and financial problems of the new countries in Africa, and thus of their central banks, fall into three broad categories:

I. These countries are still, compared to western countries of the same size and importance, *undersupplied* with the necessary financial institutions of all types. These have to be built out in a manner adapted to the needs of the country in question. And information about them must be spread among the population.

II. The monetary and financial authorities have to *create* within the country an *atmosphere* which furthers economic development while maintaining *control* of the situation so that neither inflation nor deflation can upset the growth of these delicately poised economies.

III. The monetary authorities have to manage the *foreign* monetary and financial relations of the country so that no balance of payments crisis can occur while at the same time encouraging the import of capital and trained personnel for development purposes.

These three aims have to be pursued all at the same time and are inevitably interrelated. Moreover, they are at times closely connected with the political attitudes of the countries concerned and cannot, therefore, be dealt with exclusively as technical questions.

CHAPTER V

THE ESTABLISHMENT OF CENTRAL BANKS AND THEIR STATUTORY OBLIGATIONS

The establishment of the central banks in the six countries under consideration was usually fairly quickly decided and carried through without any transition period. The latter, however, is found in both Rhodesia and Nyasaland and in the Republic of the Sudan. The interesting and profitable experiences made during that time either contributed to the form the statutes of the central bank were given and/or allowed preliminary measures to be taken towards the establishment of the central bank. In the countries where there was no interregnum, a special investigation was usually made by experts from the Bank of England or the Banque de France. These not only helped to draft the statutes, but supplied from their organizations personnel either as advisers or for key positions in the new banks. The central banks all show traces of their origin, though frequently subsequent changes in the statutes and the ever greater replacements of the expatriates by Africans has considerably changed their character since their establishment.

The first central bank to be established was the Bank of Rhodesia and Nyasaland by Act of March 13, 1956. It started operations at the end of the same month. Subsequently central banks were established as follows:

	Date of law	*Start of operation*
The State Bank of Ghana	March 1, 1957	March 1957
The Central Bank of Nigeria	May 15, 1958	July 1958
The Bank of Tunisia	September 19, 1958	November 1958
The Bank of Sudan	December 1, 1959	February 1960

The Bank of Morocco is older, having been set up under the treaty of Algeciras of April 7, 1906, but it too received new statutes on July 30, 1959.

In the cases of Ghana, Nigeria and Rhodesia, the new central banks were the successors of currency boards.[1] These latter were, at

[1] The West African Currency Board, established in 1912, operated in Gambia, Sierra Leone, Ghana (formerly the Gold Coast) and Nigeria, while the Central Africa Currency Board, established in 1954, had competence in Northern and Southern Rhodesia and Nyasaland. It had operated since 1938 as the Southern Rhodesia Currency Board.

that time, exclusively currency issuing institutions, without even a fiduciary issue; nor did they possess powers to formulate and execute monetary policy in the regions in which they were competent. When issuing West African or Central African currency, they did so only against the receipt of the same amount of sterling in London, or supplied sterling for West or Central African currency. (Evidently currency is understood here to include coin and note holdings of commercial and other banks.) The exchange was effected at a fixed rate (subject to commission). It was thus essentially foreign trade earnings, which decided the amount of currency in circulation in the territory in question. The currency was also thereby assured a sterling backing of one hundred per cent.[1]

Already at the end of the Second World War, expatriate experts[2] and the new leaders of the African states in formation started discussing the monetary situation created by the Currency Board system. In view of the increasing internal need for a local currency and the increasing desire on the part of the countries to be able to have an active domestic monetary policy several suggestions were made. Some experts advocated the establishment of central banks,[3] whereas others considered that the rate of development of these territories would be slow and that a reform and an elaboration of the Currency Board system would be all that was required.[4]

Then came requests from the countries themselves for investigations. Mr. H. C. B. Mynors was asked already in 1948 to examine the position in Southern Rhodesia. He came to the conclusion that an elaboration of the Currency Board system was more appropriate at that time than the establishment of a central bank. The chairman of the Central Africa Currency Board was to be an expert, who would also act as adviser to the government and maintain close relations with other financial institutions. In Ghana (then the Gold Coast) an investigation was made by Sir Cecil Trevor in 1951. The result was the establishment of the Bank of the Gold Coast, which was to deal exclusively with African customers. The ordinary commercial banks were already then being accused of not lending—or not lending enough—to African customers and this new bank was an attempt at satisfying the demand for special attention to this problem. In fact the Bank of the Gold Coast did very little business.

[1] J. B. Loynes, *The West African Currency Board*, 1912–62, London, 1962.

[2] Sir G. L. M. Clauson, 'The British Colonial Currency System,' *Economic Journal*, 1944, pp. 1–25.

[3] J. Mars, 'The Monetary and Banking System and the Loan Market of Nigeria,' published in *Mining, Commerce and Finance in Nigeria*, ed. Margery Perham, London, 1948, pp. 177–224. Ida Greaves, 'Colonial Trade and Payments,' *Economica* February/March 1957, pp. 47–58.

[4] W. T. Newlyn and D. C. Rowan, *Money and Banking in Colonial Africa*, Oxford, 1954, pp. 267–92.

In Nigeria, there was a proposition in 1954 that the post of an adviser to the government on Rhodesian lines be created, but this suggestion was not adopted.

The next step was the actual establishment of the new central banks.

The very considerable economic development of the Rhodesias after 1945, as well as the important immigration, had created the need for a more developed monetary system. The Chairman of the Currency Board, in his capacity as adviser to the government, recognized that a central bank would not only contribute to progress by being able to help in the formation of a money and capital market, but also that its establishment would be necessary in order gradually to build up the means by which the monetary development would be controlled. He, therefore, not only supervised and assisted with the creation of the Bank of Rhodesia and Nyasaland, in 1956, but he also was its first Governor.

The statutes of the Bank differ considerably from those of other new central banks; there is, for instance, no main clause which gives directives for the institution's policy making. The Bank is merely empowered to do certain things in the monetary and financial sphere —reading these statutes in conjunction with those of central banks in newly independent countries, the impression is gained that the Bank of Rhodesia and Nyasaland was conceived as an agent—this perhaps being a natural result of its growth out of the Currency Board. All this has not prevented the Bank of Rhodesia and Nyasaland from functioning as a real central bank, a policy-making institution.

In Ghana and Nigeria, the establishment of the central banks was closely linked with either complete or internal independence. Basically, it was the feeling that only through the possession of a central bank would the two countries achieve monetary independence (autonomy). There was also a strong desire to have an indigenous monetary policy to promote economic growth. This required an independent policy-making institution, a bank of issue, which could control the monetary conditions of the country. It also implied breaking away from the West African Currency Board system. The status symbol a central bank is supposed to be, was also an argument in its favour.

The Central Bank of Nigeria started operations on July 1, 1958. It had been preceded by a consultative investigation led by Mr. J. B. Loynes, of the Bank of England. The statutes drafted closely resemble those of other new central banks in the sterling area. Their main feature was that the close link to sterling, which had existed under the Currency Board system, was maintained as sterling was made, with gold, the only reserve currency. A subsequent amendment to the statutes (April 1962) has since removed this restriction. The actual and desired greater differentiation in the pattern of Nigerian trade fully justified a greater spread in the foreign exchange reserves. Gold and dollars were acquired each to the amount of 10 per cent of total official reserves. This is also a hedge against possible revaluations.[1] More basically, it also reflects the desire of the new countries in Africa to free themselves from too great a dependence on the state of the internal economy of any one country. The second point of interest is that the original statutes underestimated the speed at which the central bank would need sharper means of control over the banking community. The expected effects of the six-year Development Plan 1962–68 have also materially changed the position. Both with respect to the enforcement of the discount rate and the liquidity ratio new clauses have also been introduced. (These have further been re-enforced by making special deposits possible.) Though these subsequent amendments have proved necessary after some three years of operation, the original statutes made the first few years of the Central Bank of Nigeria not only constructive, but allowed it to lay a firm foundation both of monetary administration and collaboration with the commercial banks.

The establishment of the Bank of Ghana was not as smooth nor has its subsequent history been as untroubled. The main point is that already when the Central Bank was established the question of amalgamating it with the present Ghana Commercial Bank (the former Bank of the Gold Coast) was raised. The authorities wisely decided on creating a true central bank without any commercial activities. But this was not the end of the matter. Twice since 1957 the whole question has again been raised, but in spite of much lobbying and behind the scenes argument, the *status quo* has fortunately been maintained.

It is really surprising that this issue has arisen three times in so short a time. When once a developing country acquires an issuing and policy-making institution of its own because it believes in its value, the advantages gained should not be lightly relinquished. Had a commercial bank with some central banking activities been the aim, a simple transformation of one of the already established commercial banks would have been the obvious solution. In view of the repeated return to the question in Ghana and elsewhere a brief discussion of the advantages of true central banks seems indicated.

The essential argument for having a central bank without commercial activities is that the basic function of the central bank is to control the monetary situation in the country. It therefore must be

[1] The DM and florin revaluations in 1961 and the preceding uncertainty have left their mark.

in a position to control the commercial and other banks and monetary institutions. This is done not only by discount policy, by the enforcement of liquidity ratios and possibly of special deposits, but also by more or less formal gentlemen's agreements. The central bank, either through the bankers' association, through special meetings or even by the most informal talks, lets its wishes, which in this case really are directives, be known. If the position of the central bank is good and it has the confidence of the banking community, this informal control is often far reaching and efficacious. Should a central bank itself be operating in the commercial field, it would either find that one department must control the other on a par with the other banks, or it would be tempted to make exceptions for its own department on the grounds of greater national interest. Both policies are difficult to enforce. The former demands a high degree of impartiality and objectivity—and even when the regulations are scrupulously and meticulously enforced the rest of the banking community will find this hard to believe. The resulting suspicions will make the task of the central bank even more difficult than already is the case. This applies doubly to the alternative policy of excepting the central bank's commercial department, for any reason, from the regulations of the monetary authority. Such a policy will only create added suspicion and jealousy and will prevent or hamper the development of a commercial banking system large enough and sound enough for the economic development of the country in question. Commercial banks are anyway likely to fight shy of a country where there is a commercial bank, which has the strong backing of the central bank, as they would consider this unfair competition. When policy considerations intervene, as they sooner or later must do, the deterrent effect becomes of even greater importance.

In the specific case of Ghana, the commercial banking system is not only established with three banks, Barclays DCO, Bank of West Africa and the Ghana Commercial Bank,[1] but the two former have an important network of branch banks. On the whole, the two first named commercial banks have managed to find profitable business. The Ghana Commercial Bank, which is restricted to dealing with Africans only, has found it difficult to make headway, in spite of various attempts in several different fields. This partial failure is not due to lack of imagination on the part of the management of the bank, but is basically due to the reason that banking in Africa is a new art and that the habit has not spread as might be desirable. The fact that banks must have depositors as well as creditors in order to function efficiently is not yet realized by the community at large.

Thus, the Ghana Commercial Bank does not yet have the sound

[1] 'New Bank for the Gold Coast,' *Barclays Bank Review*, May 1953, pp. 36–7.

foundation of large deposits which an ordinary commercial bank can usually count on. To some extent, it is the difficulties the Ghana Commercial Bank has experienced that have given rise to the constant demand that the amalgamation with the Central Bank should take place. Such a solution has, moreover, seemed a natural one to many of the leading personalities because the two organizations have often had senior managers formed in the opposite tradition. They have invoked Professor Richard Sayers' argument that in order to stimulate commercial banking in a developing country, the central bank *might*, for a transition period only, operate in the commercial field. When the latter was well established, however, the central bank should 'retire gracefully'. Sayers expressly mentions that under normal conditions, when adequate and efficient banking services are available, the central bank should be a straight bank of issue. As sufficient banking facilities are certainly available in Ghana, Sayers' major argument is applicable.[1]

The central banks also do not need to participate in commercial banking in order to have detailed and rapid information about the state of the business in the country. They all obtain it through the Clearing House, which they all set up as one of their first measures. This was usually done in collaboration with the local Bankers' Association or Committee. It proved to be a badly needed technical device, which expedited interbank clearing quickly in countries where distances make communication both slow and costly. All parties have profited, the commercial and other banks by an efficient service, the central banks by the information with which it supplies them.

In the Republic of the Sudan there was a transition period between the monetary administration as it existed under the Anglo-Egyptian Condominium and the establishment of a central bank, the Bank of Sudan, in February 1960. After political independence a Currency Board was created on June 17, 1956, to issue immediately the new national currency, as preparations for the central bank had barely been started.[2] The Currency Board[3] which had had Sudanese,

[1] Richard S. Sayers, *Central Banking after Bagehot*, Oxford, 1957, esp. pp. 108–33. 'Central Banking in Underdeveloped Countries': 'If there are no gaps (in the commercial banking system), well and good, it (the central bank) should then stand aside,' p. 118.

[2] In 1956–57 the Federal Reserve System had a Central Banking Mission in the Sudan, which explains the American influence there has been on the structure of the Sudanese banking system. For a picture of Sudanese monetary and financial problems at the time see Andrew F. Brimmer, 'Banking and Finance in the Sudan,' *South African Journal of Economics*, Vol. 28, No. 1 (March 1960), pp. 23–34.

[3] Z. Siemienski, *The Sudan Currency Board*, Ministry of Finance and Economics, Economic Section, Khartoum, 1957, pp. 5 ff. Also see Reports of Sudan Currency Board, 1st to 4th (December 31, 1957, June 30, 1958, June 30, 1959, and February 21, 1960), Khartoum S.C.B./2–5.

British, Egyptian and Swedish members on its board, supervising the currency exchange, used the National Bank of Egypt in Khartoum as its agent. It took over the Currency Reserve Fund, i.e. the cover for the initial issue, 50 per cent in (unredeemable) Treasury Bills and 50 per cent in sterling assets supplied by the government. During its over three years of existence it neither accepted deposits nor gave loans; though it was thus not a maker of monetary policy, it laid an important foundation for the Bank of Sudan. Moreover, during the period of the functioning of the Currency Board, the Economic Section of the Ministry of Finance took measures to assure the training of the future senior employees of the envisaged central bank. It also started the collection of essential economic and monetary information, which now is collected and partly published by the Bank of Sudan. Thus, the new Central Bank had a head start over its sister organizations in other developing countries, several of the most important first tasks having been fully or partly tackled.

The Bank of Sudan took over at its inception the foreign exchange reserves of the government and the assets and liabilities of both the Sudan Currency Board and the National Bank of Egypt (which ceased operations in the Sudan). As a counterpart for the holding of foreign exchange reserves, the government was credited with domestic equivalent in value to the sterling securities, Treasury Bills and other assets involved.[1] At the time the Sudan considered itself a *de facto* member of the sterling area, a position which has since been abandoned.

In contrast to most of the newly founded central banks of Africa, the Bank of Sudan found that among its assets was an advance to the commercial banks. Usually all commercial banks are expatriate banks and completely independent of the central bank, and one of the main objectives of monetary management has to be the obtention of control over the commercial and other banking system. Some of the commercial banks operating in the Sudan were also independent and they even held substantial deposits with the Bank of Sudan. Other commercial banks had borrowed. These advances could only be obtained against foreign securities, which the domestic banks do not possess, or against actual cotton, which is strongly seasonal, so that the whole system was fairly unwieldy. While part of the outstanding advances were repaid during the course of the summer as the cotton crop receipts came in, towards the end of 1960, the commercial banks had again increased their borrowings at the Bank of Sudan. Their liquidity had been decreased by the transfer of very large deposits, corresponding to the government part of the income from the cotton crop, to the Bank of Sudan.

[1] Bank of Sudan, *Economic Bulletin and Financial Bulletin*, January–March 1960, pp. 11 ff.

The commercial banks themselves had partly used their temporary high liquidity to advance credits to importers, credits which were slow in being repaid, due mainly to an overstocking of textiles.

Thus the Bank of Sudan had the position from the start of being a lender of last resort. It took the consequence of this situation and introduced the discounting of bills. Bills of trade are in general usage and are therefore a familiar instrument. Their discounting by the Bank of Sudan enables the banks to obtain credit under a flexible system, which considerably simplifies their operations, especially for the banks without external backing. On the other hand, the introduction of such a system allows the Bank of Sudan not only to retain but to extend control of the internal credit system, thereby re-enforcing the instruments of monetary control.

The establishment of the central banks in Tunisia and Morocco differed considerably from that of the four banks discussed above. These two countries belonged at the time to the French Franc Area which implied not only a monetary difference but also a different social heritage. Consequently, the statutes of these banks show another outlook both in the organization of the central bank and in the relations to the government and with respect to the control of credit. These differences reflect largely the superficially different structure the countries of the French area acquired and are justified inasmuch as they reflect the peculiarities of the countries in question. Throughout the following, it will be necessary to be conscious of the two heritages the African countries have received. There are, however, already signs that they are partially being transformed into a national—or perhaps an African—heritage, the earlier marked differences becoming attenuated. In part, this is due to the ever increasing integration of these countries into the world economy as well as the exigencies imposed on them by the similarity of their aims, fast economic development under stable monetary and financial conditions.

The Central Bank of Tunisia started its activities in November 1958, at which moment the dinar was put into circulation. Earlier in the same year negotiations with French representatives and those of the Banque d'Algérie et de Tunisie, which previously had managed Tunisian monetary affairs, had established a *modus vivendi* for the new central bank. Special help and assistance was given with the staff training and organization problems so that two years later the Central Bank was being run entirely by Tunisians.

Tunisia, as a newly independent country, naturally desired to have her own central bank. There was, however, also dissatisfaction with the policy followed by the Banque d'Algérie et de Tunisie. The Tunisian Government considered that a central bank should do more to further economic growth and the statutes of the new central bank contain a clause stipulating that the bank must support the government's economic policy. On the other hand, it is under the obligation of advising the President of the Republic as to any measure that might jeopardize the monetary stability[1]—the provision of this clause of the statutes thus being put negatively. The strong affirmation that the central bank is responsible for monetary stability and the maintenance of the value of the currency common to all other statutes discussed is missing in the case of Tunisia. These aims are, however, constantly being mentioned by the leading people as a *sine qua non* for peaceful economic development. They are, moreover, partially safeguarded by the limitation on credits that can be made to the government by the central bank. These may not be greater than 5 per cent of ordinary revenue and for not more than 240 days of any calendar year.

While the Central Bank of Tunisia was established as a new bank, the Banque du Maroc was the successor of a long banking tradition when it was legally instituted on June 30, 1959. Its predecessor was the State Bank of Morocco (Banque d'Etat du Maroc), which had been set up as a private international institution by the treaty of Algeciras in 1906. This bank was both a bank of issue and a commercial bank. The twelve participating countries, however, gradually withdrew so that after the First World War the majority of the share capital was in the hands of French financial institutions.

After political independence in 1956, the new government in Morocco fairly soon wished to have a central bank owned by itself and the sole task of which was to be the monetary control and development of the country. This was in no way a criticism of the policy of the Banque d'Etat but corresponded to the spirit of the time.

Thus, the Banque du Maroc came into being as a public institution whose capital is subscribed in its entirety by the state. The new central bank received all the normal obligations and powers. It issues the currency, the newly introduced dirham, and holds and administers the centralized foreign exchange reserves, which involves the bank as an adviser on import control policy. It is the government's banker and broker and carries the accounts of all public institutions. It may on occasion be delegated to administer certain of these special institutions. It may also subscribe to the issues of certain selected financial institutions either under special legal sanction or of those directly under the control of the state. Moreover, the Banque du Maroc was to support and advise on the economic, financial and development policy of the government and it is adviser to it in all financial matters notably in negotiations with foreign powers and international financial institutions. It may also on its

[1] Law No. 50–90 of September 19, 1958, Art. 34, § 3.

own initiative advise the government on any matters pertaining to its own spheres of activities.

In both Tunisia and Morocco the central bank has a commercial banking department.[1] This is largely traditional and seems to cause no difficulties. The departments reinforce the central bank's attempt to direct credit into new fields, where it is badly needed. To this extent the banking system in both countries has gaps and the argument that the stage is transitional could be invoked. Efforts are being made to build out financial intermediaries for both agriculture and small industry and trade.[2]

The fact that the 'Banque du Maroc' was the absolute successor of a bank well equipped with staff and other amenities greatly facilitated its initial stages. It could concentrate directly and immediately on policy-making issues. To some extent these advantages were also available in the case of the Bank of Sudan, which has used the period of the Currency Board to build up its staff. The Ministry of Finance had taken important measures to assure the formation of suitable officers for senior and middle ranks. Selected candidates were sent to central banks and universities abroad for training. It was arranged that the former local branch of the Bank of Egypt should let its technical staff (partly Sudanese) be taken over. Gaps were filled by a policy of 'secondment'. The foreign central banks, with which the Sudanese Central Bank had close contacts, were asked to *lend* senior officials, mostly technical, for a period of approximately two years. These men are not only highly qualified, but chosen for their capacity to explain and *teach* their own speciality. This system, which has proved to be very efficient, is liked by the Sudanese because the individual in question, knowing his career is in his own bank (and arrangements have been made that his promotion is not retarded by his foreign assignment) will have no incentive to remain once his contract is over. Moreover, the Bank of Sudan inherited from the Ministry of Finance two foreign economic advisers, who both know the country well and who have had the tact and the diplomacy to execute their tasks while gaining and maintaining the confidence of their Sudanese colleagues.

The use of foreign advisers is a practice not restricted to developing countries alone, but is well established as the best means of obtaining, for shorter or longer periods, specialized information and help among the industrialized countries of the western world and Europe in particular. In the monetary, economic and financial field the Bank for International Settlements, Basle (Switzerland) was especially prominent during the first ten years after the War—as was

[1] The Bank of Rhodesia and Nyasaland does not use its statutory powers to act as a commercial bank.

[2] Cp. p. 157.

the OEEC in Paris (France)—while the United Nations and other international institutions in this and other fields bear proof of the great value such expert assistance can be, even in European countries. In fact most of the countries under discussion have used foreign experts either as advisers or as members of the staffs of their new central banks in order to fill the gaps during the first few years and/or to assist African staff later.

One set of countries, of which Ghana, Nigeria and to some extent Morocco are examples, appointed expatriates, Bank of England, Deutsche Bundesbank or commercial bank men to senior positions. Part of their technical staffs they were able to obtain locally, the two long-established commercial banks, Barclays DCO and Bank of West Africa, generously putting some of their best African employees at the disposal of the new central banks—a debt which is gratefully acknowledged. The gaps were filled by on the job training. But more than once senior officials, Governors or Deputy Governors found themselves at the cash desk, explaining, teaching and generally expediting matters. The senior expatriate officials are all trying to train hand-picked Africans for the senior positions. They hope to have made themselves superfluous in approximately five years' time after the founding of the central banks. On the other hand, when the Tunisians created their central bank, they immediately appointed Tunisians to senior positions. These men at first had a few French technical advisers. But by agreement with the Banque de France, Tunisians were trained in Tunisia for the technical jobs and in France for more senior jobs. This intensive programme worked well enough to allow the last Frenchman to leave the Central Bank of Tunisia some two years after its establishment.

All three methods of mixing foreign and African staff are attempts to make the new central banks fully African as quickly as possible,[1] while assuring that the people taking over have sufficient knowledge of central banking practice and policy to assure that these new countries will have monetary order.

It is still too early to know how well this policy will succeed in practice. Few African senior officials have yet been in their positions long enough to have had time to show their capacities. At technical level (which is already largely African) the work is done—if more slowly and with relatively more checking staff than in Europe.

Unfortunately the policy of 'Africanization', which in some countries has recently been accelerated, has led to the premature removal of highly qualified and leading expatriate personnel from central banks and ministries of finance—as well as elsewhere. Moreover, a more than acceptable number of the new African appointees

[1] At the time of writing the Bank of Rhodesia and Nyasaland was still a completely European bank.

have been chosen for their political and not their technical qualifications. It therefore remains to be seen how far the new appointees, both at technical and policy making level, are going to be able to handle the task ahead of them.

It is still too early to judge how the new central banks will finally succeed in managing the positive policy creation which will be necessary in years to come. They are still at the stage of building up the fundamentals of their positions, while the full range of powers, which will accrue to them eventually, are still only latent, irrespective of whether they are specifically granted in their statutes or whether they belong to the traditional sphere of central banking policy. It is, however, of interest to try to estimate what the present position of the central banks is, both in relation to their specific powers and the hopes of the countries in which they operate. Thus the study of the statutory obligations and competences affecting general policy that have been given to the new central banks is especially relevant. In this section the general provisions will be discussed, while the specific relations to the government and to the financial intermediaries will be examined in subsequent sections.

The statutes of these central banks of the six countries are relatively brief and flexible and grant broad powers in the field of discount policy, commercial bank reserve requirements and open market operations. This stands in sharp contrast to the central bank statutes of developing countries drawn up immediately after World War II, which tended to legislate monetary policy. In the African case, major reliance is placed on central banking procedures as developed in older countries rather than on special powers or new and complex control devices.[1]

The main objects of the central banks are similar whether they have received their banking heritage from Britain or France. The fact that they are differently formulated and weighted does not change the essence. These objects are stated as:

(1) to issue legal currency,
(2) to maintain external reserves,
(3) to influence the credit situation with a view of maintaining:
  (*a*) monetary stability in the country,
  (*b*) the external value of the currency,
(4) to act as banker to the government,
(5) to act as financial adviser to the government—with the specific object of warning the government of any threat to the value of the currency (Tunisia),

[1] Federal Reserve Bank of New York, 'International Development: The New Central Banks, *Monthly Review*, October 1960 (Vol. 42, No. 10), pp. 181–3.

(6) to assist in the development of a sound monetary, credit and banking system,
(7) to further the orderly and balanced economic development of the country.

Even when all these objects are not specifically stated (and no statute names all of them) a careful reading of the document concerned and especially of the detailed provisions, shows that all these aims are more or less explicitly enjoined on each individual central bank.[1]

The points of outstanding interest are that the basic policy function of all central banks, namely the maintenance of the *internal and external value* of the currency has been specifically enjoined. The close practical—as well as theoretical—connection between the internal and external value of a currency, has been demonstrated so frequently that it is unnecessary to expand upon this aspect here. That the preoccupation of certain countries such as Morocco, the Sudan and Tunisia with development problems should have been reflected in the statutes of their central banks is natural and is in no way incompatible with monetary stability and the maintenance of the external and internal value of the currency. In some situations, at certain times, this may, however, require a very careful monetary policy on the part of the central bank and full co-operation on the part of the ministry of finance. Prevention is, however, the lesser of two evils, the alternative being inflation, balance of payments crisis and possibly devaluation with all the concomitant repercussions. And the central banks were founded by intent and by law to prevent such a cataclysm.

Having been given specific obligations the central banks were also given a number of competences. These vary more from country to country than do the obligations—in some cases the competences are not in keeping with the obligations to such an extent that a speedy revision of the statutes is necessary. In fact, some revisions have already taken place, especially in Ghana and in Nigeria. In most cases the revision of the statutes—or the revisions which will prove necessary in the future—pertain to four main points, namely the definition of the value of the currency, the composition of the foreign reserve, the rules for rediscounting (i.e. making bank rate effective) and the provisions for liquidity ratios and/or special deposits, i.e. re-enforcing the central bank's means of control over the banking system.

In the original statutes in Ghana, Nigeria and Rhodesia the value of the currency was related to that of the pound sterling. Since then in Nigeria, the pounds are now defined according to international

[1] See Appendix I, p. 295, for text of main clauses in statutes.

custom in grammes of fine gold. In Tunisia and Morocco, the value of the dinar and the dirham are both, in special laws, defined in grammes of fine gold. Previously to the introduction of the new currencies, parity with the French franc had been the rule. In Morocco the newly fixed parity involved a devaluation, a devaluation of the French franc not having been followed previously.

The composition of the foreign reserves and especially that part forming the backing for the currency reserves has been altered. The original statutes of the Central Bank of Ghana and those of Nigeria stated that the foreign currency reserves had to be held in gold and sterling assets of various types. The new amendments in Nigeria and Ghana allow the external assets to be held, apart from gold, in assets in or of 'any country outside Nigeria where the currency is sterling or is freely convertible into gold or sterling'[1] or bills of exchange 'on any place outside Ghana, payable in convertible currency' and securities of governments 'expressed in convertible currencies'.[2] Thus, both countries have enlarged the type of assets in which the foreign exchange reserve can be held, to include assets in foreign currencies, though the way they have to be convertible is defined differently. This new move corresponds to the desired and actual changing pattern of trade and the wish not to be economically dependent on one country. The various speculative movements in connection with assumed and actual revaluations in 1960/61—however unmotivated these were—have increased the wish of these countries to achieve economic as well as political independence. The original statutes in the Sudan, Rhodesia, Tunisia and Morocco all allow the foreign reserve to be held in gold or foreign currencies.

The revision of the statutes to allow bank rate to be more effective and to introduce liquidity ratios was necessitated by the fact that the banking system developed much faster than originally foreseen. This has been the case in Nigeria, where the central bank found it needed more power, and where there was a good opportunity to revise the statutes in connection with the start of the new six-year development plan. In the case of the Sudan, the statutes did not need altering, but the introduction of discount and other facilities was done by administrative order. In fact, the actual way the statutes are drafted usually is such that, if the central bank has the support and moral backing of the government, it can enforce its authority. Where such backing is lacking, even the best statutes remain inoperative. This applies to the provisions for making bank rate effective, to liquidity ratios and/or special deposits.

[1] Amendment to the Central Bank of Nigeria Act, 1958, 19/3/1962; § 2.

[2] Bank of Ghana (Amendment) Act, 1961; § 2. 'Convertible currency means currency which can be exchanged by its holder for gold or other currency,' § 1 (1).

Thus the statutes of the new central banks in these six African countries are such that, with or without revision, the central bank can operate effectively. Whether it does so or not, depends on far less tangible factors than the statutes. Each central bank must earn the position it holds in the country and can only give the government the full support it can expect, if in return its authority is upheld.

CHAPTER VI

CENTRAL BANK POLICY: LAYING A FOUNDATION

The first measures of new central banks were all aimed at laying a sound foundation for future policy making. The statutes they had received gave them certain powers, which, however, would remain ephemeral unless translated into practical action. The difficult question of finding and training a suitable staff had to be solved, at least on a temporary basis, immediately, for the day-to-day work of the central banks could not wait. Thus the new central banks had hardly been set up before they found themselves coping with some very difficult problems. Chief among these were a currency exchange, the taking over of the foreign reserves and the administration of exchange control, the start of its functions as banker to the government and the establishment of research departments.

(*a*) CURRENCY EXCHANGE

An exchange of currency, of the notes and coins in circulation was considered necessary in all countries studied except the Rhodesias and Nyasaland, where the Central Bank in this respect was the natural successor of the Central Africa Currency Board. Sovereign countries usually consider that a national currency is one of their special prerogatives and this attitude appears to be justified when the country is a reasonably distinct economic unit. A national currency, however, is not essential to an autonomous credit policy though, when the currency is the same for several political entities, it does tend to circulate freely in the whole area.

That such international and inter-regional flows are frequent is shown by the experience of the currency boards. The exports of Central Africa Currency Board notes were directed towards the neighbouring parts of Portuguese East Africa, while West African Board currency circulated fairly freely in neighbouring French territories. Inter-regionally, within the area of the two Currency Boards, there were exports and imports of currency from and to Rhodesia and Nyasaland, while there seems to have been a steady movement of currency from Gambia and Sierra Leone towards

Ghana and Nigeria, a movement which has continued into present times.[1] In French West Africa there have long been very important flows of FAO francs not only within the area but into all other West African countries from Guinea to Nigeria. This movement follows the important inter-regional and international trade in fish, timber and labour from the Niger loop to the west and south.[2] So important in fact is this free movement of trade in the economy of that part of the world that the new political independence of the individual countries was not allowed to lead to its monetary fragmentation.[3] The necessity to exchange currencies at several frontiers would probably act as an important deterrent to trade. In the six countries, however, which are larger and economically viable, national currencies were introduced.

In Morocco and Tunisia the dirham and the dinar were issued to replace Moroccan and Tunisian francs that had previously been in circulation. The rate of exchange was one to one and was effected surprisingly quickly. This was partly due to the fact that all the money banks—irrespective of type—in the two countries acted as agents to the central banks for this operation. Also the Moroccan and Tunisian do not hoard notes and coins to the same extent as is done elsewhere, but prefer to keep their savings in gold or precious gems—not to mention their herds. An additional factor of importance is the widespread state bus service which reaches into the most isolated districts and which makes possible the flow of money as well as trade.

The exchange of currency in Ghana and Nigeria was also needed in order to obtain the foreign exchange reserves from the West African Currency Board. The new central banks in West Africa received at pounds sterling 1:1 value for each of the West African Board pounds handed in an exchange which has now almost been fully effected. The chief delaying factor is the habit of the people to hoard notes and coins and then not to realize that these notes are no longer valid. How complicated a currency exchange is in countries where the amount and structure of the currency in circulation is unknown and where a considerable portion of the money-using public is illiterate, is almost incomprehensible. Thanks to careful preparation, good publicity and lots of work, the currency exchanges were effected smoothly and surprisingly quickly. This also applies to the Sudan where the currency exchange, as mentioned above, was

[1] J. B. Loynes, *Report on the Future of the Currencies of Sierra Leone and the Gambia*, Government Printer, Sierra Leone, 1961, p. 8.

[2] Jean Tricart, Les échanges entre la zone forestière de la Côte d'Ivoire et les savanes soudanaises In *Les cahiers d'outre-mer*, no. 35, 9me année, Juillet/Septembre, 1956, pp. 219 ff.

[3] Banque Centrale des Etats de l'Afrique de l'Ouest; *Rapport d'Activité* 1961, Paris, pp. 47 ff.

effected by the Currency Board, which functioned for some three years before the Bank of Sudan came into being. The latter has continued to issue and reissue the Currency Board notes; in due course new notes will be printed in the name of the Bank of Sudan.[1] The number of banks in the country having been small, the Provincial, District and Local Government Treasurers also helped with the currency exchange which took place fairly quickly, namely in three months for notes (April 8 to July 7, 1957), though a limited exchange period of some three months was allowed subsequently for bona fide holders, who had missed the official period.[2] The exchange of coins, however, took much longer and was not completed till May 31, 1958.

The Sudanese pound as issued was given a decimal structure being sub-divided 'into one hundred equal units, each of which shall be called a piastre' and 'each piastre shall be divided into ten equal units each of which shall be called a millieme'.[3] Both dirham and dinar have also been given decimal structures. In Ghana and Nigeria the traditional pound was issued, with the result that there is a constant demand for a revision. In Ghana, in 1961 a formal request was made by the government to the Bank of Ghana to effect a change over to a decimal basis. In Nigeria, the discussion has not gone much further than newspaper articles.[4] While other sterling countries have already some time ago changed to a decimal system,[5] those which are now considering such a step might be well advised to await the governmental decision based on the Halsbury Committee's report of September 1962. The majority recommended the decimalization of the pound because of its international standing while the minority advocated the decimalization of the 10 shilling. These are the main ways of decimalizing a pound and it would not add to the cohesion of the international monetary system or simplify exchange operations if every possible alternative were implemented, a different one in each country decimalizing under the apparent object of rationalization.[6] In fact, the various movements in Ghana and Nigeria have so far not led to any result, partly due to the lack of sufficient a number of experts in decimalization and

1 Bank of Sudan, *Economic and Financial Bulletin*, October–December, 1960, p. 26.

2 *First Report of the Sudan Currency Board for the period ending* 31*st December*, 1957, p. 4.

3 *The Currency Act* 1956, § 3 abc.

4 Dr S. A. Aluko, 'Decimal Currency for Nigeria', *Morning Post*, January 17, 1962.

5 South Africa (2 Rand equal £1; 1 Rand equals 100 cents) and most of the British West Indies (not Jamaica), Australia, New Zealand etc.

6 For the most frequently advocated systems see John Hunsworth, 'Decimalization for Britain? Case not Proven', *The Banker*, August 1961, pp. 534–42.

partly because the problem, in comparison with others, is relatively unimportant.

The proper time to have introduced such an innovation would have been at the moment of the currency exchange. A vital consideration is the upsetting effect a change in the currency can have, especially in countries where a modern monetary system still does not have the full confidence of the whole population. In the newer African countries the penny and even the halfpenny play an important part in price setting; and it is difficult to decimalize in such a way that the penny is maintained without giving up the pound. The British West Indies system (WI$4·80 equal to £1; WI$1 equals 100 cents; 1 cent equals 1 halfpenny) has laid the stress on the maintenance of the small coin, but sacrificed the pound. Thereby the upward movement of the prices of necessities was avoided, an increase which takes place when the penny counterpart is really worth 2·4 pence, as is the case when the pound is decimalized, or 1·2 pence when the 10 shilling is decimalized. The main choice seems, however, to lie between these two alternatives and the use of half cents when decimalizing to 10 shillings and half and quarter cents when decimalizing to pounds might mitigate against price increases.

Characteristic of the currency in circulation in all these countries is the fact that it is subject to more or less important seasonal variations due to the necessity to move the crops. These variations are most pronounced in countries with monocultures such as Ghana (cocoa) and the Sudan (cotton). Already in Nigeria, with three main crops (cocoa, groundnut and palm oil) the timing of which is different, the seasonal variations are less marked. In Tunisia and Morocco, with several crops, and in Rhodesia, with its important mining community, the currency in circulation and the money supply is much more stable. However, in all countries important differences are seen in the movements of coins, notes and deposits as they essentially serve different sectors of the community.

Table IV shows the composition of the money supply in the six countries at the lowest and highest annual point of the seasonal variations. As expected, in Ghana, the Sudan and Nigeria, the composition of the money supply changes very considerably, while in the other three countries there is much greater stability. Naturally, these changes mean that the central banks have to be equipped with the right sort of currency, coins and notes and the required denominations to meet the demand. As the denominations required gradually change through time with the increasing monetization of the countries, whether due to geographical spread or to a deepening of the monetary system due to changes in habits[1], the central bank must

[1] Cp. p. 200.

TABLE IV

Coins, Notes and Deposits at Seasonal High and Low

	Ghana	Morocco	Nigeria	Rhodesia	Sudan	Tunisia
	Percentages of Total Money Supply					
Low						
Coins	56·4	1·4	19·1	5·5	55·5	1·4
Notes		41·3	43·5	21·0		39·0
Deposits	43·6	57·3	37·4	73·5	44·5	59·6
Total Money Supply	100	100	100	100	100	100
High						
Coins	61·6	1·4	21·7	5·5	60·3	1·5
Notes		40·7	44·0	20·8		40·5
Deposits	38·4	57·9	34·3	73·7	39·7	50·0
Total Money Supply	100	100	100	100	100	100

Money Supply according to IMF definition; figures averaged for several years (5–6 except Tunisia 3.)

SOURCES: Note to Graphs p. 81.

constantly revise its currency policy. This often involves it in some very considerable investments of both capital and staff. The transport of coins and notes is difficult when a country is large such as is the case in Morocco, Nigeria, the Sudan and Rhodesia. The central bank, therefore, finds itself faced with a demand that it open branches, with considerable deposits of coin and currency. While the economy of the country badly needs such facilities, it is difficult to meet the requirements, in view of staff shortages and the very important security measures that have to be taken. The latter also often make the utilization of an agent impossible. Moreover, the operation is hardly the most profitable; on the other hand, such measures tend to decrease the cost of transfer of currency, which reduces the cost of running a modern monetary system.

It is probably only possible to realize fully how large the seasonal variations of the money supply are from a graphical presentation. Graphs I–VI show the changes in the money supply, in coins, notes and deposits for the six countries. The lowest point for the year of the money supply has been taken as the basis; thus the graphs do not all cover the calendar year, but the monetary year of each country which varies from case to case. The trend has also been eliminated and the seasonal variation as presented is an average of the longest series available for each country.

Monthly Changes in Money Supply, Deposits, Notes and Coins, Trend Eliminated

GRAPH I

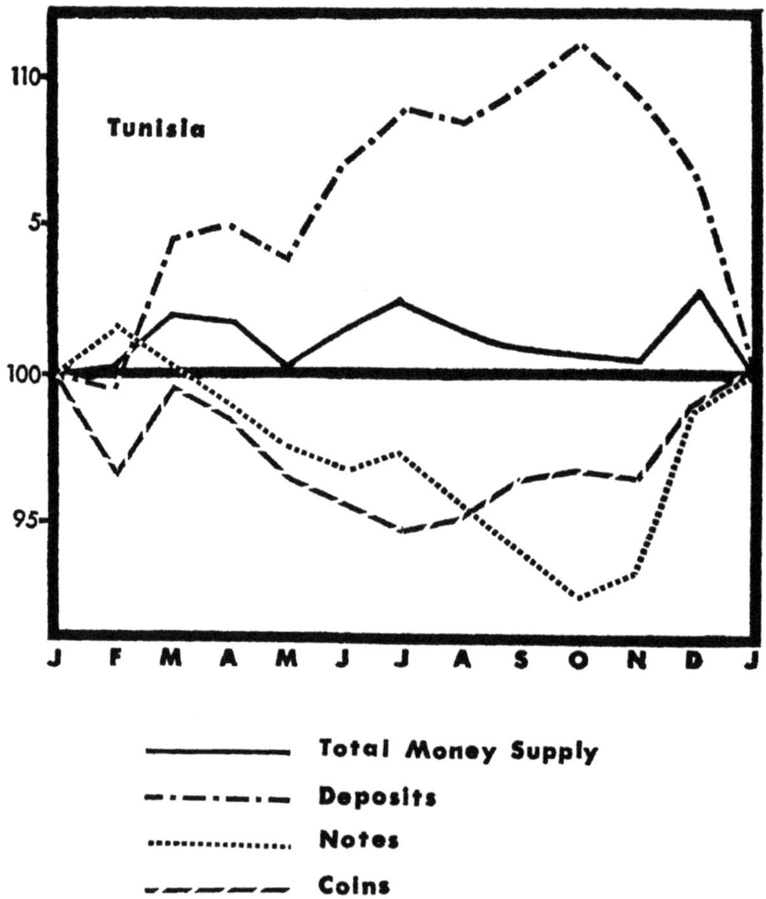

GRAPH II

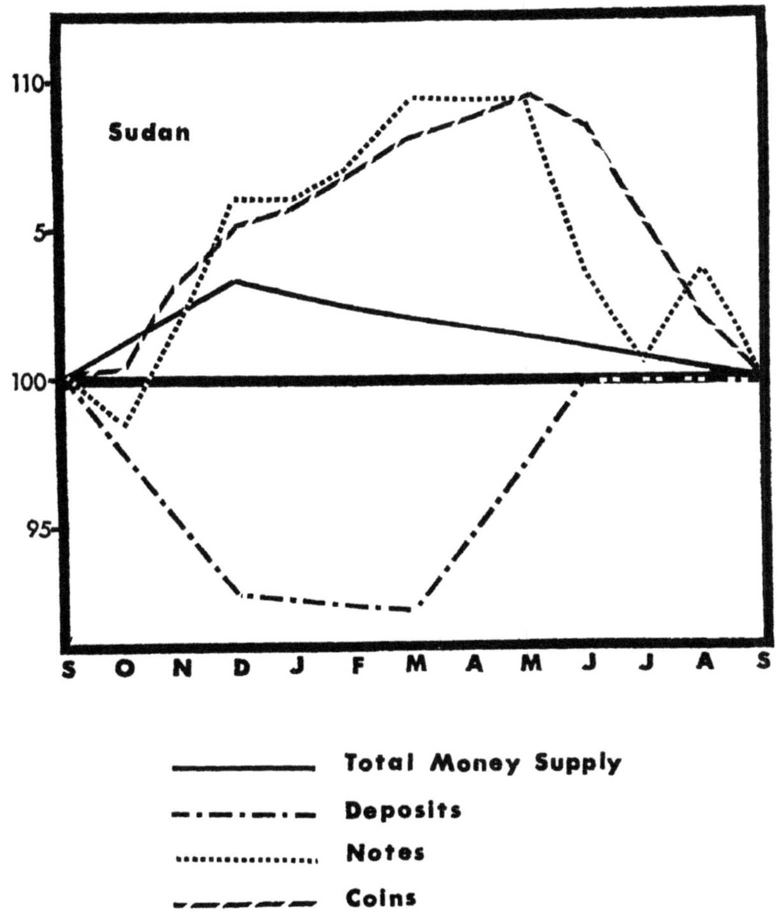
Sudan
110
5
100
95
S O N D J F M A M J J A S
Total Money Supply
Deposits
Notes
Coins

GRAPH III

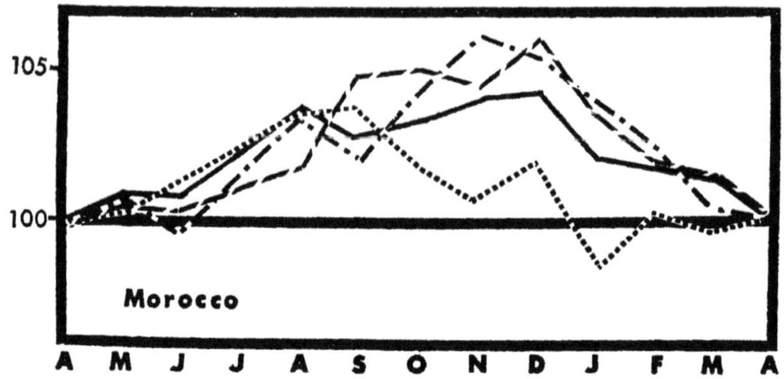

GRAPH IV

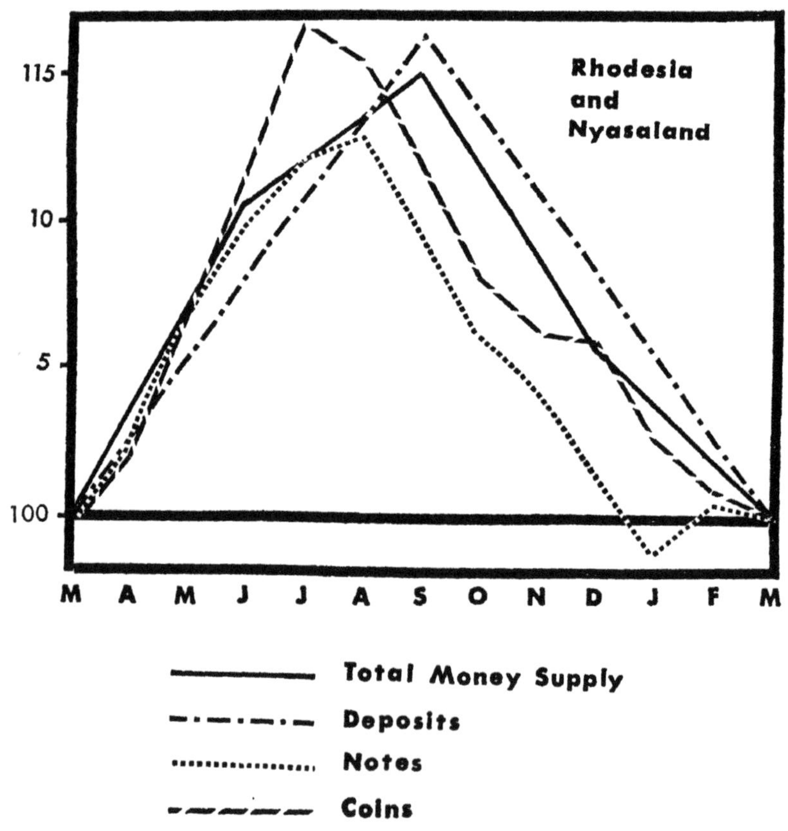

GRAPH V

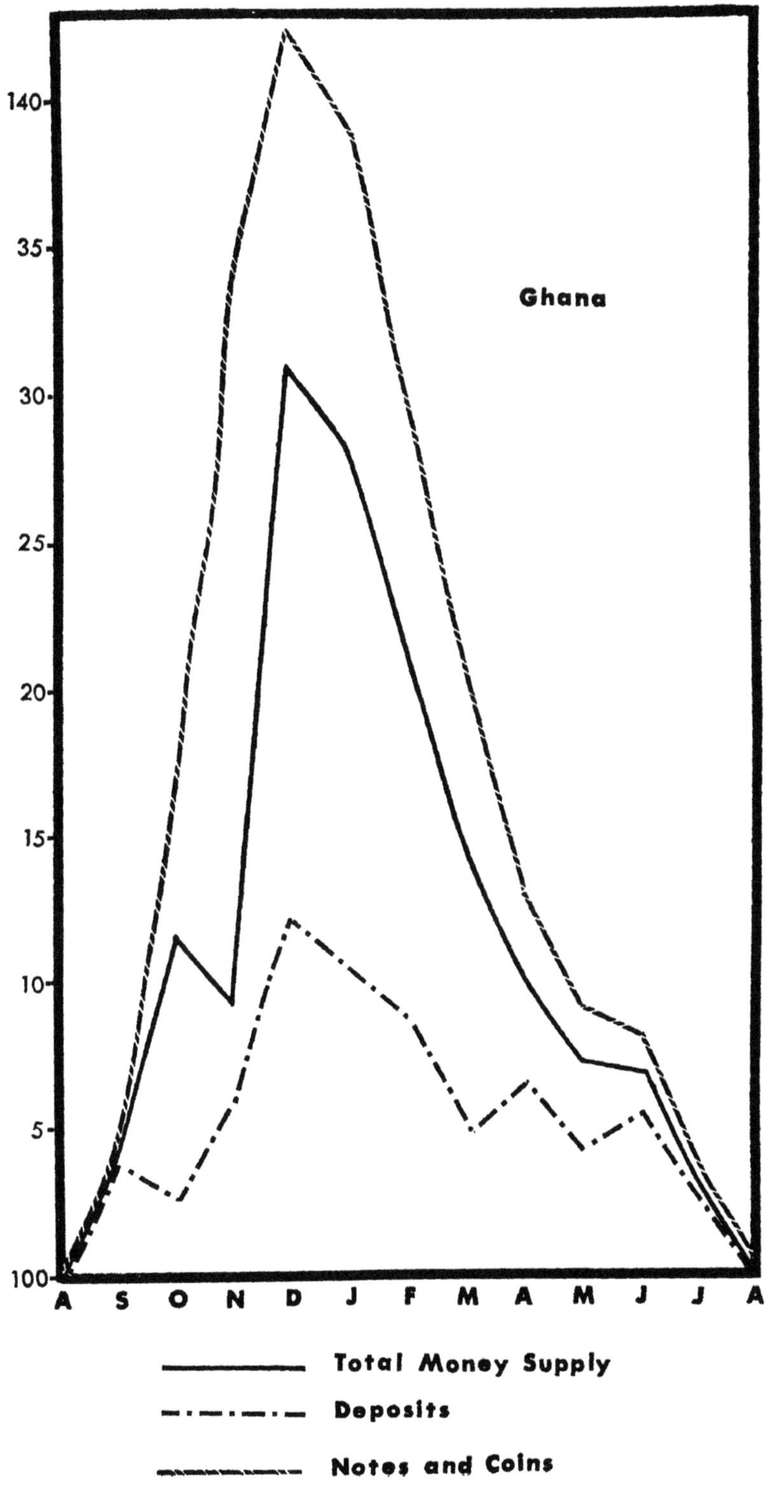

140
35
30
25
20
15
10
5
100
Ghana
A S O N D J F M A M J J A
Total Money Supply
Deposits
Notes and Coins

GRAPH VI

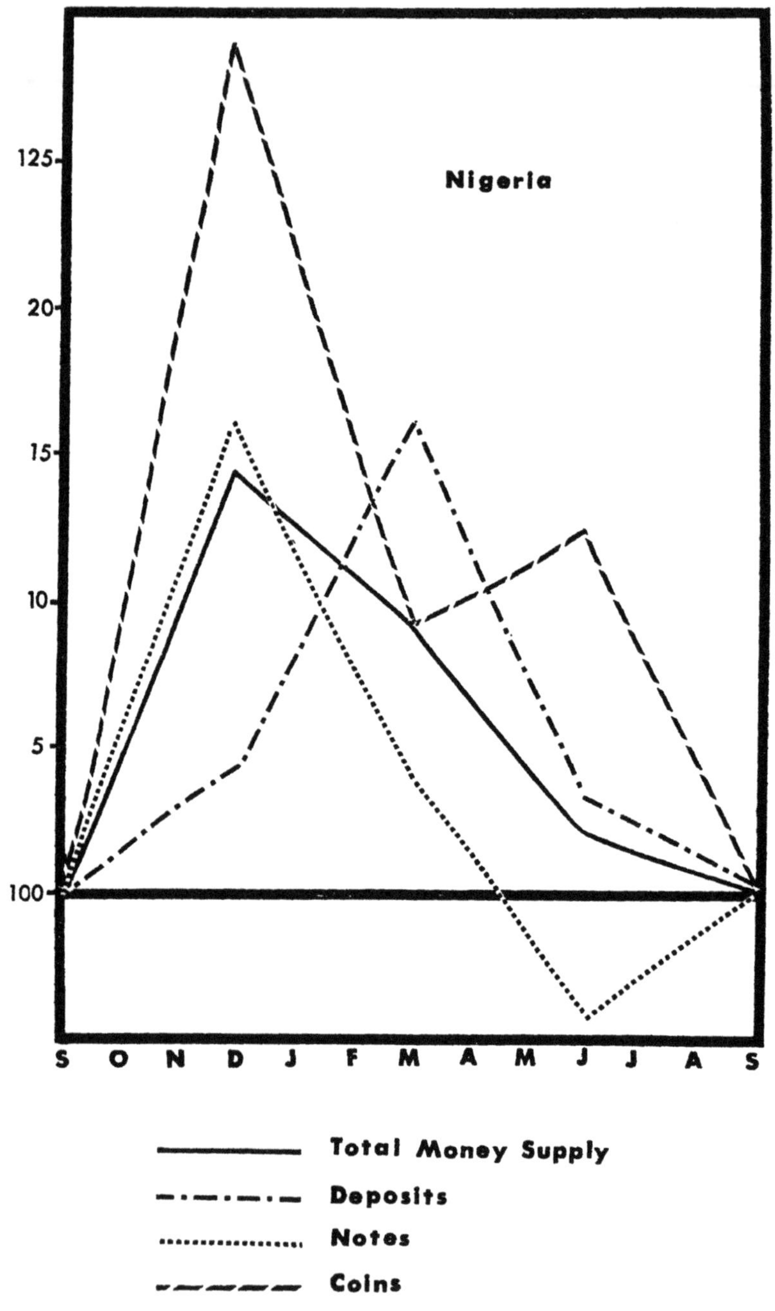
Nigeria
125
20
15
10
5
100
S O N D J F M A M J J A S
Total Money Supply
Deposits
Notes
Coins

For these graphs the trend of the series has been eliminated.

SOURCES:

Ghana:	*Quarterly Digest of Statistics.*
Morocco:	*Bulletin Mensuel de la Banque du Maroc.*
Nigeria:	*Digest of Statistics.*
Rhodesia and Nyasaland:	*Monthly Digest of Statistics.*
Sudan:	Bank of Sudan, Report for the Year ending December 31, 1960.
Tunisia:	*Bulletin de la Banque Centrale de Tunisie and Bulletin de Statistique et d'Etudes Economiques.*

In Ghana (Graph V) the whole seasonal movement of the money supply is dominated by the cocoa crop. Notes and coins (separate series are not published) are used to buy up the crop from the farmers and they increase in the autumn, rising to a maximum at the end of the year (Christmas also having a certain effect), then fall sharply as goods are bought, taxes met and debts repaid. The movement in deposits reflects at a lag and, in a very minor key, the influence of the over-riding factor. In Nigeria (Graph VI) too, there is a maximum in notes, coins and the total money supply at the end of the year, reflecting the peak periods of the sale of crops. These are cocoa in October, palm oil in November and groundnuts in November/December. The preference of the farmers for coin (now shillings, formerly pennies) as opposed to notes is striking. Over the last ten years, however, the larger farmers, especially in the south, have learnt to accept notes instead of coin. This shows a certain change in habits as notes can be eaten by termites, while coin cannot; thus the more progressive farmers are either spending their income, using special strong boxes, or possibly even depositing their income in banks. They are certainly not burying it in the ground! Deposits show a different maximum, namely March. This coincided with the return of the coin and notes and the most important tax payments, which also explains the intervening fall in coin in circulation. The rise in June again reflects the last spurt of trade supported by the mid-year crop before the assets of the previous season have been exhausted. Deposits fall from December onwards as assets are used for purchases and payments of all kinds.

The seasonal movement in the Sudan (Graph II) shows a very special picture. The total money supply appears to be subject to only small variations. This is misleading as the strong increase in notes and coins is compensated for by a marked decrease in deposits. Another remarkable point is that the seasonal increase in notes is as large as that of coin. In most of these countries coins still dominate. This is partly to be explained by the fairly important number of more progressive cotton growers in the relative neighbourhood of Khartoum, who presumably are prepared to take notes, while coins reach essentially the widespread outlying districts. Especially the gum arabic purchases (at their peak in January) and the purchase of hides and cattle would largely be effected by coin. The cotton season for purchases from domestic producers is January to May and also reflects the highest months of the note and coin in circulation. Deposits, on the other hand, show almost the opposite movement. They are drawn down to supply the notes and coin and also to secure imports. As part of the import control regulations, importers have to deposit at the Bank of Sudan the Sudanese counterpart of their purchases abroad in order to secure the import licence. For certain categories the full amount has to be deposited, for others more or less. Thus importers draw down their deposits in expectation of the demand for goods that will be arising when the crops have been harvested. As the Sudan is a relatively isolated country, delays of six–nine months between order and sale are not surprising, this explaining largely the movement of the curve of deposits. The other factor influencing deposits is the payment at the end of the cotton season of the taxes thereon to the government.

In Rhodesia and Nyasaland (Graph IV) with its mixed population, the movements are what would be expected. Coin circulation rises to a maximum in July when the number of seasonal workers on the plantations is at its height, while the notes used for the marketing of the crops lag somewhat behind. The return of coins and notes to the banks at a lag of some two months is clearly shown in the movement of deposits. The total money supply clearly reflects the movement of the other series.

The situation in Morocco and Tunisia is completely different (Graphs I and III). In both countries there is practically no connection between deposits on the one hand and notes and coins on the other, or between coins and notes. They all are used basically by different sections of the population and only overlap marginally. Notes in Morocco are used essentially for moving the crops. They show an increase from April to September when the crops are sold, fall in October–November when taxes are paid (the tertib), rise again somewhat in February when the olives are collected. During this period, too, coins are at their maximum, taxes apparently having little effect and the olive crop an important one. In a bad year, the lesser harvest affects chiefly the note circulation, and has little effect on the coin circulation. Deposits are affected mainly by capital flows to and from France and the USA and the payment of taxes. In Tunisia the divergence between deposits and notes and coin is still more marked. They mirror each other, the notes and coin being at their maximum during the olive harvest, when deposits are at their minimum. Thus, the total money supply being an average, gives a very poor picture of the seasonal movements of currency in these two countries.

The currency exchanges were not only in themselves important technical steps that had to be effected smoothly by the new central banks, but the administration of the currency issuing function with its marked seasonal changes required especial attention. More important are the policy-making aspects of the currency in circulation. These will be discussed below[1] as they are one of the main tools of the central banks for keeping price stability in otherwise under-monetized countries and require, to be effective, the co-operation of the ministries of finance, the marketing boards and the authorities controlling production, imports and distribution.

(*b*) FOREIGN EXCHANGE RESERVES

All the new central banks became responsible holders of all or part of the foreign reserves of the country. In some cases this was intimately connected with the currency exchange and the issuing function of the central bank. By 1962 the central banks in most countries had become almost the sole holders of foreign exchange, apart from the working balances of deposit money banks and sometimes the Treasury.

In Ghana, Nigeria and Rhodesia the governments, the marketing boards and private companies which owned important (sterling) assets had been in the habit of holding and administrating these foreign assets on their own. The lack of a central bank had made such a practice unavoidable. When the central banks were formed, it was not immediately obvious that they should have these assets transferred to them. Governments (including the regional ones in Nigeria) and the marketing boards valued their autonomy. With the passage of time, the assets held independently decreased, partly because of the fall in the external price of the exports of these countries and partly because both planned and unplanned economic development required a considerable expenditure of foreign exchange. The marketing boards found that they were short of the means necessary to finance the purchase of the crops[2] and turned to the central bank for help and assistance. The central banks then usually took the opportunity of strengthening their own position.

The often important assets held by central, federal or regional

[1] Cp. p. 211 ff.

[2] 'Beginning November 1960 the Bank's (Bank of Ghana) foreign assets also include sterling bills drawn by the Cocoa Marketing Board on its marketing subsidiary in the UK in order to finance the purchase of the cocoa crop. Previously the financing was obtained by running down the Board's liquid sterling assets and in 1959 this was combined with loans from the Commercial Banks.' IMF, *International Financial Statistics*, March 1962, p. 131.

governments allowed these to exercise an autonomy with respect to investment and planning policy which sometimes led them to neglect the essential consultation, co-operation and harmonization of policies between all the country's financial and monetary interests. The development plans, sometimes unnecessarily ambitious, certainly contributed to the running down of these assets. But in all countries a gradual realization has grown up that co-operation and consultation between ministries of finance (and planning or economics) and the central bank are necessary for the conservation of the foreign assets of a country. It is now understood that financial and monetary policy must be seen as a whole and that it must not be mutually antagonistic. Thus, there is everywhere greater cohesion than there was only a few years ago. The increasingly greater economic planning has also shown that the foreign reserves of the country have to be wisely husbanded and that there is much to be said for having them concentrated in the hands of the central bank. Then one account shows the total position and the advisability of entering into new commitments can be more easily estimated. Thus in Nigeria, in connection with the introduction of the new six-year development plan, an effort was made to collect the foreign reserves of the regional governments and marketing boards in the Central Bank of Nigeria. The holders were to be given compensation in domestic assets. Necessarily innumerable technical questions[1] had to be solved for such a transaction to take place, but in principle all holders agreed that this was the only sensible policy and the Central Bank of Nigeria's position was correspondingly strengthened, so that it better could discharge its duties towards the country.

In Rhodesia the position is quite different because the main foreign (sterling) assets not in the hands of the Bank of Rhodesia are held by the important, essentially expatriate mining companies. Since these have been registered in Rhodesia (1953–54), their assets have been included in the foreign assets of the country. It is felt that there is here a certain dilemma, and that these assets are not freely available to the government or the monetary authorities in the same way as the Nigerian assets might be. Therefore, it is sometimes argued that these long term assets should not be included in Rhodesia's foreign exchange reserve. It is a moot point. Obviously any total mobilizing of assets would hardly be successful; but even in Nigeria the consent of the holders had to be secured. It is very much in the interests of the mining companies to support any sensible development policy in Rhodesia. These are strong arguments for the inclusion of the assets of the mining companies in the total assets of Rhodesia.

[1] Rate of transfer, purchase, maturity; value of income, liquidity of compensating assets, their availability, the availability of foreign assets, etc.

A similar problem is apparent in all the countries where the largest banks have often been expatriate. They held in some cases —especially in Ghana, Morocco, Nigeria and Rhodesia—important foreign reserves and there has often been not inconsiderable criticism that these large working balances were depriving the country in which they operated.[1] In fact, before the existence of the central banks, the expatriate banks had to hold foreign assets sufficient to meet the commercial and financial demands. Their foreign connections made them very flexible as, in times of stringency, they could draw on the assets of the world markets, especially London and Paris. Since the establishment of the central banks, the increase in the number of indigenous banks to which certain accounts have often been transferred, and the formulation of national economic policies, the expatriate banks have found that much reduced working balances are needed. This movement is clearly shown in the figures of Table V (next page).

The foreign exchange holdings of the Sudan were held by the National Bank of Egypt, Cairo, till 1949–50 when a separate foreign reserve was set up for the Sudan. At the time of the currency exchange, the stocks of notes and coins were the property of the Sudan Government, which concluded agreements with the Egyptian and British Governments (about 40 per cent of the coins were found to be British). In the case of Egypt the 'Financial Agreement, 1957' also covered the outstanding amounts due to the National Bank of Egypt, Khartoum by their Cairo office and the total outstanding debt of the Sudan Government in respect of advances made by Egypt prior to 1937–38 for development purposes. The Sudan Government received from Egypt sterling £20 million (nominal value) in British Government securities in part settlement; the remainder of the amount was put on a 'special account', which is being repaid gradually by deliveries of goods from Egypt and by the use of this special account for capital remittances by the Sudan.[2] The rest of its foreign assets the Bank of Sudan received from the government, which was credited with domestic currency equivalent in value to the sterling securities.

The foreign exchange reserves of Morocco and Tunisia have, since their establishment, been concentrated in the hands of the new central banks. There are no official holdings of foreign reserves apart from the US assets, which are part of the foreign aid being given to both countries. These assets, the counterpart of which is often delivered in kind, are usually recorded separately. The structure of the foreign reserves differs from that of the other countries discussed;

1 Edward Nevin, *Capital Funds in Underdeveloped Countries*, London, 1961, pp. 49–51.

2 Bank of Sudan, *Economic Bulletin*, October/December 1960, pp. 24–5.

TABLE V

Gold and Foreign Exchange Reserves

End of Period; Millions of US Dollars

		1951	1952	1953	1954	1955	1956	1957	1958	1959	1960	1961	1962
Ghana	*	374	379	409	514	532	484	434	450	427	382	186	209
	†	396	413	453	558	584	532	483	507	480	448	211	223
Morocco	*	31	39	42	69	94	84	120	130	141	205	183	170
	†	94	99	119	156	166	142	117	168	184	264	220	219
Nigeria	*				624‡	656‡	647‡	644	559	498	448	368	320
	†				683‡	737‡	718‡	681	599	568	508	470	381
Rhodesia	*	126	130	162	150	178	181	213	207	221	195	226	231
	†	322	233	262	279	279	314	310	311				
Sudan	*	240	185	178	170	152	192	121	88	158	191	177	169
	†	276	211	186	178	165	204	127	94	163	193	179	170
Tunisia	*								47	85	85	74	62
	†								58	97	97	77	68

SOURCES: International Financial Statistics; Nigerian Digest of Statistics.
Morocco 'Etudes et Statistiques'—in 1957 the Deposit Money Banks had a negative holding.

* Monetary Authority and other official.
† Plus reserves of Deposits Money Banks.
‡ March.

they depend upon special agreements between Tunisia and Morocco and the French authorities, which have very considerably modified the former system by which their foreign exchange reserves formed part of the french franc assets at the French Treasury or the Bank of France.

'Tunisia's net position was structurally in surplus. In order to retain for its own benefit the foreign exchange reserve resulting from its transactions with countries outside the French franc area, rather than let that reserve benefit the other countries in the area, Tunisia asked in September 1959 to have its assets at the "Office de Stabilisation" put into a separate account. A statistical account records its in-payments; it was credited at the outset with $15 million so as to allow for the foreign exchange brought in by Tunisia in the course of past years. The administration of this account has given rise to quite serious practical difficulties; it is based on declarations by the banks which deal on the Paris exchange market as intermediaries for Tunisian banks. At the same time the exchange originating from certain financial transactions is kept at Tunis or with foreign correspondents.

'Morocco also no longer participates, except very partially, in the French franc area's pool of exchange. After the stoppage of the operating account, it asked to be allowed to procure on the Paris market, against French francs, the non-French foreign exchange which it needed for its commercial payments; this was on the understanding that, by way of *quid pro quo*, it would sell in Paris its surpluses of non-French currencies deriving from commercial transactions. In respect of its other current payments, and of capital transactions, Morocco has become completely independent. Formerly the reserves of the "Banque du Maroc" consisted only of gold and of franc assets; now they accumulate in the form of balances with numerous correspondents abroad. That does not of course rule out recourse to the Paris market for all kinds of exchange transactions.'[1]

The administration of the holding of foreign assets has been a point which has caused some discussion not only in Morocco and Tunisia. The sterling area countries used to have their assets invested for them and the bulk was placed in long term British securities.[2]

[1] Jean-Pierre Gern, 'Morocco and Tunisia on the Threshold of Monetary Autonomy. *Zeitschrift des Instituts für Weltwirtschaft*, Vol. 90, No. 1, 1963, p. 134. Also in Basle Centre Publication Series A, No. 39.

[2] The Ghana Government appointed a committee in 1958 to advise it on the investment policy of the sterling assets. It was composed of Lord Piercy, Lord Rennell of Morgan, Grenfell & Co., Mr Alfred Eggleston, the Governor of the Bank of Ghana and Dr Goldschlager. The then Minister of Finance, K. A. Gbedemah, said that the maturities of the investments should be synchronized with the capital expenditure under the five-year plan. Moreover he indicated that there would be no aversion to holding part of the assets in equity if this was advised as the best method of maintaining the purchasing power of the assets. Equally a suggestion for a switch into dollar or other foreign currency securities would be considered. *The Banker*, April 1958, pp. 209–10.

As the important surpluses of foreign exchange were earned in the first half of the 1950's, a period of low interest rates in the United Kingdom, a large part of these assets were, by the end of 1960, quoted considerably under par because of the new high interest rate policy. And many of the countries either could not or would not wait till the maturity of the stock, when the full nominal value would be available. Partly due to this experience and partly to the rumours of revaluations, several countries have gradually started differentiating their foreign asset holdings. The official reasons given for these moves are the changing pattern of trade, desired or actual, and the advisability of not being so dependent on the internal economy of one country. The Sudan and Nigeria have switched some of their sterling assets into dollar and gold assets—with the full understanding of the British authorities. Many countries are also keeping part of their current earnings in other foreign currencies in somewhat inflated working balances. To some extent these are also being converted into dollar, a marked preference for short-term paper being evinced.

Closely connected with the gestation of the foreign exchange reserves is the question of the administration of foreign exchange control, which exists more or less liberally applied in all six countries. Legally this function is usually exercised by the Minister of Finance on behalf of the government. He normally delegates the administration of foreign exchange control to the central bank, as only there is the necessary day-to-day knowledge of the situation to be found. Either as part of the central bank itself or as a closely affiliated and subordinated office can the control be exercised with some probability of success. This is doubly necessary when foreign exchange control is being used as a deliberate tool of monetary policy, when for instance the domestic counterpart of the foreign exchange has to be deposited on order instead of on obtention. Moreover, the central bank officials are a hand-picked group of officers on whose integrity and impartiality full reliance can be placed. Their training in efficiency is usually the best in the country and constitutes a certain guarantee that irritating and discouraging administrative delays do not arise. The efficiency attained depends, however, largely on the proportion of automatically granted licences, which in turn is an effect of both policy and the formulation of the law; the more liberal, the more efficient. Above all there should not be frequent or erratic changes in the regulations. This can be avoided if the general monetary, financial and commercial policy of the country is well integrated.

The successful stewardship of the foreign exchange reserves of any country should be such that all current commercial and financial transactions can be effected without difficulty. Therefore a suitably large working balance should at all times be available. The adequate size for any given country depends upon numerous factors. Apart from proper policy measures, the extent to which the economy is open, the variability of exports, imports and their prices and above all 'the opinions of the relevant authorities, national and international, concerning this adequacy'[1] have all to be taken into consideration. An often-mentioned standard is a year's worth of imports. Few developing countries seem to be able to maintain so high a working balance and when mobilizing their assets for their development plans, they often set their aims lower. Nigeria, for instance, has deliberately contented herself with minimum reserves equal to four months' worth of imports, which 'is less than the figure adopted by many countries; equally it exceeds the figure of some others, but I believe that, given our own particular circumstances, it is just about right.'[2] In fact the total reserves of the country, as opposed to those of the central bank, were then more than twice this or some nine months' imports.

How slender the actual free reserves of a country can become depends partly upon the legal provisions for foreign exchange as a part of the backing of the currency in circulation. These provisions are more than just a legal restriction; they are usually necessary to retain the essential confidence in the currency. Thus, a foreign exchange reserve set at a minimum of four months has to be reduced by the foreign reserve needed for the currency backing. This may be, in fact is, in Nigeria around two months' worth of imports. And the currency in circulation is tending to increase, not least because of the developments plan. Thus, if minimums are ever reached, Nigeria would, in fact, only have two months' worth of free reserves, an amount which informed opinion would certainly consider inadequate.[3]

As is seen in Table V, the position deteriorated considerably during the last three years, the reserves of all countries having decreased, while their imports have, in fact, mostly been increasing. Though there appears still in most cases to be a comfortable margin between the total foreign reserve and that needed as backing for the currency in circulation (and demand (sight) liabilities) most countries have, for development purposes, committed very important parts of their foreign reserve. While it is almost impossible to estimate exactly in each case how important these commitments are, that they amount to half or more of the apparent free reserve is probable.

[1] IMF Staff Papers, *The Adequacy of Monetary Reserves*, Vol. III, No. 2, October 1953, pp. 181–227.

[2] Chief Festus Sam Okotie-Eboh, *The Mobilization Budget*, FDP 735/362/1, 200, p. 9.

[3] Cp. p. 225.

One of the reasons why foreign reserves are still as high as they are today is that the Ministers of Finance during the first years had a very cautious policy. They wanted to maintain the currency backing at 100 per cent or just under this high figure. Often judged too conservative in this respect, with demands that a fiduciary issue be created to help finance the economic development, they stood firm. As till end of 1960 there was no indication that finance was the bottleneck in these countries, the policy was justified. The reserves are needed now. And in the early years the Ministers of Finance could expect the subsequently experienced increase in the currency circulation due to both the deepening and the geographic spread of the monetary system. In fact this movement will continue, possibly further hastened by a more rapid economic development and, at worst, by an increase in prices. Therefore, the size of the necessary legal backing of the currency circulation will tend to increase, further reducing the free reserves.[1]

The foreign exchange reserves of the six countries under discussion are not too large for the purposes they are supposed to serve. While these will be discussed in greater detail below, it suffices to note here that the manner in which the central bank administers the available reserves is of great importance. Of even greater importance is its general policy which can have a decisive effect on the changes in the available reserves.

(*c*) BANKER TO THE GOVERNMENT

The central banks in Africa had one obvious duty and that was to be the bankers of the governments. This has also been made one of their obligations in their statutes. In practice, though not always by statute, they usually act as bankers to the state institutions, such as the development corporations, post offices and special agencies. However, in some countries all or part of the accounts of official institutions have been given to the government sponsored commercial bank (Ghana, Tunisia). This has been done either in an effort to strengthen the national commercial bank or because its services were already so efficient. The central bank usually provides its services free of charge to the government and sometimes, though rarely, to the state institutions.

[1] Nevin, loc. cit., p. 13 to p. 21. He argues that the foreign exchange reserves are one of the sources of savings available to the developing countries. He advocates a substantial fiduciary issue possibly averaging 50 per cent deliberately induced to liberate this part for domestic capital investment. While most countries have already used their surplus reserves (over and above 100 per cent coverage) in this way, they were chary of relaxing further than to some 80 per cent. This was due to the realization that with economic development (and sometimes monetization) the high coverage, maintained absolutely, would soon be a much smaller fraction of the total money supply—an argument not discussed by Mr Nevin.

It was obvious from the start that as banker to the government, the central bank should take over the latter's internal accounts. What was not always so obvious was that it should also have the government's foreign exchange reserve.

As explained above, several governments maintained their own reserve for some time; in fact, the Central Bank of Nigeria received them only in 1962,[1] some four years after its establishment.

Being banker to the government means not merely acting as sort of accounting agent for the government's cash position. It also means at times supplying the government with shorter or longer term advances, either on current account or as the counterpart of Treasury Bills or even Government Bonds. These need to be underwritten and issued on both the internal, and possibly the external money and capital markets. Each of these transactions involves policy making, both with respect to current policy, and in a developing country, in respect of the essential but slow task of building up a money and capital market. The ways and means of dealing with the latter task will be discussed below.[2]

The important point here is the more or less inflationary effect credits from a central bank have on the economy. When the borrower is the government, the case is both clear and has been carefully studied. This was done for European conditions in wartime, a laboratory example of strained inflationary financing. During the war efficient physical controls, chiefly rationing, price and wage control, kept inflation latent. The moment the moral pressure of winning the war was removed, the physical controls became more or less inoperative and the post-war inflations developed. Unfortunately, the dangers of especially central bank credit are not as well known as could be desired and the implications for policy are sometimes disregarded when they prove inconvenient. This is a special temptation when a country wants to speed up economic development and has reached the point where finance, and especially internally raised finance, becomes a bottleneck. It therefore seems to be pertinent to discuss briefly the main points in respect of the central bank.

While there are several ways in which a government can secure the funds it needs—and it is assumed that it will only raise them in order to spend them—these methods can be divided into two distinct categories according to

'what happens to the total amount of money (cash and bank balances) in the hands of the public and to the liquidity of the banking system as a whole. Perhaps the most practical single dis-

[1] Chief Festus, loc. cit., p. 10.

[2] Cp. p. 172.

tinction is between those operations which absorb part of the money volume already in the hands of the public and those which add to that volume.'[1]

Behind this way of looking at the problem is the assumption that money 'in the hands of the public', represents latent purchasing power and that it is liable to be used. This is especially the case in a fast developing economy or would apply to wartime conditions especially if nothing were done to counteract such a tendency. Thus, an increase or a decrease of the money supply is equivalent to an increase or a decrease—sometimes even multiple—of purchasing power and absorbs or releases goods and services.[2]

Using the resulting increases or decreases of the money volume as the criterion, there are five methods of raising finance. The first three, taxation, borrowing genuine savings from the public and borrowing funds accumulated in the past[3] absorb money from the public. These methods are therefore neutral in respect to the economy as a whole. The other two methods of financing expenditure both add to the volume of money. They are borrowing from the commercial banks[4] and direct borrowing from the central bank.

'The greatest danger attaches to direct borrowing by the government from the central bank, thus swelling the money volume and money income of the community and either expanding the note circulation or increasing the liquidity of the banking system. In the latter case, the banks, having to carry the costs of increased deposits and in many cases to pay interest on funds deposited with them, may seek to acquire more revenue producing assets and further increase the volume of their lending, thus entering on a secondary expansion of credit.'[5]

The extent to which the above will increase the volume of money, depends both on the banking system of the country in question and on the economic conditions at the time the loans are made.

The clearest case of an increase in the supply of money is direct borrowing from the central bank. It may be assumed that the government borrows in order to spend. If then, the government secures a credit of 100 millions of newly created money at the central bank it will use this to pay for goods and services. The primary

[1] BIS, 12*th Annual Report*, p. 15.

[2] A. C. Pigou, 'Types of War Inflation', *Economic Journal*, December 1941, pp. 439–48.

[3] Borrowing past savings has the effect of reducing the lending capacity of the institution or individuals in question for other purposes.

[4] Cp p. 136ff.

[5] BIS, loc. cit. p. 14.

effect will be that some part of the credit, say 30 million, will be paid out in the shape of notes and coins and increase the volume of currency in circulation; the remainder will be paid by means of drafts to private persons, firms, etc., who will deposit the other 70 million at the commercial banks. These banks in their turn will receive as the counterpart of these new deposits a claim on the central bank of 70 million. The secondary effect of the loan will depend on the practice of the banking system in respect to reserve ratios. Usually the commercial banks' claim on the central bank will form part of their reserve ratios (formal or informal) and therefore be the basis for a multiple expansion. Such an expansion will be especially probable when the effective demand for credit is high—or if, as pointed out, the banks are actively trying to find revenue earning assets.

Thus direct borrowing by the government from the central bank will increase the money supply in the first place by an expansion in the note circulation and in the volume of deposits, the sum of their increase being equal to the size of the original credit. In the second place, the increase in the commercial banks' reserve ratio through the counterpart draft of the new deposits at the central bank will allow a multiple expansion of the money volume depending on the customs or laws applying to the reserve ratio.

Evidently, the effective demand for credit by the public—or the government—for loans from the commercial banks is a key factor. If either the applicants for credit cannot meet the standards set by the commercial banks—though these will tend to relax them under the above circumstances—or if there is virtually no demand for credit on the part of the public, the secondary inflationary effects will not materialize. However, even if at the time no effective demand for credit exists, the commercial banks will have become more liquid and the government's initial expenditure is likely, especially in a developing economy, to give rise to a demand for credit at some later stage.[1] The commercial banks will then be in a position to meet it, provided that the central bank has not changed the requirements of the reserve ratio. To do this to an extent that would be in proportion to the size of the original credit to the government is usually difficult to effect.

Developing countries normally do not lack (latent) inflationary pressures. The general stepping up of activity, with a corresponding increase in the velocity of money, the foreign loans—to the extent the counterpart is not delivered in kind—the inevitable partial bottlenecks which have a price increasing effect all pile up the pressure. Moreover, there is the yearly influence of the price and the size of

[1] For example, the government builds a feeder road; the local transport entrepreneur eventually increases his fleet to twice its former size.

the (cash) crops, which always takes more money out into the country with no necessary real counterpart. The central bank, as the cornerstone of the monetary system, is thus constantly under pressure to release more currency and credit for circulation. This demand should correspond to the normal demands of trade, and to that extent it is necessary for the economic growth of the country. Any additional demands are likely to be inflationary. A government's demands for finance, especially if these are more than purely temporary, are apt to be additional to the normal needs of trade. It is therefore necessary for both the central bank and the Minister of Finance as the government's representative, to know exactly what the implications of such a policy are. Only then can, in the light of the actual internal and external position of the country, the wisdom of such a step be gauged.

The drafters of the statutes of the new central banks in Africa, irrespective of their monetary areas, were all, thanks to their war and post-war experience, very conscious of the danger inherent in central bank credits to governments. They knew well that what started as advances in respect of temporary deficiencies of budget revenue could easily be stretched for purposes initially unintended. Thus, the absolute size of the credits allowed is narrowly circumscribed, though made flexible by being related to the size of the current budget revenue. Thus the governments can legally receive 5–20 per cent of current revenue as advances from the central bank. In some countries this credit may only be for six months, or it has to be repaid within the current financial year or within six months thereof. Moreover, the 20 per cent mentioned above includes direct purchases of Treasury Bills. The regulations are, therefore, quite restrictive, and on the whole they have been respected, even if window dressing occasionally occurs. Both the Sudan and Morocco are countries where the governments' own assets at the central bank far exceed their debts, whereas in Ghana and in Tunisia the opposite is the case.

The temptation of borrowing too much from the central bank is becoming an issue.[1] Till 1961–62 internal finance was not a bottleneck. The situation is changing rapidly and the countries are carefully surveying their internal and external assets, while wondering how far they will stretch.

(*d*) RESEARCH DEPARTMENTS

One of the most important tasks of the new central banks was the establishment of their own research departments. These were badly needed as the new central banks usually did not have even the most elementary statistical monetary and financial information on their

[1] Cp. p. 227.

own countries. The research departments had all to start by collecting statistical information on such things as the number of banks and their branches, till-money, deposits, advances, their distribution by branch and size, the asset holdings and the many other series necessary for formulating the policy making of the central banks. The practical statistical problems have often been enormous—the central banks departments have, however, succeeded in establishing surprisingly reliable series, even if their scope and detail still need to be enlarged. Naturally, the most modern break-downs have, where possible, been used and often the most modern mechanical aids—by elimination of the human factor accuracy is much higher.

The staff problems for the research departments were in some ways less acute than in the rest of the central banks. The department, however important, even essential, was not a policy-making department and could therefore more easily have foreign experts, either seconded or appointed outright. The ground that had to be broken was not new in principle, it was the same basic material that had to be produced everywhere in considerable quantities before original analysis could be undertaken. Though the central bank had usually been legally empowered to obtain information from commercial banks and other financial intermediaries, the lack of systematic and simplified classification did not facilitate the task. Moreover, many financial intermediaries were not used to the modern statistical approach and, even when more than willing to co-operate, they found the information requested hard to compile and present accurately. The work required a special type of economist with a marked statistical sense and an infinity of patience. In most countries the basic series are by now available and the collection of the statistics is a more or less automatic procedure.

Thus the new problem of detailed current analysis of the economic situation, to have as a basis for monetary policy, is arising. So far, the analyses that have been done, have been mainly the work of non-African specialists. In the near future, the new African experts will be increasingly active. Some of them are brilliant. But they have rarely had the quite specialized training that can only be acquired by several years of work in the research department of an established central bank. They have often visited European and other central banks for shorter periods or had a year as an International Monetary Fund-trainee or at the staff college of the International Bank for Reconstruction and Development. Their main training has, however, usually been acquired at universities of many different types. Moreover, their intellectual and temperamental approach sometimes tends to put economic growth at the forefront of their thinking. They often neither know nor have they understood the dangers that are inherent in any policy that is not well balanced in respect to all aspects of the economy. The effect the new economists will have on the economic policy making in their individual countries will be interesting to observe. Naturally, the actual policy makers usually have a certain influence.

An important, but perhaps not obvious, job that the members of research departments as well as the senior staff of the central banks had to undertake, was the economic enlightenment of the population. The work of the new central banks is namely made doubly difficult by certain characteristics of the economies in which they operate. Chief among these is the lack of comprehension for monetary and financial questions which is often found even in the highest ranks of the administration. While luckily enough, ministries of finance have usually had as ministers and senior administrators African or expatriate experts, the administrators in other ministries may not know, and therefore not recognize, the limits as well as the possibilities of autonomous monetary policy. When this lack of knowledge leaves the monetary and financial decisions in the hands of a small group of experts, the inherent weakness of the situation may temporarily be overcome. However, as the economy of the country develops, the central bank has to operate on a much wider field. Its various activities bring it into contact with increasingly wider circles, which will not have had the benefit of even the very rudimentary knowledge of such questions as is found in the Western World. The new central banks, therefore, have the additional task of spreading the necessary basic knowledge both to special groups of administrators and above all to the population as a whole.

The senior central bank staff and the members of the research departments have often been active in writing articles, inspiring journalists and above all in giving radio talks. The wireless has become in African countries the most important means of spreading information to a broad cross-section of the population. It reaches areas where newspapers are a rarity and persons who either cannot read or who would not use their knowledge for a 'serious' article. Before currency exchanges, when introducing new measures, such as Treasury Bills or Government Bonds, central bank officials have given radio talks explaining the measure for the man in the street. On other occasions central bank officials have arranged and taken part in round-table discussions on a new budget or even run a series of talks on a basic economic information. The more factual and useful the latter can be, the greater the echo it is liable to find. Skilfully drawn up, much general knowledge can be built into such a series of lectures.

To reach a specialized group of administrators and senior officials other means are usually required, if only because they need more detailed information. Formal and informal discussions between central bank officials and their closest collaborators is one of the best ways of clarifying issues. More general as well as current problems can be discussed at meetings of Economic Societies, Chambers of Commerce and Bankers Associations. The education of future administrators in both general economic and legal problems should be done at universities and technical high-schools by a series of general courses for all faculties.[1] In this way the new middle classes will receive the general knowledge they will need both in their private as well as in their public capacities. Future senior officials or ministers with a specialized background such as medicine, agronomy or engineering, would have the general knowledge and understanding in order to be able to take collective responsibility for the ministries or the cabinet on general policy.

The research departments of the central banks have proved increasingly necessary for general research, public relations and for economic analysis. The publications of the central banks are valuable sources of information for government, administration and the business section of the community. They are usually reliable and unsensational; as such they are valued at home and abroad.

[1] Cp. p. 122.

CHAPTER VII

CENTRAL BANK POLICY: MAKING IT EFFECTIVE

While a detailed discussion of monetary policy must be reserved for Part IV, which will attempt to build out the context in which the Central Banks have to operate, there are certain aspects of central bank policy, which must be included in this chapter.

The basic and most important problem that faces any new central bank in a developing country is how to implement and make effective the implicit or explicit injunction to assist in the economic development of the country. The main qualification here seems to be imagination for, on the one hand, new and kaleidoscopic problems have to be tackled promptly with tact and vision, while, on the other, the high principles of central banking standard must be maintained.

In their attempts to maintain the external and internal value of the currency, while controlling the monetary situation without hampering economic growth, the central banks find themselves faced with two separate, though connected branches of policy. The one is the policy they pursue towards the commercial banks and other financial intermediaries, the other is the policy as adviser to the government. Evidently these two aspects are closely interconnected as the authorities' major policy decisions and implementations will react on the system of financial intermediaries. Therefore, the two policies must be consistent or unwanted and unexpected contradictions will be created, which will negate the total policy.

There is thus no breach between so-called traditional prerogatives and policies and the new, dynamic attributes. This applies to the whole gamut of transactions and obligations from being banker to the government, to the control of commercial banks and other financial intermediaries,[1] to the development of financial institutions of all kinds,[2] to the issuing and marketing of different kinds of paper.

[1] The new central banks usually alone (and sometimes in conjunction with the Ministry of Finance) enforce the bank law and often the insurance law as well.

[2] The Banking Act (July 1, 1960) in the Federation of Rhodesia and Nyasaland has deliberately eased the rules of 'eligibility', by giving a larger field of action to financial institutions, which cannot be qualified as banks, this in order both to render the financial system more flexible and to give opportunities to Africans. However, any future bank (defined as any institution accepting deposits from the public) must obtain a licence.

However, the technical means used are different and here we are mainly concerned with the policy towards the commercial banks and the financial intermediaries. The tools at the disposal of central banks in Africa are much the same as those which have become traditional in the financially more mature countries. They are liquidity ratios, rediscounting facilities, credit 'rationing', which actually in Morocco and Tunisia means controlling the direction in which credit is given, interest rate policy and embryonic open market operations. While the statutes of the central banks empower them to use these means, it has often proved, for several reasons, difficult to put them into effect.

The new central bank almost always has its capital entirely subscribed by the government. This is, however, a detail compared to the distribution of competences in the statutes. Moreover, the personality of the governor is decisive for whether the central banks have sufficient independence to fulfill their purposes. Most governments—however 'new'—realize that it is to their detriment to jeopardize the currency and with it the monetary and financial stability of the country and therefore tend to support the central bank in public, whatever family differences there may have been behind the scenes.

The question of the control of the central bank over the commercial banks (and other financial intermediaries) is one of the most difficult. Ideally, the informal contacts of commercial bank managers and the governor of the central bank should be sufficient to make the policy of the central bank both understood and followed.[1] In fact, it is proved time and again that this high moral position is only acquired by the combination of personality and latent powers.[2] The government's respect for the central bank contributes immeasurably to its authority.

Thus the central bank should, however, be able to count on a position of formal and real authority. In positions of difficulty, however, effective weapons are needed.

Foremost among these weapons are liquidity ratios[3]—also called

[1] 'The Bank (of Rhodesia and Nyasaland) has relied more on moral suasion reinforced by the powers to fix statutory deposits and liquidity ratios. For example, during the second quarter of 1956, it requested the banks to restrain lending for the speculative acquisition or erection of fixed property and for non-essential imports, and there was a further request in more general terms in January 1958, which was not withdrawn until February 1959. This latter was part of a general squeeze on credit.' Bank of Rhodesia and Nyasaland, *Annual Report* 1961, p. 3.

[2] It is important that the commercial banks know that the board of the central bank will allow the latter to enforce regulations when they are needed.

[3] Sir Theodor Gregory, *The Present Position of Central Banks*, Stamp Memorial Lecture, London 1955, p. 21. For comments see Richard S. Sayers, 'The Variations of the Cash Reserve Requirements' in *Central Banking after Bagehot*, Oxford 1957, pp. 85–91.

variable reserve ratios—customary in financially mature countries, enforceable by law in emerging countries. These are supposed to guarantee the interests of the depositor and, of all the monetary weapons, have most nearly retained their original purpose. However both the size and the composition of the liquidity ratio allow it to be used as an instrument of monetary policy.

The size of the liquidity ratio is usually of 30 per cent or higher. In most countries it can be varied according to the demands of the situation. Some banking laws differentiate the ratio according to the type of bank or financial intermediary, in other countries the regulation is less flexible. A proposal which is often made is that different ratios should apply to expatriate and indigenous banks on the grounds that the former are more liquid.

'This proposal is, of course, discriminatory between the two classes of banks but could presumably be justified as it is in line with the Government's policy of aiding the development of the indigenous banks. More serious perhaps is the fact that this proposal is discriminatory towards banks of the same class, because although expatriate banks are as a whole more liquid than indigenous banks this may not be so in the case of individual banks.'[1]

The argument is, thus, refuted by those who make the proposals. But the idea is constantly being raised and, in order not to 'discriminate', is often based on a size measure (capital, turnover, etc.). As many important international commercial banks often have only one agency in African countries, put in to deal with specialized interests, these expatriate banks would be on a par with the smallest indigenous banks—an absurd situation.[2] Moreover, the original idea, of safety for the depositors, is the *sine qua non* for the development of indigenous banking. In order to establish confidence, the argument could easily be reversed, as Africans seem to realize that new and inexperienced bankers are more likely to make investment mistakes than well-established and experienced institutions. Thus a differentiation according to type of bank, commercial or deposit, or according to the type of financial intermediary, bank, building society, merchant bank or hire-purchase institution, is the more rational approach.

In fact, liquidity ratios have been well above the minimum specified. In Ghana, the liquidity ratio has varied from a maximum of 65

1 Early draft (photostat copy) of articles of Charles V. Brown, Jr., 'The Supply of Bank Money in Nigeria. *The Banker's Magazine*, November and December 1960, pp. 1 and 11.

2 The provision that, if foreign assets are included in the liquidity ratio, the central bank may limit the proportion, should be sufficient to eliminate the advantage some expatriate banks are supposed to have.

per cent in December 1958 to 44 per cent in 1960 and 32 per cent in 1961, while cash ratios were respectively 17, 19 and 12 per cent.[1] By December 1962 the liquidity ratio had risen to 50 per cent and the cash ratio to 16 per cent. Decreased economic activity had increased liquid assets while the increase in deposits had been slight. In Rhodesia and Nyasaland the liquidity ratio was 34·7 at the end of 1960, 34·2 in 1961 and 36·2 in 1962. Exchange control, early proceeds from tobacco sales and a lower level of advances than the previous year led to the higher liquidity ratio.[2] In Tunisia, though no liquidity ratio is fixed in the central bank statutes, attention is paid to the ratio obtaining between quickly mobilizable assets compared to all assets. This was in 1960, 1961 and 1962 in the private sector 44, 37 and 32 per cent, in the semi-state sector 24, 16 and 22 per cent, giving an overall relationship of 34, 25 and 25 per cent respectively. The semi-state institutions tend to specialize on medium and long term loans.[3]

The composition of the liquidity ratio varies but usually consists of all or any of the following assets all of which must be unencumbered; the first two items are the 'cash ratio':

(*a*) notes and coin which are legal tender in the country in question,
(*b*) balances at the central bank,
(*c*) balances (and/or Treasury Bills) held abroad (usually UK), up to a certain proportion set by central bank,
(*d*) Treasury Bills (domestic),
(*e*) inland bills of exchange and promissory notes rediscountable at central bank—up to a given proportion determined by the central bank,
(*f*) net balances at any domestic bank.

In the case of Rhodesia and Nyasaland part of the liquidity ratio (also called reserve ratio) has to be held as a deposit with the central bank. The latter is also the case in the Sudan, though the central bank may specify other forms at its discretion.

The composition of the liquidity ratio, by its inclusion of Treasury Bills, can be so designed as to further and assist in the creation of internal money markets. However, the embryonic instruments of a money and capital market must be available, otherwise only deposits at the central bank can be used for reserve ratio requirements. Moreover, reserve ratio requirements can be varied through time so as to correspond to the needs of the money and capital markets—and it is possible to have such a flexible system without endangering either the currency or the interest rate system. In such an exercise

[1] Bank of Ghana, *Quarterly Economic Bulletins*.
[2] Bank of Rhodesia and Nyasaland, *Annual Reports*.
[3] Banque Centrale de Tunisie, *Rapports Annuels*.

the central bank has contributed both to one of its traditional functions, the control of commercial banks and has also assisted in development by first furthering an institution. However, care must be taken that the liquidity ratio does not become debased into a means of assuring the government a market—and a permanent holding—for its Treasury Bills. Such a policy was attempted in some European countries after the last war. A bitter lesson was learnt, that the liquidity ratio is a monetary measure and as such should be kept flexible.

The utility of liquidity ratios as a monetary weapon in export-oriented countries has been attacked as not being very efficient. The demand for commercial bank credit is relatively small so that changes in liquidity ratios do not have enough influence. The essential purveyor of purchasing power is the money supply due to the seasonal payment of the cash crops—and over the latter there is none or little control.[1] The reflection of this demand is in (seasonal) imports and therefore a prepayment of part or all the cost of imports (often affected ahead of time in view of the expected demand) would help control this increase in purchasing power. Such advance deposits on imports would influence both 'the desired cash balances of the private sector' and second would 'withdraw purchasing power from that sector'.[2] While this is perfectly correct and possible to put into practice, it assumes permanent import licensing. This would build into the system an undesirable rigidity. It also complicates administration—which is usually a weak point. It is, however, an effective alternative or complement to liquidity ratios and has been practised in the Sudan, where there were no rediscounting facilities.

In fact, the central bank has a much simpler way of controlling the commercial banks, namely by their rediscounting. This normal measure of control exists in all the countries under discussion, which were all familiar with the bill of exchange or commercial bill, which had been introduced for foreign trade purposes at an early date. Its existence is not merely necessary for the central bank's control over the banks and the money economy, it being a smooth and elegant way of making the central bank the lender of last resort, but also because it is needed in order to assure a flexible supply of credit to the economy.

How important this is is shown by the conditions which existed in the Sudan before the introduction of discounting facilities early in 1962. The commercial banks could only obtain credit against foreign securities, which the indigenous banks did not possess, or actual cotton. The latter system was a bit unwieldy. There were also restrictions, which had to be administered by the commercial banks,

[1] Cp. p. 74 ff.

[2] Olakanpo, loc. cit., p. 404.

on advances in the categories 'imports, retail trade, personnel and professional'. These restrictions were mainly in order to make more difficult the financing of excessive stocks of imported goods. With the introduction of rediscounting the Bank of Sudan's control over credit expansion of the banks could be exercised through the control of availability and cost of central bank credit to them—thus making qualitative credit control no longer necessary.[1]

The discounting of bills from commercial banks started in April 1961. Since then banks that have been using other forms of credit with the Bank of Sudan have been able to choose either to avail themselves of the same forms of credit as previously (against cotton or foreign securities) or to present bills for discount within the overall limits of their credit lines with the Bank of Sudan. In addition to commercial bills, the Bank of Sudan also accepts bills issued by banks' customers to the order of a commercial bank in respect of advances secured by exportable produce of the Sudan. The inclusion of this category of bills was justified by the relative scarcity of the genuine commercial bill and the need to provide an easy means for the re-financing of the banks' advances to customers in respect of exports. The latter are seasonal, more so than appears from the overall banking figures, as the seasons partly cancel each other out. Naturally each harvest needs its own financing.[2]

Rediscounting of trade bills is also usual in Morocco, Tunisia and Rhodesia and is on the increase in Ghana and Nigeria. Naturally, the main customers are the indigenous banks, who do not have outside resources. The large expatriate banks, British, French, Egyptian, Arab or other, which have access to the financial centres of the world are less dependent on the local central bank. This corresponds to the best international banking practice where commercial banks, public or private, first have recourse to their partners in other countries, only then to their central bank. As the economy matures the indigenous banks will acquire good foreign contacts, so that they only need to have recourse to the central bank in the last resort, while the expatriate banks will become relatively less dominant in the financial structure of the country. In spite of this, as banks with a special link to an abundant flow of credit, which can be diverted to the country in question for temporary finance (crop, etc.), they should always prove a valuable asset. Thus when the resources of the international commercial banking system are exhausted, the central banks of the world truly become the lender of last resort.

[1] Bank of Sudan, *Economic Bulletin and Financial Bulletin*, January–March 1961.

[2] Bank of Sudan, Circular letter to banks containing conditions for the discount of bills of exchange or promissory notes and for loans against the collateral of such bills and notes. Khartoum, March 1961.

While in all countries the commercial banks as a whole have recourse to the central bank, individual banks may be liquid enough to be independent, or only to require its assistance at the height of the export season. However, the combination of liquidity ratios, rediscounting and the gradually increasing dominance of the central banks, should mean that these odd cases are no danger. It is very much in the interests of the commercial banks themselves to support any sensible central bank policy. And the commercial banks that might be liquid enough to be able to be independent of the central bank, are exactly those which are most likely to realize this and, therefore, those whose loyal collaboration is assured.

It has been shown above how directional control of credit was used in the Sudan as a stop-gap measure, before the discounting of bills was introduced. In this case it was used exclusively to prevent certain types of credit financing (chiefly the carrying of inflated stocks of imported goods) from becoming too large. In Morocco and Tunisia the directional control of credit for the purpose of altering the structure of credit is perhaps the main tool of the central banks. It complements the activity of the governments both with respect to the government plan and essentially in the financing of the semi-public institutions, which have been created to stimulate activity in agriculture and industry.

The organization of the banking system is somewhat different in Morocco and a short description is necessary as an introduction. The Banque du Maroc was made the official controller of the legal dispositions and the regulations pertaining to the banking profession and to the organization of the money and capital markets.[1] The commercial and other banks are organized into a Comité des Banques, which also has two sub-committees, the Comité du Crédit et du Marché Financier and a professional committee (salaries, organization, etc.).

In the Comité des Banques the Banque du Maroc plays a dominating part.

'Son influence, appuyée par les moyens dont il dispose institutionnellement plus que par la lettre de la réglementation, lui permet, lorsque la nécessité en apparaît, de faire prévaloir le point de vue de l'intérêt général et de conduire le Comité à user de son pouvoir réglementaire dans le sens nécessaire à l'application d'une politique du crédit cohérente. D'autre part, l'Institut d'Emission assure les arbitrages nécessaires dans les débats qui peuvent intervenir lorsque

[1] Statutes § 13.—These powers were previously the prerogative of the Ministry of Finance.

le Comité des Banques, comme le Comité du Crédit et du Marché Financier, sont saisis de certains problèmes à titre consultatif.'[1]

Thus the influence of the central bank is important, allowing it to use 'moral suasion' while the banks themselves are also consulted. The Comité des Banques in Morocco is an ancient institution and its existence has been legally confirmed several times by the banking law.[2] Thus the internal cohesion of the banking community in Morocco is very pronounced and is more formal and far-reaching than is the case in countries where there are rather new Bankers' Associations.

It is in this context that the Banque du Maroc exercises its credit control. The practical administration of the latter was, however, formally revised in 1959 and the new system was officially implemented from the beginning of 1960. Each bank was accorded an upper limit to its rediscounting facilities at the Banque du Maroc. These ceilings represent the upper limit to which commercial bills and other credit instruments can be rediscounted. An exception, because of its seasonal character, is made for credits financing the stocking of cereals (grains). Also excepted are certain medium term credits where the Banque du Maroc can determine whether the credit will be given in the first place.[3]

The rediscounting of medium term credits (up to five years) is one of the peculiarities of the central banks of Morocco and Tunisia and it is intimately connected with the directional control of credit. It is done in order to assure sufficient varied financial resources for agriculture, construction and even for industry. There is no lack of overall finance in these countries, the recourse to the central banks is always below the ceilings. But the quality of credit available often leaves certain sectors short and the rediscounting of medium term paper is one of the means of redistributing available resources. This can also safely be done as there is no monetary pressure in these countries.

In Tunisia the central bank has an even more dominating position

[1] Banque du Maroc, 'La réglementation des activités banciares au Maroc', *Etudes et Statistiques*, Bulletin Mensuel, October 1960, p. 31: 'Through its influence, which is more strengthened by the institutional means available than by the regulation, it is in a position to make, if necessary, the general interest prevail and the committee use its statutory power in the direction needed to pursue a coherent credit policy. Moreover, the Banque du Maroc is able to arbitrate in debates, which may arise when both the Comité des Banques and the Comité du Crédit et du Marché Financier have to deal with certain problems as consultants.'

[2] *Réglementation et organisation de la profession bancaire* (roneographed). Dahir January 31, 1943, revised January 15, 1954, January 17, 1955 and April 16, 1955.

[3] Banque du Maroc, *Rapport Annuel* 1960, pp. 44–5.

in the whole credit structure. In 1961 it rediscounted some 25 per cent of total short term credits, 28 per cent of medium term credits. This important help naturally made it possible for specialized institutions to invest a greater proportion of their own funds in medium and long term loans. This is confirmed by the fact that the chief applicants for credit facilities were the semi-public institutions which applied for 47 per cent more credit facilities, and mainly short term, than the previous year.[1]

It is naturally possible for a central bank to affect the structure of credit by its discount or rediscount policy without necessarily having a full system of credit control.[2] Especially where there is a variety of institutions specializing in various types of financing, the easing of credit for one part of their activity, say short term, will liberate funds for medium or long term investment. Naturally, it is a policy that requires very careful handling, especially in countries where there is high pressure on the country's financial and real resources, implying powerful latent inflationary tendencies. However, such a flexible discount or rediscount policy, imaginatively conducted, should be able to ease bottlenecks within the structure of credit, without necessarily resulting in more overall credit being mobilized.

Various discount or rediscount rates for different types of institutions and/or credits would be one of the more formal technical means of achieving such a policy. Such differences have not been applied, as uniform rates are traditional. There would, however, not be any basic reason why such a differentiation should not be tried, especially as it would tend to re-enforce the efficacy of the interest rate policy of the central bank.

The interest rate policy of the central banks in the six countries under discussion is not as effective as in financially mature countries.[3] This is due to the smallness of the monetary sector relative to the whole economy, the dominating position of cash crops and the very small number of financial intermediaries, especially the lack of effective money and capital markets, making supporting open market operations impossible. There are, therefore, few changes in bank rate though they are not unknown. It is, however, questionable as to whether changes of a half per cent have much influence.

The Rhodesian attitude to the possibilities of interest rate policy is the most positive of all the countries under discussion. However, in spite of the fact that this country has the most differentiated

[1] Banque Centrale de Tunisie, La distribution du crédit. *Rapport Annuel* 1961, pp. 81–93.

[2] Directional credit control is usually disliked by the commercial banks, who feel, especially when the demand for credit is large, that it is they who have to bear the onus of saying 'no' to the general public.

[3] Cp. p. 233.

monetary system, the attitude is still very reserved and cautious as is shown by the following quotation:

'It is through its discount rate and as the lender of last resort that the Bank sets the general pattern of interest rates throughout the financial sphere. The Bank first quoted its discount rate at $4\frac{1}{2}$ per cent on 1st August, 1957, shortly before it assumed responsibility for managing the Treasury Bill tender on behalf of the Federal Government. The rate remained unchanged until 1960 when it was raised on 3rd August to 5 per cent, and, on 29th June, 1961, to $5\frac{1}{2}$ per cent.

'As in other countries, the level of bank rate exerts an influence on other rates and it is therefore likely to affect the level of credit throughout the financial system. However, it cannot be so effective an instrument of control as in more highly developed centres.'[1]

In Ghana changes in bank rate have also taken place, it being $4\frac{13}{16}$in March 1960, rising to a maximum of $5\frac{13}{16}$ in June to fall to 4 in December. By July 1961 it had reached $4\frac{1}{2}$ per cent where it has remained stable.[2] The movements were mainly reflections of the price of money in London and the stable rate, the breaking of the link through foreign exchange control.

A limiting factor is, moreover, the transfer charge on funds to abroad, London and Paris, a factor that has to be taken into account. Several attempts have been made to liberate the countries from this link, which is often considered onerous. The introduction of exchange control has sometimes been seen as a means to break the link. It is possible that its actual importance is over-estimated, especially now when there are domestic investment possibilities at rates which are often higher than those obtainable in London. Only very important changes in interest rates abroad are likely to make it profitable to invest abroad because domestic returns have to be majored by the transfer charge.

While the field in which effective interest rate policy by the central bank is growing slowly, the heavy superstructure of the natural interest rates has a soporific effect. Very high and traditional rates of interest (profit) have often made the individual capitalist indifferent to 'moderate' rates and to their changes. Only a rapid increase in savings invested through money or capital markets, where the return is seen and calculated, can break the iron grip of usurious rates.

One of the main arguments for the creation of money and capital markets[3] is that by their very existence they should stimulate savings

[1] Bank of Rhodesia and Nyasaland, *Annual Report* 1961, p. 3.

[2] Bank of Ghana, *Quarterly Economic Bulletin*, September and December 1962, p. 46.

[3] Cp. p. 172.

and make both liquid funds and investment capital available at reasonable rates of interest. The central banks have everywhere attempted either to create money and capital markets (Ghana and Nigeria) or to support markets already in existence (Morocco, Rhodesia and Tunisia) or plan to enlarge the possibilities (Sudan). The central banks have themselves a specific interest in the creation of these markets as they should eventually give them a new monetary weapon, namely open market operations.

The existing money and capital markets have in fact been too narrow to allow a very active policy. However, the very existence of the central banks has improved matters because they handle the tender for Treasury Bills.[1] This allows a certain flexibility here which has not been entirely without effect. By introducing a system of open bidding the supply and demand for short term money could find an equilibrium reflecting market conditions. The central bank could also adjust the issue so as to take advantage of market conditions. Thus the first issues of Treasury Bills in Ghana (spring 1960 £G2 million a month) and Nigeria (£N2 million in April and £N1 million in May and June 1960) were in fact launched at a time when, owing to the seasonal influence of the cocoa harvest, the banks and the Cocoa Marketing Boards have liquid resources to spare, while on the other hand, the government is particularly short of funds.

The issue of government bonds is also increasing the number and quantity of financial instruments available. The capital market should, however, not be exhausted by the government's capital requirements, which are increasing everywhere because of the size of the new development plans. One of its main functions should be the supply of risk capital for productive investment, whether industrial or agricultural. This implies eventually having a stock exchange and they exist on a modest scale in Morocco, Nigeria and Rhodesia. In Ghana, the Sudan and Tunisia brokers meet periodically in order to effect the purchase and sale of the small number of shares offered. As more saleable equities appear on the markets such *ad hoc* arrangements can easily be expanded and formalized.

The most positive influence of the central bank in a new economy may easily be the activity it can and should develop as adviser to the government. The statutes of the central banks specifically stipulate this function and in the case of Tunisia enlarge it to an obligation of warning the government of any condition, which might endanger monetary stability. Both the preventive and the positive aspects of the advisory capacity should be developed by the central bank with the full co-operation of the government and its official institutions.

In countries where highly specialized skills combined with a

[1] There are none in the Sudan.

broader view are even rarer than they are in more mature countries, the Governor, Vice-Governor and the Advisers, if any, of the central bank represent hand-picked, trained and discriminating persons. They are also by their functions, and the statutes re-emphasize it, uncommitted to any vested or sectional interests. They are bound to safeguard the stability of the currency, while promoting economic growth and development.

Moreover, the central bank is the executor of monetary policy by all the various operational means at its disposal. It has a unique position in that it has close contact with the markets, while having the judgement of an impartial observer. It should be able to judge better than any one else the effect that can be obtained by any given measure designed to affect the monetary aspects of the economy.

It would therefore be hard to find more fitting advisers to the government on all issues pertaining to economic and financial matters, all of which will ultimately affect the monetary situation. By following the best traditions of financially mature countries, whether continental, British or the US, the Governor of the central bank has always been the adviser to the (sometimes changing) minister of finance and through him to the government. For important matters a sub-committee of the cabinet or even the total cabinet would normally seek the opinion of the Governor of the central bank.

Even more important than official appearances are the informal contacts of the Governor of the central bank with the government and the senior civil service especially at the ministry of finance and at the ministry of economic planning. Here the matter in hand can be discussed before the memorandum on it is drafted and it is always easier to adjust opinions in the give and take of an easy discussion.

Some Governors of central banks, moreover, find both the time and the energy to be chairman (or adviser) to a variety of committees such as those on economic planning. This can really only be possible where the persons concerned are outstanding and where the central bank is supplied with above average staff and not too serious problems arise.

With all these intertwining activities the question arises of 'the degree of final responsibility borne by the Central Bank for policy decisions still varies to some extent in different countries. . . . But whatever may be the precise definition of statutory responsibilities, and the exact division between the functions of principal and of agent, it has seemed to me of recent years that the practice, and indeed the philosophy, of relationship between Government and Central Bank has tended to become more uniform in the major centres. The conception, fairly widespread fifty years ago, that the Central Bank should get on with its own business and not pay too much regard to politics or Governments, has steadily given way to the different conception that, though retaining much independence in its operations and in its thinking, the Central Bank should act in the closest harmony with Government. . . . And everywhere it has become increasingly recognized that monetary policy and general fiscal and economic policy are part of the same picture, in which the final responsibilities must lie with Parliaments. . . . Central Bank leaders would agree, I think, with equal insistence that they cannot properly carry out their responsibilities unless they enjoy a large measure of independence from Government both in their technical operations and in their policy thinking. The importance of independence in operational matters is obvious enough. The need for an independent approach to policy may be more controversial, but I submit that it is no whit less important.'[1]

The independent approach to policy making on the part of the central bank representatives can be a most useful check on the more political and committed approach of the politicians. While the latter—according to modern practice—must take the final and full responsibility for the policy pursued, it is valuable to them to have it pointed out that the consequences of a policy they may desire for certain reasons, probably will have side effects, at least, which may be anything but desirable. Furthermore, there are occasions when radical changes in policy are necessary. If it is for the greater good of the country, it may then be necessary to have called to one's notice that 'It is the job of the politician to make the economic necessity politically possible'.[2] It is the central bank which can point this out long before the country need rely on foreign or international economic experts and advisers.

It is in its advisory capacity to the government that the dynamism and imagination of the new central bank can come into its own. Whether this is apparent or not depends, however, on the contrast effect with the government and especially the minister of finance. If the latter is a hot-head, who pays no attention to the realities of the situation, the central bank will appear in its—traditionally—conservative role. If the minister of finance is himself conservative and lacking in imagination, the central bank may be using its energies to put some dynamism into his activities. Both these extreme cases have actually arisen in the six countries under investigation. Naturally the general public usually only sees the combined effect of the co-ordinated policy of central bank and ministry of finance and therefore is badly placed to judge the real position taken on any question by any one of the two parties concerned.

Normally, however, such unusual extreme cases are rare and the

[1] Lord Cobbold, *Some Thoughts on Central Banking*. Stamp Memorial Lecture, London, 1962, pp. 6–7.

[2] Wilhelm Röpke, autos epha.

frequent consultations revolve around matters where the principle is more or less agreed, while the technical means of executing it offer several alternatives. The central bank is apt to advocate the one that, from the point of view of the stability of the currency, is most preferable. As this often involves considerable technical knowledge, the central bank's opinion should be weighed carefully. Moreover, few Governors are unable to explain the essence of the fascinating points involved to an interested audience. While it may not always be possible to accept the central bank's attitude, whenever more important confidence or monetary effects can be expected, its opinion should be allowed to weigh heavily when taking a final decision.

The discussion of the means of control available to the central banks in these six countries shows that even at best, the sphere of operations and the intensity of control that can be expected of a central bank in an emerging and, thus by definition, financially immature country, is circumscribed. The monetary economy is still too limited and too narrow, it has not yet gained the depth that allows refined interest rate techniques or liquidity ratios and open market operations to be effective. If the central bank is to contribute actively to the deepening of the monetary system, it has also to help towards the development and growth of the economy, and this it can do best as adviser to the government.

CHAPTER VIII

SUMMARY AND CONCLUSION

The establishment of central banks gave a focal point to the monetary systems of the six countries under discussion. The central banks immediately mustered the existing financial intermediaries and this in itself gave a certain flexibility and direction to the monetary economy. However, full operational and policy efficiency has to be earned also by a central bank. Though more progress has been achieved than could have been expected in the few short years, there is still a long way to go. The worst problems probably lie in the future and it is then that the patient and constructive work of these initial years will be put to the test.

The central bank had primarily to secure its operational foundation. The introduction of the national currency was one of the first measures. It was not only needed because of political considerations, but in order to have a well-defined money supply. The currency exchange led to the taking over of the foreign assets of the country. Sometimes this was achieved directly when the central bank acquired immediately all the foreign reserves. Elsewhere the central bank only acquired the amounts relative to the backing of the currency, while independent holders retained their foreign assets. Their later centralization at the bank required a further measure. In several countries the acquisition of the foreign reserves involved also the administration and enforcement of foreign exchange control. Another of the central bank's main functions was taking over of the government accounts and often also those of public and semi-public institutions. This step was not merely a routine matter where the central bank acted as a sort of agent to the government, but was often enlarged to the handling of government short and long term debt. In its turn this involved helping in the creation of money and capital markets, which in themselves were also necessary as collectors of capital, indicators of interest rates and additional, if future, monetary weapons, because they would allow open market operations. In order to have the necessary information on the state of the economy, the central banks had to set up research departments which, in the beginning, were often not more than glorified statistical offices and which, only after some years of existence, could start monetary analysis.

Making central bank policy effective towards the financial intermediaries required a different type of action. The enforcement of liquidity ratios and/or directional control of credit, either as a stop-gap measure or a permanent one, were major innovations. The introduction of discount or rediscount facilities of commercial bills and/or promissory notes made the central bank the lender of last resort, and assured a more flexible and smoother method of supplying credit to the economy. Not merely the facility with which credit could be obtained, but the terms on which it was available became the start of an interest rate policy, which, however, is less efficacious in these countries than in financially more mature economies. One of the reasons is that the money and capital markets are still embryonic and do not allow supporting open market operations. The other main reason is the importance of issue of new money for the cash crops. The central banks are attempting to influence the domestic price paid to the producers. Their contribution to the formation of a more differentiated economy, where the domestic sector takes a dominating position, should also alter the relative importance of the new money issued for the cash crops, making it a marginal, not a major, factor.

Apart from making the right type of credit available in sufficient quantities for the various sectors of the economy, the central bank's biggest contribution to economic growth is in its function as adviser to the government. Here the central bank is an objective and uncommitted expert on the monetary effects of the government development plans, the means by which they can be financed and the stresses and strains to which they are liable to expose the economies. By seeking the minimalization of the latter they can help to assure a smoother and more continuous rate of economic growth.

PART THREE

CHAPTER IX

FINANCIAL INTERMEDIARIES AND THE STRUCTURE OF CREDIT

The variety, the number and the extent to which commercial banks and other financial intermediaries are subject to the control of the central bank differs greatly among the six countries under investigation. This is the case in spite of the fact that these countries are all relatively advanced as emerging African countries and, compared to the continent as a whole, relatively homogeneous. The density of financial intermediaries in the individual countries varies, however, with the history of monetary development, the speed at which trade grew up, and the degree of differentiation in the economy due to the availability of natural resources and/or the demands made by an indigenous or an expatriate population.

While it is impossible here to discuss even briefly the history of the establishment of the various commercial banks and other financial intermediaries, it can be assumed that till the mid or late 1950's, financial institutions were established in Africa in response to a need for the type of institution in question. The needs were created by the ever-increasing trade with Africa, the demand of the expatriate population and the colonial government to have available the banking facilities they normally had in their country of origin, as well as the desire to get round the cumbersome and sometimes costly method of shipping out currency. Thus, the establishment of the first bank in Lagos, on the West Coast of Africa in 1892, came in direct response to the advice that a bank was 'an urgent necessity' in view of the 'serious inconvenience (due) to the lack of banking facilities'.[1] Later, the possibility of current and future profits attracted other banks of various nationalities. Still in 1945–53, the marked boom in Morocco led to the formation of new expatriate financial institutions, the existence of which was justified by the apparent possibilities of both immediate gain and long term operational opportunity.

Since the new conception of engineering deliberate economic growth has been the major objective, the fundamental motivations

[1] Albert Adomakoh, 'The Evolution of Currency and Banking in West African Countries, in *Jahrbücher für Nationalökonomie und Statistik*, Vol. 174, No. 6, 1962, p. 510. Also in Basle Centre Publication Series A, No. 42.

leading to the establishment of banks or other financial intermediaries has changed. On the one hand you encounter the desire to have a 'national' institution of a given type, irrespective of whether there already exist sufficient institutions of this type or not. Sometimes the motivation is a 'prestige' reason, sometimes it is believed that national institutions will look after African interests better[1] and sometimes the newly created institutions really fill a gap in the structure of the available financial intermediaries that a country at that stage of 'dynamic' growth would need.

Far more important is, however, the idea that by establishing an institution you can create a need for that institution, or use it for some ultimate purpose. The creating of these financial institutions is seen as part of the dynamization of the process of development. Under this theory they are established ahead of the time when a 'natural' demand for them would arise. They are seen, as they by their very nature are, as means to an end.

Their deliberate establishment as part of the growth and development process is thus also seen as the means of attaining something the economy in question very much needs, both immediately and in the future, desires. This argument maintains that a commercial bank will further internal and external trade, a savings bank engender savings, a development bank create flourishing private enterprise, a Stock Exchange bring into being a capital market.

Assuming firstly that the establishment of the institution has been correctly judged with a view to the stage reached by the economic development of the country, the basic and sometimes unconscious assumption is that the financial intermediary in question will have a very active policy. While institutions established in response to a need for them have, metaphorically, been able to sit back and let business come to them, the new institutions in Africa have not only to go out and find the business, but often they have to create the business. This requires more than just good sales talk. It demands on the part of the financial intermediary a basically active and constructive policy, which harmonizes with the major aims of the economic growth of the country in question. Thus, financial intermediaries will find that they must plan and work to create their own future sphere of activity, while, if possible, earning their living in the present.

Whereas several of the newly created financial intermediaries, such as some development banks, find that with an imaginative policy they can more or less immediately find a useful sphere of present and future activity, others have much greater difficulty in

[1] For some of the criticism levelled at earlier institutions see Thomas Balogh, 'Structure économique africaine', *Revue Economique*, Vol. XIV, No. 2, March 1963.

justifying their existence. Sometimes this is due to over-crowding. Apart from the occasional failure due to lack of imagination, flexibility or experience on the part of the management, many of these borderline financial institutions have a degree of sophistication which is too pronounced for the stage of economic and financial development attained by the country in question.

The need for imagination in the management of any financial institution or intermediary must not mean a relaxation of the requirements of the soundness of the business undertaken. But, within this limit new methods (or techniques) of granting loans,often with the collaboration of other authorities, could give additional flexibility to the credit system. This is not an utopian dream. Here and there new methods have successfully been tried and will in part be discussed below.[1] Sometimes they require a staff of consultants, costly from the point of view of the individual bank or institution. However, collaboration between several banks or other institutions would be a possible solution. Moreover, it is more than probable that such extra-operating costs could be financed by international agencies on a loan or grant basis. An efficiently run system, that could mobilize domestic assets and pass them on to viable productive enterprises, would probably be considered as one of the most constructive investments in future development.

An additional problem is that often the interest rate structure of developing countries is such that it makes certain types of constructive loans (e.g. to agriculture) too expensive for the creditor. This type of problem can be solved by the setting up of special funds for the purpose. Whether these funds are financed by internal savings or taxes (i.e. directly or indirectly through the government) or by foreign lending agencies is, from the domestic point of view, immaterial. It is only when the loans given can be expected to cause a direct or indirect (multiplier or accelerator) demand for foreign exchange that partial or full financing by foreign lending agencies should seriously be considered. An approach of this kind can be justified for certain purposes because, with the changes brought by development, the 'natural' structure of interest rates (and profits) can be expected to change. While most projects must take the current structure of the latter into account, there are certain desirable relatively long term spheres of development which should be favoured by cheaper credit. Their choice requires, however, a very sure hand.

There is, unfortunately, no absolute measure as to what type of financial intermediary is suitable for any given economy in a process of development and growth. Any decision will always depend upon relative evaluation. It is evidently fairly clear that a country pos-

[1] Nevin, loc. cit., has made the techniques that can be attempted the central theme of his newly published book.

sessing only one commercial bank is unlikely to be in immediate need of a Stock Exchange. On the other hand it becomes very difficult to estimate at what point a country already fairly well equipped with financial intermediaries of several kinds may start to need an acceptance house.

The decisions which have to be taken by the authorities are simplified in very many cases as it is often only a question of licensing the financial institution. This giving of permission to operate, however complicated the preceding negotiations may have been, has usually relieved the authorities of the task of judging the profitability prospects of the enterprise. If an individual or existing firm (domestic, African or expatriate) calculates that, in the given context, the establishment of the financial intermediary is worth while (either on an immediate or future profit basis or in order to safeguard future markets), there is a high probability that the project is well founded, as private persons or firms cannot afford to risk an investment in capital, personnel, effort and time on an apparently non-profitable investment. In fact, the monetary and financial authorities have usually viewed with favour the establishment of a variety of new financial intermediaries, provided these have conformed to the minimum requirements of the banking or insurance laws (or before the latter existed, any standard they set themselves).

The authorities have, however, a much more difficult task when they decide to establish a financial intermediary or institution which is ahead of the degree of development of the country, or which fills a need, sometimes glaring (such as agricultural credit) which no one else would undertake.

The criterion of immediate profitability is in this case not always a sure guide as the sphere of operations has to be built up. Among the factors that must be taken into consideration are the expected growth and development potentialities of the country, the existing and prospective structure of financial intermediaries and the demands that can be anticipated upon the latter by the former. This pattern is closely connected with the direction that has been given to the country's growth and development by the overall framework within which the authorities are working. The discussion of these aspects in the introduction applies here[1] especially as to the interaction and mutual compatibility between the starting point and the possibility of choice of policy.

The selection of the financial intermediaries to be established must be in line with the 'chosen' policy. If, for instance, the economic growth of the country is expected to be fairly autarchic a relatively broad network of banks and other institutions for the domestic market would appear more suitable, while, if the amount of foreign

[1] Cp. p. 21 ff.

trade is likely to be important, export–import banks may be more strategic in the development process. In fact, both types of institutions are likely to be necessary because developing countries are usually highly dependent on foreign trade, while they are all attempting to build up at least a domestic, if not an export industry. Because of the historical importance of international trade in these countries, the financial intermediaries for financing it are usually available. Some countries, for good or bad reasons, are bent on altering these ways and means. More urgent seems to be the creation of institutions for financing the domestic development, whether agricultural, industrial or perhaps even commercial—though the latter sphere often seems to be more or less well financed either by self-financing or by an internal vertical credit system, not to mention the usury which is so ubiquitous and which is such a heavy burden for the population, and shackle to modern development. Only the establishment of a network of suitable financial intermediaries, the spreading of the knowledge of their usage among the population and the building up of 'creditworthy' individuals can alleviate this abuse, while laying a constructive foundation for the future.

Much has been said in the chapter on central banks[1] about the need to use all the means of modern advertising (radio, newspapers, speeches, discussion groups, etc.) to spread objective and factual information about banking and other financial methods and techniques throughout the population.[2] The (expatriate) commercial banks have of recent years played a considerable part in disseminating information, not least by advertisements in newspapers. The savings banks, including the co-operative and post office, have recently joined the movement, not merely to increase their deposits but also as part of savings campaigns initiated by the governments.

1 Cp. p. 96 ff.

2 This is a problem also in developed countries and is shown by the following extract from the Swedish-International Press Bureau, August 10, 1962. 'The number of cheque accounts in Sweden's commercial banks has increased from 170,000 in 1957 to 433,000 in 1961 and a continued rise is being recorded this year, according to a report by the Swedish Banks Association.

The rapid increase is principally due to a more general introduction of wage and salary payments by means of cheques. In 1961 alone the number of accounts rose by 90,000.

Parallel with the increase in the number of cheque accounts the cases of cheque fraud have also shown a rise, although not on an alarming scale, the report says, while pointing out that the rate of abuse is comparatively low from an international point of view. Joint reporting of abuse, quick barring of accounts and *detailed information given to new account holders are methods used to counteract fraudulent practice.*

Even in the United States the need of economic education is considered acute. See E. Sherman Adams, 'The Problem of Economic Illiteracy'. Text of an address given by Vice-President, First National City Bank before the Annual Dinner of the Chamber of Commerce, New York, October 9, 1962.

These latter, too, are beginning to advertise their saving and premium bonds. Most of this information is being directed to the whole population, the propaganda being largely in pictorial form, not merely as an advertising device but also in order to take into account the unfamiliarity of certain sections of the population with the printed word.

As African societies are, however, very heterogeneous, if only because of the speed with which the modern economy has been introduced and, therefore, the very varying degree to which it has been assimilated by various sections of the population as well as individuals, this information should be spread as selectively as possible. The presumptive share holder will need quite a different type of information from the savings bond buyer or the new insurance policy holder or the individual venturing to open a current account. Moreover, in this transition period of rapid change, the illiterate 'mammie' or cocoa farmer may well be wealthy enough to buy both shares, bonds and run a savings account. And these apparent abnormalities should as far as possible be taken into account.

There is one group of persons who should, however, be selected for special attention. These are the students of the universities, technical colleges and other institutions of advanced learning. They are the presumptive future leaders of the country whether 'elite' or 'upper middle class' in the intellectual sense. They will probably not only have their own incomes to administer, but that of firms, organizations and even governments. They should be given the basic necessary information, banking, financial and possibly legal, while they are in a group that can be reached. This could be done fairly easily for students of all faculties.[1] Few universities in 'developed' countries have such a system, much to the regret of many faculty members and future employers, and its general introduction in Africa would give the individuals as well as the countries a head start over most other continents.

One of the main reasons why information about banking, stocks and shares, insurances should be spread broadly and effectively is that, the whole system being new and unfamiliar, the population does not understand how it can and should be used. It is this lack of comprehension that is at the root of the many complaints about the so-called reluctance of the commercial banks and insurance companies to accept African clients. Both the expatriate *and* indigenous banks, which also have to conform to ordinary banking standards so as to avoid bankruptcy, must require that their clients accept the basic principles of banking and insurance in their dealings

[1] Erin E. Jucker-Fleetwood, 'Banks at Universities of Developing Countries' *Schweizerische Zeitschrift für Volkswirtschaft und Statistik*, Vol. 96, No. 2, 1960 pp. 235–7. Also in Basle Centre Publication Series A, No. 30.

with these institutions. Even the most liberal government sponsored loan schemes become inordinately expensive if they cannot operate as revolving funds. This means that they have to be able to count on repayments being effected as foreseen. For all these reasons progress in the banking and financial intermediary field can only be achieved if coupled with increasing information and education on the way these institutions work and the manner in which they can be utilized.

The governments in Africa are themselves in favour of a more differentiated and wider network of financial intermediaries. The reason is not only because they see these institutions as a means to accelerate the introduction of a modern economy but because they hope and expect that they can thereby create domestic savings.

One of the few points on which all economic experts agree, whether theoreticians, administrators or policy makers, is that the major part of the capital needed for the development of each single country will have to come from that country. International credits, loans and grants, even if expanded to several times their present volume (and it is questionable whether this would be in the best interests of the developing countries themselves) can only be a marginal—though essential—contribution.[1] The amounts of capital needed are so huge that only domestic savings can supply the requisite volume. As economic growth and development gets under way, it should be perfectly possible to obtain not inconsiderable domestic savings—which by definition are then invested. All historical studies prove this, even those of the most recently emerged countries such as Japan. In the communist countries—which do not borrow internationally—all capital is raised internally by a system of indirect taxation so complex that it reaches all goods and production processes.[2] It has the effect of keeping the standard of living at any given (relatively low) level. For various reasons, the governments of Africa have rejected such a system and expect to be able to obtain the domestic savings their countries need by other, more flexible means. One of their main allies in this campaign they see correctly in the system of banks and other financial intermediaries, which are not only potential sellers of saving and premium bonds, but collectors of both savings and liquid funds. These amounts form the greater part of the domestic capital and credit available but they can be supplemented by the credit creating capacity of both the central bank and the commercial banks.

[1] Alexander K. Cairncross, 'The Contribution of Foreign and Domestic Capital to Economic Development' in *Factors in Economic Development*, London 1962, pp. 39–74.

[2] Wolfgang Stolper, *The Structure of the East German Economy*. Harvard, 1960, p. 256 ff.

Before discussing the role of various types of financial intermediaries it is interesting to examine the structure of credit. Table VI gives the percentage distribution of credit (loans and advances) extended by institutions registered under the banking law. Only five countries are given as it proved impossible to obtain a comparable breakdown for Morocco. The credit structure as shown, covers essentially short and medium term loans.

Automatically excluded is credit given in trade bills discounted in foreign centres and naturally all the private domestic system of loans and credit. In certain sectors these two exceptions are important. In Rhodesia, for example, much of the foreign trade is effected by foreign finance, while in all countries there is a tendency for certain creditworthy individuals to act as intermediaries between the banking sector and their less creditworthy countrymen. This is especially marked in the Sudan, but probably is fairly ubiquitous. No legal intervention is possible as these persons use their private fortunes for their financial transactions, obtaining bank credit for their commercial and industrial activities. As they carry a certain risk, though lessened by their knowledge of the persons involved, this credit is much more expensive than that advanced by the banks. As it is still sought, it presumably is put to profitable use and contributes to the flow of credit in the country. Naturally, it cannot be directed, but follows fairly closely the market demands. While sometimes going to excess, it does help to attenuate the bottlenecks in production, services and transport that otherwise would arise. Its main use is in the shadowy but all important sector between the original domestic economy and the modern sector. The activity of these private financial intermediaries is, therefore, a useful activity that should disappear on its own as both banking facilities and creditworthiness increase.

In spite of these not inconsiderable omissions, the structure of credit as shown in Table VI leads to some interesting conclusions.

In both Ghana and the Sudan—and Nigeria probably has much the same credit structure—the very small amount of credit advanced to agriculture is startling. This sector is the most important for both food and export production and occupies 65 per cent or more of the population in these countries. Though agricultural banks are being introduced, these have as yet to make their mark. They are finding the same difficulties as the commercial banks have done, no clear titles to land plus antiquated production methods—and therefore uncertain harvests and returns. Collaboration between the agricultural banks and the development plans of the governments should lead to rapid improvement as is shown in the case of Tunisia. Rhodesia has always had a corps of large-scale farmers, whose credit standing was good; the problems facing this country with the

TABLE VI

*Structure of Credit**

	Ghana	Nigeria	Rhodesia	Sudan	Tunisia
		percentage	distribution:	December 1961	
1. Agriculture, Forestry, Fishing	2·7	21·1§	15·6	1·4	10·3
2. Mining and Quarrying	0·6	0·9	1·7	—	1·5
3. Metallurgy and Engineering	—		8·4	—	4·6
4. Manufacturing	1·8	5·5	16·9	13·8	60·0
5. Marketing (essentially export)	43·5†	—	—	46·8	
6. Wholesale and Retail trade (incl. imports)	17·8	32·4	15·4	17·7	
7. Motor vehicle	2·9	—	3·6		
8. Building and Construction	1·9	9·2	3·0	—	8·1
9. Financial Institutions	—	4·1	14·2	—	—
10. Transport and Communications	—	—	0·4	—	8·2‡
11. Government Service	0·1	1·4	0·5	—	—
12. Other	28·7	25·4	20·1	20·3	7·3
	100·0	100·0	100·0	100·0	100·0

SOURCES:

Ghana: Bank of Ghana, *Quarterly Economic Bulletin*, March 1962, p. 10.
Nigeria: Central Bank of Nigeria, *Annual Report and Statement of Accounts*, 1962, p. 27.
Rhodesia: Central Statistical Office, *Monthly Digest of Statistics*, p.68.
Sudan: Bank of Sudan, *Economic and Financial Bulletin*, July–September, 1962, p. 34.
Tunisia: Banque Centrale de Tunisie, *Rapport Annuel 1961*, pp. 85 and 95.

* Loans and Advances from Registered Institutions; excludes Advances by the Agricultural Bank of the Sudan.
† Advances from Government 42·8.
‡ Includes electricity.
§ Includes finance for export crops.

increase in the number of African farmers, will probably be similar to those of the other countries.

The credits advanced to industry, metallurgy and engineering and manufacturing, are also very modest considering that these credits are among the most productive and that the furtherance of these sectors is the most ardently desired by the countries concerned. Both to increase *per capita* income and to counteract unemployment, industry is considered as the most promising sector. Naturally the banks can only advance 'working capital', either short or medium term. The basic capital for industry must come from other sources. Development Banks[1] of various kinds have been established to help promote industry by supplying capital, consortiums and technical help. The relatively short time they have been working is reflected in the low demand for working capital in all countries except the Sudan, where a recent industrial effort has been made.

Wholesale and retail trade is well represented and so is the important sector called 'marketing' which essentially finances exports. Both in Ghana and the Sudan this sector takes, at the peak of the export season, nearly half of the credit available. In Ghana the position is so strained that nearly the total of this amount, 42·8 out of 43·5 per cent had to come from government sources. This extra burden was wished on to the country by itself, as it preferred to do its own financing instead of using the international financial centres, chiefly London, as it had previously. Thus more profitable alternative uses of the credit available was restricted and the government finances had to bear a burden, which hampered its other activities, while the inflationary effects, both direct and indirect, of such a policy had to be faced.

Other items in the structure of credit show the lack of development both in the country and in the use made of financial institutions. This is notable in the small advances to construction, mortgage loans being difficult because the titles to land are not clear. It is probable that the item 'other', which covers largely personal and professional advances, really is a misnomer and that a substantial proportion of these credits are really being used for other purposes.

The credit structure of these African countries shows up the weak spots and the deficiencies the financial intermediaries, old and new, have to remedy. Not only can an appropriate network of commercial banks and other financial intermediaries collect liquid funds and savings but they can also help to distribute these to the most dynamic sectors. This requires, however, a financial education of the population at large and its various sections, while new and more flexible means of granting credit have to be devised without infringing on

[1] See p. 141.

the necessary high business standards. Then the available institutions can be correctly and fully used, provided they can function in a context where both the governments' development policy, the legal system and the progress made by the economy in general is such that they are given a productive field in which to operate.

CHAPTER X

COMMERCIAL BANKS[1]

The commercial banks are usually the most important contributors of credit to the economy. In several countries, where the financial intermediaries have only recently been established and are still not functioning properly, the commercial banks were in 1962 still responsible for the total, or by far the greatest proportion, of the short and medium term credits advanced to the private economy. Only in Morocco and Tunisia are the contributions of the commercial banks smaller, due to the large number of state and public institutions that have been established to divert credit into new fields, fields which needed stimulating. Thus in Tunisia the private banks only contribute some 50–55 per cent, while much the same proportion is probably to be found in Morocco. The commercial banks are thus the most important source of short and medium term credit to African economies and this in spite of the establishment of a variety of specialized financial intermediaries.

The reasons for this position are partly historical, in that the commercial banks were the first banks established in these countries. Already at the turn of the century, there were commercial banks in Ghana, Morocco, Nigeria, Rhodesia and Tunisia. Before the first war they were established in the Sudan.[2] As commerce and trade expanded, more commercial banks opened branches and agencies in these countries. They specialized primarily on financing export trade but had the full range of banking facilities for the use of both the authorities and individuals. As the economies expanded and a domestic sector developed, a variety of commercial banks were attracted to these countries, while those which were already established opened numerous branches and agencies.

[1] It would have been desirable to discuss the whole of this chapter on the breakdown of credit structure, instead of institutions. In view of the way the statistics are made available, this is not possible. The institutions are, however, often specialized in one or more fields, so that they roughly correspond to types of credit.

[2] *Ghana:* Bank of British West Africa Ltd., 1894.
Morocco: Banco Salvador Hassan y Hijos, 1865.
Nigeria: African Banking Corporation, 1892.
Rhodesia: Standard Bank Ltd., 1892. *Sudan:* Anglo Egyptian Bank Ltd., 1913.
Tunisia: Banque de Tunisie and Banque Franco-Tunisienne. Both 1879.

In fact, during the decade of the 1950's, the expansion in both the number of commercial banks and in the number of their branch offices was very marked.[1] It seems improbable that a greater density of commercial bank branches is needed at the present state of economic development. Many of the branch offices, especially in Ghana and Morocco but also elsewhere, are not earning their keep. They are essentially investments in the future. As the standard of living rises, as new agricultural and industrial activity reaches their locations, these branch offices should, however, become integrated into the surrounding economy. The coverage by branch banks being relatively dense, future expansion should probably, except for certain key points and in Rhodesia generally, be more or less adapted to the development.

Most of the commercial banks in African countries are expatriate in as much as they are themselves branch offices of important international commercial banks. Many of them have, however, either become incorporated in their country of activity or have acquired domestic capital and made nationals members of their boards.

Moreover, there are now also African commercial banks.[2] In Nigeria there are several commercial banks all established by private Nigerian enterprise. Four other countries have deliberately created one each in order to have national commercial banks. They are:

Ghana:	The Ghana Commercial Bank (1953).
Morocco:	The Banque Marocaine du Commerce Extérieur (1959).
Sudan:	The Sudan Commercial Bank (1960).
Tunisia:	Société Tunisienne de Banque (1958).

Each of these banks has been established with the moral and sometimes the financial assistance of the government. The latter may have taken the form of a subscription to the share capital (Morocco 51 per cent) or the transfer of the assets of public institutions (Tunisia, Ghana). The enthusiasm the establishment of a national institution created made it often possible to obtain share capital for these banks when the state of the economy was such that any issue of shares appeared doomed to failure. Thus the capital of the Société Tunisienne de Banque was easily collected while the Sudan

[1] *Ghana:*	1960:	3	Commercial banks, 101 Branch offices.
Morocco:	1959:	36*	Commercial banks, 182 Branch offices (*all banks).
Nigeria:	1961:	12	Commercial banks, 203 Branch offices.
Rhodesia:	1959:	5	Commercial banks, 200 Branch offices.
Sudan:	1961:	7	Commercial banks, 31 Branch offices.
Tunisia:	1960:	5	Commercial banks, 47 Branch offices.

[2] For an African view of banking and its difficulty see Appendix II giving quotations from the *Ghana Parliamentary Debate* of August 24, 1960, on the Ghana Commercial Bank.

Commercial Bank had its capital of £500,000 over-subscribed with 19,000 shareholders of which 11,000 had holdings of £1—10 shares.

The legal status of a bank and the origin of its capital, important though it may be as a symbol, is in fact a secondary consideration. The cardinal question is the policy followed.

Within the last few years there has been a radical change in the policy outlook of the expatriate commercial banks. While previously they invested a considerable part of the surplus funds at their disposal abroad, these funds are now regularly being invested in the country, working balances only being held with correspondents abroad, as is also the practice of the domestic banks.[1] Not only has the creation of Treasury Bills and government stock given the means to invest in the country but also the growing domestic sector, with its demands for short and medium term credit, has enlarged the possibilities of normal banking business. The expatriate banks have, moreover, already several years ago, made considerable financial investments in their country of operation (if only by their branch banks[2] and the personnel they have trained)[3] as well as in goodwill and connections. They realize that their own future is closely bound up with the growth of the economy and they are fully prepared to assist in this process, provided they are given reasonable security.

The criticism still being levelled at the commercial banks because of 'export of domestic funds' is on the whole outdated for the six

[1] Cp. Table V, p. 86.

[2] In the 1920's the opening of a branch office up-country meant not only that its manager had to live in a disease-ridden region—without, of course, enjoying such conveniences as refrigeration and air-conditioning, which are practically vital necessities for Europeans—but also that he had to manage without a telephone (these being, of course, non-existent in those parts) and was furthermore obliged to guard his banknotes not only against thieves but also against termites, which made the safe custody of money a particularly difficult matter. The transporting of money was also a most arduous task, owing to the lack of roads, railways and air communications. The difficulties were further increased by the fact that the money circulation consisted almost entirely of coins. These conditions explain why the banks for a long time had only a very small number of branches.

[3] The commercial banks started already early to train Africans for banking, at first for clerical work later also for more senior positions. This takes place in banking schools specially established in the banks' own premises. The difficulty of the task can hardly be imagined unless one realizes that the local method of calculation is completely different from the decimal system. The success of the efforts made is, however, demonstrated by the fact that today there are branches which are wholly African from the manager down. The more promising African candidates for senior positions are often given the opportunity to have a tour of duty and/or training in Europe or America either at the banks' own offices or connections abroad or in the various banking schools. The commercial banks had started this training early enough to be able to supply the new central banks with some first-rate staff, a debt which is gratefully acknowledged.

countries under discussion.[1] On the contrary, the advantages of having commercial banks which are in a position easily to mobilize funds abroad in time of domestic stringency should be appreciated. The domestic banks have to build up these contacts in order to be fully operative. The success achieved by the Société Tunisienne de Banque and the Banque Marocaine du Commerce Extérieur in this respect, shows that it is not a task beyond the capacity of the new commercial banks.

The sudden growth in the demand deposits of commercial banks during the 1950's is shown in Table VII.[2] The Sudan shows the biggest change with an increase of 700 per cent, while both Ghana and Nigeria record over 300 per cent. Morocco and Tunisia have more modest increases which would probably not exist if foreign exchange control had not been introduced. The repatriation of funds on independence when the former French civil servants and others left, would then have been even more important. For similar reasons there is a fall in demand deposits in Rhodesia, 1954–60.

The loans and advances given by commercial banks are, in the case of Ghana, Morocco and Rhodesia smaller than demand deposits. If seasonal loans for moving the crops were eliminated from the series for Nigeria and the Sudan, the positive difference would be much smaller. In fact there is reason to believe that first-class commercial banks[3] find it difficult to secure enough creditworthy borrowers. The analysis of the structure of credit (see Table VI) also confirmed that, apart from agriculture, mining and distribution, there is little outlet for working capital or medium term loans in manufacturing (except in Rhodesia), construction or to other financial intermediaries, all appropriate fields for commercial bank activity. Various reasons are given for this lack of clients. The scarcity of well conceived and constructed projects, the lack of security (land tenure has normally not been defined, stocks and shares are in their infancy as are insurance policies) and past experience has made bankers chary. From the point of view of the commercial bankers, who, true to their calling, would like to have more business, the bottleneck is, for the time being, in the quality of the potential borrowers, not in the amount of finance available.

Evidently it suits no one concerned that this hiatus exists. The bankers have difficulty in investing their money. There is a whole series of Africans who feel they have unfairly been refused credit. And the governments cast covetous eyes on the available deposits

[1] This criticism comes equally from nationals and expatriates.

[2] The growth in demand deposits has, however, probably not kept pace with the number of accounts or, in some countries, the number of branch offices.

[3] Banks which do not have a first-class reputation complain, on the other hand, of a lack of deposits.

TABLE VII

Demand Deposits, Loans and Advances of Commercial Banks

	Demand Deposits End of Period	Loans and Advances End of Period		Demand Deposits End of Period	Loans and Advances End of Period
Ghana:			*Rhodesia:*		
1950 £ million .	8·8	5·2	1954 £ million .	83·5	28·4
1960 . .	23·6	19·9	1960 . .	63·5	52·2
1961 . .	48·1	47·1	1961 . .	63·1	51·0
1962 . .	39·2	30·5	1962 . .	62·4	50·8
Morocco:			*Sudan:*		
1950 Dh million	606·8	475·4	1950 £ million .	3·0	1·1
1960 . .	1404·0	1097·7	1960 . .	14·8	34·8
1961 . .	1326·5	1254·0	1961 . .	17·4	39·0
1962 . .	1444·2†	1364·0	1962 . .	20·0	46·6
Nigeria:			*Tunisia:*		
1950 £ million ·	13·2	4·3	1953 D million.	27·5*	46·4
1960 . .	41·1	57·0	1960 . .	47·9	68·3
1961 . .	41·7	60·0	1961 . .	48·9	79·4
1962 . .	45·3	80·4	1962 . .	58·8	82·0

* Includes small savings deposits.
† November 1962.

SOURCES:

Ghana: International Monetary Fund, *International Financial Statistics.*
Morocco: Banque du Maroc, *Bulletin Economique et Social.*
Nigeria: Digest of Statistics, and Central Bank of Nigeria.
Rhodesia: Monthly Digest of Statistics.
Sudan: International Monetary Fund, *International Financial Statistics.*
Tunisia: International Monetary Fund, *International Financial Statistics* and *Annuaire Statistique* 1959.

and encourage—to use a mild term—the commercial banks to hold Treasury Bills. This stalemate exists in countries where governments are at least paying lip service to the importance of the private entrepreneur and the enterprises he should start and keep going while supplying working capital is the basic activity of the commercial banks.

Apart from better general education for the whole population in banking and financial matters, which have already been discussed above, the coupling of credit-giving with technical advice is probably the most creative solution. A detailed description of such a method is given under the heading 'Development Banks'.[1] These latter can, however, usually only supply the investment capital, while the working capital must come from the commercial banks. Therefore, collaboration between the consultants of the Development Bank (or similar institutions, e.g. development corporations) and the bankers of commercial banks should be not only feasible but normal and regular routine. Naturally, commercial bankers have often acted as consultants and many of them have valuable experience in the field. However, the scale is certainly too small. Moreover, the profitability of an enterprise is, other things being equal, increasingly becoming dependent upon the evaluation of different technical processes, which require a technical scientific knowledge, which the banker usually does not possess.

Another variant of the same idea would be if the Development Bank (or similar institution) and the commercial banks combined to have a corps of consultants. Such an approach to the problem of utilizing the available expertise would go to the root of the problem, and not just deal with the symptom. In none of the six countries is there so little indigenous entrepreneurship that projects are entirely lacking. But they very seldom meet the standard that a bank, indigenous or expatriate, must require. If a corps of consultants could straighten out these projects, they could act as catalysts. When a pattern was established, they could even point out profitable and feasible gaps. The assumption behind this argument is that the governments, when making their development plans, leave room for private enterprise.[2]

This co-ordination is achieved in the case of the Société de Banque Tunisienne (STB). This bank is both a commercial and a development bank,[3] though it keeps a clear demarcation between the two activities. The policy is not only based on theoretical considerations, but also on the fact that the bank cannot obtain deposits tied for a certain time. However, when a medium or long term loan for capital

[1] Cp. p. 147.
[2] Cp. p. 219.
[3] Cp. p. 146.

investment purposes has been accorded to an enterprise, the bank promises its client also to open a short term credit line for working capital. The amounts involved in the latter are relatively high and while they are formally short term, they can be renewed indefinitely. The necessity of continued applications for renewal, gives the bank's experts an opportunity to discuss the enterprise's affairs and assist in the follow-up and supervision of the long term commitments.

Increasingly important is the STB's participation in the financing of foreign trade. In all countries this was normally the first historical interest of the commercial banks and they have maintained their activity at the side of the greatly expanded other services. Only Morocco has a special bank, the newly created Banque Marocaine du Commerce Extérieur 'chargée de trouver de nouveaux débouchés pour nos exportations et d'aider à l'exécution de nos programmes d'importation et d'exportation'.[1] Thus over and above the ordinary banking services, this bank makes studies of possible foreign markets and runs an insurance service for foreign trade.[2]

In all countries the commercial banks as a whole have resort to the central bank through discounting or rediscounting of bills of exchange and other credit instruments or through direct loans. This was not an obvious situation when the central banks were established but has developed through the latters' policy.[3] It allows the central bank increasingly to finance the needs of trade, both the seasonal needs of crop finance and the longer term needs of an expanding economy, the expansion of which is often about to be enhanced by the secondary effects of the development plans. It is also the easiest and safest way to issue and distribute a fiduciary issue.[4]

The pressure on the central bank is relieved in the Rhodesias and Nyasaland and in Nigeria by the existence of British type Acceptance Houses and Merchant Banks. These also give the commercial banks an opportunity to rediscount trade bills with them, thus helping to build up a money market on the lines of those of the City of London. As both indigenous as well as foreign banks have access to these facilities, these Acceptance Houses and Merchant Banks should be able to assist indigenous banks considerably. They replace, to some extent, foreign facilities and should eventually be able to make a significant contribution to easing the flow of short term credit for a variety of purposes.

The other main credit instrument used by the commercial banks for

[1] 'Charged with finding new markets for our exports and assisting in our programmes of exports and imports.' Throne speech of November 18, 1959, of S. M. Mohammed V quoted in Banque Marocaine du Commerce Extérieur, *Rapport sur le premier exercice social.* Casablanca, 1961, p. 4.

[2] loc. cit., p. 12.

[3] Cp. p. 102.

[4] Cp. p. 229.

TABLE VIII

Commercial Banks: Assets and Liabilities

	Balance at Central Bank	Borrowings from Central Bank end of period	Holding Commercial Bills	Holding Treasury Bills
Ghana:				
1957 £ million	—	—	0·2	0·6
1960	3·1	0·2	4·0	4·6
1961	0·6	—	0·6	6·7
1962	2·1	—	1·0	18·1
Morocco:				
1950 Dh million	—	—	—	221·1†
1960	—	98·0	297·8*	340·4†
1961	—	144·0	353·0	263·9†
1962	—	210·0	342·4	365·6
Nigeria:				
1959 £ million	1·0	—	0·6	—
1960	1·5	1·8	1·2	1·8
1961	3·4	7·0	1·1	3·0
1962	1·4	14·8	3·1	3·4
Rhodesia:				
1956 £ million	0·1	—	8·9	—
1957	8·6	2·0	11·1	0·8
1960	4·8	1·1	6·7	—
1961	5·2	2·0	7·0	0·2
1962	5·3	0·8	6·3	1·8
Sudan:				
1956 £ million	6·8‡	3·6‡	—	—§
1960	6·1	2·1	—	—
1961	6·0	6·8	—	—
1962	4·5	4·3	—	—
Tunisia:				
1960 D million	1·9	11·4	—	9·5†
1961	2·9	17·4	—	10·7†
1962	4·0	13·1	—	12·8†

* January 1961.
† Effets publiques.
‡ At National Bank of Egypt.
§ No Treasury Bills exist.

SOURCES:

Ghana: *Quarterly Economic Bulletin* (March 1962) and *Economic Survey* 1961.
Morocco: *Bulletin Economique et Social* and IFS.
Nigeria: Bank of Nigeria, *Annual Report*, Consolidated Statement of Commercial Banks and privately communicated information.
Rhodesia: *Monthly Digest of Statistics.*
Sudan: IMF, *International Financial Statistics*, and Bank of Sudan, *Annual Report*, and Banque Centrale de Tunisie, *Annual Reports.*
Tunisia: IMF, *International Financial Statistics*, and Banque Centrale de Tunisie, *Annual Reports.*

having recourse to the central bank is Treasury Bills. The commercial banks' holding of Treasury Bills varies from country to country, but where the commercial banks had little alternative use for their assets and the government was under financial pressure they are considerable.[1] While the government naturally needs certain credit facilities, there is always the danger that, if it calls up, even apparently temporarily, funds which should be reserved for the growth of the private sectors of the economy, the expansion of the latter may be seriously retarded for lack of funds. It has unfortunately proved very difficult even in financially mature countries to consolidate an important volume of Treasury Bills.[2] Such a consolidation is likely to prove doubly difficult in a developing country.

The borrowing of commercial bank credit by the government is not without its dangers because it adds to the supply of money with no corresponding reduction.

'Borrowing from commercial banks, either by selling them government securities or by taking up direct credits, corresponds to no reduction in either the spending power of the community or the volume of money (cash and bank balances) in the hands of the public. On the contrary, spending by the government of funds borrowed from commercial banks will increase the money income of the community and the total of cash and bank balances.'[3]

The extent to which government borrowing from the commercial banks increases the money supply, depends very largely on the particular conditions at the time the loans are made. Four cases can be distinguished:

[1] A case in point is Ghana.

[2] *Report of the Committee on the Working of the Monetary System* (the so-called Radcliffe Report), Cmnd. 827, HMSO, London, 1959, §§ 542–90. Also Alex K. Cairncross, *Monetary Policy in a Mixed Economy*, Wicksell Lectures, Stockholm, 1960, p. 13 ff.

[3] Bank for International Settlements, 12*th Annual Report*, p. 14.

(1) If the public is saving by means of bank deposits—current or saving—and the funds the government borrows correspond to these deposits, then there is no primary increase in the active money supply. If the loan takes the form of long term government securities or special Treasury Bills, which cannot be included in the reserve ratio, there is also no secondary expansion.
(2) If, however, in the case stated under (1), the Treasury Bills bought by the commercial banks may be included in the liquid reserves, they may be the basis of a multiple expansion of the supply of credit.
(3) The commercial banks buy their government securities or Treasury Bills with newly created credit, based on a previous expansion of their reserve ratios. This creates new money but may decrease the bank's power to lend to other (non-government) borrowers. If the newly acquired securities do not form part of the reserve ratio, there is no secondary expansion.
(4) The primary conditions of (3) and the secondary conditions of (2) apply and there is both a primary and a secondary expansion of the money supply.

The commercial banks are thus hybrids; they can either leave the money volume unchanged or create new money. Which will be done depends on the size of their deposits and that of their reserve ratios.

The commercial banks have, moreover, the power to dampen the actual theoretically possible expansion of real savings.

'The . . . proposition is equally important, and much less generally understood. While apart from the cases of compulsion just discussed, the public decides the amount of real savings which it is prepared to put at the disposal of industry through the banks, it needs the co-operation of the banks to make its decision effective. If, in the face of an increased willingness on the part of the public to perform this particular kind of saving, the banks fail to take appropriate action, then the potential saving will go to waste. It will be dissipated in the form of lower prices and increased consumption by the public at large. The bank can prevent this undesigned result if, and only if, it makes new loans or investments on a sufficient scale to prevent prices from falling and ensure that the public really does the saving which it intends to do. By acting in this way the bank is behaving not as a burglar but as a benefactor: it is not imposing unsought burdens on the people, but enabling their thrifty intentions to bear fruit.'[1]

[1] Sir Dennis H. Robertson, *Essays in Monetary Theory*, London, 1940, p. 44.

The above quotation bears the stamp of the lesson of the depression of the 1930's. It has since been realized that the control of the credit creation facilities of the commercial banks must, at least at times of inflationary pressure, be curbed by liquidity ratios and sometimes special deposits.

The developing countries, with their latent inflationary pressures, have here a very nice question of judgement for monetary policy. If the credit creating possibilities of the commercial banks in respect to the general public are curbed, it may apparently diminish overall monetary pressure, especially if the public sector is expanding rapidly. However, such a 'planned' expansion is apt to create a series of real bottlenecks which can have an important price increasing effect. This applies especially to secondary (induced) demand, which is liable to be directed towards a very large number of goods and services.

The domestic sector of the economy should, to a large extent, be able to satisfy quite a few of these demands, provided it has sufficient funds (credit) at its disposal. The domestic sector is, it seems, usually under-rated because it does not always flower into factories. Especially the important but shadowy sector between the modern and the traditional sectors tends to work in very small units of production or service suppliers. It still has its importance both with respect to its relative productivity and to its capacity of filling a variety of needs. As usually the 'entrepreneurs' here are indigenous, it is also a domestic training ground for modern entrepreneurs.

The individual producers involved, however, seldom have the creditworthiness recognized by commercial banks, but they can usually indirectly tap bank credit through some intermediary. Should, therefore, bank credit for the private sector be unduly restricted in comparison to the facilities available to the public sector, the apparent overall monetary equilibrium may hide sectoral disequilibria, which in themselves are inflationary.

The commercial banks are often the main executors of the directional control of credit sometimes attempted by central banks. Though such a measure is often combined with both 'moral suasion' and the limitation of the commercial banks' credit facilities at the central bank for certain categories of loans, it is very hard to enforce when the natural demand for credit is low. The commercial banks then never come near to utilizing their full credit lines at the central bank and the latter finds it difficult to administer such a control. What demands for credit do arise have to be satisfied simply to keep some activity going in the economy. On the other hand, when there is an important demand for credit, the commercial banks often feel that it is unfair for them to be burdened with the onus of saying 'no' to the general public. This is especially the case when they are asked to do so in the sectors they themselves consider the most profitable and the safest, in favour of far less attractive business. A general control of credit through liquidity ratios and rediscounting is therefore preferable to detailed rules. Neglected sectors, especially agriculture, should be looked after by specialized institutions. This applies also to the raising of capital for industrial and other ventures which, if they are sound, would then have no difficulty in obtaining working capital. The latest reforms in the credit system (Morocco, Sudan) have thus all gone in the direction of the substitution of more general credit measures for detailed administrative practices.

The most efficient measure of control is the application of liquidity ratios.[1] Any well-run commercial bank has to have a certain proportion of cash and immediately cashable assets. This is needed both for the protection of the bank itself and for that of its clients. While the proportions necessary vary according to each individual bank's business, location and the payment habits of its clients, a cash ratio of around 8 per cent and a liquidity ratio of around 30 per cent of total liabilities is considered about normal and in conformity with sound commercial banking. Central banks have, in their turn, learnt that by varying both the size of the required liquidity ratio and the type of assets that can be held under this heading, they can materially influence the liquidity of the commercial banks. These measures affect both the absolute liquidity of the commercial banks and their credit creating capacity.[2] Evidently, liquidity ratios tend to be more efficient in times of fairly brisk demand for credit from the general public than when an effective demand is lacking.[3] A reduction of the liquidity ratio theoretically makes the commercial banker more willing to lend. Even if he does not reduce his interest rate (and charge) he may relax his requirements on the creditworthiness of his borrowers or be prepared to make a bigger effort to turn part of his 'fringe of unsatisfied borrowers' into creditworthy prospects. He is not, however, a magician and has always the not entirely harmless alternative of investing in Treasury Bills or government bonds.

Special deposits can be and are used to some extent. They supplement the effect of liquidity ratios and have the advantage of really

[1] The actual liquidity ratios have been as follows:

	Ghana:	Nigeria:	Rhodesia:
1957	55	—	—
1958	65	—	—
1959	50	33·0	—
1960	44	40·5	34·7
1961	32	47·9	34·2
1962	50	29·1	36·2

[2] In an emergency, part of the assets held in the liquidity ratio can be made ineligible for secondary credit expansion.

[3] This can be due to all or any of the following: a depressed state of the economy, to self-financing (rare in Africa), to a lack of creditworthy borrowers.

sterilizing the funds involved. However, this is only the case if the central bank does not let itself be bludgeoned into transferring the assets to the government either directly or indirectly by buying government paper. This obnoxious practice is unfortunately not unknown in financially mature countries and leads to disaster because it completely falsifies the monetary policy.

The prepayment of part or the total of import orders has some very fervent advocators[1] and is sometimes also used in practice (previously in the Sudan). Theoretically it is a neat way of dealing with the large swings in purchasing power caused by the export crops. It is also reasonably efficient in practice. However, it assumes permanent controls, import and foreign exchange control, and it requires quite some administration—chiefly by the commercial banks. For these reasons, it should really only be treated as an emergency measure, if at all, as all permanent monetary measures that build on controls tend to perpetuate the distortions in the economy while giving the authorities a possibly fatal respite before they have to deal with the fundamental issues.

As the economy of the African countries becomes more mature the role played by the commercial banks will gradually increase absolutely while diminishing relatively. Other financial intermediaries will start to play an important part especially in the sphere of medium and long term credit and capital. The commercial banks' essential role in these countries will not be diminished, but the present tendency of expecting them to undertake to supply credit and capital to sectors and in directions for which they are not equipped will stop. Other specialized institutions, which have already largely been established, will take over these tasks and the commercial banks will only really be expected to operate in the field where they can make their largest contribution, namely short term credit.

[1] J. O. W. Olakanpo, loc. cit., pp. 406–7.

CHAPTER XI

DEVELOPMENT BANKS

The development bank, whether industrial, agricultural or even commercial, is essentially a post World War II institution. Naturally it had forerunners, but it was only in the late 1940's and early 1950's that the basically new conception was implemented. The bank was not merely to supply medium and long term funds, but to attempt to achieve an active policy as a founder of private entrepreneurial enterprises in conformity with the development policy of a government and nation. And this attempt was to be made in countries where the preconditions for natural economic growth were often lacking. The bank was seen as an institution that often itself had to create the preconditions for its own activity, it was considered at its foundation as a dynamizing factor.

The distinguishing hallmark of the development bank is, however, that it only seeks to support and promote economically profitable enterprises, whether in industry, commerce or (sometimes exceptionally) agriculture. Thus also institutionally it conforms to the theory expected to give the fastest development.[1] The universal application of this criterion was emphasized also by Mr. Khruschchev, who stressed that 'with regard to an individual enterprise the question of profit is of great importance as an economic indicator of its efficiency'.[2] In this he was in agreement with Per Jacobsson who maintained, 'In a truly competitive market system profits should be regarded as a sign of the capacity to furnish the goods and services required by consumers; just as losses should be a sign of the inability to furnish the goods and services which are required, or of bad judgement as to the trend of effective demand'.[3] The development bank, by its insistence on this criterion, is basically different from the development corporations and some other institutions, which were prepared to promote projects even if they needed subsidizing over longer or shorter periods.

The development bank of the 1960's is a very sophisticated

[1] Cp. p. 257.

[2] Nikita Khruschchev, speech made before the Central Committee of the Communist Party, Moscow, November 24, 1962.

[3] Per Jacobsson, *The Market Economy in the World of Today*, Jayne Lectures for 1961, American Philosophical Society, Philadelphia, 1961, p. 18.

institution compared to some of the earlier forms it has taken.[1] In Africa some of the pioneering precursors have not been called banks but development corporations, while a number of various institutions surviving from the pre-war or pre-independence periods have not only contributed substantial amounts of capital, but have collected valuable experience which the managers of present-day development banks can draw upon as a guide to their activities.

The most important development banks in the countries under discussion are the following:[2]

Ghana:	Ghana National Investment Bank, established 1963.
Morocco:	Banque Nationale pour le Développement Economique, established 1959.
Nigeria:	Investment Company of Nigeria (ICON), established 1959 (to be turned into full-scale development bank with larger capital), and several development corporations.
Sudan:	Industrial Bank of Sudan, established 1961.
Tunisia:	Société Tunisienne de Banque, established 1958.

Ghana: The decision to establish this bank was taken in 1962 and the statutes were confirmed early in 1963.[3] The bank is expected to have a capital totalling £G10 million. £G7·5 million is to be subscribed by the government and £G2·5 million preference shares are eventually to be sold to the public. Only part (one third) of the government subscription is to be paid up immediately. The government is also to put a £G10 million loan at the bank's disposal. The bank may also borrow abroad from recognized institutions and governments. The bank hopes to start operation in the course of 1963. Its main function is to 'provide finance in the form of long-term or medium-term loans with or without security or by purchasing or subscribing for shares or other securities or by acquiring any other interest' (§4a). Moreover, each application is to be considered strictly on its financial and economic merits (§14) and safeguards to assure this have been included.

Morocco: The Banque Nationale pour le Développement Econo-

[1] William Diamond, *Development Banks*. The Economic Development Institute. IBRD Baltimore, 1957, pp. 19–40 and pp. 89–124; and Yves Guillaume, 'Banques de développement', *Bulletin Economique et Social du Maroc*, Vol. XXII, No. 81, 1959, pp. 55–66.

[2] There is no typical industrial development bank in Rhodesia. An Industrial Promotion Corporation of Rhodesia and Nyasaland was privately formed in 1960 with a capital of £1 million. It is especially to assist with the raising of funds for starting or expanding projects and to supply, where necessary, managerial and technical advice. Its investments amounted in 1960 to £82,000, 1961 to £360,000 and 1962 to £488,000. Bank of Rhodesia and Nyasaland, *Annual Report* 1961, pp. 10–11 and *Annual Report* 1962, p. 16.

[3] National Investment Bank Bill 1963 and Bye-Laws.

mique (BNDE)[1] was established in 1959 both to assist in the national economic development and to replace the former system of industrial credits, the links of which to France had largely been broken by independence.

The BNDE has an authorized share capital of Dh20 million of which 15 million Dirham has been paid up. The government and public corporations subscribed half the shares, while Moroccan banks and foreign banks subscribed 25 per cent each. Moreover, the BNDE can borrow at long term on the market, a facility which has been resorted to the extent of Dh27 million. A further source of finance is the rediscounting at the Banque du Maroc of the medium term credits granted. The government has also undertaken to advance credits to a maximum of Dh30 million. Reliance on this source of finance has never exceeded Dh6 million and has since been reduced. In December 1962 the BNDE received loans from the International Bank for Reconstruction and Development and the International Finance Corporation. The former loan amounts to US $15 million in foreign exchange, while the IFC invests Dh7·5 million (US $1·5 million) in share stock of the BNDE representing three-quarters of a new stock issue.

The BNDE has as its statutory object 'the assistance of the economic development of Morocco', but in fact it restricts its activity chiefly to private industrial or commercial enterprises. Its financial assistance is for investment (equipment), not working capital, and its loans may not be shorter than two years. In fact, its medium term loans are usually of five years duration, while long term loans (to private enterprise) should be repaid in fifteen years; both are given at 7 per cent plus 2 per cent commission, which very considerably increases the price of the loans, especially long term loans. Moreover, the BNDE does not lend less than Dh50,000 on any one project; if not satisfied with the profitability of the undertaking it can require a state guarantee.

By the end of 1962, thus in four years, the BNDE had effected 142 operations totalling Dh212 million; Dh62 million were on long term and the bulk of the rest was on medium term. The distribution of these loans was such that over 30 per cent was in engineering industry, some 29 per cent in electricity, mines and petrol and some 18 per cent in chemistry. The other loans are small in very diversified branches.

Like most development banks the BNDE has a specialized department to study the projects and to check the manner in which the loan is utilized. Particular stress is laid on the way the total project

1 Sources: *Statutes and Annual Reports* of the Banque Nationale de Développement Economique and Banque du Maroc; *Etudes et Statistiques*, Bulletin Mensuel.

is executed. A special clause in the Bank's contracts allows it to withdraw should the creditors not fulfil all their obligations.

The BNDE may also take participations which it has done in the tourist industry, in the 'Maroc Equipment', a pre-finance research institute, and in three banks of which the Banque Marocaine du Commerce Extérieur is the best known.[1] Moreover, the BNDE administers, as agent for the government, several funds for regional or special economic reconstruction.

Nigeria: Negotiations are under way to transform the Investment Company of Nigeria (ICON) into a fully fledged development bank with a larger and possibly wider international capital.[2]

ICON was set up in 1959 with a paid-up capital of £1 million subscribed by Nigerian, British, Canadian, American, Swiss, French and Dutch companies, individuals and firms.[3] Its Board of Directors consists of well-known Nigerian and European businessmen who have a wide range of technical and managerial experience in industry and commerce and who represent successful private enterprise.

Apart from the normal functions usually undertaken by a development bank and which are discussed below, ICON has also actively participated in the formation and running of the Lagos Stock Exchange 'by facilitating the buying of stocks and shares'. This activity was believed to increase the amount of private capital available to private industry and this approach has apparently been successful.[4] ICON's activities have also taken the form of underwriting issues or conversions of shares and securities in Nigerian companies.

The overall commitments of ICON amounted by December 31, 1960, to a total of £307,000 of which investments and loans amounted to £122,000. By the end of 1961 total commitments were up by another £700,000.

ICON has been the only organization in Nigeria which has attempted to finance industry and commerce with private capital. The many development corporations and other organizations with similar activities obtained their capital from governments (British or Nigerian) or from marketing boards. Several projects established have proved successful but none of these organizations could pro-

[1] Participations play an important part in the financing of industry in Morocco. Two specialized public institutions, The Bureau de Recherches et de Participations Minières (established in 1928) and the Bureau d'Etudes et de Participations Industrielles (established in 1957) known as the BEPI both take participations.

[2] Reconstruction completed January 1964: new name Nigerian Industrial Development Bank Ltd; paid-up capital £2.250.000 to which also the IFC and private institutions outside Nigeria have subscribed.

[3] ICON: *A Key to Development*, Lagos, 1960.

[4] Cp. p. 177.

vide either the technical assistance or the true objectivity that is natural to a development bank.

Sudan: The Industrial Bank of the Sudan was inaugurated in November 1961. The share capital amounts to £S3 million of which the government subscribed £S500,000. In addition the government is to lend the Bank £S500,000 to be repaid in thirty equal half-yearly instalments commencing fifteen and a half years after disbursement. The purpose of the bank, which started operations in August 1962, is to encourage the establishment, expansion and modernization of private industrial enterprises in the Sudan and to encourage and promote the participation of private capital both internal and external. By the end of 1962 the Bank had announced 'three small loans for the manufacturing of macaroni products and air coolers and for car maintenance'.[1]

Tunisia: In February 1957, thus within a year of independence, a campaign was launched, inviting the public to subscribe to a fund for the support of a nation-wide industrialization programme. Owing to the low saving capacity of the public at that time the major subscribers to the fund were large industrial and commercial enterprises. The sum collected was D1.434.000 of which D320.000 went into some thirteen medium sized[2] industrial undertakings while the greater part went into the following institutions and enterprises:

Société Tunisienne de Banque	200.000Dinars
Société Nationale d'Investissement	215.000
Banque Nationale Agricole	134.000
Compagnie Tunisienne de Navigation	70.000
Industrie de la Cellulose	495.000
	1.114.000

The activities of the two latter companies are obvious and the two banks are discussed below.

The Société Nationale d'Investissement (SNI) was to act on the one hand as a holding company in order to buy shares of new companies, thus supplying otherwise unavailable risk capital. On the other it was to help these companies in negotiations with the government and local and international banks. Moreover, it was to study all projects that could lead to new industrial, commercial and agricultural enterprise.[3] The projects are supposed to benefit directly

[1] Bank of Sudan, *Annual Report* 1961, p. 28, and 1962, p. 34.

[2] Ten of these industries received letters of guarantee of D15,000 to D30,000 ($357–$714). One received D110.000 ($2,619), while two needed only D5,000 ($119).

[3] Statutes de la Société Nationale d'Investissements.

the national economy; saw mills, sugar refineries, road transportation, phosphates and hotels—the latter for the foreign exchange—have all been studied and initiated. It is also the SNI which grants foreign enterprises with letters of guarantee. The SNI is interested chiefly in large-scale projects and should find that it can usefully co-operate with the industrial aspects of the Development Plan.

Early in 1957, the Tunisian Government, dissatisfied with the marked stringency of the internal market, decided to create an all Tunisian Bank under the name of Société Tunisienne de Banque (STB). The STB[1] had immediately to take on three separate functions: it acts as an ordinary commercial bank, accepting deposits, granting short and medium term loans, negotiating and rediscounting all types of papers and securities, etc.; it has to function as a development bank financing, often initiating and guiding new industrial undertakings and finally was entrusted both with the handling of the government's Building Programme and the Special Revolving Loan Fund of $5 million given by the Development Loan Fund, Washington, in 1961.

This unusual combination of commercial and development bank has in this individual case proved more than justified. The STB was immediately popular and its deposits grew surprisingly quickly, thus providing the working capital for the new industrial projects. In fact the STB has usually advanced over one-quarter of all Tunisian credit outstanding and thus holds a key position in the country's financial structure and not least in the flow of imports and exports.

With regard to the Building Programme the STB could grant loans up to 80 per cent of construction costs at rates of 5½ per cent for medium and 7·65 per cent on long term loans. So as to have the funds necessary to implement the programme, the STB was authorized by the government to float a D2 million bond loan. This successful issue allowed nearly a thousand loans to be granted for various construction projects by the end of 1961.

The STB has, moreover, made use of her right to purchase stocks in newly established enterprises. By December 31, 1961, these participations amounted to D515,362,270. Some thirteen important companies have been assisted. The STB participation usually remains around one-tenth of total capital, though in some cases it has over 50 per cent.[2]

The common denominator of all modern development banks is the stress laid on the department called in Ghana the Development

[1] Capitalized at D 400,000 with 80,000 shares of D5 each held by some 1,200 shareholders.

[2] The Banque Nationale d'Investissement (1959), a former subsidiary of the STB, was later turned into a development bank and is now an amiable competitor to the STB.

Service Institute. This is a department which consists of experts on all the various aspects of industrial entrepreneurship from accounting to raw material and market problems and possessing a keen appreciation for the economic importance of the technical process envisaged.[1]

In some cases, as foreseen in Ghana, the Development Service Institute not only has an advisory capacity for the clients but its advice is binding on the Bank as to 'the technical, market and economic feasibility of the projects'.[2] The experience of the Société Tunisienne de Banque shows that the selection of the projects to be financed is very complicated. Not only must the suitability of the project from the national point of view be evaluated, but also the applicant's creditworthiness requires careful consideration. Modern entrepreneurship is a new skill in developing countries and persons with a good idea may not have the necessary knowledge or experience to set up an acceptable loan application.[3] The STB found that it had then to assist the firm or entrepreneur in question with technical advice, thus often saving a valuable project.

New entrepreneurs also seldom have the capacity to establish a realistic and exact cost calculation. They usually need help with this at the very start. Moreover, they frequently are unfamiliar with modern accounting methods and are unable to keep the necessary books. Part of the secret of the success of the Société Tunisienne de Banque is that its experts frequently review the books of the firms which it has assisted; thus it is able to keep in touch with their position and to give, when needed and in good time, advice and help.

It is possible that development banks could go one step further and contribute actively to good management by arranging for future managers to have their final training abroad—till there are enough domestic enterprises. Such training should only be envisaged for an already qualified person. It should also preferably be acquired in a recognized firm of the branch in question and in a position as close as possible to the one which will have to be filled.

The primordial importance of good management of enterprises in developing countries cannot be overstressed.[4] It is not only a question

[1] With the modern advance in technology the choice of process may make all the difference to the profitability of the enterprise. This can even apply to small industry.

[2] Bye-Laws, § 8.

[3] Appendix V, p. 318, for text of typical loan application.

[4] Xenophon Zolotas, Governor of the Bank of Greece, considers management, administrative as well as Schumpeterian, as of both primordial importance and the worst bottleneck. He therefore proposed in his *Economic Development and Private Enterprise* (Bank of Greece Papers and Lectures, No. 10, Athens, 1962, pp. 18–30) that industrial Development Corporations should be set up in developing countries in order to concentrate exclusively on the training of management

of decision taking and directing with or without technical (engineering) knowledge. The productivity of the individual worker—this basic and essential factor—is intimately connected with the attitude of management to labour. All newer studies show that the assumed lower productivity per worker in Africa has been greatly overestimated.[1] There are factories in Africa with the same capital investment in machinery, etc., per worker as is normal in Europe and America and they achieve very much the same degree of worker productivity. But where this is accomplished management has usually taken special measures.[2]

The development banks usually aim at establishing carefully selected small and medium sized industries to be set up with the dual purpose of providing key industries while helping to train both entrepreneurial material and skilled workers. This stress on a large variety of smaller purely industrial projects is realistic. So often economic development is envisaged as large dams and large factories only. The studies of Western economic development, however, show that the small and medium sized industries were an essential support for the more spectacular investments. Not only did they supply the day-to-day needs in the secondary and tertiary sector but they were also the breeding ground of outstanding entrepreneurs, engineers and inventors.

Modern technology assists developing countries in the formation of small and medium sized industry in a surprisingly large number of ways. There are four reasons:

1. Modern industry is not based on coal—it can use electricity, detrol, natural gas or even atomic energy. Thus its location is more or less independent.

2. Modern road transport—the truck has made the former link to the railway and the canal (or waterway) superfluous, further increasing the mobility of industry.

3. The developing countries can buy the most modern machines—they do not have to make the inventions themselves. This gives them an enormous advantage—they only have to learn to use—and manage—the machines.

and possibly project preparation. All financing should be done by the ordinary banking system. A similar proposal for a training centre for management was made for the Sudan. ILO Expanded Programme of Technical Assistance, *Report to the Government of the Republic of Sudan on a Productivity Mission* (January–April 1959), Geneva, 1960 (ILO/TAP/Sudan/R2).

[1] See also P. Kilby, African Labour Productivity Reconsidered, *Economic Journal*, June 1961.

[2] International study on West African conditions done by staff members of the Basle Centre for Economic and Financial Research. Its conclusions are summarized in Appendix III, p. 311.

4. The bogey of size that first the moving band and then automation introduced is not the only technological development. While it is fully justified for certain large units, electricity plants, huge mass-scale production (cars, etc.) it certainly does not have universal application. There are many structural changes which operate in the opposite direction and lead even in European countries to a deconcentration of plants and a diminution in the size of single industries.[1]

This applies even to steel and iron production where extremely interesting structural changes in the method of production are taking place. In a very near future the production of steel and iron goods will become deconcentrated. Small and medium sized plants to make special objects—such as screws, piping and the thousand and one specialties needed—could easily be run independently of each other and will become typical in Europe and elsewhere.[2] They would base their production on cheaply available iron or even steel, processed in Liberia, Gabon, South Africa, etc.

The same type of technological change is taking place for textiles, plastics and many other consumer commodities, the most profitable and easiest type of production for most developing countries.

An analysis of the size of existing and planned industry confirms both the fact that small and medium sized industry is technically feasible in African countries and that it corresponds to market conditions as well as available entrepreneurial scope.

In Table IX a breakdown of industrial enterprises in Nigeria and Tunisia both existing in 1962 and planned is given according to the size of invested capital. For Nigeria federal industrial undertakings have been excluded. These are usually very large-scale (invested capital £5 million or more) and are at present beyond the scope of private finance even when assisted by a Development Bank sometimes collaborating with the government. Moreover, the size of major industry justified in a country of over 40 million inhabitants would not be justified in a country with only some 4 million.

The material on which the table is based has been privately communicated and in neither case is it completely exhaustive. The samples are, however, large enough to give a good survey of the *structure* of industry. If anything the bias of the sample in both cases is that it neglects to some extent small industry (especially

[1] This is in sharp contrast to the widely held belief that modern industrial techniques require large or even very large plants and thus discriminate against developing countries. For the disaggregation effects in industrialized countries see Edgar Salin, 'Die neue Etappe der industriellen Revolution' in *Lynkeus*, Tubingen, 1963, pp. 345–58, and esp. p. 355 ff.

[2] E. W. Mommsen (Managing Director of Phoenix Rhein-Rohr), 'Die Strukturwandlung der europäischen Rohstoffimporte'. An Address delivered at Basle University, May 24, 1962. Published in *Kyklos, Internationale Zeitschrift für Sozialwissenschaften*, Vol. XV, 1962, Fasc. 4, pp. 259–75.

TABLE IX

*Existing and Planned Industrial Units in Nigeria and Tunisia**

	Number of Industries		Capital Invested		Average Capital Investment	
	Existing†	Planned	Existing	Planned	Existing	Planned
	in per cent		in per cent			
Nigeria						
£N‡						
– 100,000	44·2	30	6·2	2·0	40,092	46,143
100,001– 500,000	40·7	26	16·9	10·6	276,333	289,167
500,001–1,000,000	2·3	23	4·1	25·3	1,000,000	750,909
1,000,001–	12·8	21	72·8	62·1	2,547,143	2,030,000
Tunisia						
Dinars‡						
– 100,000	66⅔	18·2	15·1	2·1	18,813	75,000
100,001– 500,000	33⅓	63·6	84·9	26·4	211,125	264,286
500,001–1,000,000	—	9·1	—	14·3	—	1,000,000
1,000,001–	—	9·1	—	57·2	—	4,000,000

SOURCE: Privately communicated basic material.

* The surveys on which these figures are based are not exhaustive but large enough to be representative. In both cases there would be a tendency for small industry to be under-represented (especially in the borderline between indigenous and modern sectors) while larger investment is well represented with the exception of Federal industry in Nigeria.

† Existing 1962.

‡ £N1 = Dinars 1,177.

borderline enterprises between the indigenous and modern sector) while giving a fairly complete survey of larger industries—with the exception of federal industry in Nigeria.

In spite of this systematic bias small industry with capital investments up to £100.000 and dinars 100.000[1] dominates numerically in both existing industry in both countries and planned industry in Nigeria. That these enterprises are on the smaller side is shown by the average capital invested, namely £40.092 and dinars 18.000 in existing industry and £46.143 or dinars 75.000 in planned industry. Next in numeric importance come the enterprises in the category of dinars and £100.001–500.000. Here too, the average capital investments are fairly low with £276.333 or dinars 211.125, while planned industry foresees average investments of £289.167 or dinars 264.286.

These figures also reveal that the average investment in each category of smaller and medium sized industry is tending to become slightly larger. The opposite is the case for the two categories of large industry, investments over dinars or £500.000 where the average investment apparently is lower for planned than for existing industry. However, the number of larger industries either existing or planned is small and can hardly be taken as an absolutely reliable statistical sample.

The large industries are really all special cases. In view of their size, it is not surprising that they at present take such an important part of total capital invested. The need for such large industrial units will probably, at least for the time being, prove fairly limited after those at present planned have been established, and the proportion of capital absorbed by them should be reduced in favour of industries with capital up to dinars or £500,000 to 1,000,000.

All the available evidence, whether from the history of the European[2] and American[3] development or that of more advanced developing countries, such as Japan[4], shows that small and medium size industry is not only the easiest to establish, but also usually the more labour intensive and the best training ground because of its variety (especially on the technical level) and the opportunity it gives to a large number of persons to learn to take managerial decisions. The progression through time is typically from light to heavy industry (and judging from current trends in Europe and America, then back to light industry). Naturally, the time taken for

1 The £N1 = Dinars 1,177. The categories in the breakdowns have thus roughly the same values.

2 A. T. Youngson, *The Possibilities of Economic Progress*, Cambridge University Press, 1959, esp. p. 107 ff.

3 George Terborgh, *The Bogey of Economic Maturity*, Chicago, 1945, p. 86 ff.

4 Norman S. Buchanan and Howard S. Ellis, *Approaches to Economic Development*, New York, 1955, pp. 173–89 and p. 267 ff., for a general discussion of the size of industrial units and their role in a developing country.

these changes can vary greatly and can be shortened especially if modern techniques are available and the prerequisite conditions favourable. The African developing countries are still at the beginning of the industrialization process and the main stress is, as it apparently should be, on a large number of light industries.[1]

To assist by partial financial participation in the establishment of light and lighter small and medium sized industries is the typical province of the Development Bank. The technical advice that has to be given in order to be successful is extensive and varies from country to country as well as from project to project. The mobilization of basically private capital for the purpose should not prove too difficult as the individual amounts needed are comparatively small and it should be possible to raise them in each individual country even if initially, assistance from abroad or from the government proves necessary.

[1] These light industries typically produce consumer goods and supply parts for other industry. As such they have also the advantage of being both important substitutes and guardians of the price levels.

CHAPTER XII

AGRICULTURAL CREDIT INSTITUTIONS

The organization of the right type and kind of agricultural credit in sufficient quantities is the perhaps hardest problem to solve in the six countries.[1] There is a vicious circle of small farmers using antiquated methods, with little or no knowledge of how to improve their yields. Even where technical knowledge is available, the titles to the land are seldom clear, the sums needed for almost any improvement are very considerable compared to the borrowing capacity of the individual and the normal credit institutions are often reluctant to venture into this very risky business.[2] Only the large-scale plantation farmer with his expert knowledge and important security has proved by experience to be 'a good risk' and thus to be free of credit raising problems. The result is that special measures have had to be taken everywhere to attempt to assure agricultural credit on reasonable terms.

In most cases it has proved necessary to have special institutions supported financially by government or international aid of one kind or another.[3] This assistance may have taken the form of share capital and/or subsidies from the government budget and/or advances from the central bank and/or credits from special funds of international or foreign institutions. These latter often replace today the funds which the former colonial governments made available.

[1] This is a problem these countries have in common with all other countries 'developed' or 'developing'.

[2] Under normal circumstances defaults on agricultural credits usually amount to some 20 per cent representing ever-increasing indebtedness of the farming community. A bad harvest due to weather (rainfall or lack of), insects or disease may mean the complete default of a whole farming community.

[3] Eugene R. Black, President of the International Bank for Reconstruction and Development in his address *Economic Development for the Peoples of Africa* Afrika Institut, the Hague, October 29, 1962, pp. 11 and 7. 'Clearly, ways must be found to attach more Africans to permanent holdings of land, and to give the African farmer both the means and the motive to increase the productiveness of his homestead. In a number of countries south of the Sahara, the Bank has been glad to support programmes aimed at these objectives' for 'The ambition of every country in Africa is to develop industry as a source of employment and higher standards of living for its people. The roads to industrialization are several, and one already being travelled in Africa is the transition that can be made from cultivating agricultural products to using them as the basis for processing and manufacturing'.

There has thus been a shift of funds and capital from other sectors into agriculture. To re-enforce the original financial arrangements, directional control of credit has often been handled in such a manner as to increase the proportion of the flow of current saving—and credit—invested into agriculture, thus through time also securing a shift in the structure of capital investment.

The second important feature of agricultural credit is that it must be combined with efficient technical help and advice. This is the best means of minimizing risks,[1] both in respect to the credit institution and the borrower. Because of the uncertainties involved when modern technical methods are not being used and also because of the costs thereof, insurance schemes are almost excluded.[2] They are not yet in operation for agriculture in Africa, though their success in countries where agriculture is highly rationalized[3] shows that at some future date they might prove to be a viable possibility. The essential problem in Africa is to improve techniques and assure their utilization through time so that better and more stable harvests and yields can be obtained. Therefore most agricultural banks or societies, whether for large or small farmers, run some kind of technical assistance. In recent years, these technical branches have either supplemented or collaborated with the government plans for the improvement and furtherance of agriculture, to the mutual benefit of both and of the farmer in particular. The technical assistance and advice offered will often cover all aspects of the operation: they include ploughing, crop rotation, improved seed, better planting and harvesting methods, the use of fertilizers and manure, animal husbandry, irrigation, afforestation and the best methods to renew the stock of crop trees (whether olive, cocoa, palm oil, vine, etc.) or the introduction of a more diversified crop with the often neglected vegetables. Large-scale irrigation schemes, involving the building of dams and the complete overhaul of an agricultural system, can usually only be secured within an overall plan. But the success of more modest counselling proves that, except in unusual circumstances, e.g. the deserts of the Sudan, much can be achieved without grandiose schemes.

The third point on which help is very often needed is marketing.[4] The individual farmer, short of cash at the end of the agricultural year, is easily tempted to sell at perhaps a cut price to obtain liquid

[1] FAO, *Agricultural Credit in Economically Underdeveloped Countries*, Rome, 1959, pp. 98–111.

[2] FAO, *Report of the Working Party on Crop and Livestock Insurance*, Bankok, Tailand, August 27 to September 7, 1956, Rome 1957.

[3] The American Bankers Association, 'Crop Insurance is Growing Fast', *Banking Journal*, December 1962, p. 82.

[4] In some countries, especially Ghana and Nigeria, marketing boards, established for other reasons, render such help unnecessary. Cp. p. 211.

funds quickly. Moreover, there are fluctuations in prices on the world markets which the individual can seldom survey and he is easy prey to the unscrupulous trader. There is a credit aspect to this problem too. If the individual farmer takes an unnecessary loss on the sale of his harvest he is no longer in a position to repay his loans, involving himself in unnecessary indebtedness and jeopardizing the credit system.

The fourth point, which cannot be neglected, is the creation of clear titles to land. Various legal methods have been tried more or less successfully. In Tunisia the main activity of the 'Crédit Foncier', founded because of the depression of the 1930's and financed by a public issue, was the registration of land. Its activity, however, will take years to complete and has partly been tided over by a certificate of ownership. Only with clear titles to land do mortgage loans become possible. Naturally the clear title need not confirm individual ownership, but can apply to collective or limited company ownership.

Whatever the individual solution for agricultural credit, all countries have found that only if a certain minimum is done on each of these points can a system of agricultural credit operate. This knowledge came by a system of trial and error and most of the African countries have made their own experiences.

In Ghana, a number of co-operatives were formed by cocoa producers in 1929 as a result of the difficulties they had experienced during the 1920's. These co-operatives were designed 'to give each other mutual assistance, especially in marketing but also on the production side.[1] The farmers could not administer the societies themselves and turned for help to the Department of Agriculture, the head of which acted in the capacity of a registrar.

'The most important question that faced the co-operatives was the very high indebtedness of the cocoa farmers, who had pledged their crops and farms during the very bad years. Already between 1918 and 1925 the government had been repeatedly petitioned by local chiefs and farmers for the establishment of an agricultural bank, which would provide them with relief from these long term indebtednesses.'[1] The Gold Coast Agricultural and Commercial Society, an unofficial government body acting for the government, replied in 1928 that the request for the establishment of a bank was rejected and recommended instead that the adoption of a co-operative credit system should be considered. Professor C. Y. Shephard outlined his reasons for favouring a system of co-operative banks, which would lend to co-operative societies not to individuals, as opposed to an agricultural bank as follows:

[1] Polly Hill, *The Gold Coast Farmer*, Oxford University Press, 1956, p. 61.

'Title deeds are not registered. Individual ownership of the land is not recognized. The right to cultivate the land may be held by an individual or a family. Boundaries are not always clearly defined. The farms are so small that the cost of inspection would be exceedingly high. If it became necessary to take possession of the farms, the cost of management would constitute a heavy charge. . . . It is unlikely that borrowers would be . . . punctual in refunding loans from government. . . . If agricultural officers undertook the duties of stimulating payment, there might arise estrangement between the department and the farmers.'[1]

Various other recommendations and reports were made but no measures were taken till 1944, when a Co-operative Bank was established. It served both as a clearing house for the marketing co-operatives and as a medium of credit and finance for organizations and individuals, whether attached to the co-operative movement or not.[2] Because of the difficulties mentioned by Shephard, this bank could not really solve the question of credit and finally in 1950 an Agricultural Loan Board was set up, which, however, did not succeed either to liquidate the indebtedness of the past or to finance the plans for the future.[3]

The reform of the co-operatives in 1944, and later in 1960, as well as the establishment of the Ghana (then Gold Coast) co-operative societies,[4] which, however, are now the principal tool of the government for furthering economic activity and, as such, are government institutions.[5]

'Under the Ghana Second Development Plan (1959–64) the government of Ghana has implemented through the agency of the Agricultural Development Corporation a series of measures designed to accelerate the modernization and increase in production of this sector of the economy.[6] Some of the activities being initiated are the encouragement of private farmer co-operatives, the establishment of co-operative plantations with the farmers, establishment of storage and processing facilities, and the establishment of research farms.

[1] C. Y. Shephard, *Report on the Economics of Peasant Agriculture in the Gold Coast*, 1933, quoted in Hill, loc. cit., p. 64.

[2] ILO, African Labour Survey, Geneva, 1958, p. 451.

[3] Elyseo J. Taylor, 'Entwicklungshilfe vom Standpunkt des Empfängers am Beispiel der Genossenschaften in der Wirtschaftsentwicklung Ghanas', *Schriftenreihe zum Handbuch der Entwicklungshilfe*, Heft 10 (Entwicklungshilfe—einmal anders), Baden-Baden, 1963, pp. 109–24. Also in Basle Centre Series A, No. 43.

[4] These are grouped in village, district and national units and give technical help as well as marketing and transport assistance.

[5] Other state co-operatives are the Market Traders Purchasing Co-operative and the Timber Marketing Board.

[6] *Ghana—Second Development Plan*, 1959–64, Government Printer, Accra, Ghana, p. 12.

Also contemplated is the organization of wholesale food distribution facilities. It is envisaged that within the Second Development Plan some £G6 million[1] will be necessary for the programme of the Agricultural Development Corporation, of which approximately £G90,000 will be spent on three co-operative schools to be erected near Accra, Kumasi and Tamale.'[2]

While the Agricultural Development Corporation should also deal with the credit side of financing the farmers, large and small, there is no indication that this system is working either on the scale or with the efficiency that would be necessary.

In Morocco and Tunisia the approach was quite different, and, though later reformed, the original organizations are still in use. Already in 1907 the 'Sociétés Tunisiennes de Prévoyance' (STP), a type of state imposed co-operative, were founded in Tunisia and a similar organization was established under the name of 'Sociétés de Prévoyance' in Morocco in 1917. These 'societies', to which originally anyone paying agricultural taxes belonged automatically, were especially organized to help the small farmer. They were widely spread geographically throughout the country and gave chiefly short term loans to farmers in the traditional sector. Later in Morocco they enlarged their activities to include credits to local artisans and house building. In both countries a national organization was later founded, the 'Caisse Centrale', while in Morocco, the larger country, regional groupings, the 'Caisses Régionales d'Epargne' were also established.

In Morocco the Sociétés de Prévoyance (of which there were eighty-two in 1959) have become the cornerstone of the new reform of agricultural credit. Transformed into the Caisse Nationale de Crédit Agricole (CNCA)[3] they essentially keep their structure while changing names at all levels and absorbing the other institutions giving agricultural credit.[4] In Tunisia, on the other hand, a Banque Nationale Agricole (BNA) was founded for credit to large and larger farmers and the sphere of activity of the STP, though reformed,[5] was limited to the small farmer (less than forty hectars in

[1] *Ghana—Second Development Plan*, loc. cit., p. 72.

[2] E. J. Taylor, loc. cit., p. 116.

[3] By dahir no. 1–60–106, December 4, 1961, Banque Marocaine du Commerce Extérieur, *Bulletin Mensuel* (No. 21), December 1961 p. 1.

[4] The other main source of agricultural credit in Morocco was the Caisse Fédérale de la Mutualité et de Coopération Agricole for medium and long term credit. In 1960 its loans outstanding were Dh 25 million. Its capital came from its own resources, advances by the state and through rediscounts at the Bank of Morocco. Certain co-operative societies also advanced credits for various purposes but the amounts involved were small.

[5] The new reform of the system requires formal adherance and the payment of dues. The societies are financed by extra tax income of the canoun and receive financial support from the government (and formerly the French Fonds de

the north, sixty in the centre and less than 100 hectars in the south). However, both organizations, in spite of minor differences, work on much the same basic plan.

The organizations are supposed to be revolving funds. The Moroccan Société de Prévoyance had a capital of dirham 190 million in 1960;[1] of this credits had been given amounting to Dh175 million in 1960. As revenue they have the tax on corn (maize).

The local Société de Prévoyance only advances short term credit basically for seed and fertilizers, minor improvement and harvesting, so that too early sales do not have to be effected. Medium term loans are given for the purchase of animals and light equipment and smaller land improvement. The central organization in Morocco gives no credits to individual farmers but to credit organizations, public institutions and co-operatives, while in Tunisia it specializes in medium and long term credit.

The technique of the long term loans of the Caisse Centrale in Tunisia is adapted to the type of planting. For instance, on olive trees the rate of interest is 1·5 per cent for the unproductive period (thirteen years) and is payable only during the twenty-first–twenty-fifth year when maximum yield should have been reached. The actual loan is repaid with the full interest of 55 per cent during the thirteenth to twenty-fifth year, the productive years. On irrigation schemes repayment starts at once. This flexibility shows a rarely found realistic attitude with respect to the repayment possibilities of the loans.

The STP also helps with the marketing of the produce, thus assuring the repayment of the loans. The borrower must use the STP marketing facilities and the amounts due are deducted from his income. Some 10 per cent of the wheat harvest and 35 per cent of the barley harvest are handled in this way. By being able to rely on a strong organization, the individual farmer is not tempted to sell out at low prices just to acquire cash. This aspect of the marketing is especially important for olive oil where the STP is always prepared to buy at a price of 180 millimes per kg; a policy which tends to stabilize the market in that it prevents sudden price falls.

The Société de Prévoyance in both countries give technical assistance to the small farmer, working as far as possible in close

Modernisation et d'Equippement). Also in 1959, the reform included the wiping out of the debts in respect of seed previous to 1954 by decree in order to alleviate the burden. Simultaneously new credits were only accorded to those who lived up to their obligations.

[1] The Dh190 million were composed as follows in millions of Dh: Reserves 30, Advances from: The Bank of Morocco 28, Government funds 100 and various loans 20 and rediscounts 12. Banque du Maroc, *Etudes et Statistiques*, October 1961, pp. 11, 13.

collaboration with the government machinery for the improvement of agriculture.

The Sudan and Tunisia have adopted the Agricultural Bank as the solution to the problem of credit to all types of farmers. In fact, they have both run into difficulties. In Tunisia these remain mainly theoretical because the STP reaches the small farmer. Highly centralized banks usually find it difficult to acquire a structure such that they have sufficient local knowledge and flexibility. The apparatus required, the specialized staff, also make such an operation highly costly.

The Tunisian 'Banque Nationale Agricole' (BNA)[1] of June 2, 1959, was founded by the government, which holds half the share capital of dinars 400 thousand. The BNA[2] is a highly centralized organization, the local branches of which transmit the demands for credit, indirectly over seventeen agencies, to headquarters in Tunis. The local branches act chiefly as technical advisers as the purpose of the BNA is to 'encourage modern methods'. Long term credits (ten–fifteen years) amounting, in December 1961, to dinar 3,000,000[3] are for the acquisition or extension of rural properties and the enlargement of the area under cultivation and are secured by mortgages. Medium term loans (two–five years), dinar 350,000,[4] are similarly secured and given for land improvement. The short term loans (nine months) at an average of 7 per cent are designed to help with the cereal harvest, the arboricultural harvest and the vines. Special credits are also given for soil improvements and plantations—the latter using the same technique as the STP. The BNA also runs a profitable commercial and foreign department. Apart from its own share capital the BNA can receive deposits also from public institutions, has a special contribution from the Revolving Fund and a loan from the Development Loan Fund.

In the Sudan the Agricultural Bank was founded in 1957[5] for the purpose of (§4) providing 'facilities for the promotion and improve-

[1] Habib Bourgiba, Speech of July 3, 1958, reprinted in *La bataille économique*, April 17, 1956, to February 5, 1960, Tunis, 1960, p. 681. 'Un important organisme bancaire . . . (qui) . . . mettra à la disposition des agriculteurs du crédit à taux d'intérêt modéré et tiendra compte de ses possibilités. Mais il importe qu'en retour le bénéficiaire soit de bonne foi. Aussi notre devise est toujours, comme je le disais tout à l'heure, d'accorder le préjugé favorable et d'attendre que nous soyons payés de retour.'

[2] Statutes, Banque Nationale Agricole. The debts of the agricultural community towards the institutions to which the BNA succeeded were transferred and have to be paid in eight years.

[3] Banque Centrale de Tunisie, *Rapport Annuel*, 1961, pp. 90 and 92.

[4] Banque Centrale de Tunisie, *Rapport Annuel*, 1961, pp. 90 and 92.

[5] *Agricultural Bank of Sudan Act*, 17/VI/1957, and *A Short Note on the Agricultural Bank of Sudan* (The Agricultural Bank of Sudan: Agricultural Loans, Rules and Regulations, and Bye-Laws). Khartoum, March 1960 (roneographed).

ment of agriculture in the Sudan and all such other activities as may be incidental, accessory, ancillary or subsidiary thereto, affording assistance in cash, kind, goods or services to approved persons who are primarily engaged in agriculture or allied or subsidiary industries. It shall be the endeavour of the Bank to distribute the facilities given by it so that the benefits may be shared as widely as possible'.

The authorized share capital was £5 million provided wholly by the government. £2 million were transferred immediately, though part of this amount consisted of transferred agricultural loans made by the government (a guarantee of repayment was taken over by the government). The remaining £3 million were to be paid subsequently with at least £500,000 paid in any year if the Bank requested it (§6). Moreover, the Agricultural Bank may raise funds, subject to the approval of the Minister of Finance and Economics in any suitable manner, or issue bonds or debentures on the guarantee of the government (§22). There is also no restriction as to whether these funds are domestic or foreign. The Bank is also empowered to accept deposits (§23).

The Agricultural Bank of the Sudan must advance credit on demand to all except closed, independent schemes such as the Gezira. Thus it must have guarantees that the money is used correctly and has, therefore, instituted a system of inspectors and experts to advise at all branches. This applies chiefly to private cotton growing along the White Nile and the Nile north of Khartoum. However, the Bank is showing great interest in the Equatorial Province (South) where coffee, pineapples and wheat can be grown. The transport problem remains.

In order to cut out the financial operations of the licensees, the Agricultural Bank has worked out the real cost of the operations. Though, for administrative reasons the credit is still given to the licensee, the whole has to be passed on to the tenants. By strict cost control, the Bank has succeeded in cutting the cost of producing cotton by some £3–4 by bale. The costs could and should be further reduced. For instance, fertilizers were unduly high and a new direct import has decreased the price for both licensee and tenant to *ca.* £18 from £25.

The Agricultural Bank gives working capital (short term) at 6 per cent plus commission and medium term at 8 per cent. It may give long term loans but this activity has been very restricted. The Agricultural Bank also charges a commission of 2–3 per cent for marketing and ginning cotton if the licensee cannot undertake this himself.

The collaboration of the Agricultural Bank with the Ministry of Agriculture is far reaching. The Ministry effects all preliminary investigations and also tests the mechanization methods (the Sudan has a labour shortage) for picking cotton and durra, the seed for quality and even height so that harvesters can be used. Both Bank and Ministry collaborate for the very important information services, especially radio talks and for the improvement of agricultural social services.

The establishment of the Agricultural Bank in the Sudan was urgently necessary because the whole system of credit to private agricultural estates (especially cotton) had broken down. The commercial banks had been deeply involved in the financing of private estate cotton growing, usually through the intermediary of local financiers, who passed the credits (with deductions) on to the licensee and who supplied the tenant farmer.

When cotton prices fell, the 1957–58 harvest was a complete failure and ended with an indebtedness of over £S4 million of the financiers to the commercial banks, this only representing a small part of the total debts outstanding. The result was that

'This vast indebtedness, mainly from the 1957–58 season and not including any deficit which may arise in the 1958–59 season, has understandably caused the commercial banks to be wary of future cotton financing while cotton prices are low. Much as they may wish to assist the industry and to obtain repayment of the arrears due to them, banks are afraid that, by making further advances at the existing level of cotton prices, they may increase, rather than reduce, the amount of debts due to them. Because of this the Committee is of the firm opinion that, without Government intervention in any of the forms suggested in the Interim Report, private cotton growers will be unable to obtain finance for the 1959–60 season.'[1]

In view of the difficulties existing in the agricultural credit field as well as the technical difficulties of setting up operations in so vast a country, the Agricultural Bank only really started having an influence in the 1959–60 season when its existence proved essential for the financing of that season's cotton harvest.

The closed agricultural schemes include the Gezira.[2] Founded before the First World War by British Concession Companies and nationalized in 1950, this cotton-growing gravity-irrigation scheme was unique of its time. Covering over 5 million acres, with some 520 thousand permanent inhabitants, and another 200 thousand seasonal, it produces some 250,000 to 400,000 bales[3] of extra long

[1] *Final Report of the Committee appointed by the Minister of Finance and Economics to consider cotton production costs in the private estates*, Khartoum, December 31, 1959, p. 17. Hasan Bashir acted as secretary to the committee.

[2] Arthur Gaitskell, loc. cit., p. 24 ff.

[3] At 420 lb. each.

staple cotton per annum or 30–40 per cent of world production. There is an exact scheme of tenant holding, repartition of costs, income (after cost deduction) between tenants, 42 per cent, Board 10 per cent, Government 42 per cent and social services and reserve funds 6 per cent. The method of cultivation (rotation: cotton, durra, lubia and fallow) is exactly prescribed and carefully supervised. Since nationalization, greater emphasis is being laid on more varied crops, vegetables, hemp, castor, etc., as well as sugar, greater increase of mechanization and use of fertilizer. Increased social services, schooling, health, community development is all contributing to increasing the standard of living[1] in an area where it has already been one of the highest of agricultural Africa south of the Sahara for several decades.

The Gezira Scheme, though it has had its financial fluctuations, has always been so basically sound as well as of such importance to the country, that it could always raise any temporary credits needed. These are deducted as costs from the joint account, balanced at the end of the selling season, before the income is distributed. The other closed schemes, such as the Managil Extension, a new neighbour to the Gezira, should be in the same favourable position with regard to credit facilities.

In Rhodesia and Nyasaland there are two banks specialized in agricultural credit, the Land and Agricultural Bank of Northern Rhodesia, founded in 1953, and the Southern Rhodesian Land Bank.[2] In December 1961 their total loans outstanding amounted to £17 million, of which £13 million was long term and £4 million medium and short term. A large proportion was given as mortgages, some £1·8 million to co-operative societies and only £2·9 million as seasonal loans to farmers.[3] These two banks lent only to the expatriate farmers.

Therefore, in 1961 an African Loan and Development Company, with a paid-up capital of £100,000 and authorized capital of £250,000, was formed under private auspices for the purpose of extending to African farmers and businessmen the normal range of financial services and credit facilities, with emphasis on short term loans.[4] This new institution is to collaborate closely with the government agencies, which are already giving the problem of shortage of finance to industry considerable attention. This is especially acute with respect to African farming for the African farmer 'is all too often handicapped by not possessing the type of security which would

[1] Press and Information Officer, *The Gezira from Within*, Khartoum, 1959, p. 35 ff.

[2] Southern Rhodesia Land Bank Act, 1947.

[3] Rhodesias and Nyasaland, *Economic Report* 1962, p. 60.

[4] Loc. cit., p. 60.

enable him to obtain commercial credit through the existing channels'.[1]

In fact, the Rhodesian expatriate farmer has always also had recourse to normal commercial bank facilities. On the one hand these farmers were owners of large estates, and had a high level of technical knowledge, and as such were considered creditworthy. On the other hand, the important mining industry was essentially self-financing, thus leaving some room for agriculture as well as industry and commerce in the ordinary credit structure.

In Nigeria what few loans were given by the banking system to agriculture came from the commercial banks and were given to the larger farmers. The big trading companies have supplemented the flow of credit for agricultural machinery of various types. What little financing agriculture otherwise received was through Development Corporations and the Regional or Federal Government Budgets, a principle which is maintained under the new development plan, though on a much larger scale.[2]

This survey of agricultural credit has shown that in no country has a satisfactory solution as yet been found. The countries where there are diversified credit institutions, either for large and small farmers (Tunisia), or for different types of estates (Sudan) probably cover the field best. But even here the cost of credit is high for agricultural purposes. The result is that, at best, the short (and medium) term needs are met, while there is a chronic deficiency of long term capital.[3] This is partly due to the scarcity of capital in these countries, reflecting a low rate of saving. What funds are available are wholly or largely supplied by the government or state institutions. The central banks often act as lenders of last resort for part of the seasonal movements of credit. While this effectively diverts funds from other sectors, the aim should be to encourage agricultural savings, as well as general savings, as a basis for agricultural expansion. Such a policy is necessarily a long term project.

In agriculture, above all, the interdependence of economic growth, development and credit facilities is evident. Many schemes have to be initiated at regional levels and require collaboration on the part of the governments in their development plans, the ministries of agriculture (fishing, forestry and animal husbandry, where these are

[1] Bank of Rhodesia and Nyasaland, *Annual Report* 1961, p. 11.

[2] Cp. p. 261.

[3] Even in Rhodesia, there is apparently a shortage. 'Once again it must be reported that the Board had to be restrictive in granting this form of assistance (long-term loans) as funds available were not sufficient to meet the legitimate demands of the agricultural industry, the outlook for 1962, is, if anything, less favourable and no relaxation can be foreseen.' Report of the Land and Agricultural Bank of Southern Rhodesia, December 31, 1961, p. 3.

separate) and the institutions offering credit facilities. The most important follow-through is probably the system of agricultural experts working among the farmers as they alone can ascertain that the changes made and the advice given is maintained till it becomes second nature.

The organization of credit facilities must remain flexible in respect to the changing status of the farmers, the introduction of new crops and should, if possible, pay attention to repayment possibilities when the production periods are long. Moreover, the institutions should be given the highest possible guarantees of repayment, so that their resources remain revolving funds. When major calamities disrupt the system, either the government or insurance should intervene to keep a steady flow of credit for the most important production in Africa, agriculture.

CHAPTER XIII

SAVINGS INSTITUTIONS AND INSURANCE

The small but growing flow of savings collected by the savings institutions in African countries in no way corresponds to their number and variety.

There are savings banks, co-operative societies of various kinds, post office savings banks, building societies and mortgage banks. Many of these were started in the first decade of the century, especially in Morocco and Tunisia, while Ghana, Nigeria and Rhodesia and Nyasaland knew this development in the 20's and 30's. The Sudan has experienced it during the last decade, a decade which also saw an acceleration of institutional establishment in most other countries. Additionally, the start of insurance, especially life insurance, has increased the means to collect savings.

The post office savings banks, because of their many offices, have, with the exception of Morocco and Tunisia, been at the forefront of the savings movement for the ordinary man.[1] This familiarity with the post office was relatively easily established. However, little attempt was made to dynamize this institution, which soon suffered from a very high number of depositors with very small accounts.[2] It is only in the last two to five years that the governments have realized that there was here a potential collector of savings. Various savings campaigns have been launched by radio, film and advertisement, some directed exclusively to the post office savings banks, others mentioning them as one of several instruments that could be used for saving. It is still too early to discern the result from these efforts.

Similarly, the various co-operative societies or banks which accept deposits[3] (and now usually have as such to be registered under the various banking laws) have also mostly many small depositors.

[1] In the territory of Rhodesia and Nyasaland there were in August 1959 250 offices and 370,000 depositors; of these 225,000 were African, while 80 per cent of the new accounts opened in 1958 were started by Africans. Banking Supplement, Rhodesian Property and Finance, *Money Market and Banking in the Federation*, August 1959, p. 23.

[2] In Nigeria, for instance, the number of depositors rose from 169,611 in 1950 to 279,401 in 1960. The average balance per account was 1950 £16·7 and 1960 £12·9. A maximum had been reached in 1955 with £20·8 when the number of depositors was 224,499. Federal Office of Statistics, *Digest of Statistics*.

[3] Chiefly in Tunisia and Morocco; Ghana and Nigeria have both known them but they have mostly been failures.

In Morocco, for instance, artisans have their special credit organizations with the regional Caisse d'Epargne et de Crédit, whose advances in 1959 were only Dh2 million and the Banque Populaire which finance small industry (80 per cent) and commerce. Their credits to the economy in 1960 amounted to Dh69 million, of which their own deposits were Dh51 million and most of the rest rediscounts at the Banque du Maroc (4) and other institutions.[1] These banks have undergone a reform in 1961 which should make them more effective and dynamic in their support of local artisan and commercial activity.

An important contribution to the flow of savings consists of the time and savings deposits of the commercial banks. These are included in the figures of other savings banks in Table X. An interesting development should be mentioned here, namely the savings accounts started by the West African banks for illiterates. These persons, who cannot read or write, are able to have accounts because the form which is used as a receipt has the imprint of the thumb and fingers of the depositor (see illustration, p. 170). The popularity of these accounts is proved by the impressive number of ledgers, and the surprisingly large totals on many of them show that there was a real need for such a handling of accounts. This is an outstanding example of the type of imagination needed in order to adapt modern banking methods to the needs of actual, but changing, situations in developing countries, without sacrificing the soundness of the system.

Savings co-operatives also profit from savings campaigns but they are usually restricted to their members or the circle of persons whose interests they support, the artisans or the small trader. With clients with only modest means, it is difficult to build up important deposits.

The mortgage bank and society has really only succeeded in the territory of Rhodesia and Nyasaland[2] and to some extent in Morocco. In the former a society was started in 1924; from 1949 onwards many were founded in response to the demand for finance for construction of all types. These societies, which numbered fourteen in 1960, were largely daughter companies of British and South African institutions. They were thus able to have a free financial policy as they were not limited to local funds. The abolition of capital exports from South Africa in 1959 considerably reduced their resources. A special effort has been made to use these institutions for financing housing for Africans. One method has been for the government to guarantee mortgages for this purpose up to

[1] Banque du Maroc, *Etudes et Statistiques*, October 1961, p. 10.

[2] The only Tunisian mortgage bank was liquidated on independence when various forms of governments subsidy and guarantee for construction were introduced.

TABLE X

*Deposits of Savings Institutions**

	Post Office Savings†	Other Savings Banks‡	Mortgage Banks and Building Societies
Ghana (£ million)			
1950	4·7	2·2	—
1955	5·3	5·0	—
1960	5·0	12·8	—
Morocco (francs milliard)			
1950	—	11·8	n.a.
1955	—	37·2	n.a.
1960	—	31·8	6·8 (1959)
Nigeria (£ million)			
1950	2·8	3·2	—
1955	4·7	10·6	—
1960	3·6	27·4	—
Rhodesia (£ million)			
1950	n.a.	n.a.	n.a.
1955	22·7	6·4	9·3
1960	33·0	10·8	28·9
Sudan (£ million)			
1950	1·4	1·2	—
1955	2·0	3·1	—
1960	3·7	9·1	—
Tunisia (Dinars million)			
1950	—	2·5	—
1955	—	5·2	—
1960	—	5·7	—

* Figures in domestic currency at end of year.
† Including savings certificates.
‡ Including savings deposits of commercial banks.

SOURCES:

Ghana: *Economic Survey*, Bank of Ghana, *Annual Report* and *Quarterly Economic Bulletin*; IMF, *International Financial Statistics*.

Morocco: *Bulletin Economique et Social du Maroc* and Banque du Maroc, *Etudes et Statistiques*.

Nigeria: *Digest of Statistics*.

Rhodesia: *Monthly Digest of Statistics*.

Sudan: IMF, *International Financial Statistics*.

Tunisia: *Annuaire Statistique* 1957–58, *Bulletin de Statistique* and Banque Centrale, *Rapport* 1960.

£2,000, while elsewhere the societies have lent funds to the government, which itself then finances the construction in question.[1]

Morocco has also had a couple of mortgage banks, which were not very active, and two public institutions. The Caisse de Prêts Immobiliers was founded in 1920 for the purpose of advancing cheap credit for housing.[2] Though founded by the government, it has the legal form of a limited company and a certain degree of independence. It can issue bonds on the market to obtain finance (1960, Dh28 million) and was till recently indistinguishable from an ordinary mortgage bank. In 1960, however, the majority of the shares (total capital Dh2·5 million) was taken over by the Caisse de Dépôt et de Gestion and the government's control increased. Some Dh40 million come from advances from the government and the central bank. The security for the loans given must not only be high, but the latter must correspond to a social aim. This is an effort to stimulate construction activity in the country in general. The loans outstanding of the Caisse de Prêts Immobiliers fell from Dh74 million in 1958 to Dh61 million in 1960. The government has therefore tightened regulations in order to stimulate the flow of credit into cheap housing.

In Ghana, Nigeria and the Sudan there has been considerable demand for mortgage banks or societies. Construction is a major activity in all these countries and its financing is always more or less difficult. To the date of writing no move had been made to deal with this problem. It is a question worthy of solution because, having built a house on credit, the individual is often forced to save on a scale he would not otherwise contemplate.

Other savings institutions, about which little is known, are deposits with hire purchase finance houses (Rhodesia) and pension funds. These latter exist everywhere to a greater or lesser degree. Often their funds have been invested abroad and are now being, at least partly, repatriated. No definite information is available on the extent, frequency or the capital value of these two types of saving.

The football pools are important collectors of savings in West Africa. They enjoy great popularity and bring in an important and growing income from penny 'savings'. From the monetary point of view they are probably the only way to skim off purchasing power from the lowest income group. The football pools have now been either nationalized or the investment abroad of their assets has been forbidden. The importance of the pools is shown by the fact that in 1960 one country alone calculated that $3 million per annum were going abroad through this agency. The love of speculation shown by the popularity of the football pools has encouraged the issue of

[1] Banking Supplement, loc. cit., pp. 15, 18, 19 and 20.

[2] Rémy Lahaye, *Les entreprises publiques au Maroc*, Rabat 1961, p. 261.

premium bonds. The forced loans introduced in Ghana in 1961 is on this basis, a detail which has, however, not made it more popular. Other, earlier attempts to introduce premium bonds failed because the issues were not well prepared.

The gradual introduction of insurance companies, and especially life insurance companies, to African countries has created a new method of saving.[1] The movement is still in its infancy and has encountered several difficulties.[2] These range from government interference, which in some cases goes much further than legitimate control of the insurance companies for the protection of the policy holders[3], to the unfamiliarity of the African with the principles of insurance. Most insurance companies in Africa, whether expatriate or African, rely heavily on foreign help; it is the reinsurance companies of the western world that have assisted with technical and moral help—such as membership of the boards. Their financial contributions have usually been negligible.[4]

The main difficulty of private life insurance policy is that the individual African seldom understands that he will obtain benefits by maintaining his policy over time. The Africans who have reached the educational standard that this perception requires, normally have pensionable employment in the civil service, larger organizations, both public and private, and at universities. Thus the life insurance policy holder, with the exception of certain leading people in self-employment, does not really calculate with the far distant future and the number of defaults often reaches the order of 30–50

[1] On December 31, 1960, the Federation of Rhodesia and Nyasaland had 108 insurance companies. Only twelve of these were dealing exclusively in life insurance, while twenty-four had both life and non-life business. The assets of life insurance amounted to £65·3 million representing 88 per cent of the total assets of all insurance companies. Approximately one-third was invested in each of government securities and mortgages. The life insurance assets had increased in 1960 by 8 per cent, while those of other insurance business had fallen slightly. Ministry of Economic Affairs, *Economic Report* 1961, Salisbury, pp. 67–8.

[2] One of these is the purely technical, namely the lack of suitable life expectancy forecasts. Jamaican actuarian tables are usually taken as a basis. With the rapid improvement in health, especially of those who tend to take life insurance, the average life expectancy is changing very rapidly, making accurate forecasts difficult.

[3] Governments have been tempted by the swelling savings as well as the not inconsiderable profits (in 1959 the premium paid in Morocco amounted to Fr. 18,2 mrd, while in 1953 they were only Fr. 1,3 mrd.). Sometimes the investment policy of the insurance companies becomes too narrowly prescribed, while on other occasions actual nationalization has been effected.

[4] The Swiss Reinsurance Company has, for instance, not only helped in the field to build up local insurance companies but has organized in Zurich a course (to be annual) in General Insurance. The course, adjusted to the needs of future insurance personnel from developing countries, includes general insurance principles, the forms of insurance, reinsurance, organization and administration of insurance companies. Swiss Insurance Training Centre, *General Information and Program for the 1st Course in General Insurance* 1961–62, Zurich, 1961.

IV Form for Illiterate Account

To BARCLAYS BANK D.C.O. .... *19* ....

.... *BRANCH*

Please **DEBIT** *to my SAVINGS BANK ACCOUNT No.* .... *the sum of* .... *receipt of which amount I hereby acknowledge by the impressions of my fingers and thumb as given hereon.*

£ ....

RECEIPT STAMP

To be cancelled by date and initials

Depositor's Name

Above sum paid over at Depositor's request and impressions made in the presence of :—

.... *Cashier.*

.... *Clerk.*

Ledger Keeper's Initials

Checking Clerk's Initials

A 29

per cent. The more successful insurance companies have, therefore, concentrated on group life insurance through firms, trade unions and other organizations. While this approach still represents a new idea and has 'to be sold', it is probably the most constructive under present circumstances. In view of the social and job mobility, reflecting the dynamic development, in African countries group life insurance should be so built out that pension rights can be switched as jobs are changed. This problem has still to be tackled, but is fundamental, as the African mentality is such that there would be a preference to renounce life insurance in favour of mobility.[1]

The investment policy of all savings institutions and insurance companies has been a matter of concern in recent years. The expatriate organizations, which dominated the field before independence, were prone to invest abroad because of the lack of suitable investment possibilities in the country of operations. This capital export naturally did not find favour with the new independent governments. These have therefore created domestic investment paper such as Treasury Bills and government stock. The policy of the savings institutions and insurance companies, irrespective of whether they are expatriate or African, has loyally been changed, so that at least most new current savings have been invested in the country. The repatriation of formerly accumulated assets is complicated, but is proceeding, sometimes under certain pressure from the governments.

The investment policy, however, is not solved merely by domestic investment. Treasury Bills and government bonds carry relatively low rates of interest, especially compared to both the income and the increase in capital value of real estate financing. In view of the high risks especially insurance has to face, a—by western standards—more than normal proportion of the funds have directly or indirectly been invested in real estate. This policy conflicts with the desire of the new governments to raise as much finance as possible for their development plans. They believe that the funds of savings institutions and insurances are particularly suitable for indirect investment in government projects.[2] This again conflicts with the interests of the private sector, the need for a steady flow of investment capital. These problems belong to those of general credit and investment policy and cannot be discussed here. Sufficient to note that savings institutions and insurance companies, because of their actual and potential value as collectors of savings, are unavoidably implicated.

[1] The Swedish pension clearing house would be a model for such a scheme.

[2] After this manuscript was finished laws were introduced in some countries making obligatory the investment in Treasury Bills and government stock of half the assets of domestic commitments.

CHAPTER XIV

MONEY AND CAPITAL MARKETS

The establishment of effective money and capital markets as opposed to Stock Exchanges was hardly possible before there was a central bank, which could handle and direct the credit instruments. The introduction of Treasury Bills and domestic government bonds was usually not undertaken before a central bank had been established as the necessary facilities were only then available.[1] This was also foreseen in the statutes the central banks were given.

Money and capital markets have two basic functions, both of which were badly needed in the six African countries. On the one hand they give more flexibility to the short term credit structure, while on the other they can promote the savings habit by making suitable instruments available. The exact line of demarcation between a short and a long term credit instrument is not clear because of the theoretical high liquidity of government bonds, while Treasury Bills are unfortunately too easily renewable. However, the traditional forms have been found efficient and the inherent dangers are so well known that it should be within the capacity of the monetary and financial authorities to achieve a policy that minimizes them.

It proved necessary to plan carefully the introduction of new credit instruments whether the first issue of Treasury Bills or short or long term government bonds or even the sale of shares. These measures, which are so commonplace to financially mature countries, are unprecedented experiments in these developing countries. If one of them were to fail, it might be months or even years before another attempt could be made, since failure would only create distrust of the new instruments. A policy of prudent restraint is therefore necessary; it is advisable to begin with rather small issues, so as to explore the availability of the various types of funds and check whether the interest rates fixed are correct. Up to now the authorities have, in most countries, rather underestimated the capacity of the market; but it is easier to follow up a first successful issue by a second than to remedy the consequences of a failure.

[1] An exception is the Rhodesias and Nyasaland, where especially local government stock was placed relatively successfully, 1946–50 some £43·6 being issued. United Nations, *Structure and Growth of Selected African Economies*, New York, 1958, p. 45.

These observations apply with particular force to the establishment of Stock Exchanges and the sale of shares. It goes without saying that shares can only be easily sold if the purchaser in turn can dispose of them without difficulty. This means that there must be some place where shares can be bought and sold, i.e. where they can change hands. In countries where worthwhile shares have, up to now only been issued in small numbers, the arrangements often are at first on a fairly modest scale. Sooner or later it is necessary to have a fully fledged Stock Exchange reasonably commensurate in size and capacity with the supply of marketable shares and the volume of domestic risk capital available. But it is most inadvisable to set up large Stock Exchanges in which the small amount of investment paper on offer could become the object of speculation, since this would merely result in the tying-up of capital which could be much more constructively employed elsewhere in the economy. This is doubly true of these new countries, since there the apparatus of monetary control is not as developed or as efficient as in financially mature countries.

A further problem is the fact that, if the shares are to constitute really good investments, the industrial and agricultural enterprises in question must be managed with skill and circumspection. If that is not the case the intrinsic value of the shares declines, and where Stock Exchanges are small this can have a disproportionately adverse effect and unjustifiably damage the reputation of the country's whole economy. It will in fact be very important how these new Stock Exchanges are run, and this depends on the capability of the indigenous authorities and the economic growth of the whole country. In this connection it should be borne in mind that it is regarded as fashionable these days to have a Stock Exchange, as this is one of the institutions of a 'modern' country. It is to be hoped, however, that the new countries will succeed in obtaining the advantages without the disadvantages.

The Stock Exchanges, of course, also create markets for the new short and long term government bonds. The risks involved will naturally be reduced if there is a large number of subscribers with plenty of capital at their disposal. Such bonds are thus sold not only to individuals but also to the 'expatriate' and local commercial banks, industry, insurance companies and Marketing Boards. With regard to the difficult matter of deciding at what interest rates these loans ought to be issued, it should be remembered that their terms must not only be based on domestic conditions but must also be such as to make them attractive to institutions and companies which normally invest their funds mainly in London and other international financial centres. It is obvious that the rates fixed will have to be a little above those customary on the international markets.

On the other hand, in view of the budgetary burden which they represent, it is important that they should not be too high.

Premium bonds have also been introduced in Ghana and are being considered elsewhere.[1] On the one hand this type of loan brings in funds which would otherwise not be attracted by normal government loans and on the other hand it would mean that, although the interest rate has still to be adapted to the exigencies of the government budget, the large prizes are able to compete with the substantial profits earned, for instance, by the building industry and other types of private enterprise. The local population's love of speculation is reflected in the enormous success of the football-pool companies. The issue of premium bonds in small denominations of, say, £2–5[2] attracts medium-sized sums which are too small to be invested in the building industry, and this would benefit not only the government's finances but also those of the individual subscribers. The drawings would, of course, have to be carried out by means of modern machines, so as not to entail the use of a large amount of skilled labour.

One of the difficulties in placing government stock is the relative lack of financial intermediaries with automatic investment needs. Life insurance companies and domestic pension funds in particular are still in their infancy and there is a definite limit to the amount of government stock that can be carried by other financial intermediaries (building societies, Merchant Bankers) and larger enterprises and banks. That time and development change this condition is shown by the experience of Rhodesia and Nyasaland where the internal government debt had risen to £147·9 millions by December 1962 representing 51·9 per cent of the total long term Public Debt of the Federal and Territorial Governments of £284·7. In 1954, the domestically placed £53·1 million were only 30·7 per cent of a Public Debt of £173·3. Of the increase in Public Debt £94·8 million had been raised internally and only some £30 million raised abroad.[3] At the same time some £38 million have been raised at home and abroad as medium (seven years) and short term debt. Moreover, the weekly Treasury Bill issue in 1961 averaged £1·9 million as against £2·3 million in 1962 corresponding to high liquidity on the short term market due, essentially, to capital movements resulting from

[1] Erin E. Jucker-Fleetwood advocated their introduction in an article, 'The Monetary and Financial Position of Ghana and Nigeria'. Basle Centre for Economic and Financial Research. Publication Series A, 29 (June 1960), p. 10. Translation of articles published in *Neue Zürcher Zeitung*, June 27 and 28, 1960.

[2] Without competing with the local football-pools, the tickets of which command a much inferior price.

[3] Rhodesia and Nyasaland, *Economic Report* 1962, p. 74, and *Monthly Digest of Statistics*, August 1963.

the Congo crisis and the subsequent introduction of foreign exchange control also towards the sterling area.

The territory of Rhodesia and Nyasaland had a head start in the formation of a money and capital market and yet 'difficulty is being found in raising capital'.[1]

This difficulty is even more apparent in other countries. In Ghana, both government stock and Treasury Bills have been issued. The first issue of the latter, £2 million, was in February 1960. In August 1961 the Treasury Bills outstanding were £10 million but seven months later (March 1962) the amount outstanding was £22 million.[2] By December 1962 the outstanding total was over £38 million. At the same time some government stock was issued internally but only £5·5 million worth,[3] showing that long term capital is hard to obtain and that the prospects of funding the large Treasury Bill float are bleak. In view of the scarcity of domestic long term capital, compulsory savings were introduced in July 1961. These National Development bonds are obligatory at a rate of 5 per cent for wage earners and 10 per cent for all other categories. The 5 shilling bonds are repayable at 6 shillings in 10 years and are a premium bond with prizes amounting to 2 per cent with half-yearly drawings. The bonds are non-cashable except for certain special cases. The cocoa farmers participate but at 10 per cent or 6 shillings a head load making their cash return per head load 54 shillings. It was hoped that in the budget year 1961–62 some £11 million would be raised from this source.

In Nigeria, too, Treasury Bills and government stock have been issued, but the rate has been much more cautious. Treasury Bills were first introduced in April 1960 with an issue of 4 million. The Treasury Bill (Amendment) Act (May 1962) raised the amount that could be outstanding at any one time to 40 per cent of estimated current federal revenue, thus raising the potential limit to £50 million in 1962–63. Fortnightly issues (instead of monthly) were also introduced and the average amount of Treasury Bills outstanding in 1962 was £21·5 million compared to £13 million in the preceding year.[4] The amount outstanding in December 1962 was £24 million or half of the total potential.

In Morocco, where the issue of short and medium term government stock is well established, bons d'équippement were issued till 1959, when they reached a maximum of frs. 25 milliards. Subsequently bons remboursables at five years were issued at the more

[1] Bank of Rhodesia and Nyasaland, *Annual Report* 1961, p. 16.

[2] Bank of Ghana, *Quarterly Economic Bulletin*, September/December 1962, p. 51.

[3] Bank of Ghana, *Annual Report* 1961–62, p. 26.

[4] Central Bank of Nigeria, *Annual Report*, March 31, 1963, p. 33.

favourable rate of 4·5625 per cent. The more favourable rate was possible because of the high liquidity of the banks. In 1960, 10 milliards were issued and in 1961 6 milliards, representing almost entirely a consolidation of the former bon d'equippement. The total of both types of bonds outstanding in December 1961 was Frs. 29·031 million of which the banks, including the central bank, held some 75 per cent. Almost the full total of short term bonds (one year) was also held by the banks and the central bank.[1] The money and capital market in Morocco consists thus entirely of medium and short term paper and is largely restricted to the banking sector.

Much the same situation is to be found in Tunisia where the current government debt is mainly short term, representing bons d'equippement and stock for settling the costs of the war. Of the former D1,247 million were issued in 1960 and D2,010 million in 1961. Of the latter the corresponding figures are D66 million and D180 million.[2]

There are plans to issue government bonds in the Sudan. The holders should be larger firms, the Post Office savings banks (which are due for a reform), etc., and it is expected that some £S½ to 1 million would be available at irregular intervals. There certainly are some sources of capital as the few share issues so far floated have usually been over-subscribed. The introduction of Treasury Bills is, on the other hand, at present unlikely. Firstly, there are no very large swings in financing in the Sudan, because other crops are harvested in the low season of the cotton cycle—giving the Sudan a unique monetary pattern. Secondly, the government has often very large liquid deposits at the Bank of Sudan, as have the commercial banks. Through Treasury Bills, the funds of the commercial banks would be transferred to the government account with the risk of increasing the psychological effect such large balances always exert.

In Ghana, the Sudan and Tunisia there are no Stock Exchanges. The number and quantity of the shares on the market do not yet justify such an introduction. This does not mean that there is no possibility of trading in shares. Various ad hoc solutions have been found. Their common denominator is that the representatives of banks meet at regular intervals in order to effect the purchase and sale of the shares they have in commission. The arrangements, with their local variations, seem to answer their purpose and, until there is a very much larger amount of saleable shares, should be sufficient for the current needs.

There are comparatively ancient Stock Exchanges in Morocco at Casablanca and in the territory of Rhodesia and Nyasaland at

[1] P. M. Dupuy, 'Le Trésor et la monnaie au Maroc en 1918 et 1962', *Bulletin Economique et Social du Maroc*, Vol. XXVI, No. 93, August 1962, pp. 92–3.

[2] Banque Centrale de Tunisie, *Rapport Annuel* 1960, p. 34, and 1961, p. 36.

Salisbury and Bulawayo.[1] These latter have some four to five brokers and quote some fifty shares and a smaller number of bonds. The shares are those of companies established in the Federation, mining, industry and commerce. The peculiarity of the Rhodesian markets is that they have Merchant Banks which both discount bills and help to issue shares. For instance in 1959, the Rhodesian Acceptances issued successfully, shares of the Rhodesian and Nyasaland Tobacco Co., Ltd. and of the Rhodesian Television. The two Stock Exchanges have had a peaceful existence with still a limited number of transactions. The same applies to the Stock Exchange at Casablanca, where the turnover of its thirty quoted shares is small. Its history has, however, been fairly checkered, reflecting both the degree to which it was dependent on expatriate capital and the economic history of Morocco. A Stock Exchange that cannot count on a fairly broad basis of internal savings is naturally in a precarious position. The proximity of a free gold market does not increase the tendency towards a fair degree of stability.

The opening of the Stock Exchange at Lagos on October 1, 1960, was fairly well prepared. The Central Bank of Nigeria had already been running a temporary, though slightly awkward method of trading in government bonds, while the first share issue in 1959 of £174,898 at £1 shares of the Nigerian Cement Company Ltd. was successful. Dealings in this share was made possible by the facilities offered by ICON, the Investment Company of Nigeria. The latter has since helped to run the Stock Exchange, which quotes shares (in January 1963, twenty-three quotations) all of well-established companies in Nigeria, and the government bonds, a third Development loan also having been issued. There is daily trading and rates had stabilized so that yields in the beginning of 1962 were around 10 per cent. Domestic issues have been cautious; for instance that of John Holt Investment Company Ltd., underwritten by ICON, was over-subscribed by more than 300 per cent; the allotted total was doubled over what was originally planned. All 600 odd applicants were private persons or smaller firms.

The Lagos Stock Exchange hopes that gradually the interest[2] and financial strength of the public will be increasing and that a larger number of quotations and issues will be possible. Especially in the private sector there is an increasing interest of existing and new enterprises seeking to establish themselves in Nigeria and who

[1] V. P. Romilly, 'The Money Market in the Federation of Rhodesia and Nyasaland, *Bankers Magazine*, December 1962, pp. 401–7.

[2] Some 10 per cent of the outlay of the Stock Exchange during its first year of operation was for advertising. It was aimed mainly at private long-term funds kept liquid on bank accounts or in cash, mainly for want of a better known alternative.

actively seek the participation of Nigerian capital. It is hoped that the existence of the Lagos Stock Exchange will facilitate both the formation of private savings and their suitable investment.

A private acceptance house was founded in September 1960, Philip Hill (Nigeria) Ltd., which hopes eventually to contribute to the issue of shares on the Nigerian market and of Nigerian shares on the London Market. This issuing activity is to be completed by Investment Management and General Financial Advice, including raising financial capital. A successful activity has been the raising of short term finance by Acceptance Credit, an innovation in Nigeria. The sums outstanding at any one time amounted in the 1961–62 season to £1·4 million, a useful addition to the crop financing, and a key development in the monetary structure of the country.

The very great importance of the financing of trade through the money market, through discountable commercial bills, acceptance credits, promissory notes, etc., has already been referred to as part of the activity of central and commercial banks. It has therefore not seemed necessary to discuss the question in this chapter, especially as the movement is still embryonic. Its theoretical and general implications are, moreover, discussed below in connection with those pertaining to the Fiduciary Issue.

The degree to which it has been possible to establish money and capital markets in the six countries of Africa has varied considerably, depending on local conditions and conceptions. Basically all countries have an easier money than capital market. Savings, the essential ingredient, are still very small. It is, therefore, always difficult to place long term loans, except in the countries where the market has been kept deliberately short. The existing Stock Exchanges have hitherto done better than might have been expected, but this is mainly due to the cautious manner in which they have been administered and the careful selection of the shares accepted for quotation. If they can prove to be reasonably stable, they will turn out to be a positive factor in encouraging domestic savings for the private sector and thus contribute greatly to economic growth and development of their countries.

CHAPTER XV

SUMMARY AND CONCLUSION

While there is every indication that primarily the commercial banks as well as other financial intermediaries have succeeded in supplying the economies of the six African countries with commercial and industrial short term credit in sufficient quantities, there has been a definite overall lack of medium and long term capital and of both short term credit and long and medium term capital for agriculture. This latter problem is not specifically African, but universal. However, the overall lack of medium and long term capital makes the position of agriculture in Africa particularly acute.

The lack of medium and long term credit and capital reflects the basic fact that savings are in short supply. This is due to the structure of the economies, the low *per capita* income and the high propensity to consume. Hitherto, the deficiency in domestic long term capital has been made up by the use of international loans and of past savings, mainly the profits of Marketing Boards and Statutory Corporations.[1] But the governments all realize that if the rate of growth of the economies is to be as high as is considered necessary, the creation of important domestic savings is absolutely essential.

There are two basic methods in which domestic savings can be increased and both are being attempted parallel to each other. On the one hand, the structure and content of the economy can be altered so as to achieve a higher *per capita* income, while, on the other, the rate at which savings are formed out of any given income can be increased. Two different techniques have been used, namely, the diversion of funds directly to productive investment (e.g. taxation and/or directional control of credit) and by encouraging the individual to save more.

The financial intermediaries are, at the side of the government financing, the best tool to supplement the latter and to help implement the desired policy. They can do so best within the framework of a market economy and can give support to the all-important private sector, which otherwise is easily neglected. This has been recognized and the governments have, on the whole, tried to give help and support to both commercial banks—the indigenous sometimes being given preference—and other financial intermediaries.

[1] Cp. p. 272.

In view of the lack of a differentiated structure of financial intermediaries, a series of specialized institutions, to assist the domestic economy and its various sectors, have been established. While they differ slightly in construction and administration, the aims of these new financial intermediaries are the same. They seek both to stimulate private industrial and agricultural activity and reform and to contribute to the necessary long term capital. Their original capital is obtained from governments and/or international institutions and/or public subscription. Additionally, they usually have the right to certain special support in the shape of government loans and/or preferential treatment when rediscounting at the central bank. Increasingly the international institutions (mainly AID, World Bank and IFC) are giving loans to development banks, thus providing finance, while letting local organizations control its investment. Moreover, it is foreseen that these development banks whether industrial or agricultural, may at a later date issue bonds on the market (and/or sell the shares they retain), thus drawing on any savings that might result from their activity.

The stimulation of savings activity is, however, not only made to depend on the results. Already at the start of the venture, the entrepreneur is expected to provide part of the necessary capital. The repayment of the loans obtained, though often adjusted to the profitability prospects of the enterprise, is enforced according to the contract, while default is prevented by supplying the necessary technical advice.

Thus the newly created development banks and agricultural banks both stimulate productive investment and accumulate savings.

Other financial intermediaries also assist in the accumulation of savings. Savings banks, including the Post Office and the commercial banks' savings deposits, building, mortgage and hire purchase societies all contribute while the newly established life insurance companies and pension (or provident) funds are probably the most promising potential collectors of long term savings. All these financial intermediaries, following the example of the older established commercial banks, use advertising to stimulate savings and either complement or supplement the government's own saving programme.

Eventually the combined efforts of all financial intermediaries should be reflected in greater ease and volume on the money and capital markets and on the Stock Exchanges. These latter only exist as yet in three of the countries and are still relatively small and not very active. Their intrinsic value lies mainly in their potentialities, which, however, must be carefully nursed into bloom.

While the broad lines of the aims of the establishment of a variety of financial intermediaries to satisfy the needs of various sectors can be summarized, the details of their manner of operating can not. Part III has attempted to describe various techniques used to achieve an accepted policy in new and developing economies where special circumstances have always to be taken into consideration. A maximum of flexibility and imagination is needed also at technical level to meet the constantly changing needs and thus ensure the success of the overall policy.

The establishment of specialized financial intermediaries to meet the needs of certain sectors of these economies has been the answer to the necessity of stimulating the economy and to creating medium and long term capital. Most of these countries seem to have now the financial intermediaries they should require (with the exception of building societies in certain countries). These new institutions will need several years of quiet but active work in the context of a stable economy if they are to be able to achieve their aims and make the contribution they undoubtedly can, to the growth and development of their countries.

PART FOUR

CHAPTER XVI

THE LIMITS OF MONETARY POLICY

Monetary policy in African countries has to take into account certain factors which on the one hand are peculiar to most developing countries and on the other are specific to Africa. Naturally, there are differences from country to country, but there is still enough homogeneity to be able to discuss the broad categories of fundamental approach.

The most important difference between developing countries and financially mature countries is that in the latter monetary policy must take into account the total liquidity position at the side of the money supply, whereas in the developing countries the state of liquidity is still largely a simple function of the money supply.[1] This is because the developing countries do not have, in their money and credit sector, an important financial superstructure with a highly differentiated credit system, such as is found in Great Britain or in the United States. In other words, the deepening of the credit system has not yet taken place.

In the developing countries the institutional structure, while usually containing all basic and fundamental organizations, is not mature in the same way. There are not innumerable types of credit organizations often financing each other, such as a commercial bank financing a holding company, which in its turn finances a hire purchase organization. All the interconnecting lines of credit do not exist, neither are the stocks and shares, short, medium and long term loans of all these organizations on the money and capital markets. There is little prospect of credit switches occurring on the provocation of very slight changes in expectations, conditions, terms or the constant need of some of these institutions (insurance companies and the like) to invest profitably. This is due to the lack of a large volume of highly differentiated near-money assets such as deposit accounts, saving certificates, building society shares and deposits, defence bonds, commercial bills, Treasury Bills, tax reserve certificates, deposits with savings banks and other short term liabilities as also hire purchase facilities and trade credits. The existence

[1] Erin E. Jucker-Fleetwood, 'The Money Supply in Mature and in Developing Countries', *The Irish Banking Review*, March 1961. Also available in Basle Centre Publication Series A, No. 38.

of these instruments of liquidity on a large scale is the hallmark of the financially mature countries.

In the developing countries and especially in Africa it is not only that the money and credit system is too new to have allowed time for deepening to take place, but that the real counterpart still does not exist. Thus the 'man in the street' does not yet have the creditworthiness—the savings, the house, the life insurance, the pension, the steady job—which alone can form the basis for this type of deepening of the credit structure. In fact, a preliminary stage has not yet been reached. This would be characterized by important indigenous creditworthy industrial, commercial and possibly agricultural groups of enterprises. Their growth has just started, but their contribution to monetary liquidity is usually very slight. The only important exceptions are the Marketing Boards, which built up important foreign assets in the 1950's and the mining companies in Rhodesia. Here too it is a question of mainly foreign assets. These latter, however, give the possibility of commanding domestic currency. The central banks do have to allow for their effective purchasing power, both internally and externally; but this can be done by private agreement with a very small number of individual enterprises and institutions. It does not require, as would be the case if they were numerous, the implementation of general measures of monetary policy.

In view of their financial structure, the developing countries thus do not have to have a monetary policy which takes into account an important volume of near money. Some countries are at an intermediate stage and either occasionally or increasingly have to adjust their policies for the growing volume of near money assets, which added to the money supply (IMF definition) gives the total liquidity position. With the maturing of the monetary and financial systems the monetary authorities must always take into account the growing importance of the near money holdings, created by the deepening of the institutional structure. The total liquidity position to the extent it exists has in fact to be considered equally with the money supply[1] when formulating policy. This involves the use of interest rates and their relative structures, the latter not only being influenced by changes in bank rate but also by selective controls or such genial handling of the money and capital markets as took place in the United States 1960–61.[2]

As has been shown in the two preceding parts, the six African

[1] Erin E. Jucker-Fleetwood, *Der Radcliffe Report*, Zeitschrift für die gesamte Staatswissenschaft, 116, Band, 3. Heft, 1960. Also in Basle Centre Publication Series A, No. 32.

[2] Robert von Roosa, 'Reconciling Internal and External Policies', *Journal of Finance*, Vol. XVIII (March 1962), p. 1.

countries under discussion have still an insignificant, though growing volume of near money assets. They therefore, when formulating monetary policy, have to concentrate, if not exclusively then largely, on the money supply.

The money supply according to the IMF definition covers notes and coins in the hands of the public plus demand deposits of banks (less interbank deposits). It is thus designed to include all the cash assets of the community while excluding the whole of the near money assets. Nearly all countries are able to furnish accurate statistics of the money supply and this makes for a fairly high degree of international comparability.[1]

The emphasis on the money supply and the currency in circulation in particular as an operative factor is further increased by a second consideration. A characteristic of the financial structures of practically all developing economies is the split between that growing sector of the economy, which utilizes money and credit and that which still uses barter or money substitutes (cattle, shells, etc.). Between these two there is an ill-defined and fluctuating intermediate area where money may be used in all transactions with persons from outside the community (traders, tax collectors, etc.), while within it barter is still the main means of exchange. Marginal differences in value might even here be settled in money. The relative size of this intermediate area varies both through time and geographically. In some countries, it is still an important factor, in others it has practically disappeared. In the six African countries it is decreasing fairly fast, but though its importance may vary, it still has to be taken into account.

Thus allowance must always be made for the gradual full monetization of those parts of the economy, which are still in the barter stage or not far removed from this stage. Here it is not a case of issuing extra-money for which there is no counterpart of goods and services. These are already present. But it does mean issuing more money than would be justified by the economic process alone. The extent to which newly issued money goes to the monetization of this sector must still be largely a matter of 'feel' on the part of competent authorities. A partial check is found in the internal price movement, when reasonably reliable indices are available for the *real* internal market (i.e. not for the consumption patterns of city dwellers, or, in some cases, expatriates). Unfortunately, nothing is yet known of the price movements at the transfer stage from barter to money and in the immediate following stage.

In spite of these difficulties the monetization of the country proceeds almost on its own as the patterns of behaviour change. The central bank must take the process into account in its currency

[1] For a discussion of the money supply definition see Appendix IV, p. 315.

issuing function both with regard to the amounts and denominations of coins and notes released.

With regard to the demand deposit part of the money supply, the central bank usually has the legal competence to enforce minimum reserve ratios and, in some cases, special deposits. The extent to which these arc or can be used vary. Naturally, if for some reason the members of the board of the central bank—who may have other interests at heart or because they are under instructions—refuse to allow the governor the enforcement of the powers, the efficiency of the central bank is gravely compromised. It is then impossible for the bank to use the gentleman's agreement as its main instrument of control. The latter usually only seems to work if the central bank has both prestige and enforceable weapons in reserve. Over and above the general tone of monetary policy must be such that it encourages the living up to the terms of the gentleman's agreement or the respecting of the minimum reserve ratio. When all the participants realize that their true interests are not really in conflict much is gained and the execution of monetary policy is greatly simplified.

The use of bank rate and the structure of interest rates as instruments of monetary policy is only feasible when there is a certain volume of near money assets in the country. Then also open market operations begin to become a possibility and the policy making capacity of the central bank is greatly enhanced. At the moment, however, most of these central banks are in a preliminary stage where their policy making is directed to the formation of 'near money' assets or to the deepening of the monetary structure.

This basically means that the central bank should promote the creation of the institutions and the instruments of a more sophisticated monetary and financial structure and encourage their use. While it is usually necessary in developing countries to create an institution before there is a real demand for it—thus reversing the manner in which the system of the present financially mature countries was built up—the institution or instrument must be adapted to the needs of the country. Its introduction must find justification in that it has an immediate, if initially small, field of activity. Otherwise there can be a period of bitter disappointment between creation and utilization, a situation which can easily lead to the disrepute of the institution or instrument and which must be guarded against. Thus, the timing of the new step requires the best possible judgement. Each new measure must also be very carefully prepared. On both these points the central bank can have an influence. It can advise on the most suitable forms, statutes and perhaps even managers. It can even advertise and promote the sale of new Treasury Bills and government bonds. If the measure has been well conceived a certain success should be immediate. The danger of failure can make a central bank over-cautious; however, such accusations as are occasionally heard are really due to others wanting to proceed too fast. It is very much in the interests of the central bank to be imaginative with respect to the deepening of the monetary system. Only thereby can it enlarge its own possibility of executing the monetary policy, which is its legal and moral responsibility.

A central bank in Africa is, however, not autonomous in its policy making. Especially with respect to the horizontal broadening of the monetary system it finds itself affected by factors more or less outside its control. Some of these it shares with central banks all over the world, some are specifically African or have special aspects. The main ones are the size and internal and external price of crops, both cash and food, wage policy and the changes in the structure of labour, government financial and budget policy, including the development plans, and the balance of payments position. All these factors affect monetary policy and at best there can only be an interaction between the position taken by the central bank and the effects of these extraneous factors. All of them imply changes in the behavioural patterns of individuals and that in countries where some of the fastest changes ever seen are taking place. One of the dramatic evidences thereof is the way with which money was introduced and the speed with which its use has spread.

CHAPTER XVII

THE HISTORY OF MONETIZATION

The history of the monetization of the African countries is so interesting and essential to an understanding of the present-day attitudes to money and monetary policy that a digression is necessary. The processes here described as a historical evolution are in some parts of Africa, and marginally in the six countries, still in operation. They have to be taken into consideration by the monetary authorities and, in fact, constitute a problem that affects their policies both in regard to currency and institutions.

Two basically different cases must be distinguished. The countries in Northern Africa, Tunisia and Morocco, were through the centuries part of the Mediterranean commercial area. The cities, at first on the coast, later inland, were already in pre-Christian times commercial centres and money was in use. Of Africa south of the Sahara very little is known. Any development similar to that in Northern Africa was almost unknown except in West Africa where it started after 1500. In spite of these differences the monetization of the rural parts of the six countries does not take place till much later. In Northern Africa, it came in the nineteenth century, in Africa south of the Sahara in the twentieth—the background for modern monetary policy is thus not too different.

The process of monetization has very wide implications. Especially in Africa south of the Sahara money is the spearhead of modern civilization. Its arrival profoundly changed the social, economic and psychological behaviour of the people. The shock-impact effect of the confrontation with the demands of a radically different system is seen today most clearly in the cities. But the revolution that has taken place in the rural areas[1] is at least as profound if less dramatic because it is tempered by the rhythm of the cycle of agricultural production. In Northern Africa, money arrived more gradually and in response to a natural demand for it rather than as the imposed system of an alien people. Thus the changes in behaviour of the rural population in Northern Africa are probably smaller than in Africa south of the Sahara.

The first known traders in Tunisia were the Phoenecians, who

[1] United Nations, *Enlargement of the Exchange Economy in Tropical Africa*, New York, 1954, II c. 4.

already in the sixteenth century BC established a trading station called Cambe, on which they based their commerce with the tribes of the coast land. The foundation of Carthage, about 814–813 BC, led to what is now modern Tunisia becoming the hinterland of the second most important city in the then known world. The Phoenecians were followed by the Greeks and the Romans, all of which introduced their own moneys. Later came the Arabs who founded Kaironan in Tunisia, and who reached Morocco in AD 684 settling it permanently in 705. They brought with them the dinar (gold), the dirham (silver) and bronze coins.[1] This monetary basis, it cannot be called a system, was subject to debasements of the coinage at the will of the sovereigns and the working of Gresham's law kept the currency in actual circulation small. There was not a great demand for currency as, in effect, it was only in the cities where a certain commercial activity effected with money took place. By 1850, commercial relations had developed with France, Great Britain and Spain. With trade came the currency of these countries, but it was the Spanish peseta which gained 'general' acceptance because it was also being used in the still small inland trade, commerce with Spain, because of geographic and historical factors, being ancient. By the end of the nineteenth century the breakdown of the silver standard, and with it of the peseta, increased the monetary disorder which led to the establishment of the Banque d'Etat.[2]

During these centuries of foreign trade the rural areas seem to have been completely untouched and the very simple and primitive existence of pre-Christian times had continued unmodified. Barter and possibly money substitutes allowed what exchange of goods there was, while the herds were the store of wealth. In the nineteenth century, however, a change seems to have taken place.[3] Its outward and visible sign was not only the important import of tea, but also its distribution throughout the country. The world market price of tea was falling throughout the century, and the former drink of the rich became widely popular. The comparatively fast spread of the consumption of tea and its companion sugar, was amongst the most active agents which changed the traditional economy to a monetary economy.[4] These imported luxuries had to be paid for in cash, and this stimulated the individual to earn it. The government found tea a profitable source of income, taxing it in 1845 at 10 per cent *ad valorem*. It was only later, however, apparently in 1856–60, that the drink really became popular and widespread. What tea and sugar

[1] André J. Marty, *Le franc marocain—Monnaie satellite*, Paris, 1957, p. 14.

[2] Cp. p. 56.

[3] J.-L. Miège, 'Origine et développement de la consommation du thé au Maroc', *Bulletin économique et social du Maroc*, Vol. XX, No. 71 (January 1957), pp· 377–98.

[4] Loc. cit, p. 378.

had accomplished was followed up by the important road network and bus transport system built up later by the French so that these countries now have a money (currency) economy for ordinary trading purposes reaching even the most isolated villages.

A study of the movement of notes at the six agencies of the Banque d'Etat in Morocco confirms the wide spread of currency.[1] The three agencies in rural areas, namely at Kenitra, Meknes and Rabat have more or less important outpayments of notes all year round and the harvests' seasonal variations are clearly reflected. In Rabat this movement is superimposed on that created by the payments of salaries and holidays. At Fes and Marrakech both commercial (and tourist) centres the inpayments dominate, whereas at Casablanca the effects of the city's commercial activity and close linkage to the general economy give important in and out movements in both directions. The growing importance of notes in the total money supply is confirmed by an increase of 27 to 34 per cent between 1950–59. Because of the small denominations, the trend of the note circulation in Morocco corresponds more nearly to that of both notes and coin in a country with a currency structure of the type found in Nigeria.

The monetization of the Sudan reflects clearly its double orientation as well as its national history. To the extent it was linked with the Arab world, and through that with the Mediterranean and Red Sea trade, coins seem to have started circulating in Northern Sudan in the latter half of the Fung Dynasty (1504–1821).[2] These were mainly the celebrated Maria Theresia Thaler and various European gold and silver coins including the Spanish peseta. The Egyptian conquest in 1821 introduced Ottoman and Egyptian coins with which requisitioned goods were paid. In response to an important increase in trade, money started circulating freely in the lower Nile districts and in the larger towns though as late as 1861 apparently it was probably still very difficult to secure their acceptance beyond Kaka—about 350 miles south of Khartoum.

From 1885 to 1916 there was a succession of various attempts at creating a domestic currency. During the siege of Khartoum, General Gordon issued notes (still to be seen in the Museum in Ondurman), which he himself signed. This first attempt at paper money was abortive as the Mahdi conquered Khartoum soon after. The latter and his successor Khalifa Abdullahi struck coins of their own, the intrinsic value of which was higher than the foreign coins also in circulation. Gresham's law again went into operation and

[1] Banque du Maroc, 'Les variations de la circulation fiduciaire', *Etudes et Statistiques*, October 1960, pp. 9–28.

[2] Bank of Sudan, 'Some Historical Notes on the Use of Currency in the Sudan', *Economic and Financial Bulletin*, October/December 1960, pp. 19–26.

these Sudanese coins largely went out of circulation to be exported as gold ingots. Counterfeiting was not unknown and also the gradual debasement of the currency around 1890 and after did not enhance its prestige. A base coinage was introduced after Ali' Dinar's revolution (1899) as he was in desperate need of finance. These emergency coins imitated the style and script of the Egyptian piaster but bore his name and mostly consisted of metal discs cut from old petroleum and kerosine tins.

The establishment of the Anglo-Egyptian Condominium led to the introduction of the Egyptian currency system, consisting of British and Turkish coins and later notes of the National Bank of Egypt. Early in 1916, a price increasing shortage of small denomination coins led to the introduction of British shillings and florins. Later all Egyptian coins were made legal tender. This system remained in force till the establishment of the Currency Board.[1]

The circulation of currency in the Sudan was on the whole restricted to the northern area and the larger towns till some time around 1900. After that it gradually spread to other areas, the eastern region probably being the first because of both the trade in gum arabic—this is the main production area—and the aftermath of the unrest during and after the First World War. This led to a certain amount of military and administrative activity on the eastern frontier in the Province of Dafur and has given us an interesting eyewitness account of the 'monetary' situation of the time.[2]

'Until the building of the first station at Kereinik money in the form of coins or paper had hardly reached Dar Masalit. Only in 1922 did it begin to trickle into El Geneina, through the pay of the soldiers and the few officials; and in the outlying districts there was still none at all. The three current media of exchange were sticks of salt; strips of homespun cotton-cloth, damur, of more or less standard length and width; and sheep or goats for larger dealings. The sticks of salt were laboriously made by anyone who cared to take the trouble, at one of the salt wells which occurred in certain places. Water from the well was allowed to evaporate until the salt was at saturation point. Then short stalks of grass, tied by one end along a string, were dipped in it and hung up to dry; dipped again and re-hung; and so on until the deposit of salt on them was about as thick as a man's finger. There was no inspector of weights and measures on the Sultan's payroll.'

'With a company of soldiers and their wives all spending money, the market (at El Geneina) began to flourish, nickel and silver coins

[1] Cp. p. 61.

[2] Reginald Davies, *The Camel's Back—Service in the Rural Sudan*. London, 1957, pp 159–60.

joining—and very gradually beginning to displace—sticks of salt and strips of damur as currency. The Sultan readily assimilated the suggestion that the market ought to be a source of revenue for municipal purposes. Notice was given daily for several weeks that after a certain date vendors of animals, grain, flour, milk, eggs or other commodities would have to pay dues for the pitches they occupied; and that these would be payable in coin. When the appointed day came there were many who had no coin with which to pay even the extremely small sums demanded. Sticks of salt, at the current rate of exchange, were accepted and subsequently sold in bulk, but offers of gourdfuls of fried locusts were firmly rejected. I never tried this dish, notwithstanding the example of Saint John the Baptist, though people told me that it was a delicacy.'[1]

Forty years have passed since then and there are several banks at El Fasher, the capital of the province and the end of the new railway. At any rate in the towns, at the markets currency is in circulation. In the southern part of the country, which is still very isolated and almost untouched, the circulation of money outside the towns must be very slight. Monetization depends essentially upon the spread of development projects; irrigation schemes give the possibility of a cash crop and the spread of industry to the towns along the Nile below Khartoum will increase both external and internal commerce. The influence of the latter spreads currency with decreasing intensity throughout the country all radiating out from Khartoum, a busy centre of industry and commerce.

By 1800 there was in West Africa a bewildering variety of currency in circulation.[2] Most popular was, here as elsewhere in Africa, the Spanish peseta (doubloon and dollar), which seems to have come into circulation at a very early date.[3] The revolt in the Spanish colonies had by 1820, however, cut off the supply of the Spanish peseta and the existing stock was enlarged by each piece being cut in four (and sometimes stamped). These cut coins were demonetized in 1839. Second in importance were probably French francs (the Napoleon and the one-franc) while 1852 United States gold coins and in 1874 Belgian, Italian and Swiss five-franc pieces were also made legal tender. British currency had some difficulty in becoming popular—an attempt in 1825 to introduce it as the only currency failed—but it gradually established itself (first in Sierra Leone) and after new currency regulations were introduced in 1880 gained ground rapidly. Unfortunately, there is little information as to the amounts involved, only isolated figures being available. There is

[1] Loc. cit., p. 165.
[2] A. Adomakoh, loc. cit., pp. 499–512.
[3] Loc. cit., p. 502.

reason to suppose, however, that around 1880 the main centres of economic activity in British West Africa were Gambia and Sierra Leone and that the rise of present-day Ghana and Nigeria came later. The inland wars had restricted activity exclusively to the coast forts and the distance from Europe kept even these small till the advent of the steamer.[1] Lagos, being even more remote, only became an independent colony as late as 1886 and the development of the hinterland restricted by internal unrest and a complete absence of roads took time. Modern monetary history of Nigeria starts only in 1912 when the West African Currency Board was established.

At that time there was still a considerable amount of primitive currency and barter. The former 'consisted of a variety of commodities, and different usages were observed among the various West African countries. However, the circulation of cowries was common to most of the countries. Cowries were in general use in Nigeria and among the Africans in the Gold Coast. No mention is made of the use of cowries in Sierra Leone, but the use of cowries there and in neighbouring French colonies adjoining Nigeria, Gold Coast and Sierra Leone may be presumed. The rate of exchange at which cowries passed seemed to vary from one country to another, in Nigeria they passed at 4,000 cowries to the shilling; in the Gold Coast the rate was 1,800 cowries per one shilling. Cowries appeared to have been in use throughout the nineteenth century, but evidence taken by the Department Committee on a special West African Currency sitting in 1912 suggested that not only were cowries in general use at the time, but barter trade was also considerable, though both of these were on the decline.'[2]

'In Southern Nigeria local differences were well marked. In the Western province hardly any primitive form of currency existed by the first decade of the twentieth century; the Committee on West African Currency reported that British silver coins were used practically throughout the Province. On the other hand, trading by barter was still carried on to a large extent in the Eastern and Central Provinces just before the First World War. British silver coins were accepted freely in only about half of the markets. Primitive forms of currency known as 'manillas' and brass and copper rods and wires, formerly legal tender, were in 1912 still in use to a considerable extent although they had been demonetized. In Northern Nigeria cowries were still in use extensively among the Africans, and trade was carried on largely by barter.'[3]

It is against this background that the change in the structure of

[1] Gustaf Adolf Wanner, loc. cit., p. 101.
[2] Adomakoh, loc. cit., p. 506.
[3] Adomakoh, loc. cit., p. 506.

Currency in Circulation in Nigeria 1912–1960

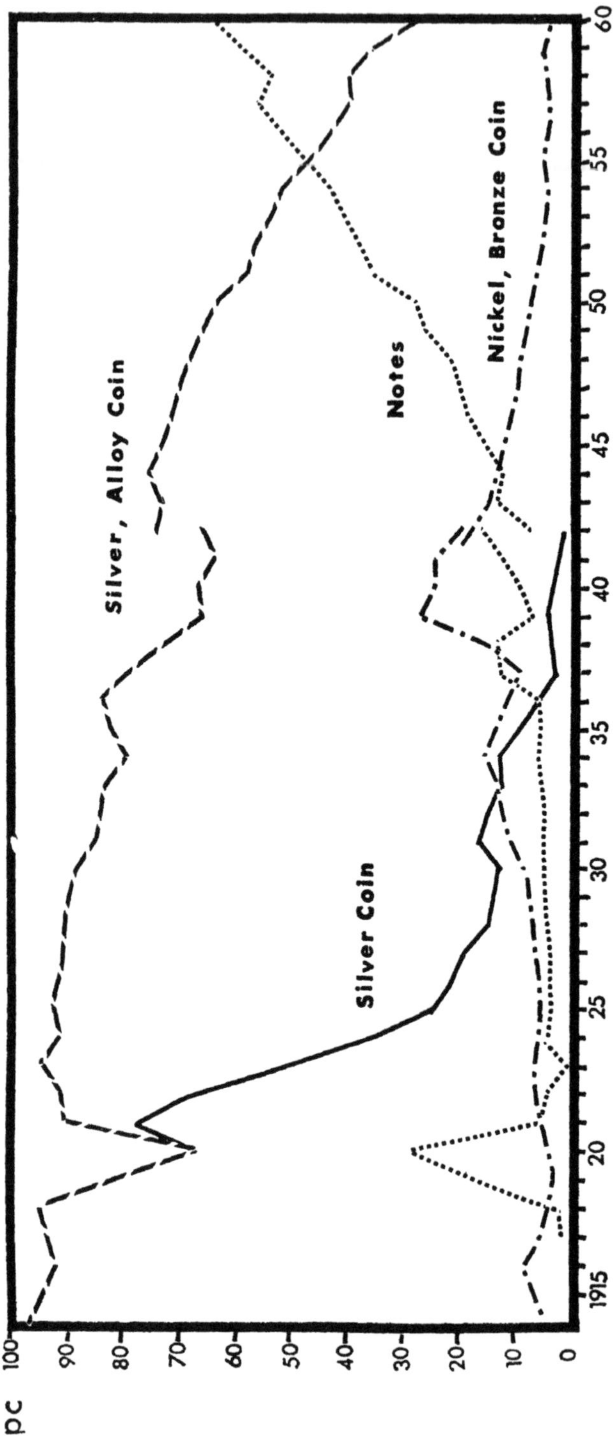

the currency in circulation in Nigeria depicted in the preceding graph[1] must be judged. In June 1914, the total amount of coin (silver, nickel and bronze) in circulation amounted to nearly £2 million. In 1960, this figure (December 31st) was £69 million, the evolution being shown in the diagram. The economic history of the world is clearly reflected, especially the price movement of raw materials. In 1920 there was the post World War I boom, then the receding demand throughout the twenties and thirties. The Second World War had marked stimulating effects and since 1950 onwards

Currency in Circulation in Nigeria 1915–1960.

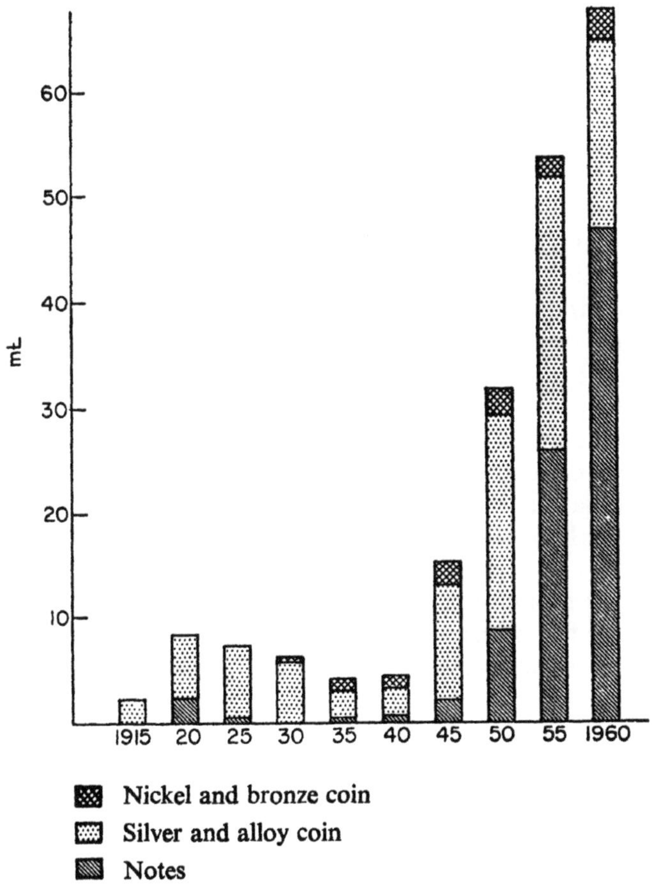

[1] The sources of the Graph and the Diagram are J. Mars, 'Money, Public Finance and External Payments' in *Mining, Commerce and Finance in Nigeria*, ed. Margery Perham, London, 1948, p. 180, and the Nigerian *Digest of Statistics*. The two series are not quite comparable. The first is based on June 30th and the second on March 31st. This helps to explain the slight discrepancies at the join. The trends should, however, be comparable.

the growing importance of internal economic development adds to the price and quantity effects of world demand for raw materials.

The graph shows how the structure of the currency in circulation altered. The use of nickel and bronze coins, though relatively small, is of great importance. The slow rise throughout the thirties going to a peak in the early war years, probably reflects clearly the growing internal monetization. When an area enters the monetary orbit, pennies are the first coins accepted and the purchasers of cash crops had to conform to this local custom. The banks had to supply large quantities of nickel and bronze coins (June is almost the lowest point of the yearly seasonal movement), which were transported out into the countryside. Some of this coin came back through trade, while the rest was often hoarded for shorter or longer periods. The next step is that the shilling or alloy coin is accepted.[1] In certain areas in Nigeria in the early 1960's shillings were still the main means of paying for the crop. However, from 1954 onwards there is an absolute as well as a relative fall in the amount of alloy coin in circulation. This indicates a welcome change in habits of (mainly) cash crop sellers, who increasingly are learning to accept notes—and even drafts on banks—thus decreasing the need for the cumbersome transport of shillings.

Notes were introduced already in 1917, but were never really popular. They were accepted in 1920 when the Currency Board, because of the high prices for raw materials, ran short of coin, but this was a temporary effect. Only during World War II did their circulation start increasing. It reflects the interaction between economic development and familiarity with more sophisticated forms of money, a familiarity which, a study of the development of commercial banking shows, is also being extended to credit instruments.

The Nigerian monetization from 1914 onwards can be taken as a typical example for Africa south of the Sahara. More or less quickly barter and money substitutes are replaced by first small denomination coins, then larger denominations followed by notes and then credit. The monetization of Ghana was similar but more rapid, due to the speedy introduction of cash transactions in the cocoa trade. Little is known of the monetary process in Rhodesia; but the important behaviour patterns of indigenous and expatriate populations have been carefully analysed.[2] The main difference with West Africa is that the labour of the African male (especially in the mines but also elsewhere) has been one of the principal monetizing factors. Of

[1] Silver coins were replaced by alloy coins throughout the twenties and the thirties.

[2] William J. Barber, *The Economy of British Central Africa*, London, 1961, esp. pp. 93 and 173–91.

basic importance for the slow monetization was the fact that, thanks to the family's subsistence economy, the wage paid to the male did not have to be able to support the family—it was a marginal increment. Moreover, this labour was largely periodic, and had its reflection in periodic disguised unemployment in agriculture. It also often involved large migrations (this is also the case in French West Africa). All these factors have probably contributed to making the average East African (according to Barber) less sensitive to economic incentive than, for instance, his West African counterpart. This seems to be an unnatural effect. At one period it was believed that all Africa was practically immune to economic incentives. This argument has been contradicted by experience acquired as soon as monetization proceeds far enough when a real consciousness is gained of the possibilities a modern economic system can offer to the individual.

The shift from a barter and money substitute system to a money and credit system is an essential precondition for modern economic development. This is so obvious that it does not really need to be discussed. Two points should perhaps be made. Only with a monetary system is it possible to obtain the prices, which are a guide to the needs of the economy. The truer the prices, the more perfect the market system and the surer the basis of calculation for private and public economic activity. The second point is that the essential savings required for economic development must be in monetary form—irrespective of whether these are voluntary or forced. Evidently they correspond to real savings, a non-consumption. But only through the intervention of money can the necessary transmutation be effected into the goods (and services) of a quite different kind needed for investment.

CHAPTER XVIII

THE PROBLEM OF MONETIZATION

As should be clear from the preceding historical description, there are four main reasons for the long term trend increase in the currency in circulation. These would seem to be:

(1) Growth of *money using* population;
(2) Deepening of monetization in marginal users;
(3) Changes in the prices of raw materials;
(4) The normal growth of the economy.

It is frequently difficult to isolate the effect of each of these factors. They are inter-related with often the same outward symptom contributing to, for instance, both the growth of the economy and to the growth of the size of the money using population.

Moreover, it is not always possible to know the primary motivating force. Is it the push of demand, the need to have cash in order to pay taxes or buy western consumer goods (textiles, sandals, bicycles, radios) or the pull of the at first gradual, later rapid expansion of paid work (plantation, road building)? The possibility of working—as opposed to trading which is fun in itself—is usually seen as a means to an end. It does not, in Africa, have (yet) the moral and social overtones with which Puritanism has endowed it in the western world. It seems probable that the need to pay taxes in cash was the first stimulus, especially in Africa south of the Sahara. At a later stage the desire for western consumer goods took the overhand—though this was the first element in Morocco.

An analysis of the changes in the composition of the Nigerian money supply, reveals the great importance that certain key consumer goods can have in spreading money. The circulation of alloy coins 1945 to 1960 correlates with the number of bicycles imported into Nigeria. Alloy coin circulation reached a maximum in 1954 while the number of bicycles imported[1] had already passed its peak in 1953. Since then both have been declining. The correlation is thus not that of constantly growing trends and therefore a reasonably good result, namely 0·83, shows a very high probability of some connection.

[1] Federation of Nigeria, *Digest of Statistics*, Lagos.

The connection was probably twofold. Because of the very high position of bicycles in the consumer preference pattern of the African, for prestige as well as transportation reasons, there was the push to seek work. The bicycle was then often taken back to the village.[1] But the bicycle owner probably carried with him also his change from his last period of work. As notes in many regions were not in common usage and there was also the danger, before safes became more common, that they would be eaten by termites, this spare cash was almost certainly at one period carried in alloy coin.

Moreover, the good cash crops (paid largely in alloy coin) in the late 1940's and up to 1954 also increased the amount of alloy in circulation and made the purchase of bicycles (as well as other things) easier.

That transport is an outward and visible sign for the flow of money is highly probable. It seems also likely that if a common denominator could be found for the available statistics on railway tonnage hauled and the number of vehicles on the roads (it is not possible to work out tonnage hauled here) a similar good correlation would be found between this figure and the increase in the note circulation during the period 1950–60.

In both cases described, the number of people using money must have been affected, while its use increased by marginal users. It seems almost impossible to isolate these two factors; they can at best be indicated. Moreover, the degree of monetization is certainly not a constant factor—a year of good harvest may mean more monetization, as may the opening up of a feeder road.

It is naturally impossible for a central bank to issue its currency and especially to adjust its long term composition on accurate analysis of this kind. Investigations are further complicated by the fact that even the statistics of currency in circulation are not on a really comparable basis for a long enough period. The only conclusion that can be drawn is that if over a series of years, one part of the money supply grows faster than the total money supply, it is probable that this is important in the monetization of that country at that time. As is shown in Table XI, in the Sudan 1958–60 deposits in circulation increased on an average by 13 per cent per annum, while the total money supply increased only by 10·5 per cent per annum. In Rhodesia and Nyasaland 1957–60 notes in circulation increased by 5·1 per cent per annum while the money supply actually decreased. In Nigeria, perhaps the most 'typical' developing country from a monetary aspect, the note supply rose by 7·1 per cent per annum while the total money supply rose by less than half or 3 per cent per annum.

[1] Eyewitnesses explain that it was often *carried* so that it would arrive bright and shiny.

This is an indication to the monetary authorities. However, their policy in this respect must still today largely be made on 'feel'; this sense for the right proportion which often is second nature to the skilled central banker.

These trends of the money supply and its composition are a reasonable indication of increased monetization both geographically and deepening. The internal price movement (cost of living) in these countries during the same period, also as trends per annum, varied from +2 per cent to −2 per cent. But in most countries there was an almost stable price level, with small increases of around 1 per cent per annum. In Ghana, Morocco, Nigeria and Tunisia the increase in the money supply did not thus affect prices. This was due to the fact that the markets were well provided with goods both produced internally and imported. These countries benefited from the freedom to import. Either there was no foreign trade and exchange control or it was very liberally administered. In the Sudan the position is reversed. Prices did not rise because of the tight control on the money supply. This was the aftermath of the 1957–58 balance of payments crisis which was so brilliantly surmounted.[1]

There is a particular price problem about which nothing is known and that is the effect that the change from barter to money has on prices. Is money so highly prized that prices fall at first, perhaps to increase later, or does monetization lead to an increase in the price level immediately? There is not sufficient evidence to do more than formulate the problem which would require a special study. Reliable price indices for African communities done separately for a 'fully' and 'newly' monetized area do not exist. Longer price indices for African communities are also rare and therefore the movement of prices can often only be indicated by the unrepresentative indices made for city dwellers (i.e. usually people who pattern their consumption on expatriates).

Another problem about which almost nothing is known is whether monetization takes place through an increase in the money supply or whether increases in velocity contribute.[2] It seems probable that increases in the money supply are the first and main factor contributing to monetization. This has been assumed here. The various ways in which monetization has been achieved[3] indicate no increase in velocity, but the actual physical spread of money. However, indigenous populations have a strong tendency to hoard money, notes as well as coin. When these are mobilized, it is reflected in an

[1] Cp. p. 246.

[2] The velocity of circulation of money 'fluctuating as a fever curve round the norm for the stage of growth of the specific country, . . . has proved a useful indicator for monetary policy'. Erin E. Jucker-Fleetwood, *Der Radcliffe Report*, loc. cit., p. 510.

[3] Cp. p. 190.

TABLE XI

Trend of Money Supply and its Composition

Trends of:	Ghana (1958–62)	Morocco (1958–62)	Nigeria (1957–62)	Rhodesia and Nyasaland (1957–62)	Sudan (1958–62)	Tunisia (1959–61)
				per cent per annum		
Total Money Supply	2·6	9·5	3·0	—3·0	10·5	16·7
Deposits	18·9	10·7	2·5	—5·7	13·0	17·1
Notes	—8·8 (Notes and Coins)	7·8	7·1	5·1	8·6 (Notes and Coins)	13·5
Coins		6·7	—4·7	1·1		3·6

SOURCES: Same as graphs.

increase in velocity; but the direction of spending would probably be towards an already monetized sector, for instance, the trader. Thus also the increased use of money by marginal users (deepening) seems unlikely to be caused by increased velocity.

While in financially mature countries there is a tendency for the relative money supply and the velocity of circulation of money to become stabilized at a fairly permanent level, such medium term stability can hardly be expected in newly monetized countries. They are still in a process of dynamic monetization and, coupled with fast economic growth, must gradually acquire a larger money supply. Thus a country with today a small relative money supply and high velocity, will in ten or twenty years have reached a different degree of monetization and thereby a larger relative money supply and a lower velocity.

Nigeria, as is seen in Table XII, is a typical case of such an evolution. Throughout the 1950's and early 1960's rapid economic development as well as monetization has taken place. The relative money supply has increased from 8·6 to 12·6 while, naturally, velocity has fallen from 11·6 to 8·0. This is the evolution as could be expected. However, the increase in the money supply has been on the high side, for prices have also been rising. While not entirely indicative of internal prices, because the city pattern of consumption is different from that of the countryside, the movement of the cost of living indices reflects to some extent the movement of prices in the whole country. The general indices have increased from the base year 1953 to December 1961 in Lagos to 141, Ibadan to 142 and in Enugu to 157.[1] In all cases food and drink, tobacco and kola, clothing and personal have increased more than the general index. This is partly due to substantial increases in indirect taxation, but there has certainly been an increase in the internal Nigerian price level, an increase which is not due to higher import prices, which have only increased by some 6–7 per cent in the same period.[2] There has thus been a domestic pressure on prices, due to the amounts of currency issued being rather larger than may strictly have been necessary.

A similar development can be expected in the Sudan. The relative money supply 1955–56, the only year for which GNP figures are available, was 10·3 and velocity was 9·7. With economic growth and increased monetization the relative money supply will probably increase, especially as the country is the largest in Africa and communications are both difficult and still rudimentary. In view of the careful monetary and financial policy pursued, prices are likely to rise less fast than in Nigeria.

[1] *Digest of Statistics* (Nigerian).
[2] *Digest of Statistics* (Nigerian).

TABLE XII

Relative Money Supply and Velocity of Circulation of Money

	Ghana		Morocco		Nigeria		Rhodesia and Nyasaland	
	RMS	V	RMS	V	RMS	V	RMS	V
1950								
1951	—	—	32·6	3·1	8·6	11·6	—	—
1952	—	—	30·2	3·3	9·9	10·1	—	—
1953	—	—	32·3	3·1	11·6	8·7	—	—
1954	—	—	33·8	3·0	11·2	9·0	29·0	3·4
1955	15·5	6·4	34·7	2·9	11·7	8·6	26·0	3·8
1956	15·7	6·4	26·1	3·8	10·0	10·0	24·9	4·0
1957	13·4	7·5	32·5	3·1	10·4	9·6	24·5	4·1
1958	13·2	7·6	30·4	3·3	10·5	9·6	22·2	4·5
1959	13·2	7·6	—	—	10·0	9·9	20·2	4·9
1960	14·4	6·9	31·3	3·2	11·7	8·5	17·6	5·7
1961	18·6	5·4	—	—	12·6	8·0	20·0	5·0
1962								

Sources: Appendix VI.

The opposite trend is discernible in Rhodesia and Nyasaland. There the relative money supply has decreased, while velocity naturally has increased. The monetized sector has actually suffered from a recession, while, on the other hand, monetization of the hitherto important non-monetized sector of the community is proceeding fairly slowly. However, the contribution of this sector to the national income is at least partly accounted for. The contribution thereto of the copper mines is also included and their financing is largely independent of the internal money supply. Unless there is a profound structural change in the composition of the economy, it seems as though any further fall in the relative money supply would be reflecting economic stagnation instead of growth. However, the money supply is here the dependent factor as a mere increase thereof would not stimulate economic growth.

The relative money supply of Morocco is the highest in the countries investigated and corresponds to that of a financially mature country such as Belgium, France, Italy and even the United States.[1] With the exception of the latter, these are also all countries where the checking system (commercial bank or post office) is not very popular and there is therefore a tendency for relatively large amounts of money to be held by individuals and smaller firms as ready cash. These countries have, with the exception of Switzerland, the highest recorded relative money supply. This high relative money supply in Morocco does not mean really sufficient monetization in the modern sense. The utilization of money is there ancient and reaches back through several thousand years.[2] Much of it is hoarded or kept in highly liquid form (bank deposits). The very high liquidity of Morocco shows that credit injections would be useless as a stimulant to the economy. It is not liquidity that is lacking. The activation of available liquidities by real economic growth is the only feasible solution.

Ghana alone of all the countries investigated had an apparently stable relative money supply at a fairly high level, 13–15. This corresponds to that of countries like Germany, Sweden, and Canada.[3] As basic monetization is also probably there the most advanced of any country south of the Sahara, the present relative money supply would probably be large enough to allow development and if there were a trend towards a greater relative money supply the change should be very gradual. The increase in the relative money supply in 1961 reflects an absolute increase of the money supply

[1] See Bank for International Settlements, *Annual Reports* 1945 onwards.

[2] Cp. p. 191.

[3] Tunisia with 1958 relative money supply of 17·4 and velocity of 5·7 falls also in this general category. The available figures cover too short a period to attempt an analysis.

of 34·5 per cent. In 1961 the main increase came in the demand deposits 'in the second half of the year, when the new budget started to exert its influence on the economy. The extraordinary rise in November and December was due to the new method of cocoa financing. Prior to 1961 the Cocoa Marketing Company was based in London and it made use of facilities offered by London banks. With the establishment of the Ghana Cocoa Marketing Company in Accra, cocoa financing was performed by Ghanaian banks, and this introduced a new strong seasonal influence on the movement of demand deposits in Ghana. But even apart from the seasonal rise there is a strong rising trend in demand deposits.'[1]

This development is clearly inflationary and explains the sudden marked rise in official internal prices, 7–10 per cent according to locality. It cannot be continued with impunity.

Thus in dynamically developing countries there will be long term changes in velocity and relative money supply. Such trends are clearly discernible even from the short series (due mainly to non-existent GNP figures) shown in Table XII. Such an evolution, however, is so marked as well as theoretically probable, that the monetary authorities can never afford not to take it into consideration.

The short term changes in velocity in the countries in question could be quite considerable. This is due to the fact that certain sections of the population have hoarded money, including, in some countries, gold. (The latter is not included in the money supply figures as used in Table XIX. The quantities are unknown, but certainly often important.) Were these hoards mobilized, an extra demand for goods might arise. Experience shows, however, that the tendency to utilize them is sluggish except in times of special crisis. In the Sudan, for instance, gold (from the harems) was forthcoming at the time of the cotton credit calamity in the early 1950's and also at the time of credit stringency in 1957–58. Such behaviour seems to be exceptional and short term and rapid changes in velocity as are found in financially mature countries[2] do not seem to be very important.

The available figures do, however, show that there are attenuated yearly changes. These correspond in Ghana and Nigeria to good and less good harvests—the main consumer of newly issued currency. The figures indicate that, in spite of all appearances to the contrary, the consumption habits of the countries are fairly stable. Otherwise, the reflection would be found in the GNP figures which would

[1] Central Bureau of Statistics, *Economic Survey 1961*, Accra, 1962, p. 90.

[2] Erin E. Jucker-Fleetwood, *The Key Role of the Velocity of Circulation of Money and Credit*, Oxford Economic Papers, October 1958. Also in Basle Centre Publication Series A, No. 22.

fluctuate more than they do.[1] In Morocco only the year 1956 shows an exceptional short term increase in velocity due to a sharp fall in the money supply because of the important net transfer, chiefly by emigrants, of Fr.M. 111 million out of Morocco.[2]

These short term changes in velocity have in fact been minor and should never hitherto have created a major source of disturbance for monetary policy. They were nearly always a passive reflection of events in other spheres. However, these countries have a latent reserve of money among the population which could be mobilized in a crisis and the existence of which can never be forgotten with impunity.

TABLE XIII

Marginal and Average Velocity of Circulation

	Velocity		
	Marginal	Average	Difference
Ghana			
1955–60	6·26	7·07	−0·81
1955–61	3·44	6·81	−3·37
Morocco			
1950–58	0·79	3·16	−2·37
Nigeria			
1950–60	6·87	9·56	−2·69
Rhodesia			
1954–61	5·03	4·42	+0·61

SOURCES:

Table XII, p. 205.

Table XIX in Appendix VI, p. 321.

The first derivative was calculated by ordinary correlation method. The correlations were much less good than for financially mature countries, giving: Ghana 0·81, Morocco 0·60, Nigeria 0·88, Rhodesia 0·37.

The remaining problem connected with the monetization of these countries is the possibility of estimating the velocity of circulation of the new money as compared to the whole stock of money. This can be done by calculating the marginal velocity (i.e. the first derivative) and comparing the average velocity.[3] The results of this calculation have been tabulated in Table XIII. It is seen that for the four

[1] See Appendix VI (GNP and Money Supply).

[2] Ministère de l'Economie Nationale, *Tableaux économiques du Maroc 1915–59*. Rabat, 1960, p. 269.

[3] Erin E. Jucker-Fleetwood, *The Key Role*, loc. cit., p. 293, the same method has been used by C. Drakatos, 'Short-Term Fluctuations in the Velocity of Circulation of Money in the UK 1954–61', *Bankers Magazine*, December 1962, pp. 408–15.

countries for which there are the basic statistics very different results are obtained.

In three of the countries, namely Ghana, Nigeria and Morocco, the marginal velocity, i.e. the velocity of new money is considerably below that of the stock of money, the average circulation. This is what would normally be expected especially in the case of Ghana and Nigeria where the average velocity is fairly high. In both countries monetization, both geographic and deepening, is still in progress.

The difference between the average velocity and the marginal velocity is not too important with 0·81 for Ghana 1955–60. If the movement of domestic prices is considered, the rate of monetization was probably more or less correct. Accra retail prices increased by 18 per cent during the period. This index includes changes in taxation[1] and it is probable that the greater part of the price increase was due to taxes and frictional factors and only very slightly to monetary factors. The change in the position when 1961 is included confirms the precariousness of the situation as described above.[2] The increase in the money supply (34·5 per cent) depressed the average and the marginal rates of velocity very considerably, and increased the difference to 3·37. This created an inflationary situation, the full effects of which are likely to be felt only when the velocities return too close to their 'normal'. As it is, prices increased by 14 per cent in one year, or nearly as much as during the six previous years.

In Nigeria the velocity of new money is considerably below that of the velocity of the stock of money with 2·69. There are indications that the price level increased considerably. There are no figures available for the whole period but 1953 to 1960 the Lagos consumer price index increased by 32 per cent, which is more than should be caused by tax increases and frictional factors. The increase in money supply was, therefore, probably contributing to the increase in prices.

In Morocco, the average velocity was low and the marginal the smallest ever recorded. The difference between them was also 2·37. It reflects the slowing down of the whole Moroccan economy. If figures were available for a later period, a slightly more favourable picture might be obtained. However, it should be clear that the supply of money is more than the country desires and any attempt to increase economic activity by credit inflation would only increase the weight of money without leading to its usage.

In the Federation of Rhodesia and Nyasaland the marginal

[1] Unfortunately, there are no price series available, nor the basis to calculate them, which would eliminate the factor of increased indirect taxation.

[2] Cp. p. 243.

velocity was higher than the average (by 0·61 points). This is unusual for a developing country. It is explained by the important fall in the relative supply of money over the period. It in turn was due to the withdrawal of important assets from the Federation, a withdrawal which, however, did not torpedo economic activity in the same manner as was the case in Morocco or even Tunisia. The price level having remained fairly stable there is reason to suppose that the country is close to being under-supplied with money.

While a comparison between the average and the marginal velocity of circulation of money can unfortunately only be effected *post factum*, it is the best measure to date of the rate at which monetization can be safely effected. In a financially mature country a position of equilibrium would be reached if, *at constant prices*, the marginal and the average velocity of circulation were the same. (This equilibrium is not necessarily a full employment equilibrium.) In a financially immature country, i.e. where monetization is still in progress, a stable monetary growth is obtained if the difference between the average and the marginal velocity of circulation is such that overall prices remain constant. The amount of money issued to enable monetization to take place should be exactly the amount which keeps overall prices stable. While this must vary from country to country, it would seem probable that the difference between the rate of circulation of new money, i.e. the marginal rate and the average velocity, should not be greater than 1·0 in order to achieve stable monetary growth.

CHAPTER XIX

FACTORS AFFECTING THE MONEY SUPPLY

CROP SIZE AND PRICE POLICY

As cash crops are the main utilizers of newly issued money, the size of the crop and the internal price are very important monetary factors, as is also the policy of Marketing Boards where these exist.

The purpose of Marketing Boards in most countries, with the exception of the Sudan, is not merely to collect internally and sell abroad a crop (at standard grades), i.e. to function as a commercial intermediary, but is to secure an internal price for the commodity in question different from the world market price. In Ghana and Nigeria the internal, or producer, price has hitherto been maintained below the world market price, leading, *inter alia*, to important accumulations of foreign exchange. In Morocco and Tunisia the policy has been to maintain a higher internal price than the world market price. This was possible because the guaranteed prices secured on the bulk of the exports to France assured these countries the same prices as were accorded to the internal French market.

The price of wheat was guaranteed and administered by the Office des Céréales, that of wine supported and that of olive oil had a minimum at which the Sociétés de Prévoyance bought directly from the farmer in order to protect him from the market fluctuations.[1] As the crops were sold abroad above the world market price, namely at the internal Tunisian price plus a margin for commercial handling, there was a counterpart in foreign exchange which could satisfy the demand for foreign (almost entirely French) goods coming from the agricultural sector.

This picture seems to be changing. The Tunisian and Moroccan export prices are, in the autumn of 1962, at least partially (for cereals) on a level with world market prices.[2] Whether this downward movement (*ca.* 20 per cent) will also affect wine and oil is still unknown. By the time the new crops come on the market, the

[1] Banque Centrale de Tunisie, *Bulletin*, April 1959, p. 7 (oil); July 1959, p. 3 (wheat); and October 1959, p. 11 (wine).

[2] Because of the level of world market prices in 1963, Morocco decided to suspend cereal exports. The area formerly used for cereal export production is according to the plans to be developed for other high yield, labour intensive crops (mainly fruit and vegetables).

Common Market negotiations may have cleared the picture. In Nigeria and Ghana the fall in the world market prices of their main exports, cocoa, palm oils and kernels and groundnuts has limited the freedom of policy of the Marketing Boards.

The price setting activities of the Marketing Boards are in all circumstances of such fundamental importance that they should be effected in co-operation with the monetary authorities, both Central Bank and Ministry of Finance, in order to assure their integration with the overall economic policy.

The question at issue is essentially the following: is the factor that most stabilizes a growing economy a stable internal price of the main crops, because other prices tend to be in relation to the former, or is it income stabilization, with lower prices for larger crops and higher prices for smaller ones? In the former case the absolute amount of money issued for the purpose of buying the crop is neglected, whereas in the second case it takes pride of place.[1] (It should perhaps be pointed out that the case at issue is not the stability of internal prices over a selling season—this is usually accepted as more or less necessary.)

The former thesis was made the policy of the Cocoa Marketing Board in Ghana, where cocoa exports amount to approximately 60 per cent of total exports, and was based upon two policy-making White Papers and the Williams Report.[2] However, 'the White Papers assumed as self-evident that fluctuations in prices cause or enhance fluctuations in producer incomes'.[3] Professor Williams's thesis, not fully expounded in the report, maintained that, because of market imperfections in the internal market, there was a tendency for traders in other commodities to set their prices according to the price of cocoa.[4] The comparatively stable prices and the compara-

[1] Curiously enough, there is some evidence to suggest that around the year 1600 'income stabilization' was the main aim of the Africans. One bean of *ca.* 8 gm. of gold was traded for one red bean irrespective of size. The size of the bean apparently is large or small according to whether the harvest is good or bad. 'So fand er (Samuel Braun, Basler Zunftmeister und Mitglied des Rates) an der Elfenbeinküste Gold, eingeschmolzen zu stetsfort genau gleichschweren Körnern im Gewicht von *ca.* 8 Gramm. Dieses Gewicht wurde dann aber im Tauschhandel nicht beachtet, vielmehr dienten als Gewichtsmass Samen, vorab rote Bohnen, die verständlicherweise je nach Ausfall der Ernte im Gewicht verschieden waren. Er bemerkt dazu, besser hätten es die Händler vor seiner Zeit (1611–1620) gehabt, sei doch "Gold nicht gewäget, nur bei Augenmäss verhandelt" worden.' W. Burkhard-Wuhrmann, 'Vom Handel in Uebersee im Strom der Zeit', *Schweizerische Zeitschrift für kaufmännisches Bildungswesen*, Vol. 49 (1955), p. 5.

[2] *Report on Cocoa Control in West Africa 1939–43 and Statement on Future Policy*, Cmd. 6554, 1944; *Statement on the Future Marketing of West African Cocoa*, Cmd. 6950, 1946.

[3] P. T. Bauer, *West African Trade—A Study of Competition, Oligopoly and Monopoly in a Changing Economy*, Cambridge, England, 1954, p. 272.

[4] Conversation with Professor J. W. William in February 1960.

tively minor fluctuations in crop size in the late 1940's and early 1950's would, however, have created conditions which would tend to lead to such a conclusion. The fallacy of the argument was shown in the 1960–61 cocoa season when the cocoa crop was nearly one-third larger than the previous year and twice the size of a normal year and was purchased at the same internal price (£G112 per ton). The increase in the coin and note circulation from the yearly maximum in December 1959 to 1960 was double any increase previously registered (£G6·2 million compared to £G2·9 million, December 1955 and 1956). The huge changes in cocoa farmers' incomes (increase of £G5·6 million to a total of £G45·4 million[1]) affected prices, foreign exchange reserves and government finances.

In Nigeria the idea of price stabilization has not been as marked as in Ghana and has tended more towards the concept of income stabilization with higher prices for small crops and lower prices for larger crops. While it is impossible to isolate the price increasing effect of the cash crops on the general level of prices, it is clear that Nigeria has never had to take the impact of a crop doubled within a year. While the Nigerian cocoa crop is important (*ca.* 20 per cent of exported crops), it is only one of many other crops, the latter having a different impact in the crucial year.

A study of the actual internal producer prices and the income paid to farmers[2] shows that neither in Ghana nor in Nigeria has it been possible really to stabilize either the internal price paid to producers or their income. Both show important swings which, however, are smaller than would have been the case had the full world market price been paid.

In both countries, however, the lower internal price as compared to the world market price, allowed the accumulation of very important reserves of foreign exchange.[3] Originally it was thought that these reserves could be used to stabilize the price of the cash crops through good years and bad. In fact, the foreign exchange surpluses have been used for development purposes as has the domestic counterpart. The assets still available from this source are little more than working balances, though in Nigeria some two Marketing Boards still have a small but welcome capital surplus. With the fall in world market prices from 1960 onwards, there was no question of stabilizing the internal prices, which have everywhere been brought down.

The question then arises as to what the break-even point of the

[1] Central Bureau of Statistics; *Economic Survey 1960*, Accra, 1961, pp. 22, 23.

[2] This study was made internally at the Basle Centre for Economic and Financial Research and was based on partly confidential material communicated by the various Marketing Boards and Departments of Agriculture.

[3] Cp. p. 86.

internal (or producer) price of the cash crops is, i.e. at what level will the internal price correspond to the (psychologically fixed) cost of production? No serious studies seem to have been made on this point. But there is a certain amount of evidence (the judgement of experienced buyers, etc.) which would indicate that production would not start falling on economic grounds (real cost of production and value put on effort) before prices had fallen to approximately half those of 1960 for the same crop and grade thereof. There is, however, universal agreement that such a fall in internal prices is not only politically unfeasible but impossible. After a long period of increasing real incomes, the population would not be prepared to make up in more work and therefore quantity produced, for prices falling to that extent. This is especially the case because the habit of increasing standards of living has penetrated far into the countryside. The younger generation begins to regard this situation as normal while the older generation has one prime consumer demand, education for its children. In places where important school fees have to be paid for both primary and secondary education (such as the Eastern Region of Nigeria) the meeting of these fees is a powerful stimulus to increased agricultural production and reform.

The very sharp criticism of the price policies of the Marketing Boards made by P. T. Bauer,[1] while substantially valid, is probably weakened for 1950–60 by the following considerations:

(i) the evident advantage of the accumulation of external and internal savings available for development;
(ii) the marked market imperfections which, when variations in incomes were small, allowed prices of one cash crop to play a decisive role;
(iii) the fact that the production period of all cash crops, except groundnuts, has been of several years' duration.

Almost all these arguments in favour of stable and low internal prices are disappearing or becoming attenuated. Not least is the increasing importance of the shorter production period for improved varieties of both cocoa and palm trees. Further, the dissemination of information about modern technical advances, such as a more or less intense use of insecticides and fertilizers, can result in a marked difference to the size of the crop in any one year. This should make the production of cash crops much more sensitive to internal price changes than they were a decade ago.

In this more sensitive economy, internal prices have recently had to be adjusted downwards, because world market prices are falling. Not only are there no reserves to carry out a stabilization policy

[1] Loc. cit., esp. pp. 263–343.

(as originally intended), but also the Marketing Boards are expected by the governments concerned to produce some, if comparatively minor, surpluses of foreign exchange and domestic savings also in the future. Whether they will be able to do so will depend largely upon the level of world market prices, as there is a limit to where internal prices can go.

There is, moreover, a high probability that increasing real incomes, or at least increasing money incomes, will become the general aim of the agricultural population of the two countries. This will probably require a more flexible policy on the part of the Marketing Boards in the future when both the size and the price of the crop are taken into account.[1] From the point of view of the monetary and financial authorities, agricultural incomes steadied to a reasonable rate of growth should be a stabilizing factor in a dynamic economy. There is one proviso: that this can be achieved at an internal price which still allows an equivalent acquisition of foreign assets (at least for that part of the crop exported). In other words, the internal price should not need to be (for any reason) superior to the world market price.[2]

The price setting activities of the Marketing Boards are the main factor in credit creation in these countries. It is therefore recognized by the central banks that they must here not only be consulted, but that their advice must be taken into account, because otherwise there is no real prospect of the central bank being able to operate an effective credit policy or that the soundness of the economy can be safeguarded. It is obviously impossible for an individual Marketing Board to be able to take into account all the factors involved, especially with regard to the effect internally on inflationary and deflationary trends and externally to world prices. The central banks were established to have this complicated overall survey of the economy and they are the only competent instance. Moreover, they have the legal and moral responsibility of maintaining equilibrium and cannot fulfil their function if autonomous institutions—however innocently—counteract the general policy.

In countries where there are no Marketing Boards or Sociétés de Prévoyance the changes in the world market price is reflected internally (sometimes inversely) in the producer countries. While there would be a theoretical possibility of varying export taxes and/or subsidies accordingly to achieve internal stabilization, this is not done in the countries under discussion. The monetary and

[1] This will not least be the case if internal price agreement schemes, independent of production control, are adhered to.

[2] Should such an eventuality arise, it might prove necessary to revise the taxation on exported cash crops in favour of the equilibrium of the balance of payments.

financial system as a whole has to deal with the changes in purchasing power by monetary and financial policy.

WAGE POLICY

Theoretically the movement of wages could be an important inflationary factor in the monetary systems of African countries. So far this has only in a few instances been the case, though increasingly political considerations and the growing strength of Labour Unions are jeopardizing the future.

The basic wages of unskilled workers are fairly stable and, compared to European standards, low. The very low productivity of unskilled workers with little or no capital equipment does not have to be demonstrated. Added to this there is in all countries a mass of would-be workers. These are usually country people who have come to the cities in the hope of a brilliant future and, therefore, also employment. This mass not only causes important social and financial problems for the city governments, but also acts as a stabilizer on the wages of unskilled workers, for the supply far exceeds the demand. Thus, the weight at the bottom of the ladder tends to keep wages low. In Ghana and Nigeria there have been certain officially accepted increases,[1] while in the Rhodesias and Nyasaland the rate of increase of African earnings is nearly twice that of European earnings, thus decreasing the gap.[2] However, in periods of unemployment measures are taken to limit the number of Africans seeking jobs.

The typical feature of the wage structure of these African countries is the important wage differentials between unskilled and skilled workers, and between different categories of the latter. These often amount to 4–6 times as much and, as an incentive to qualify oneself, are excellent. Theoretically, these differences in wage rates should be completely neutral from the monetary point of view, because they stem from greater productivity. But, unfortunately, a not inconsiderable number of these qualified workers are to be found in relatively unproductive branches, administration and services, and not exactly in industry or agriculture. It is a moot point as to

[1] Central Bureau of Statistics, *Economic Survey 1961*: 'The large increases in 1960 were due mainly to a general increase in wage rate from July 1, 1960, when the minimum wage rate was raised to 6s 6d a day. This was accompanied by a general rise of 1s a day to all employees earning up to £G610 per annum. This accounts for the very large increases in such branches as mining, manufacturing, and construction.' Accra, 1962, p. 82, §250. *Financial Times*, January 11, 1963: 'The Nigerian Civil Service Workers Union has demanded a wage increase of 20 per cent in view of the rising cost of living in the country. The Union claims that the recent economic measures introduced to meet the six-year development scheme have increased the prices of consumer goods.'

[2] Ministry of Economic Affairs, *Economic Report 1961*, p. 25.

whether these high wages do not increase the monetary pressure in the country. This is unquestionably the case when promotion has been obtained by favouritism and not qualification. The problem of status is intimately linked with the desire for work of certain kinds and productive employment has hitherto not been very fashionable.

It is unfortunately a typical experience that technical colleges have none or few applicants for the courses to become foremen, electricians, plumbers, etc. Everybody wants to be an engineer. In fact some 3–10 technical men are needed for every engineer and far from everybody is capable of qualifying for the upper brackets of technical and administrative professions.

This sociological resistance ought in time to be overcome as a profession fills up; then unemployment within it will rise and/or the economic return fall. Eventually this should encourage people to enter other professions and trades. However, the sociological resistance is probably greater in the developing countries than it is in Europe or America because of the (imagined) loss of caste or face involved. And sociological valuations have not yet changed fast enough to adapt to the demands of a modern economy.

The Trade Unions would have an important constructive method of improving the lot of African workers, namely, by assisting them in all possible ways to acquire skills. Then higher wages would be not merely automatic but justified. The skilled worker would also have increased status based on a real contribution to the growth of the economy—which is the only tenable long term criterion.

The senior Trade Union officials always argue that they in no way wish, by their more or less effective demands for higher wages, to force them so that such a wage increase would affect prices. They often hope that price control will look after matters. This is rather a dangerous way of arguing. In these African countries, where the administrative apparatus is usually hardly able to carry the burden of its ordinary duties, price control has never worked well.[1] Thus any unjustified increase in basic wages is bound to have a price-increasing effect. The wage increases obtained by individual workers when they become more qualified should, however, be easily carried by the developing economy.

GOVERNMENT FINANCIAL POLICY

The financing of the government budget(s) and the development plan is probably potentially the most serious threat to the monetary and financial stability of the developing countries.

Everywhere the taxable capacity of the countries is low compared

[1] In Europe it does not work—even in wartime—without its counterpart, rationing, which is doubly inconceivable in Africa.

to financially mature countries of the same population and strength. Direct personal taxation is almost unknown and by far the largest part of the governments' income comes from indirect taxation of imports and/or exports and excise. There is a strict upper limit to import duties and excise as very high rates easily lead to lower absolute returns, while the yield of export duties depends upon the outcome of the harvest and the world market situation. Thus the current budget must be kept within strict limits if it is to be able to produce a surplus available for financing the development plan. The current budget, in its turn, is under constant pressure as it almost always has to absorb the running costs of a large part of the schemes of the development plan.

Hitherto these African countries have, on the whole, been able to maintain their surplus on the current budget and it has been used to finance part of the development plan. The pressure is, however, increasing, while it is improbable that the taxable capacity of the countries will increase in proportion. A considerable effort will, therefore, be needed to keep current budget expenditure down by the greatest attention to saving measures and the elimination of unnecessary expenditure. The bottlenecks in the shape of the lack of teachers, doctors, nurses and other technical personnel which have hitherto prevented voted estimates from being fully spent are rapidly being overcome and the budget as presented to parliament will in future be nearer to the cash position than it has ever been before. With the lag in expenditure eliminated the balance of the current budget becomes of primary importance. The existence of a surplus will, moreover, be necessary for many years to come as a contribution towards the financing of capital expenditure, whether an official plan exists or not.

There are three main sources of capital for the financing of a development plan, namely the (dwindling) surplus on the current budget, domestic savings and foreign loans and grants.

Most development plans have relied heavily on foreign sources of capital, sometimes up to 50 per cent of the total. The development countries tend to be caught in the vicious circle of having to make a plan before knowing how much foreign capital they can count on and not being able to make a valid plan before having this information. Partly for this reason the development plans tend to be too large compared to available capital resources. They will almost everywhere have to be either prolonged, say, from six to eight years or have marginal projects eliminated. (It would be easier to do either or both if there were less political 'éclat' round the plans.) Each individual developing country seems to have expected the volume of internationally available capital to be larger than it actually is. Unfortunately it is limited for a variety of reasons, and the developing countries are in competition against each other. Even the 'fairest' distribution would leave most developing countries with less than they had hoped to receive. It is, therefore, essential that no projects relying on foreign capital are started before there is a firm commitment for the necessary finance. Otherwise the project might remain unfinished or balance of payments difficulties are liable to arise due to the temptation to use credit financing and/or to misappropriate domestic capital.

The domestic capital available for financing the development plans is even more limited than is apparent from its very small volume. No development plan is likely to succeed unless a private sector is allowed to grow up at its side. This private sector stretches from the most modern to the important shadowy sector between the traditional and the modern sectors. If these are deprived of capital and credit, because the government plan has appropriated all available financial resources, it will never come into being. Only an absolute increase in domestic savings will alleviate the situation and supply all sectors with more capital.

The encouragement of domestic savings is probably the single most effective way of assuring the sound financing of the development plans. If these cannot be increased, the temptation is to have resort to credit financing.

Credit financing of government expenditure, whether for development purposes or to cover so-called short term deficits, is usually a boomerang unless the country in question is also suffering from a marked cyclical depression. No credit injections (a euphemism for inflation) can act as spur to economic or industrial development. It cannot produce more technically trained people. This difficult problem must be solved by intelligent international co-operation—and even then it will take time. Moreover, no increase in liquidity will produce Schumpetrian entrepreneurship, where this basic characteristic is lacking. There are Africans—especially in the north but also elsewhere—who prefer to hold liquid assets rather than to use them, if the latter requires a personal effort. No more goods and services will suddenly appear because credit facilities have been extended. In fact, available goods and supplies might easily be withdrawn from the market because of an expectation of higher prices later on. At the same time the will of the population to save will be weakened because of the obvious negative returns.

The monetary and financial authorities have thus to keep the current budget in surplus and to finance the development plan from available domestic and foreign capital. The apparently easy way out of unjustified borrowing will stifle the private sector while credit creation either at the central or the commercial banks, is the start of inflation with its uncomfortable or even disastrous consequences.

BALANCE OF PAYMENTS

The balance of payments can both cause and reflect monetary disequilibria.

In the former instance, if the trouble is temporary, the monetary authorities may well consider that the domestic economy should not be subjected to the normally ensuing restrictive credit policy. They would then support the internal market, filling any foreign exchange gap by either drawing on existing reserves or borrowing abroad. The latter measure might be almost automatic at commercial bank level (providing the countries applying foreign exchange allow it) or at more official level, such as applying for financial assistance from the International Monetary Fund. The Fund has in fact made it its policy freely to help developing countries in difficulties because of falls in raw material prices.[1] When these look like being temporary, there is no reason why an otherwise healthy and dynamic economy should have its pace retarded.

The responsibility for avoiding externally created non-temporary balance of payments problems for the developing countries rests largely on the industrialized countries. By co-operation and enlightened credit policies as well as liberal trade policies they help developing countries as well as the industrialized countries themselves. The developing countries have, however, to contribute to the international effort as far as they are able by maintaining monetary and financial equilibrium, differentiating their economies both internally and externally and, when and if it applies, enforcing whatever measures are needed under price stabilizing commodity agreements.

The most serious balance of payments problems are the internally caused disequilibria, because they easily become permanent and prevent all further real growth. The internally caused disequilibria invariably result from too high a level of effective domestic demand. The root cause is usually over-dimensioned government expenditure either on current and/or capital account. Such expenditure, moreover, causes secondary (multiplier) effects. Depending on the structure of demand and its change of direction with higher incomes as well as on the structure and capacity of the domestic economy, the new effective demand is channelled towards imported goods. This 'foreign trade multiplier' varies greatly according to country. It seems to lie between 30–80 per cent for the countries under discussion. The modern sectors of the domestic economy are small, under-differentiated and often have no spare capacity. Apart from

[1] Per Jacobsson, *Opening Address, Presentation of XVII Annual Report*, Summary Proceedings, Annual Meeting, 1962, IMF, Washington, 1962, pp. 16–33.

the goods that, therefore, have to be imported, there is also a certain prestige value in buying foreign goods even though they are heavily taxed in favour of their domestic counterpart. The attempts made to contain the demand for foreign goods (and services) by import and foreign exchange control are rarely successful.[1] They all give rise to smuggling (from that 'within the law' to the illegal) to deceit and to the non-repatriation of profits. Whatever effective demand can be contained within the country, pushes prices up.

In order to restore the balance of payments equilibrium when the cause is internal, a very deliberate policy has to be applied. This usually includes several of the following measures:

(1) Surplus on the current budget with any remaining deficits on the capital budget financed by current (not past) savings.

(2) Credit restriction, more or less severely applied.

(3) Wage and salary stabilization. This may be a purely temporary measure, till internal equilibrium is again achieved. In order to facilitate such a policy, the government budget should be brought into surplus (or balance) by cutting down unnecessary expenditure and not increasing indirect taxes unless these are unnaturally low.

(4) In certain cases by the import of relatively more consumer goods (as opposed to capital goods) in order to prevent (or brake) an internal price rise. Large stocks of consumer goods which could be run down would naturally be an alternative. A temporary shift in the composition of goods imported can have a stabilizing effect internally, especially if the position has not already got too far out of hand. A few months' delay in the import of capital goods, provided these are properly selected, should be possible without any appreciable loss of production.[2] This problem is essentially one of timing and a shift in import composition during a few months can be of decisive importance.[3]

(5) No measure should cause a slowing down of productive investment projects already started. On the other hand, the postponement of new projects, especially in infrastructure but also in productive investment (because of the two to three year period before they are productive) can be a valuable help in reducing temporarily over-inflated internal demand.

Such a packaged deal of measures, though far from easy to enforce, usually restores internal equilibrium surprisingly quickly. It is all

[1] Cp. p. 290.

[2] There are too many instances of, say, machinery being imported at great speed and then lying crated in warehouses because the factory buildings have not been completed.

[3] This is one of the effects a flexible and effective interest rate policy should achieve.

the more effective the sooner it is introduced. Then the economy has again a sure basis for its continued growth. Ideally, the monetary and financial authorities should succeed in keeping the internal situation so well in hand that internally created balance of payments disequilibria are avoided.

CHAPTER XX

THE FIDUCIARY ISSUE

A recurring problem in African countries is the thorny one of the fiduciary issue, i.e. the part of the currency in circulation which is unbacked by a foreign reserve. Especially in Ghana and Nigeria, the initial policy of maintaining a 100 per cent foreign exchange backing for the currency in circulation came in for much criticism. It was considered that these assets could in part, at least, be used for economic development purposes. As these countries are now reaching a point where the financing of development is really becoming an issue, the question has become acute. In other countries, there is a similar problem, but it is less apparent, because there was never a 100 per cent backing.

The question is not, however, whether either Ghana or Nigeria are justified in allowing themselves a fiduciary issue. Except in countries with special factors entering into consideration and as varied as Switzerland and Kuwait, it is normal that note circulations do not have full foreign exchange or gold coverage.

All financially mature countries have fiduciary issues and there is no reason why the developing countries should not have them provided that they can be acquired safely. This means that neither should the stability of the currency be jeopardized nor the foreign exchange and gold reserves be reduced to a level so low that there is neither freedom of action nor confidence at home and abroad. The question is thus the manner in which the fiduciary issue is acquired and the size it attains. Both problems are closely linked to each other and to the difficult ones of transition from financial immaturity to financial maturity, a process that takes years.

The argument for a fiduciary issue is that there is always a certain part of the currency circulation that corresponds to the domestic economy and that it never under any circumstances will be presented for conversion.[1] This 'hard core' does in fact exist and it would only be presented for conversion under conditions of galloping inflation when convertibility has anyway been suspended. Typical of these conditions are Germany, 1918–24, and the United

[1] Nevin, loc. cit., p. 15.

States during the Civil War.[1] Short of wartime conditions or gross mismanagement of the monetary system such situations are considered as abnormal. Therefore a fiduciary issue, backed by securities of all kinds, can correspond to this 'hard core' of domestic currency.

In developing countries, especially in Africa, there is, however, only a very small, though growing, domestic sector, while all these countries are amongst the most dependent on foreign trade. Any given money supply or section thereof can therefore fluctuate sharply, an overall or sectorial increase in velocity keeping its volume up and allowing a smaller money supply to effect the same number of transactions, while the released currency tries to find its way into foreign demand. And there is evidence to suggest that these African countries have latent possibilities to increase velocity. It is therefore not possible to calculate even theoretically the size of the domestic economy and adjust the fiduciary issue to this part of the economy. A considerable margin should therefore be retained. Thus the size of the fiduciary issue that they can safely allow themselves is relatively small compared to financially mature countries, while the proportion of foreign exchange and gold reserve they must allow themselves is relatively high.

The second point is that all these countries are growing economies even if their *de facto* growth is slower than their theoretical growth. With the increase of the national income—especially *per capita*—they will, for a longer or shorter period, need an increase in the supply of currency—quite apart from monetization. It is likely that, at some future date, the rate of increase of currency will decrease relatively as credit, and not currency, becomes the main carrier of expansion. When this stage will be reached, cannot at present be estimated; but such a change in payments habits will not reduce, but probably increase, the need of foreign exchange coverage. The actual position will, however, depend upon the direction taken by the newly created demand, whether towards domestically produced or imported goods.

These two points add up to the third determinant, namely the position of the balance of payments.[2] As open economies, developing countries and the African ones in particular are very vulnerable. Their hitherto mainly raw material exports are their lifeblood while their pattern of demand is increasingly geared to imported manufactures both for capital and current consumption. The deliberate

[1] Rolf E. Lüke, *Von der Stabilisierung zur Krise*. Basle Centre for Economic and Financial Research Series B, No. 3, Zürich, 1958, pp. 3–20. P. Cagan, 'The Monetary Dynamics of Hyperinflation', John J. Klein, 'German Money and Prices, 1932–44', and Eugene M. Lerner, 'Inflation in the Confederacy', the last three in Milton Friedman (ed.), *Studies in the Quantity Theory of Money*, Chicago, 1956, pp. 25–117, 121–59 and 163–75.

[2] Cp. p. 285 for detailed discussion.

creation of industry, mainly for the domestic market, can often in the long run relieve the pressure on the balance of payments. Few other measures (import control, etc.) are efficient, though the taxation of luxury imports or general turnover taxes can help keep the monetary and, therefore, demand balance. The size of the foreign exchange reserve must also be related to the balance of payments as is reflected in the habit of giving the size of the foreign reserves of a country as so many months' worth of imports. The difficulty is that such a presentation is often misleading as it is the total reserves that are usually given and not the 'free' reserves. While theoretically it is possible to regard all reserves as free, in actual fact there is a minimum which for internal as well as external confidence reasons cannot be so considered. This is evident even for as financially mature a country as Great Britain; and is doubly the case for the developing countries. It is therefore necessary for the central banks to attempt to manage their foreign reserves in such a manner that the free reserves are large enough to carry the normal fluctuations of the balance of payments, leaving a hard core of reserves. The legally stipulated minimum foreign exchange reserve is usually taken as representing this hard core. While the varying structure of the developing countries makes any general rule unrealistic, the international credit standing of any country will depend more upon the wisdom of the general monetary, financial, and growth policies followed. These will have to include a very careful husbandry of the available reserves, a husbandry achieved mainly through general policies.

With respect to the fiduciary issue, the growth of the economy is a limiting factor. The present currency backing (for confidence and balance of payments reasons) will have to grow as the currency issue grows. What today seems a more than sufficient reserve, maintained absolutely, will in a very few years be only sufficient to cover the note issue.

The problems involved are exemplified in the following mathematical presentation. The growth rate of the national income at current market prices (6·9 per cent p.a.) and of the currency in circulation (9·75 per cent p.a.) have both been patterned on the Nigerian experience 1951–60 in order to use a realistic case. There is no guarantee that the same growth rates are to be expected in future. However, even at slightly different rates of growth, the same principle is likely to persist for many years to come, both in Nigeria and elsewhere.

As Table XIV shows, the growth of the currency in circulation over ten or twenty years is likely to be appreciable. The proportion of Gross National Product and currency in circulation is also based on Nigeria. For confidence and balance of payments as well as legal

TABLE XIV

Foreign Reserve Backing of Currency in Circulation

	Gross National Income	Currency in Circulation	Foreign Reserve Coverage at			
Growth Rate	6·9	9·75	25	40	50	80
				per cent		
			£ million			
Year 1	1·000	80·0	20	32	40	64
Year 10	1·949	203·0	51	81	102	162
Year 20	3·799	514·0	129	206	258	412

reasons Central Bank demand liabilities and currency circulation should have a foreign exchange and gold backing of a certain proportion. The actual amounts needed are shown for different assumptions. Hitherto 80 per cent has been considered necessary, though in his budget speech in 1962, Chief Festus indicated that it would be possible gradually to descend towards 40 per cent,[1] which is the legal stipulation, while economists usually discuss a 50 per cent ratio.

The actual total reserves of Nigeria held by all official institutions and not only the Central Bank at the end of December 1961 were £N152 million (and at the end of December 1962 some £N130 million). With a coverage of 80 per cent requiring some £N64 million there were free reserves of some £N88 million. But in ten years' time a coverage of 40 per cent would require £N81 million, thus £N17 million more than an 80 per cent note coverage in 1961. As a 40 per cent note coverage is on the low side, especially for confidence reasons at home and abroad, a 50 per cent coverage in ten years should be aimed at; this would leave 'free' reserves of only some £N50 million in 1961 and £N28 million in 1962.

There is naturally little likelihood, short of a world war, that the absolute reserves of Nigeria and elsewhere will increase, except temporarily. Raw material prices have been falling, though now seem to have stabilized again (summer 1963) so that the 20 per cent average decrease assumed in the calculations of the development plan might be somewhat over-cautious. Moreover, the development plans will place a burden on the foreign reserves, even if the full total of desired foreign loans is obtained. If they are not forthcoming, the burden is likely to be even greater, unless certain marginal items of the development plans are eliminated. An increase in foreign reserves is therefore hardly to be expected.

The Central Bank should therefore manage the foreign reserves in such a way that already now the backing needed for the currency

[1] Okotie Eboh, loc. cit., p. 8.

in circulation in, say, ten years is reserved. The percentage aimed at is the monetary authorities' own choice. But even a 40 per cent coverage in ten years' time means a larger absolute amount than an 80 per cent coverage in year one under the assumption that the same growth rates of gross national product at market prices and currency in circulation are maintained. Should they be increased, the absolute amount of foreign reserve available for the coverage of the currency in circulation will be larger.

The second consequence of Table XIV is that a fiduciary issue is necessary in developing countries unless the economy is going to be hampered by a lack of money—even without allowing for monetization, which is extra. Evidently, in a long period, payments habits change but usually fairly slowly, even in developing countries. It is therefore pertinent to discuss the ways and means by which a fiduciary issue should be created.

In most developing countries the ministers of finance are always finding themselves under pressure from their cabinet colleagues and economic theoreticians, not to mention 'informed' public opinion, to use the fiduciary issue as part of the finance for the development plan. This would in fact mean that the central bank should undertake to take over government bonds, while crediting the government account with a corresponding amount.[1] To make this measure more acceptable it is sometimes suggested that it should be spread over a certain time, with the central bank slowly selling off the government bonds to the investing public. In essence this changes nothing in the criticism brought below. If the bonds prove saleable, they could be sold directly to insurance companies and other investors thus collecting true current savings. Otherwise the bonds would only compete with other financial investments for the available finance and, if the pace were forced, the probability is that they would be bought by the secondary credit they themselves have helped to create. Naturally such an absorption of credit would prevent it going into other directions—but it cannot by any means be considered sound finance.

The first group of consequences of using government bonds to expand the fiduciary issue would be:

(*a*) that the government would have a draft on the central bank available to finance its development programme. It would be credit creation in the truest sense of the word—exactly the course the

[1] One of the arguments employed to justify using the fiduciary issue for government financing is that the central bank must possess government stock and Treasury Bills so as to be able to intervene on the money and capital markets. This is undoubtedly true, but the central bank should be able to choose when and how it acquires these assets. Its decision should be determined by *monetary* and not financial considerations.

drafters of the statutes of the central banks have been at such pains to prevent.[1] This is because it would represent an absolute increase in the amount of monetary demand, with no counterpart either in goods, foreign exchange or non-consumption (saving);

(*b*) Moreover, this method of financing would also tend to create a secondary credit expansion, inasmuch as deposits with the central bank can be the basis for a multiple credit expansion on the part of the commercial banks.[2] While the subsequent sale of the government bonds by the central bank should reduce the commercial banks' deposits with the central bank, and thus in like measure reduce the multiple credit creation, the time factor between the two transactions allows for an inflationary period, the effects of which may not be reversible;

(*c*) There would be no counterpart in foreign exchange, while there is no guarantee that the amount raised would be spent in the country.

The full consequences of financing government expenditure at the central bank must always be carefully considered. Should the authorities, in spite of everything, decide that this is the only (sometimes politically) possible measure, the amounts raised should be comparatively small and their timing should be judiciously adjusted in relation to the economy as a whole. Naturally, the possibility of raising funds at commercial bank level should first have been investigated and utilized. The apparent lack of credit really reflects the lack of resources. Prefinancing of the government by the central bank in order to assure growth sounds feasible. It is such an explosive measure in a booming economy, however, that only the most skilful policies can counteract its permanent obnoxious effects.[3] Therefore, at times when physical, financial and foreign exchange resources are strained, the mobilization of central bank credit for investment

[1] Cp. p. 94.

[2] For fuller discussion see p. 136.

[3] In Tunisia in 1962 the support extended by the Central Bank in the financing of investment by the government contributed towards raising economic activity to a relatively high level, close enough to the one envisaged by the Tunisian three-year plan. Through its short-term and medium-term advances, and through the loans contracted abroad on behalf of the government, the Bank enabled the Treasury to *anticipate its future resources* and to make substantial investment outlays immediately. In order to avoid an excessive expansion of the money supply, the Bank adjusted its credit policy. As a result of these measures and of the increase in the gross domestic product, monetary stability was maintained, despite the increase in credits to the Treasury. The Annual Report of the Central Bank of Tunisia (p. 104) emphasizes that if this stability is to be secured the Treasury's expenditure must be sizably reduced. Otherwise, the contemplated increase in bank credits to the private sector and the expected rise in the foreign exchange reserves might exert cumulative inflationary pressures which could only be counteracted by recourse to a policy of greater austerity.

purposes instead of domestic or foreign current or even past savings should if possible be avoided.

The second consequence of using an increase of the fiduciary issue for investment purposes is that such a policy represents, to a considerable extent, a misappropriation of the fiduciary issue. Its prime purpose is to support the expansion of domestic trade, which will come in the wake of economic growth in general and the development plans in particular. Such steady support for the domestic economy will be supplementary to seasonal and growing demands for the credit needed to move the crops and which, in future, will probably be domestically financed to an ever increasing extent.

While the credit situation has hitherto not been tight, the demands for credit are growing and, as the development plans really get under way, the pressure will increase. Essentially, this demand for domestic credit from the commercial banks will be due, largely, to the secondary reactions (the multiplier and accelerator effects) of the development plans. By and large, the development plans themselves, financed out of current income (budget revenue), current or past savings (including accumulated foreign reserves) and foreign loans and grants should not create such demand for domestic credit. A certain amount of pre-financing[1] might be necessary and the new industries will eventually need working capital. The first and main demand should, however, be from trader, transport and other tertiary industry, which will be supplying the newly employed persons, whose additional demands will require facilities of all kinds.[2] The need for credit this demand will generate, may be considerable and the commercial banks are the natural suppliers.

The commercial banks themselves do not, however, have unlimited funds at their disposal. Their deposits are not growing so fast that they themselves can be expected to cover the new demands for credit. The commercial banks will therefore find that they increasingly have to have recourse to the central bank, chiefly through discounting and rediscounting of commercial bills of exchange, promissory notes, warrants and other credit instruments. They will also, increasingly, offer Treasury Bills for rediscounting, especially in those countries where a certain pressure has been used to encourage the commercial banks to hold fairly high proportions of Treasury Bills.

This recourse to the central bank will give the latter an increasing control over the market. It makes it easier for the central bank to supply the economy with the credit it needs and this will proportionately enlarge the fiduciary issue.

1 A contractor has landed an order for buildings and must complete his stock.

2 It is probable that under such circumstances the applicants for credit will prove 'more' creditworthy. Some of the demands for credit may, moreover, be indirect, and therefore be hard to analyse and evaluate.

The commercial bill is, luckily, a current credit instrument in African countries, thanks to the importance of international trade. This is a considerable advantage, which should be fostered. The relative merit of the commercial bill compared to Treasury Bills has been discussed in the Report of the Commission of Inquiry into Banking, Currency and Credit of Ireland (1938) where, in a pregnant passage, the central importance of the commercial bill is stressed.

'The disappearance of the commercial bill all over the world, its place being taken by other methods of financing, is a modern phenomenon, which, from the point of view of central banking policy, is rather to be deplored. In a number of markets Treasury bills (i.e. short-dated Government bills) have taken the place of commercial bills as a basis for rediscount by central banks, but they less closely reflect current business developments. They are not self-liquidating; they lend themselves more easily to abuse, in that rediscounting of Treasury bills may be an indirect method of government financing of an inflationary character. If credit difficulties arise, commercial bills may up to a point be allowed to run off without renewal, business people obtaining credit facilities from other sources, eventually from abroad. Treasury bills, on the other hand, must always be repaid by the Government, and if the market does not absorb them and the Government has no funds at its disposal, the central bank may be compelled, not only to retain those it has, but to accept a larger amount in order to prevent a government default. When credit institutions hold Treasury bills maturing, say, over three months, they are always able to procure funds by not renewing the bills, and the power of control which can be exerted by the central bank is in that way reduced.'[1]

The practice of the commercial bank of letting the holdings of discounted commercial bills mature without replacing them in times of monetary crisis is well established. It is probably the smoothest method of regulating the credit market. It allows the commercial banks to become more liquid so that they do not have to curtail credit accommodation to their own customers (i.e. current account holders) but only to 'strangers', while they build up their cash holdings both in tills and at the central bank. It relieves them of the necessity to rediscount at the central bank (directly or indirectly) and decreases the pressure to which the central bank might otherwise be exposed.[2] Naturally, bill brokers—or in countries where

[1] *Reports of the Commission of Inquiry into Banking, Currency and Credit*, No. 2628, Stationery Office, Dublin, Ireland, 1938, p. 226.

[2] Evidence given by Mr Alderman Salomons before the House of Commons select committee in 1858. Quoted in *Lombard Street* by Walter Bagehot, 14th edition, London, 1915 (1st edition 1873), p. 319 ff. See also Bagehot's commentary, pp. 265–83.

these are not available, the commercial banks themselves—might have to (re)discount at the central bank. This, especially if their holdings of bills is such that a large proportion thereof does not mature within a very short future. Basically the same system is current practice, supplemented by the Treasury Bill.[1] That the latter tends to swamp the credit market is unfortunately undeniable.[2] Such a development is one of the greatest dangers to which the newer developing countries are exposed.

The danger of having a credit market swamped by Treasury Bills can be mitigated not only by trying to keep the volume of the latter in check but by actively encouraging the commercial bill. The latter or promissory notes, etc., are not only used in foreign trade but in inland trade. It is one of the best means of financing the varying needs of the private sector and, by encouraging the latter, relieves the government of some of the executive and financial burden—thus decreasing the need for Treasury Bills. In the middle of the nineteenth century the inland commercial bill was the main means of financing internal trade in Great Britain. As conditions changed, communications improved, and the banking system was extended, the bank loan and overdraft slowly replaced the inland trade bill.[3] Its convenience allowed the commercial trade bill to maintain its position in the financing of international trade and commerce.

In more modern times, the Bank of Finland used inland commercial bills as backing for the fiduciary issue. They started to be included in 1921 when they were 42·5 per cent of the supplementary cover. By 1936 they were 90·3 per cent thereof; the remainder was made up of foreign notes and coupons and foreign bills.[4] This inclusion of inland and foreign commercial bills as the supplementary note cover was the consequence of the reforms taken 1921–25 to stabilize the currency.

With the prospect of fairly rapid economic growth, the African developing countries are going to need a fiduciary issue as the currency in circulation will have to be enlarged. The present 80 or 100 per cent backing in gold and foreign exchange will therefore have to be reduced. This does not, however, necessarily mean that the absolute size of this backing can be reduced with safety. It is far more probable that the amount that today represents 80 per cent will, unchanged, only be 40 per cent in a fairly small number of years, i.e. the absolute amount will merely become relatively smaller. The idea, therefore, that there are 'free' reserves in valuable foreign

1 Richard Sayers, *Modern Banking*, 3rd edition, Oxford, 1951, pp. 91–123.

2 *Committee on the Working of the Monetary System*, loc. cit. §§399–474. A. K. Cairncross, *Monetary Policy*, loc. cit., pp. 13–41.

3 R. G. Hawtrey, *A Century of Bank Rate*, London, 1938, pp. 54–6.

4 A. E. Tudeer, *The Bank of Finland* 1912–36, Helsingfors, 1940, pp. 386–7.

currency, that could, or should, be used for the financing of the development plan, is largely erroneous.

The use to which the growing fiduciary issue is put is of great importance. Ideally it should expand according to the needs of internal (and external) financing and largely be issued by means of the discounting or rediscounting of commercial bills. The existence of the latter makes a money and credit market much more flexible than when there is an over-proportion of Treasury Bills. The creation of a fiduciary issue, exclusively or mainly, by means of Treasury Bills or government stock would not only weigh down the market, but would also be inherently inflationary, at both primary and secondary level. Moreover, such a policy would be a misappropriation of funds needed by the private sector; the normal financing of the internal market would be imperilled and this would help prevent the creation of a domestic sector.

CHAPTER XXI

INTEREST RATE POLICY AND OPEN MARKET OPERATIONS

The policy of the monetary and financial authorities towards interest rates depends in developing countries even more on their general structure than is the case in financially mature countries. Here the absolute level of rates must usually be taken into account because of domestic market considerations and those pertaining to international flows of capital and liquid funds. The most recent developments in the United States and Great Britain are the new techniques for changing the structures of interest rates so as to be able to deal with both considerations when they are in conflict.[1] These difficult technical questions do not arise in developing countries. While developing countries are much freer in respect to the absolute level of their interest rates—even if relations to their main financial centres abroad must be taken into account—they have structures of interest rates and profits which are peculiarly their own and which are one of the most startling differences between them and the financially mature countries.

Comparative interest rates are a notoriously illusive subject for study, especially when the countries being compared have radically different basic structures and maturities. In the first place the relative importance of rates is different and a change, for instance, in bank rate may mean a fundamental change of policy in one country and hardly have any repercussions in another. Moreover, the work done by any given rate in any one country may be completely different. Commercial Bank rates for three months' loans to prime customers may, to varying extents, really be long term rates. Added to this, there is a change through time. In financially mature countries, there is both a short term and a medium term change in absolute levels and possibly structures while in developing countries the time change seems to be medium to long term and basically on structures. Through time therefore the size of the flow of assets affected by each rate is apt to change and differently in each country or each type of country.

In spite of these objections, it is interesting to compare the structure of interest and profit rates in a developing country with

[1] BIS, 32*nd Annual Report* (*1961-62*), p. 62.

those in typically financially mature countries. As representatives of financially mature countries Great Britain, Switzerland and Germany have been taken. The structure of interest rates and profits of a developing country is based on Ghana, Nigeria and the Sudan.[1] On investigation they proved to be remarkably similar, at any rate in the summer of 1961, the reference date of Table XV.

While the whole level of the official interest rates is higher in the developing country than in Switzerland, the difference is not larger than those which are to be found among the relatively financially mature countries themselves. The level of interest rates in Germany and Great Britain is much the same or higher than in the developing country. Such variations in interest rate levels are natural when the supply of savings and other capital is relatively small in comparison to the demand for such funds.

The really startling difference in the interest rate structure is, however, to be found in the profit rates. In financially more mature countries, these returns are comparatively low, even in the case of housing, which is in short term supply practically everywhere. But a return of 8–12 per cent (of course, an average hides extremes in both directions) is considered a very high return on such a safe investment.

This 8–12 per cent return to be expected on housing must be contrasted with a rate of 12–25 (to 33⅓) per cent in the developing country. Similarly, investments in industry may give a return of negative[2] to 10 per cent and these returns were falling everywhere in financially mature countries,[3] whereas the (admitted and therefore minimum) return in this developing country is 12–25 per cent p.a. There is as yet no sign that these returns are falling—in fact, as demand rises in the country they may even be increasing. Similarly, trade in consumers goods, where the variation in returns is particularly wide, shows in the financially mature country some 5–12 per cent, whereas in the developing country the return (a minimum again) is of the order of 15 per cent.

[1] The comparatively low level of interest rates existing today in financially mature countries is a recent development. The highest bank rates during the period 1925–29 were the following: Switzerland 4, France 4½, Netherlands 5½, Belgium 7½, Great Britain 6½, Sweden 5½, Germany 10. Bank rates of 10 to 13 per cent were usual in the financially immature countries of Europe, namely, Albania, Austria, Hungary, Estonia, Roumania, Danzig, Poland, Bulgaria and Greece. Naturally all other rates were adjusted to bank rate. Bank of International Settlements, *7th Annual Report* (April 1936–March 1937), p. 69.

[2] When income and capital taxes are taken into account.

[3] By 1962 the sharp fall in profits per unit had become a major problem. Supply had caught up with demand—thus making price increases difficult—while it proved difficult to cut costs especially in the face of granted and pending wage demands.

TABLE XV

Interest Rates and Profit Rates

	Developing Country	Great Britain	Switzerland	Germany
		*in per cent p.a.**		
Bank rate	4·75	5	2	3
Discount	4·25	$5\frac{3}{8}$–6	—	$2\frac{5}{8}$
Call money	—	$3\frac{3}{8}$	1	—
Treasury Bills	4·75	4·44	—	2·25
Yield Government Bonds	5	6·079 ($2\frac{1}{2}$ consols)	2·84	5·7
Mortgage rates	7†+charge	6·25	3·75–4·25	7·8
Commercial Banks:				
3–6 months: prime customers	6–$6\frac{1}{2}$	6	$4\frac{1}{2}+\frac{1}{2}$ charge	
others	7–$7\frac{1}{2}$	7 (up to)	$4\frac{1}{2}+1$ charge	$7\frac{1}{2}$–9
medium term (2–5 years)	8–10		3·75–4 no charge	
Yield Stock Exchange:				
(first-class securities)	10	4·3	3·3	5–6
Profit rates (minimum):				
Trade (consumer goods)	15	n.a.	5–15	n.a.
Investment (industrial)	20	n.a.	–10	n.a.
Housing	12–25–$33\frac{1}{3}$	n.a.	8–12	n.a.

* May 1961—a first version of this table was presented at an address entitled: ***Interest Rates, Prices and the Relationship between Government Expenditure and Foreign Exchange Reserve***, and delivered before the Economic Society in Accra, Ghana, on June 25, 1961.

† When given.

SOURCE:

Developing country composite of Ghana, Nigeria and the Sudan based on original research.
Financially mature countries: conventional sources.

Now why is there this very great difference? Well, there are at least three reasons:

1. The developing country has a much smaller relative stock of already existing capital equipment. It has, relative to its population and that population's (including government's) demand far less houses, industries, shops, etc., than has the financially mature country. People in Europe may not like living in houses some 100 or more years old, but those houses are there and can still be lived in. The very fact that they exist, means that there is a brake on the demand for new houses and therefore also on their price—even in times of housing shortage. It is exactly the same principle by which the price of the new cocoa crop is affected by the existence and size of the carry-over from the last year's crop.

2. Financially mature countries are relatively well supplied with all types of capital, even of risk capital.

The capital supply of a country is *not* a homogeneous concept. On the contrary, there are many different types of capital.

The small saver, for instance, who manages to save, say, 10 shillings or £1 a week is going to be very careful of where he invests it. This capital is definitely not risk capital, if he himself can help it. He will probably entrust it to a bank, saving, mortgage or commercial bank. These banks, conscious of their responsibility to their depositors will not invest in risky projects. They will certainly want to place a part of their funds in something really sure, such as the Treasury Bills and bonds of a stable and financially sound government. Another part of the funds at their disposal might be used for loans to prime borrowers, i.e. to really creditworthy borrowers. This means people who have preferably both security to offer and whose past record of repaying their debts show them to be worthy of confidence. Naturally a banker of experience who knows and can assess his clients old and new, has a certain freedom in his loan policy as he can spread his risks in a way no small saver can. But he is restricted to certain limits according to the definition by which a banker is a man who lends out money and gets it back.

Another part of the capital stock of a country is short term only. Large companies, or marketing boards, etc., may at certain periods of the year have very considerable funds to deposit for three, six or nine months. These can be put into Treasury Bills, or through the intermediary of the banks, be used as working capital by other firms. But these sums must be repaid when the depositor again needs the funds in order to be able to move the crop or participate in trade. Thus, this short term capital cannot be used for long term investment, nor can it be considered as long term risk capital.

Risk capital is the capital which people are prepared to put into either their own or friends' businesses, investments, housing or into shares.

When total savings in a country are small, it is necessary that there be a high rate of return on risk savings in order to stimulate a sufficient number of savers to risk their hard saved capital in investments which are not absolutely safe. And developing countries have relatively small total savings—and the amount of risk capital available, even at high rates of return, is in short supply. The high profits usually increase the amount of risk capital available as they usually become part of saving, i.e. the capital which can be used for entrepreneurial activity—either by private individuals or the government.

3. The third factor why profit rates are higher in developing countries is that there is relatively little entrepreneurship, i.e. in developing countries there are relatively few persons with the know-how and the taste for starting and running new industries, new agriculture and new projects of all types. It was an Austrian economist, Joseph Schumpeter, who some thirty years ago stressed the essential importance of entrepreneurship in the economies of European countries. This contribution to theory made him famous, long before the world's attention had been turned to the problems of developing countries. Real entrepreneurship is so scarce a commodity even in developed countries that it is cosseted and cared for—and naturally commands its price. And this is not only the case in Western countries. The Soviet Union has realized that not only its scientists but also the managers of its factories and the people with ideas and the capacity to carry them out effectively are precious people. In fact they are people of the same type, with the same knowledge, drive and administrative capacity as those running industries and projects in the West. In this planned economy, these entrepreneurs command salaries which are much higher than those which can be earned in the Western world. The difference in earnings between people in similar senior positions in Europe and in the Soviet Union is of the order of anything from two to ten times or more in favour of the Soviet Union.

In countries where the economic system is freer, i.e. where it is not rigorously planned throughout, the entrepreneur's reward is at least partly reflected in the profitableness of his enterprise. Thus where he is rare, the return, as measured by his profits, is high.[1]

While there is little accurate information, it is known that in these developing countries personal loans can be obtained outside the modern credit system at rates of 33⅓–50 per cent and higher. Only through time will the latter's existence modify these rates. The

[1] For a positive but realistic discussion of these problems see Nathan Rosenberg, 'Capital Formation in Underdeveloped Countries', The *American Economic Review*, Vol. L, No. 4 (September 1960), pp. 706–15.

The increasing credit standing of the individual is decisive, making him a candidate for loans in the modern credit system. This peculiar pattern of high, even very high, interest rates ($21\frac{2}{3}$–$43\frac{1}{3}$–$173\frac{1}{3}$ per cent p.a.) for short term personal loans existing concurrently with low rates ($4\frac{7}{8}$–$8\frac{3}{8}$ per cent p.a.) for long term loans on organized markets has existed at various times throughout history, but probably had the largest differential in the fourteenth century in Europe.[1] The rates quoted above apply to this period. The reasons for the discrepancy were much the same as those which apply to developing countries today.

The peculiar interest rate and profit structure of developing countries is frequently made responsible for the fact that 'unnecessary' or 'incorrect' investments are supposed to be made on a large scale in developing countries. This thesis seems to base upon the assumption that, as capital is limited, it should be used for investments which would lead to maximum 'growth' or 'social welfare' or some such criterion. It completely neglects the following considerations:

(1) The administrative problems of directing all credit flows and investments.

(2) The fact that, thanks to development plans, budget policy and capital imports, etc., a not negligible part of the total capital at the disposal of a developing country is used for fundamental investments. Whether these investments are beneficial depends on the viability of development policy as followed by the government.[2] At any rate, these measures do in fact make it possible to disregard in part the interest rate structure of the developing country itself. The capital imports add new capital absolutely while taxation probably redirects into investment funds which otherwise would largely have been used for consumption purposes. At the present relatively low level of taxation and with the present high propensity to consume in developing countries, government taxation probably interferes less with the investment process and private saving than is the case in financially mature countries.

(3) The fact that private domestic capital is invested in highly profitable undertakings means:

(*a*) that there is an effective demand for this type of investment, e.g. houses, a demand that otherwise would be unsatisfied and which would increase price levels.

[1] Sidney Homer, *A History of Interest Rates*, New Brunswick, N.J., 1963, esp. pp. 69–111.

[2] Cp. p. 256.

(*b*) that the high profit rates lead to rapid accumulation of new capital. While it is impossible to prove statistically for lack of any data, observation leads to the conclusion that the profits made especially in housing and commerce tend to be reinvested, at least as long as important profits can be made.

The use of private domestic capital in the most profitable enterprises, therefore, not only satisfies a real need but also increases the amount of capital available.[1]

(4) The investment of private domestic capital in very profitable enterprises leads to (temporary) points of saturation and therefore alterations in the structure of interest and profit rates.

For example, housing may have commanded a high return in a given city. A saturation point is reached for buildings of that type and price, returns fall, possibly considerably.[2] Profits on housing then are below those in industrial or commercial undertakings. The domestic capitalists divert (part or all) of their new capital to these branches. Should neither connections nor available know-how make possible such an investment, it becomes attractive to invest in the stocks and shares to be bought on the Stock Exchange. With yields at some 10 per cent such investments (also as a spreading of risks) are becoming ever more popular. Both in the case of direct investments or, if the capitalist's share holding is important enough, he may find himself member of a board of directors and thus become involved in entrepreneurship.

With the change in the structure of interest and profit rates, there is a shift towards longer term investment corresponding to the fall in the highest rates of return.

It therefore seems probable that much of the criticism levelled at the investment pattern of developing countries is unjustified. On the whole, the combination for government and semi-government projects and the use of market mechanisms in the private investment saving sector create both basic investments and a maximum of new capital. The investment of the latter gradually increases the stock of capital and thereby decreases the rates of return, bringing longer

[1] Already in 1956 Okwara O. Amogu wrote about Nigeria, 'It is therefore not a true picture to imagine a country teeming with opportunities for "business" development, which are frustrated by the propensity to hoard savings. There is very real willingness to employ savings productively, but sociological and political factors tend to channel the savings into uses which are less obviously (though not less truly) "productive". For instance, a great deal of saving is employed on constructing the educational system.' Institute of Social and Economic Research, University College of the West Indies, Jamaica, 'Savings in an African Economy', *Social and Economic Studies*, Vol. 5, No. 2, June 1956, pp. 202–9, esp. p. 208.

[2] This has happened both in Salisbury (Rhodesia) and Lagos (Nigeria).

term and more capital intensive projects within the scope of the domestic capitalist.

The natural fall in certain interest or profit rates described above takes time. It frequently happens that a country, wishing to speed up development, finds it difficult to raise capital, especially industrial, agricultural and commercial, for private domestic projects at suitable rates.

Here an overall or specialized Development Bank[1] which can combine foreign capital, possibly a government subsidy and some domestic capital (if only as an obligatory contribution by its clients) can prove the intermediate solution. Not only can it lend at rates inferior to what would normally be the case according to the structure of rates in the country, but it can usually help to ensure the profitable investment of the capital thanks to its advisory service. Thus by an institutional measure it proves possible to remedy the basic situation by providing more capital in the first place from abroad and in the second by assuring profits that can then be invested or reinvested.

The natural fall in interest rates does not, however, always lead to investments in longer term, lower interest rate enterprises. In some developing countries—of which Morocco is an example—a lack of highly profitable investments will merely increase liquidity as private individuals consider, say, a 10 per cent return, too small to bother about. Innumerable partial explanations have been given ranging from a lack of business opportunities through fears of nationalization to a lack of propensity to earn (and spend). A satisfactory solution to the problem might point to a natural way of mobilizing the assets. Failing this, a more active policy on the part of institutions and governments to replace the hoarded funds becomes necessary to try to stabilize the economy. Such a policy is not without its dangers, as the hoarded funds could be rapidly mobilized in a given and unknown situation without the authorities being in a position to control the effects. But more important is the fact that 'low' interest rates do not seem to stimulate entrepreneurial activity—which is a checkmate situation that can only be dealt with by specialized methods and means.

The means that might be used to stimulate entrepreneurial activity in countries where this is apparently not natural in the first or even second generation go far beyond the confines of monetary and financial policy or even economic policy as a whole. The methods pertaining to these policies are discussed at various points in this book. The broader problem can only be indicated. There is reason to believe, however, that a combination of enlightened liberalism (or even tempered radicalism) and inspiring leadership can so alter

[1] Cp. p. 141.

the basic attitude of the elite, whether new or of the old aristocracy, that fundamental resistances and traditional inertia can be overcome.

The technical limits to the interest rate policy of the central banks have already been discussed. Basically, the problem is that the commercial banks and other financial intermediaries are only gradually becoming dependent on the central bank while the amount of paper in the market available for discount or rediscount is restricted. Even when rather more is available, there is often a preponderance of Treasury Bills, which are a double-edged sword. The question thus arises whether the central bank can reinforce its interest rate policy by 'open market operations'.

As should have become clear by the discussion on money and capital markets, the latter are still so small compared to the size of the country that open market operations are just about excluded. In the first place, already minute transactions have a terrific impact because the markets are so narrow. Therefore, if any intervention ever takes place, it is merely to steady existing rates. These purchases of government stock are usually very modest as the total issued is small and most holders are permanent investors. Secondly, even if a real effect were obtained on the Stock Exchange, the economic effect would be slight, while the blow to the confidence of the investors could be fundamentally destructive. The capital markets of the developing countries are still very tender plants and it will take quite some time till they have matured enough for anyone to pluck some fruits from them in the shape of effective open market operations.

The developing countries under discussion have an interest rate structure which differs very considerably from that of financially mature countries. Not only is the general level of interest rates somewhat higher but the spread of rates is very much wider. This difference depends on the basic economy with its general lack of long term investment capital and therefore high interest rates for the capital available. Thus the private sectors tend to invest only in high yield relatively short term undertakings (including real estate). The reinvestment of profits can gradually lead to a saturation point and direct investment into lower yield, longer term investments, provided the rate is still attractive in that country. The presumed 'misdirection of investment' because of the interest structure is therefore probably over-rated. Moreover, through foreign loans, development plans and institutions such as development banks, the domestic interest rate structure is broken and investments can take place according to the criterion established by the overall economic aims of the country.

CHAPTER XXII

THE EVOLUTION OF MONETARY POLICY

Basically monetary policy in African countries consists of using the available intruments, within the limits of the constraints imposed by the structure of the economy, to maintain stable monetary conditions without hampering growth. By making credit available to productive, as opposed to speculative (or other non-productive), sectors, fundamental economic growth, provided it exists, can continue unhampered even in conditions of overall monetary stringency. The relatively modest tightenings of monetary conditions that have taken place in Africa could not be called monetary stringencies. They have, however, shown that monetary policy has a useful part to play even in these developing countries.

Of the six countries under discussion only three, Tunisia, the Rhodesias and the Republic of the Sudan have used monetary policy proper in order to control more than seasonal fluctuations. These countries have been faced with periods of overcharged economic activity which threatened the smooth functioning of the internal economy and the balance of payments situation.

The other countries fall into three categories.

1. In Nigeria, there has as yet been no need to use monetary policy proper, though it is probable that situations where it must be brought into play lie in the near future. As far as possible, the instruments and institutions for its implementation have been prepared and built out. This is stressed in the Annual Report for 1962 of the Central Bank of Nigeria. It is pointed out that the Central Bank 'entered a new phase of growth during 1962, continuing to expand and diversify its normal banking activities and at the same time achieving significant progress in developing monetary and credit policies and techniques for making them effective. These steps, in conjunction with the changes effected during the early part of 1962 in the legislation governing the operation of the Central Bank and the activities of the banking system, place the Central Bank in a stronger position to deal with the many economic and financial problems that may be expected as the new Six-Year National Development Programme is implemented.'[1]

[1] Central Bank of Nigeria, *Annual Report and Statement of Accounts* for the year ended December 31, 1962, p. 3.

2. In Ghana, monetary policy proper has not been used, because this delicate instrument was powerless in face of the credit demands of the government and the credits required for the internal financing of the cocoa crop. Price levels have increased in spite of 'price control', as has the money supply and the balance of payments has been under considerable pressure. Recourse was made in August 1962 to the International Monetary Fund for assistance amounting to \$14·25 million paid half in dollars and half in sterling. This represents some 35 per cent of the total Ghanaian tranche of \$40·5 million. The official reason given for the application was the fall on world markets of cocoa prices. It is the policy of the International Monetary Fund to assist, when they need it, raw material producing countries, especially those of the monoculture type. That the representatives of the Fund had realized that the internal situation of the country left something to be desired, is shown in the summary and extract of their report. 'It urged the Ghana Government to pursue cautious financial policies that will reduce the excessive internal demand and ease the strain on the balance of payments; and to reduce as rapidly as the balance of payments position permits the restrictions on current trade and payment.'[1] Basically, there has been a lack of co-operation between the monetary and financial authorities. While the monetary authorities protested in private at the rate of monetary expansion, they were forced to assist the financial authorities far more liberally than they considered suitable. The domestically created monetary demand is reflected in the deficit of the balance of trade in the period 1961–62. The official fall in reserves was given as £30 million in the period July 1961 to June 1962. However, the introduction of import and foreign exchange control in the second half of 1961 apparently had some effect, the balance of trade for the six months January to June 1962 showing a small surplus. Unless, however, the monetary situation is brought in hand quickly and smoothly, it is possible that Ghana becomes one of the first countries in Africa which will need to have recourse to the strictest financial discipline in order not to cripple its economic growth.

3. In Morocco the monetary authorities have had to face the harder problem of helping to stimulate the economy. This they have attempted to do in close collaboration with the Ministries of Finance and Economic Planning. Their main tool has been the directional control of credit, by which attempts were made to direct credit and capital into the Cinderella spheres of activity. Thus, especially agriculture has been favoured as well as domestic industry, sometimes through development banks. The government has often advanced

[1] IMF consultations quoted in Bank of Ghana, *Quarterly Bulletin*, June 1962, p. 5.

part or all of the capital and/or guaranteed rediscount facilities at the central bank.[1] While this policy has not been entirely without effect, overcoming the structural problems of development as well as those due to the business recession of the 1950's is a very difficult task. It touches all spheres of activity and is much greater than can be mastered by monetary policy alone. The fact that the commercial and other banks do not utilize their full credit lines at the central banks shows that it is not monetary stringency which is hampering growth and development. The reasons for the limited success of the policy are manifold and embrace national characteristics and sociological attitudes as well as strictly economic and monetary factors. Of the latter there is perhaps one main consideration.[2] The low monetization of the traditional agricultural and artisan sectors is due largely to the almost closed circuits of the flow of money in modern sectors. (The modern sectors in Morocco and Tunisia seem to be much more isolated than is the case in the other four countries under discussion.) The result is that the traditional agriculturalist and artisan has no monetary resources with which he can improve his creditworthiness. It also means that any general increase in the supply of credit and capital is unlikely to reach him unless deliberately directed. The Development Plan as well as the various agricultural credit societies are all trying to help the traditional artisan and agriculturalist, but the reforms proposed will take years to really come to fruition.

In the three countries described above the central banks have not been able to use monetary policy proper because of the context in which they were operating. Either the economy had not yet reached a degree of development such that monetary policy was efficacious, or the over-riding claims of the financial authorities have impeded the use of monetary policy, even as elementary a proposition as a limitation of credit.

Tunisia started using monetary policy early in 1962. This was done to counteract the important advances given to the government to meet development expenditure especially in agriculture. Previously the Tunisian situation had been much the same as that of Morocco. But in 1961 and early 1962 the increase in credit was reflected by a deterioration of the balance of trade and payments, which was aggravated by the low rates of interest in Tunisia. Thus on October 1, 1962, the bank rate was raised to 4 per cent (from 3 per cent). The whole structure of rates adjusted itself, though certain categories of investors were given a preferential rate.[3] The rates for savings,

[1] Cp. p. 64 and p. 146.

[2] Jean-Pierre Gern, *Les voies ouvertes*, loc. cit., pp. 32–59.

[3] Banque Centrale de Tunisie, *Rapport Annuel* 1962, p. 70 ff.

deposits, etc., have, however, in particular been raised. While the Banque Centrale de Tunisie emphasizes the need of better balance in the monetary sector, it remains to be seen whether the measures taken will have the desired effect.

The situation in Rhodesia has been very different. The Bank of Rhodesia and Nyasaland has used both Bank Rate and alterations of the Treasury Bill issue in order both to change the level of interest rates and to maintain stability in the money market. In August 1960 Bank Rate was increased from its original level of 4½ per cent (since 1957) to 5 per cent. This increase in discount rate was an attempt to counteract the outflow of funds, which was caused by the political uncertainties. The pressure increased, however, and Exchange Control was introduced in February 1961. It was designed to prevent the export of the large volume of liquid funds in the hands of residents in the Rhodesias and Nyasaland.[1] All current transactions such as imports and, with safeguards, travel and education abroad, were freely administered by the commercial banks and only capital transactions of residents were prohibited. Non-residents were allowed full freedom also in respect to capital transactions.

The result of the introduction of Exchange Control was an important increase of funds on the money market as well as in time deposits with commercial banks, discount houses and the savings institutions. In order to maintain order on the money market the Central Bank varied the size of the Treasury Bill tender. It is with some satisfaction that the Central Bank states that 'With the high degree of liquidity that prevailed in the Federation during 1962, it was fortunate that there was a money market sufficiently developed to absorb it.'[2]

The policy was re-enforced by a further increase in discount rate to 5½ per cent in June 1961. It was only in May 1962 that discount rate was reduced to 5 per cent, to be reduced further in January 1963 to 4½ per cent.

The main difficulty has been the high liquidity of the money market combined with a shortage of long term capital for investment purposes. The political uncertainties have discouraged investments and the contrast with the economic boom in the 1950's has made the slowing down of economic activity possibly appear fairly serious. The Bank of Rhodesia and Nyasaland insists that it is merely a return to 'normal conditions'. However, the combination of political uncertainty and recession conditions has not encouraged long term capital investment by residents or by foreigners. The Federal Government has therefore under-balanced its budget, as have the Territorial Governments. While the deficits have been met

1 Ministry of Economic Affairs, *Economic Report* 1961, p. 43.

2 Bank of Rhodesia and Nyasaland, *Annual Report* 1962, p. 6.

from the accumulated surplus, four Federal loans were issued in 1962, all of which were fully subscribed. Together they raised $15·0 million and helped to relieve the pressure on the money market. The Central Bank was thus able to reduce its discount rate as soon as some of the high liquidity had been permanently invested in the Federal loans. As other rates follow bank rate, this measure was designed to be an encouragement to investment.

As should be clear from the above, monetary policy in the Rhodesias and Nyasaland has been used and has proved reasonably successful. At least it has been able to maintain a high degree of order on the money market at a time when, without the intervention of the Central Bank, there would probably have been confusion. Moreover, the Central Bank has attempted to bring down rates so as to make long term capital investment more attractive. The monetary policy of the central bank has, however, had the support of other factors, both exchange control and government finance. Monetary policy in itself would probably not have been sufficient but, because it was being used, the other measures taken could be mildly administered.

In the Republic of the Sudan there was an interesting attempt to use monetary policy as a help in combating a balance of payments crisis already before the establishment of the Central Bank in 1960. In 1957 and 1958 the price of cotton on world markets fell sharply and the Sudan was unable to compensate for this by increasing the quantity of cotton exported. As receipts from exports is the dominant determinant of the national income of the Sudan[1], sharp reactions were quickly encountered especially in dwindling foreign exchange reserves. As 1956 had still enjoyed relatively good cotton prices, the income of which is spent a year later, there was a high import bill in 1957. The depletion of the foreign exchange reserve amounted to some £S24 million[2] or more than one-third of the country's foreign assets. In this situation four main measures were taken, two monetary and two financial.

1. The rate of interest was increased by the Khartoum Branch of the National Bank of Egypt; this increase was also enforced by the commercial banks.

2. By agreement with the commercial banks these latter imposed rigorous quantitative credit restrictions on loans and advances for imports and for professional and personal purposes. The original regulations were re-enforced after a few months, as those first imposed did not prove as efficacious as expected. At the end of 1959

[1] Z. M. Kubinski, *Public Finance for Stability and Growth in an Underdeveloped Export Economy*, Amsterdam, 1961, pp. 24–7.

[2] IMF, *International Financial Statistics.*

bank advances were £S2·5 million below the level of the end of 1958.[1]

3. The government maintained its expenditure on current account at the same level in 1958–59 as in 1957–58. Because of reduced revenue, due to the fall in exports, there was a larger overall deficit or nearly the entire amount of the development budget of £S15 million.[2]

4. The deficit in the overall budget was financed almost entirely by drawings on foreign loans and grants, i.e. not by depleting existing reserves. In 1959 a sum of £S12·6 million was raised in this manner. The long term loan came from the IBRD £7·0 million, while on medium term both a British ECGD credit of £1·6 million and a Western German credit of £S0·6 million were obtained. The grants came from American Aid with £S0·9 million for projects and £S2·1 million for non-project. Additionally an International Monetary Fund drawing of £S0·4 million was resorted to; in 1958 assistance from this source had already been utilized to the extent of £S1·7 million in 1958.[3]

The result of these efforts was that in 1960 the internal position had been restored, while the external position improved rapidly in view of the recovery of cotton prices and the sale of not only the total current cotton crop but also of the carry-over from the two previous years. Additionally the gum arabic production and prices were both very good, further increasing the country's foreign receipts. As a consequence, the credit restrictions were liberally administered and the government budget showed a surplus. Subsequently credit restrictions were abolished, while government finances could expand on both the current budget and the development budget.

The Sudanese example of the use of monetary and financial policy for restoring equilibrium is very instructive. It contains all the elements necessary for achieving the object in view, namely the control of domestic demand both private, through restrictions on credit, and public, by moderation in government financing. Realistically no attempt was made to restrict credit for productive purposes except through an increase in the cost of credit. The extra-finance needed to be able to maintain investment in progress was obtained from abroad as loans and grants. This was possible in view of the overall credit standing of the Sudan, a position the vigorous internal measures enhanced. That these, which included monetary measures, could be taken at a time when a central bank did not exist shows

[1] Bank of Sudan, *Annual Report* 1960, p. 61.

[2] Ministry of Finance and Economics, *Economic Survey* 1960, p. 43.

[3] Ministry of Finance and Economics, loc. cit., p. 34.

that the possibilities of monetary control are greater in developing countries than is usually believed.

One of the reasons why severe credit controls on imports were possible is that the bulk of the imports of the Sudan are 'non-essential'. In view of the low level of industrialization, few raw materials are imported. Essentially the Sudan is self-supporting with regard to food and most food items imported (with the possible exception of, at that time, sugar) are luxury items. The danger was, of course, that import restrictions would send domestic prices up. However, the control of imports was effected through credit control, which automatically decreased the money supply, while the purchasing power of especially the cotton producers had been cut because of the low cotton prices.[1] In fact, the cost of living index for Khartoum (base 1958) remained stable in spite of the creation of certain local and fairly severe price increasing bottlenecks. Consumption patterns in Khartoum are the most dependent on imports. Wholesale prices which possibly are a better indicator of general level of prices fell from a maximum in 1957. It is thus seen that the internal price level did not increase as a result of the restriction on imports because there was a simultaneous restriction in internal effective demand.

The restriction of imports and especially of consumer goods imports is often recommended as the most desirable method of preventing a balance of payments crisis and/or saving precious foreign exchange for more important purposes such as the import of development goods (machinery, etc.). The danger that is so frequently overlooked is that the result will often be an increase in internal prices as the effective internal demand is seldom cut to a corresponding measure. The wage bill is normally growing (even if wage rates are pegged) as more people obtain steady employment and more qualified persons enter the labour market. There is also no guarantee that the administered prices paid to primary producers have been adjusted to the situation. The often high indirect taxation on imported goods helps to diminish the purchasing power in the hands of consumers. However, experience has shown that such measures are not as efficacious as they might be.

There is also no sign that the non-availability of foreign goods increases domestic savings. A limitation of imports must therefore be accompanied by appropriate measures to limit internal purchasing power. These measures may be financial through changes in taxation,

[1] There is no Marketing Board for cotton in the Sudan so that the producers enjoy both the benefits and disadvantages of fluctuating world market prices. While a persuasive plea can be made for the establishment of a Marketing Board (see Kubinski, loc. cit., p. 60 ff), the difficulties of the existing Marketing Boards seem to leave the question open. Cp. p. 211.

price setting with regard to primary produces and/or monetary, leading to a decrease in credit. The latter measures may be general so as to encourage thrift throughout the economy and/or personal and professional. Whichever combination of the measures is chosen in the actual situation, there is reason to believe that monetary measures are liable also to be efficacious as they have proved to be in the case of the Republic of the Sudan.

The review of monetary policy in the six African countries under discussion has shown that monetary policy can be a valuable aid in keeping and restoring monetary stability in economies of this type. While it is perfectly possible to use monetary policy even when its more delicate and intricate tools are missing, as the structure of these economies becomes more complicated it is essential to establish these instruments and institutions. The more differentiated the latter are, the more probable it is that the monetary authorities can use selective controls to contain internal effective demand in the less necessary sectors, while leaving the stimulus of liberal credit conditions in the long and medium term productive sectors. By such a policy the monetary authorities should be able to restrict credit without hampering growth. Naturally there may be occasions when, apart from selective control of credit, general monetary measures such as changes in interest rates are necessary to encourage thrift throughout the economy in times of over-active booms or to encourage investment and enterprise in recessions. A liberal credit policy cannot, however, on its own create enterprise and economic growth. The latter depends upon circumstances which go far beyond the confines of monetary and financial policy. When aiming at encouraging economic activity the monetary authorities find they have to collaborate as closely with the financial authorities as they have to in times of over-activity.

In fact, no monetary policy, however brilliant, can succeed on its own. It is always dependent upon the collaboration of the financial authorities as the current and development budgets are usually the most important internal source of changes in the monetary and financial structure of the country. The degree of collaboration, understanding and internal confidence shown by the two authorities for each other's different perspectives and their appreciation of the limits set by the need to maintain a stable internal value of the currency are decisive for the smooth development of the economy of the country.

PART FIVE

CHAPTER XXIII

MODERN AFRICAN DEVELOPMENT PLANS

The fundamental importance of government finances and the manner of their gestation has been clearly revealed by the discussion of monetary instruments and policy. Only if these latter can function in an economy free from the strains and stresses due to the financing of the budget, whether the ordinary or the development budget, can they hope to be efficacious. Then also the major problems arising from the disturbance of the balance of payments due to direct or indirect demand created by government deficits and/or credit creation can be eliminated. Especially in developing countries, without the flexibility available from an important domestic sector, the balance of payments is a true reflection of the combined results of the monetary and financial policy pursued by the authorities.

There is a close connection between the structure of the development plan and the means available to finance it. When the former aims, and aims successfully, at producing a maximum financial return, which also means an optimum of production of resources, the increase in money incomes in the country in question should be at a maximum. The subsequent apportionment of the new income, as well as existing income, between consumption and investment becomes largely an administrative matter. Taxation is probably the major determinant as it is decisive for government income. The government revenue is limited by the taxable capacity of the country. Growth, collection reforms and suitably chosen taxation can materially assist in increasing government revenue. However, as this revenue is limited, it should be used only for the purposes for which there is no alternative coverage. One of the more important limits on the taxable capacity of any country, developed or developing, is the point where taxation results in negative returns on incentive and private savings. As revenue is limited, strict economy and careful dispositions on the ordinary budget are necessary as its absolute size and future growth are limiting factors on the development plan to the extent that the ordinary budget has to carry recurrent expenditures. There is thus a close interdependence between development plan, ordinary budget taxation and the private sector in respect of growth as well as of finance.

DEVELOPMENT PLANS

The aim and purpose of all development plans is, and always has been, specific or general economic growth. By 1960 the latter had become the major aim of all countries and most countries, whether classified as developed or developing, were consciously and deliberately acquiring policies and sometimes plans designed to further economic growth.

The new factor is not really a basic change in the policies of governments, for they had, since the industrial revolution, more or less consciously laid their policies so as to promote economic growth.[1] After World War II, however, a popular demand for the concretization of the idea of economic growth arose and therefore it became one of the main tenets of all political programmes. The aim of economic growth is therefore now common to political parties of all shades from the most conservative to the communist. The big differences in opinion are found, not in the aim, but in the methods by which it is to be attained. While wide variations are still found in the theoretical approach, the solving of concrete cases, the practical policies that can be applied to any given country at any given stage of development, are usually circumscribed by psychological, physical and/or financial realistics which have to be respected. This initial basis of concrete fact gives any viable policy a limited number of possible alternatives and choices. Their number is also reduced by the correct interpretation of experience—made applicable to varying situations by the deductions of theory—if any given aim or set of aims is to be attained.

The main difference between the industrialized countries and those known as developing is that the former already have a basic investment not only in housing, infrastructure and production units but also in a literate and comparatively highly educated population. Mechanical and technical knowledge is widespread and simplifies the retraining necessary to meet the challenge of automation. The concomittant investments are possible as a relatively high rate of savings is normal. Moreover, the social revolution of the twentieth century and the material prosperity of the post-war period has largely eliminated class differences and 'forced savings', whether raised by the government or through creeping inflation do not blatantly increase social differences. However great the change

[1] During the nineteenth century the prevailing ideas in Europe and the United States required from the authorities peace, order—legal, monetary and financial, and as little interference as possible in the workings of the economy so as not to curb or even destroy the initiative and drive which was believed to be the prerequisite for economic growth. The results show that for that time the policy achieved its end.

needed for economic growth in the developed countries, it is not more than an evolution.

The developing countries, on the other hand, need a change of structure which affects every aspect of the economy and social system. They have comparatively little accumulated capital resources geared to the practical necessities of economic growth. Their populations need education and technical and mechanical ability generally has to be acquired by all citizens not only those who work in these branches. The social differences are much more marked than in the industrialized countries and could become more important. This would especially be the case if inflation were to make the rich richer and the poor poorer. The incomes are low, therefore the propensity to consume is high and there is little saving and comparatively low taxable capacity. Some countries seem to have few natural resources, while in others they often still have to be exploited. The amount of capital needed for economic growth under these conditions is potentially enormous. Available resources have therefore to be used with the greatest possible wisdom and they have to be coupled with the technical ability and practical conditions which make them bring the highest possible return in the broadest sense of the term.

The latest African development plans which are all now target plans have paid considerable attention to the fact that resources of all types, financial as well as real and technical, are limited. The manner in which the plans have been drawn up has on the whole shown that there is a realization that only the most careful husbandry of the limited resources is likely to bring about the rate of 4 to 5 per cent growth p.a. which it is believed can both maintain the present standard of living of the growing populations, while allowing a small but sustained increase through time.

The reason for this new perception is that the current plans have the character of a gigantic balance sheet between, on the one hand, the desired real and other assets and, on the other, their financial cost. Even a superficial examination normally revealed a glaring discrepancy between the two accounts in the first draft of the plan. The desired real assets had to be scaled down to somewhere near the amount that could be financed. The exercise in itself was salutary as it brought home the realities of the situation and also stressed the need of distributing the available financial resources between the sectors in such a manner that maximum growth was achieved.

Before full comprehension was reached it was often necessary to explain that there is an intimate connection between the real and the financial balance. In an equilibrium situation (i.e. where savings equal investment) the goods and services available correspond at ruling prices to the available financial assets. No increase in nominal financial assets is capable of increasing the sum total of goods and services. The only result is an, at best, temporary distortion of their distribution. As all the African countries are, moreover, open economies and thus highly dependent on world trade, attempts to increase nominal domestic financial assets would either result in pressure on the balance of payments and an unnecessary running down of foreign exchange or, if effective import control were possible, in an upward pressure of prices on the domestic market. This basic and simple thesis, so familiar to economists, often sounds at first like 'abracadabra' to the uninitiated but is essential both for the successful establishment and the execution of a development plan.

The latest development plans[1] in the six countries of Africa have consisted, either explicitly or implicitly, of four parts:

(1) An inventory of domestically available physical and technical resources, i.e. on the actual situation. It includes a consideration of balance of trade and payments. The assessment is often very difficult as domestic statistics, though improving, still leave much to be desired. The inventory gives the working basis for an aggregate model that, correctly designed and handled, is the key for the whole plan.

(2) A priority plan for the investments. This plan aims at some kind of balance both intersectorially, i.e. between infrastructure, agriculture, industry, education, etc., and within each sector. Moreover, it usually also contains a break-down into private and public sectors.[2] The latter division is unfortunately not always considered necessary. In fact, few governments are able to execute a completely balanced plan. They can, however, usually rely on the private sector to respond to the 'imbalances', especially in certain fields, provided both real and financial assets have been reserved for the private sector.

(3) A plan for financing the investments based on actually available domestic and foreign resources. It normally consists of an inventory of past and current savings, a (conservative) projection of domestic financial resources, both savings and government revenue, becoming available within the years covered by the plan and, usually an optimistic estimate of the foreign capital that will become available. The pleasant assumption that some 50 per cent of the investments will be financed by foreign capital is usually over-

[1] Wolfgang F. Stolper, *Comprehensive Development Planning*. A paper prepared for the Economic Commission for Africa Working Party in Addis Ababa, January 15 to 27, 1962. Professor Stolper was at the time Economic Adviser to the Federal Ministry of Economic Development, Lagos, and in charge of the Economic Planning Unit for the Nigerian Development Plan 1962–68.

[2] In the latest plans the private sector amounts to in Ghana, 1963–68, 42 per cent; Nigeria, 1962–68, 44 per cent; and Sudan, 1961–70, 40 per cent.

optimistic and is only realized for a very few countries and/or projects.

(4) A plan to increase domestically available financial resources. This normally includes the increase of import duties on luxury goods and on manufactures the domestic production of which is recent; the increase of excise on alcohol, tobacco, entertainment, etc.; the introduction of direct taxation on higher income brackets (even PAYE-systems) more with a view to the future than for immediate revenue purposes. Additionally, as discussed above, savings campaigns are included as well as the amplification of the financial intermediaries.

The new attention being paid to the financing of the development plan has emphasized the fact that the major part of the financial resources will have to come from the developing country itself. Thereby new stress has been laid on the need of securing a maximum current income and thereby a maximum of current savings, government revenue and consumption. Current income can, however, only come from productive sectors, essentially agriculture but also industry and they have both been given priority. The new policy is now the tested result of experience as well as conforming to the theories of both the advocates of growth and of financial stability.

The theories of the experts on both financing and on economic growth have thus led to the same conclusion. They both explain that concentration on the most productive sectors are the best guarantee for fast and steady growth. The experts on growth stress the speed of growth, which is obtained by assuring the allocation of existing (physical) resources in such a manner as to assure a maximum increase in their future availability. The financial experts emphasize steady growth which is secured by the smoothest possible financing.

Both have become advocates of the fact that the only criterion for investment is real profitability.[1] Profitability alone maximizes income (output), minimizes costs (input). Thus this criterion must be applied above all to government and semi-government projects. This is not always easy to enforce for the social and political pressures in all countries today tend to weight the plan in favour of

[1] Stolper, loc. cit., p. 9 ff; Jacobsson, loc. cit., *The Market Economy* . . ., pp. 1–18; S. Chakravarty, *The Logic of Investment Planning*, Amsterdam, 1959; Wolfgang Stolper's review thereof in *Weltwirtschaftliches Archiv*, Vol. LXXXV, pp. 69–80; S. Daniel Neumark, 'Economic Development and Economic Incentives', The *South African Journal of Economics*, Vol. 26, No. 1, March 1958, pp. 55–63; R. E. Baldwin, 'Having regard to the low money incomes of Africans and the scarcity of foreign capital for development purposes, what contribution financial and otherwise can Africans make towards the economic development of their countries?' *Nyasaland Economic Symposium*, July 18–28, 1962, esp. pp. 10–12.

either labour intensive projects and/or welfare projects and/or even conspicuous investment. At the same time the fastest possible economic growth is ardently desired. In the private sphere profitability is automatically enforced provided no subsidies or permanent protectionist measures are taken. The latter could consist of non-time-limited import duties, import quotas or even outright import prohibitions. All such measures mean a loss of economic efficiency, and thereby a net physical and financial loss to the country (or region) in question. Naturally, in view of the fact that domestic efficiency often must be increased, time-limited infant industry import duties can be very useful.[1]

That profitability must be properly calculated with the true cost of labour, capital, rent and administration is clear. Some difficult problems often arise in this respect. The technical process chosen is, in a modern economy, often a decisive factor. When the capital intensive process is the more profitable, there is an economic loss if a labour intensive process is favoured for political reasons. The developing countries have at the moment sufficient labour intensive needs, especially in the sphere of agricultural reform, one of the worst bottlenecks, where experts of all types are needed.[2] The cost of the capital employed should be its real cost; capital from foreign grants should be costed, at least, at the normal rate for government loans.[3] In view of the changing structure of the developing country it is sometimes necessary to use shadow prices instead of actual prices.[4]

While it is always possible to calculate the true economic cost of any project,[5] whether infrastructure or productive, it is often very difficult politically to leave aside obvious infrastructure projects. This is doubly the case as they are comparatively easy to plan and

[1] Cp. p. 22.

[2] There is a general problem in most countries of the employment of primary and sometimes secondary school leavers. The basic need to provide employment is recognized in most plans. 'But in the few years ahead industry can't expand fast enough to provide the necessary employment: agriculture is the key, together with the services that might develop for a prosperous agriculture and prosperous farmers' . . . the main hope is to attract 'young men and women from the towns back to improved methods of farming, with living amenities which can compete with urban ones.' *West Africa*, 'They Prefer Soft Jobs', No. 2406, Saturday, July 13, 1963, p. 769.

[3] Cp. p. 233.

[4] E.g., an oil refinery (e.g. Nigeria) or sugar factory (e.g. Sudan) is planned on the basis of the internal production of petrol or cane, still both, however, at pilot plant stage. When available at normal production rate their cost price should fall. This price can be estimated, at least approximately, ahead of time and is of material importance for the costing of the oil refinery or the sugar factory.

[5] This criterion has always been enforced by the World Bank and is also applicable to loans or grants under IDA terms; the easing applies exclusively to the balance of payments aspects.

execute and a new bridge or road, a new ministry or a hospital, is a monument to 'progress'. By the early 1960's, however, the six countries already had at least a minimum equipment of infrastructure. This was due to the work done both before development plans and programmes were considered necessary and by the first of these executed during the late 1940's and throughout the 1950's. It is therefore politically easier now when establishing the plans to concentrate more on the essential productive sectors.

The fundamental need of furthering the productive sectors was strongly stressed in 1963 by the Minister of Finance of Nigeria as follows:

> 'It is quite easy to expend vast sums of money upon projects only to find the economy stagnating or even going backwards if the projects themselves are ill chosen and do not contribute to growth.'[1]

THE EVOLUTION OF DEVELOPMENT PLANS

The current method of overall target planning for a country or region so as to allocate physical and financial resources to its different sectors, including the private sector, is new in Africa. The earlier 'plans' were only partial and referred at first either to an augmented infrastructure programme[2] or to the utilization of foreign loans.[3] Progressively the plans expanded to include agricultural reform and industrialization. They were still, however, glorified government projects, now separated into current and development (capital) budgets.

These plans often had many defects. Especially in the mid and late fifties, there was the danger that the governments, in their desire to achieve the fastest possible growth, should attempt to organize the whole economy. The assumption was that as the governments' own earlier efforts in infrastructure had shown a much more satisfactory rate of realization than those of the private sectors in agri-

[1] Chief Festus S. Okotie-Eboh, Budget Speech, '*The Modernization Budget*', Federal Ministry of Information, Lagos, 1963, p. 38.

[2] For instance, the infrastructure of Morocco, built out during 1949–53, was in direct response to the needs of the country's then booming economic activity.

[3] Northern Nigeria in 1946–48 is a case in point. The Commonwealth Development Corporation gave funds for development. The civil servants then drew up a plan of action based on the locally available materials (raw materials of any kind were at that time very scarce) and aimed at improving the most fundamental needs of the region. Cement was locally available, while starvation three months a year and water-carried worms damaging the population's health were the main problems. The cement was used to build roads, thus securing better distribution of food and other goods both regionally and from the south, and to build cement-lined wells. Thus the health of the population was improved, their working capacity greatly increased and the groundnut crop rose by some 300 per cent in five years.

culture and industry, the governments themselves were better equipped to ensure fast economic growth. However, when the governments attempted agricultural reform and nationalized industry it soon became apparent that their rate of realization of projects was not better, and often worse, than private efforts while the cost involved was nearly prohibitive. The difficulties were due, on the one hand, to the inherent complexity of especially agricultural reform and, on the other, to the weight of administration and the latter's tendency not to pay strict attention to costs. The governments themselves have streamlined and increased their investment plans in the productive sectors. Moreover, the latest development plans respect the private sector in both agriculture and industry and both physical and financial resources are at its disposal. In some countries governments are ceasing to establish new industrial projects or even withdrawing from especially industry while they are devising new means of support for private enterprise such as Development Banks[1] and infant industry taxation and import duty concessions.

The earlier plans, with their emphasis on infrastructure have, however, given most countries a certain equipment of roads, bridges, ports, railways, administrative buildings, hospitals and even schools, colleges and universities. Such investments are evidently not direct producers of income or goods but any country needs a minimum equipment in infrastructure.[2] Now that it is to some extent available a higher proportion of actual expenditure can be used for the valuable productive schemes.

In all countries the structure of planned expenditure has greatly changed as is shown in the examples given in Table XVI. Productive schemes and especially agriculture and irrigation are now considered the most important. Second come industry and related sectors, in countries where unemployment is high (Morocco), construction (also because of its high multiplier effect). Everywhere administration, public utilities are receiving a decreasing proportion of planned expenditure. In some countries this fall in proportion also reflects

[1] Cp. p. 141.

[2] It is a moot point whether less infrastructure and more productive investment at an earlier stage would have speeded the countries' economic growth or whether the indirect benefits from infrastructure at that time were so high that it was the most advisable investment. Most proponents of the former argument forget that the absorption rate of these countries was, for technical reasons, very low and that it was never possible to spend the full financial assets voted even on 'easy' infrastructure projects. (Exception: Morocco, 1949–53, where under general boom conditions, more than twice the planned expenditure was actually invested.) That profitable productive investment was possible at an early stage is, however, shown by the privately mounted Gezira Cotton Scheme in the Sudan and by the also private indigenous cocoa growing in West Africa. Both are of fundamental importance fo the economies of these countries.

TABLE XVI

Government Capital Expenditure in Development Plans

<table>
<tr><th></th><th>Agriculture</th><th>Industry</th><th>Electricity</th><th>Transport and Communications</th><th>Education</th><th>Health</th><th>Other</th></tr>
<tr><td></td><td colspan="7">Percentage distribution</td></tr>
<tr><td>Ghana</td><td></td><td></td><td></td><td></td><td></td><td></td><td></td></tr>
<tr><td>1959–64</td><td>7</td><td>8</td><td>31</td><td>15</td><td>9</td><td>13</td><td>17</td></tr>
<tr><td>Morocco</td><td></td><td></td><td></td><td></td><td></td><td></td><td></td></tr>
<tr><td>1958–59</td><td>35</td><td>4</td><td>2</td><td>15</td><td>10</td><td>3</td><td>31</td></tr>
<tr><td>1960–64</td><td>32</td><td>28</td><td>1</td><td>8</td><td>5</td><td>1</td><td>25</td></tr>
<tr><td>Nigeria (Fed.)</td><td></td><td></td><td></td><td></td><td></td><td></td><td></td></tr>
<tr><td>1955–60</td><td>3</td><td>2</td><td>8</td><td>61</td><td>4</td><td>3</td><td>19</td></tr>
<tr><td>1955–62</td><td>1</td><td>1</td><td>7</td><td>56</td><td>6</td><td>2</td><td>27</td></tr>
<tr><td>1962–68</td><td>12</td><td>16</td><td>15</td><td>26</td><td>10</td><td>3</td><td>18</td></tr>
<tr><td>Rhodesia and Nyasaland (Fed.)</td><td></td><td></td><td></td><td></td><td></td><td></td><td></td></tr>
<tr><td>1957–61</td><td>3</td><td>—</td><td>45</td><td>41</td><td>4</td><td>4</td><td>3</td></tr>
<tr><td>1959–63</td><td>2</td><td>—</td><td>44</td><td>35</td><td>8</td><td>6</td><td>5</td></tr>
<tr><td>Sudan</td><td></td><td></td><td></td><td></td><td></td><td></td><td></td></tr>
<tr><td>1959–61</td><td>39</td><td>2</td><td>2</td><td>36</td><td colspan="2">13</td><td>8</td></tr>
<tr><td>1961–70</td><td>30</td><td colspan="2">15</td><td>22</td><td colspan="2">30</td><td>3</td></tr>
</table>

SOURCE: UN Economic Bulletin for Africa, Vol. I, No. 1, p. 75, and Vol. II, No. 2, p. 22.

Fed. of Nigeria, *Federal Government Development Programme 1962–68*.
Republic of the Sudan, *Economic Report*.
Rudolf Stucken, *Entwicklungsbedingungen und Entwicklungschancen der Republik Sudan*, p. 254.

an absolute decrease.[1] Social services, including both health and education, are often stable or perhaps decreasing. These planned investments are of course only a minor fraction of total expenditure on these items as the recurring expenditure is on the current budget and in many countries is also partly covered by private contributions. Social pressures for improved health and educational facilities are understandable but over-expenditure here will deflect capital from productive schemes and materially retard economic growth.[2]

The realization of the plans has not always been up to standard. This applies both overall and to individual sectors. Even in the execution of the most modern plans 'easy' infrastructure and sometimes health schemes tend to be fulfilled or even over-fulfilled while productive schemes and especially agriculture and to some extent industry are way below their targets. Naturally, in the sectors where the governments have been active longest, the worst technical bottlenecks have now largely been overcome. The main efforts have now to be shifted to the newer and more difficult sectors, sectors where social resistances are likely to be important and where administration has to be flexible, discerning and reassuring.

The rate of realization of plans varies very considerably between countries. Morocco with its double difficulty of surmounting a cyclical depression and stimulating fundamental economic growth is under great strain. The marked lack of intersectorial streams of income further increases the country's problems and some disappointing experiences with large scale industrial government projects have turned interest towards increased efforts to modernize agriculture.[3] With an apparently excellent start Tunisia has had to

[1] Most of the countries now have the houses of parliaments, courts, ministries, etc., that they need. Similarly the basic road network often exists and only feeder roads are now necessary.

[2] The introduction of important social services, especially unemployment benefits and pensions, however admirable in themselves should be deferred as long as possible. They would only mean expenditure on current consumption of government revenue, which is strictly limited owing to low taxable capacity. The working of the 'large family' in Africa still means that real need is rare. The 'voluntary' contributions to family assistance are effected out of that part of income the authorities at present are not able to take in taxes and therefore do not reduce capital for investment purposes in the same way. Their effect on private savings has not been investigated; social customs would probably greatly reduce the probability of a compensatory increase in private savings.

[3] Cp. Gern, loc. cit., 'Morocco and Tunisia on the Threshold of Monetary Autonomy', and F. G. Probst, 'La Planification au Maroc', internal manuscript based on Bremer Ausschuss für Wirtschaftsforschung, *Pläne von Entwicklungsländern*, Darmstadt, 1960; Commissariat Général au Plan, *Deuxième Plan de Modernisation et d'Equipement—Maroc*, Rabat, 1954; Ministère de l'Economie Nationale, *L'Evolution Economique du Maroc dans le cadre du 2ème Plan Quadriennal*, Rabat, 1958; *Plan Biennal d'Equipement* 1958–59, Rabat, 1958; *Plan Quinquennal* 1960–64, Rabat, 1960; and related material.

slow down somewhat and also concentrate on agricultural development.[1] Ghana has revised her plans several times and the latest plan is expected in 1963. The earlier plans were heavily weighted towards infrastructure and education. They were supplemented by a series of measures, state co-operatives and Development Corporations which brought most economic sectors (including commerce and transport) under government control.[2] The new plan is supposed to be more specific while leaving plenty of room for a private sector. The Nigerian Development Plan 1962–68 fulfilled on paper the requirements of modern planning but was, however, probably larger than might comfortably be financed in the six years even if the 50 per cent foreign capital contribution became available and the priorities of the productive sectors were realized.[3] In fact it has proved more difficult to raise foreign capital than envisaged and the priorities have not so far been maintained.[4] The new and very carefully prepared Sudanese Development Plan was published in 1963. It succeeds three development programmes and an interim period during which major projects of the coming plan were initiated and some even completed. The major projects seem to have been sensibly chosen for their context (Managil irrigation scheme, Roseires dam, Sennar hydro-electric power scheme, sugar and textile factories) while the quiet 'routine' development work of the various ministries including the Agricultural and related ministries seems to be proceeding effectively.[5] Considerable foreign financial support has therefore already been attracted.

The reasons for the important differences in performance in different countries are almost impossible to analyse. The plans themselves have seldom been at fault. Essential seems to be the capacity to organize[6] public and private administrative agencies in

[1] Erin E. Jucker-Fleetwood, *Financial Position and Development Projects in Tunisia*, Basle Centre Series A, No. 31, pp. 1–11.

[2] Jucker-Fleetwood, loc. cit., *The Monetary and Financial Position in Ghana and Nigeria* and *Ghana's Budget for* 1961–62, Basle Centre Series A, No. 37, and Taylor, loc. cit, pp. 109–24.

[3] Erin E. Jucker-Fleetwood, *Nigeria's Six-Year Development Plan*, Basle Centre Series A, No. 42, pp. 1–12.

[4] Okotie-Eboh, Modernization Budget, loc. cit., pp. 24–27.

[5] Erin E. Jucker-Fleetwood, *Economic and Financial Aspects of the Republic of the Sudan*, Basle Centre Series A, No. 35, pp. 6–8.

[6] 'Organization aids knowledge; it has many forms, e.g. that of a single business, that of various businesses in the same trade, that of various trades, relatively to one another and that of the State providing security and help for the many.' Alfred Marshall, *The Principles of Economics*, Book IV, 8th edition London, 1925, see p. 115 and pp. 240–313.

In spite of the importance which Marshall gave to organization, he probably underestimated its crucial role in growth and development (which he discusses under the terms: progress and change) because the England of his time was

such a manner that consistent,[1] persistent and effective action is taken until any single project or group of projects is terminated. Constant changes in (detailed) plans and in executive personnel seems to be very detrimental because practically no results are then ever obtained. Insufficient multiplier and accelerator effects are often blamed on lack of initiative. In fact, while most trained persons can expect, sooner or later, to be employed in government administration—which often acts as a glorified anti-unemployment agency—they will not develop entrepreneurial or productive activity. Only absolute necessity will compel even trained persons to take the responsibility and face the work involved in private enterprise and production.

The newest planning technique now used in Africa indicates in which sectors of the economy successful investment is likely to bring the highest return and thereby the fastest economic growth. It is a rational approach which, however, cannot measure the imponderable social and psychological resistances investment and reform in those sectors might encounter. The success of any project will therefore depend mostly on the quality of the executive officers whether public or private. Their professional standard and capacity for leadership is decisive for the success of any single project and its ultimate contribution to the sum total of several projects. By example and encouragement the executive officers can increase the likelihood of productive and remunerative activity permeating the economy. In this way the considered economic and financial plans of the chief executive will also really lead to fast and steady economic growth.

perhaps the best 'organized' country in the world. If his inclusion of organization as a factor of production was justified in that country at that time, how very much more essential is its consideration in the developing countries of the mid-1900, where so many aspects of social and economic life have still to be created. The whole continent having been a latecomer, this applies especially to the African countries. It seems as if experts of many different persuasions are finally realizing that 'organization' is there the main bottleneck; R. E. Baldwin, F. Harbison, P. G. H. Hopkins, B. F. Hoselitz and other speakers at the Nyasaland Economic Symposium, July 18–28, 1962, emphasized this point.

[1] Albert O. Hirschman, *The Strategy of Economic Development*, Yale, 1958 especially pp. 11–28.

CHAPTER XXIV

THE FINANCING OF DEVELOPMENT PLANS

The judicious administration of government finances is all the more necessary as they are limiting factors on the amount of finance available for growth and development. Especially the constantly increasing ordinary budget and the relatively low rate of taxable capacity are barriers against which every minister of finance sooner or later takes up arms.

The ordinary budget in African countries normally reflects the following tendencies:

(1) Increases in direct expenditure due to improved services and facilities such as health, education, animal husbandry and agriculture, etc. These are linked both to the increase in population and to the current amelioration in facilities.

(2) A reflection of the development plan, to the extent that the upkeep and running costs of projects financed by capital outlay falls on the ordinary budget. Examples are the upkeep of the transport system (expansive because of inclement weather conditions) and the running costs of hospitals, universities, etc. There are indications that this reflection averages out at some 25 per cent per annum of the capital outlay.

(3) A deliberate budgeted surplus on current account to use towards the financing of the development budget.

(4) A larger actual surplus on current account than budgeted. This safety factor seems to be disappearing because the technical bottlenecks that prevented budgeted expenditure from being effected are being overcome. The positive difference between the actual and the budgeted surplus is becoming increasingly smaller.

(5) A reflection of the balance of payments. The majority of taxes are indirect and include a high proportion of export and import taxes. The higher the foreign trade turnover, the higher the government's income.

The overall picture is thus one of constantly increasing expenditure on the ordinary budget and various steps have been taken to try to contain it. These measures, which have had varying degrees of success, consist mainly of the following:

(1) Strict attention to maximum economy throughout the administration. This has included attempts at securing maximum efficiency of administrative personnel by training senior, highly qualified persons also in the supervision of subordinates. This should decrease (at least theoretically) the number of subordinates needed while attempts are made to require a higher degree of proficiency throughout the personnel.

(2) Reducing the salaries of senior civil servants and others in government employ to a level appropriate to the structure of the country in question. Formerly these emoluments were patterned on the salaries of expatriate civil servants who needed an inducement to live in tropical climates, were scarce by any standard and, while being few in number, needed to earn at least what they could earn in their home countries. Now that the African civil services have just about been completely Africanized these arguments are all invalidated. The expatriate experts employed for specific jobs have, of course, to be paid at the international level. Usually, however, it is possible to come to some arrangement whereby the difference between the domestic and the world market salary level is borne by a third party.

(3) Choosing for government development investment, including utilities, projects that do not require any current support from the ordinary budget. This is largely an administrative measure. Railways, ports, local transport, post office, electricity, etc., can be economically independent in as much as they should be able to cover their expenses (including amortization and replacement) and, in some cases, show a profit. Under such circumstances they can even raise additional capital for expansion on domestic or even international markets.[1] Thus they additionally relieve the pressure of capital demands made on the government. In order to achieve this economic viability the utilities must be run at maximum efficiency and charge the full economic price of the services they offer. Any subsidy, for, say, supposedly 'welfare' purposes tends to decrease efficiency, increase demand for the utility beyond its economic capacity and results in a less than economic optimum distribution of services. Moreover, it is a burden on the recurring expenditure of the ordinary budget. This applies even more strongly to industrial investments, whether undertaken by the government or private persons that have to be subsidized in any way whatsoever.

(4) Making some charge for medical and general health services and also for education. These items are some of the most important recurring expenditures on the ordinary budget especially as health and education are subject to almost unlimited demand if wholly

[1] The £4,250,000 London placing of the Nigerian Ports Authority in July 1963 is a case in point.

free.[1] Even a small contribution is apt to keep demand within limits and certainly helps to relieve the ordinary budget expenditure.[2] The charges are, moreover, paid out of a part of income which cannot at present be reached by ordinary taxation. Thus they not only contribute to the financial costs over and above what would otherwise be available but can act as a measure to help control monetary demand. There are also indications that the charges are 'incentive creating'. The dream of free health and educational facilities shows considerable idealism; it is unfortunately impractical in most countries at present because of the enormous recurring costs.

These four measures are probably the most important when trying to contain the growth of the ordinary budget as they all tend to secure the maximum output for the minimum cost. From the specific angle of the finance for development purposes, points (3) and (4) are the most important. The weight of recurring charges for the upkeep and running costs of any investment project contemplated may easily make the latter unfeasible. If the recurrent costs can be carried by the project itself the question is eliminated. The containment of the absolute size and rate of growth of expenditure on the ordinary budget, points (1) and (2), will make room for projects which cannot pay for themselves (e.g. upkeep of road system). These measures are necessary in view of the limit set by the taxable capacity of the country as a whole, i.e. to the greater part of government revenue.

The taxable capacity of most developing countries and African countries in particular is at present low. The *per capita* money product as well as the *per capita* Gross National Product is low and its distribution does not make its taxation easier. The administrative problems as well as the cost of collection are high on all but the simplest taxes. It is therefore not surprising that some 15–20 per cent of Gross National Product is considered as the at present highest taxable proportion.[3] The reform of both taxation and collection methods should, however, lead to an increase in what can be raised even in poor countries to some 20 to 25 per cent of Gross National

[1] The retreat from completely free, especially medical care but also education, in the financially mature countries shows that even there the financial burden is too large.

[2] It is possible that preventative medical care should if possible be free and be compensated for by higher charges on other health services. Such a measure need not cause difficult administrative problems as schools, industries, mother and child care centres are easily recognized units. The purpose would be to encourage health. The medium and long term gain, not only financially, would probably be enormous.

[3] Around 1960 government revenue as a percentage of GNP was in Ghana 17 in Morocco 12, in Nigeria 11 and in the Sudan 20.

TABLE XVII

Structure of Central Government Current Revenue

	Ghana 1960–61	*Morocco* 1961	*Nigeria* 1961–62	*Rhodesia* 1961–62	*Sudan* 1960–61	*Tunisia* 1961
			Percentage			
Indirect taxes	55·4	57·9	68·3	24·0	58·7*	74·4*
Direct taxation	10·7	15·0	6·6	41·2	2·8	19·5
'Voluntary Contributions'	13·2	—	—	—	—	—
Other	20·7	27·1	25·1	34·8†	38·5†	6·1
	100·0	100·0	100·0	100·0	100·0	100·0

* Includes revenue from government monopolies.

† High proportion of charges on health and education and profit from government participation in enterprise.

SOURCES:

Ghana: Economic Survey 1962.
Morocco: Bulletin Economique et Social.
Nigeria: Digest of Statistics.
Rhodesia: Digest of Statistics 1961–62.
Sudan: Economic Survey.
Tunisia: Jean-Pierre Gern, 'Morocco and Tunisia on the Threshold of Monetary Autonomy', *Zeitschrift des Instituts für Weltwirtschaft*, Vol. 90, No. 1, 1963. Also in Basle Centre Series A, No. 39.

Product, 'Without producing serious adverse economic effects so long as the government commands the support of the people *and* there is a fairly high ratio of foreign trade to Domestic Product'.[1]

The present composition of government revenue is shown in Table XVII. Noteworthy is the very high proportion obtained from indirect taxes. These are mainly import taxes and excise, export taxes revenue having fallen relatively and sometimes absolutely throughout the 1950's in most countries. The decline has been due partly to lower world market prices for raw materials abroad and partly to no increases in export taxes in order to keep exports as competitive as possible. Import duties on the other hand have been raised very considerably and rates of 33½ to 100 per cent are now common, though capital equipment is usually either exempted or charged at a nominal rate. The three reasons for these increases are revenue, protection of domestic industry and relieving the pressure on the balance of payments. The other major reform is the introduction and/or improvement in the collection of direct personal taxation (as opposed to company taxation which has long existed).[2] The introduction of PAYE systems in Ghana in 1962 and in parts of Nigeria has apparently been a success. Personal taxation should be according to a reasonable progressive scale, in order to secure for the government an increasing proportion of the new money incomes. The cost of collection is often high, but direct personal taxation must be considered more as a measure introduced for its future utility than for the comparatively low present yield.

One of the more difficult problems is the taxation of the very large section of the population which has low incomes. Naturally some part of their purchasing power is taken by indirect taxes but the demand pattern of lower income groups is such that taxed 'luxury' items are a relatively minor proportion of consumption.[3] Charges on health services and educational facilities find here their justification. Moreover, a flat rate personal tax of some kind is often raised,

[1] D. Walker, 'In General Terms what is the Taxable Capacity in an Underdeveloped Country', *Nyasaland Economic Symposium*, July 18–28, 1962, especially p. 24.

[2] P. J. Gill, 'Future Taxation Policy in an Independent East Africa', The *East African Economics Review*, Vol. 9, No. 1, June 1962, pp. 1–15. Nicholas Kaldor, 'Taxation for Economic Development,' The *Journal of Modern African Studies*, 1.1 (1963), pp. 7–23. The introduction of compulsory saving as was introduced in Ghana is discussed as an additional contribution to the levies on income. U Tun Wai, 'Taxation Problems and Policies of Underdeveloped Countries' *IMF Staff Papers*, Vol. IX, No. 3 (November 1962), pp. 428–48.

[3] P. L. P. Davey, 'Household Budgets in Rural Areas', The *Economic Bulletin* (Ghana), Vol. VII, No. 1, 1963, pp. 17–28; P. T. F. Golding, 'An Enquiry into Household Expenditure and Consumption and Sale of Household Produce in Ghana, The *Economic Bulletin* (Ghana), Vol. VI, No. 4, 1962, pp. 11–33.

usually for the benefit of the local, district or regional government.[1] This avoids the difficult question of the assessment of non-monetary wealth, though it is not an unsolvable problem.[2] The necessity of taxing persons whose incomes are lower than the feasible direct personal income tax minimum is necessary both to restrain demand and to secure government, central, regional or local revenue. This in fact means limiting the increase in the standard of living so that part of the growth in money incomes is directed towards saving and investment. Economic growth will probably mean the creation of many jobs paid at fairly low rates and this new purchasing power cannot be left untapped. Evidently the taxation of low incomes cannot be too rigorous. This would be disincentive and could materially affect the development of the shadowy sector between the traditional and the modern, a sector from which many growth impulses spring.

The size of local and regional budget varies considerably, so do the objects for which these administrations are competent. In Nigeria, with its highly autonomous Regions, these budgets are very large and important. Here, as in other countries, part of the centrally collected revenue is distributed according to a more or less complicated formula. The claim of Regions to, say, that part of revenue raised on the export of its produce seems justified. On the other hand, if the revenue from personal taxes, fines, etc., which largely fall to the local and district administrations, could be raised so that their expenditure were fully covered by this type of taxation, the central government would have more funds available. Due to the very important differences in local population, wealth and needs it is impossible to establish generally such a system. The poorer districts will always need some additional support. The more local units, however, that can balance their budgets without assistance from the central government, the easier the latter's position.

The principle that the current budgets of the governments are fully covered by current income has been adhered to both in theory and largely also in practice. The current budget, moreover, normally produces a surplus, a surplus which is credited to the development budget for investment purposes. On the occasions when it has not been possible to achieve a surplus, the position has quickly been remedied

[1] Hajo Lohrmann, 'Local Finance in Africa', unpublished internal Basle Centre manuscript; G. Oka Orewa, Taxation in Western Nigeria, *Nigerian Social and Economic Studies*, No. 4, Oxford, 1962; N. A. Cox-George, *Finance and Development in West Africa—The Sierra Leone Experience*, London, 1961; I. D. Cameron and B. K. Cooper, *The West African Councillor*, Oxford, 1961.

[2] Ursula Hicks, loc. cit., especially pp. 321–67. 'In underdeveloped conditions taxes can often more easily be assessed and collected locally', p. 277. In a speech at Basle University on June 10, 1959, Professor Hicks stressed the point that one must show people that taxes pay for something *they* want locally.

either by a decrease in government development expenditure (the Sudan 1957–58 and 1958–59) or by an increase of taxation (Ghana 1960–61). The surplus on the current budget represents current savings for investment and is one of the important and one of the safest means of financing the development budget.

DOMESTIC FINANCING

Not merely the economic but also the political and social future of a country and its government depends upon the manner in which the domestic financing of the development plan is assured. When it is so smooth that it is almost imperceptible in the general economic picture, the constructive efforts of individuals and institutions, whether governmental or private, can come to fruition. On the other hand, any measures that add financial and thereby economic disturbances to the already profound revolution involved in growth and development increase social and political instability and also retard economic growth.[1] The increasing attention being paid by the authorities to the means of financing the plans is, therefore, one of the fundamental prerequisites for fast and steady growth.

That the major part of practically all the development plans of developing countries have to be financed out of domestic resources is gradually becoming clear. The assumption that 50 per cent of the total costs can be obtained from abroad remains a hypothesis for even the most creditworthy borrowing countries. Obtaining foreign capital for one third of the total costs seems to be a much more realistic proposition. This leaves some 66 per cent to be financed from domestic sources. As most development plans are ambitious and therefore large in relation to the resources, both real and financial, of the country in question a very considerable effort is required to assure smooth domestic financing.

Domestic financial resources available for financing a development plan are:

I '*Savings*' *out of current income*

(1) Surplus carried over from the government's ordinary (recurrent) budget; its size depends on both government revenue and the containment of the ordinary budget.[2]

[1] The literature is voluminous. Some outstanding contributions are: Graeme S. Dorrance, *The Effect of Inflation on Economic Development*, IMF Staff Papers, Vol. X, No. 1, March 1963, pp. 1–47. *Monthly Review*, Federal Reserve Bank of New York; 'Creeping Inflation', Vol. 41, No. 6, p. 86, and 'Inflation and Economic Development,' Vol. 41, No. 8, pp. 122—7.

[2] See discussion in UN *Economic Bulletin for Africa*, Vol. 1, No. 2, Chapter 1: Public Finance in African countries, pp. 1–28, esp. p. 10. Addis Ababa, June 1961.

(2) Internal borrowing out of current income; both the total size of the money income and its distribution will materially affect the propensity to save. So will the variety and suitability of the instruments of saving.

(3) Current expected income of Marketing Boards and/or Statutory Corporations and/or their counterparts. These have to be run with a maximum efficiency in order to produce current income. In the case of the Marketing Boards and their counterparts it is the world market price of export commodities that is decisive for the internal producer price cannot be decreased below a certain (perhaps variable) psychological minimum.

II *Past savings*

(1) Mobilization of domestically owned foreign exchange reserves. This has been the classical means of financing development throughout the 1950's. Most African countries had acquired sizeable foreign reserves in the immediate post-war years and they have been using these assets to finance their economic development. These reserves have now largely been used up and the remainder is seldom much more than a comfortable working balance. However, some small part of these reserves might still be mobilized; especially as the African countries seldom have as yet important foreign indebtedness.

(2) Government reserve funds and, in some countries, Marketing Boards reserve funds. Government reserve funds, mainly the carry-over of unspent appropriations, is disappearing as the technical bottlenecks are being overcome. Marketing Boards' reserve funds were supposed to be available for domestic price stabilization if the world market price dropped below the internal producer price. Marketing Boards are, therefore, often reluctant to commit their reserves for development purposes; however, the idea of domestic price stabilization has been abandoned for the present.

'Savings' out of current income are the safest and smoothest means of financing the development plan. Every effort should be made to maximize them. As already discussed above, the manner in which the development plan has been established will contribute materially not only to the economic growth of the country but also to the growth of the financial assets of the country. The higher the proportion of productive, truly profitable schemes the greater the current money income produced. Then both government revenue and private saving[1] will tend towards a maximum. To further promote both special measures have to be taken, but they should be well within the capacity of developing countries.

[1] Cp. p. 165.

The mobilization of past savings is not a 'neutral' monetary measure. From the domestic point of view these funds have in fact been hoarded and their utilization may bring about latent inflationary pressures. This applies especially to domestic past savings used for local expenditure. The direction taken by the new demand generated is decisive for its effect. If a large part is turned towards easily available domestic produce (especially food) the effect will be slight. It is probable, however, that a part, and possibly a larger part, of the new demand will be turned towards foreign goods and reflect in the balance of payments. (This is especially the case as past savings are likely to be used during the first few years of the operation of the plan and before industry for the domestic market has reached the production stage.) The import of a corresponding amount of foreign goods—to maintain domestic price stability—is then usually unavoidable. Naturally, the mobilization of foreign reserves for the import of capital goods from abroad will have no effect. But the accumulated foreign reserves and the past savings are two sides of the same coin; the use of the foreign reserves for imports of capital goods to finance the plan may not leave enough free foreign exchange to meet the indirect demand for imported goods engendered by the use of past domestic savings for development purposes. How far such a policy can be pursued with impunity is one of the difficult assessments the Central Bank has to make in order to be able to advise the Minister of Finance. There are no rigid rules; the domestic economic structure and the intangibles of the reaction of the population will vary from country to country.

The pressure exerted by the need to finance domestically a large part of an ambitious development plan has caused most developing countries to consider the possibility of domestic credit creation. Of the two possible sources, commercial banks and central bank, the latter has been the most discussed. Briefly it is argued that the backing for the liabilities (including currency) of say 80 per cent ties up capital which could usefully be used to finance the development plan. The creation of a fiduciary issue, by the specific means of the central bank taking over government bonds, is the means by which this financing should be effected. All the dangers[1] of the inflationary effect of such a policy are often disregarded. So is also the fact that an increase in the reserves of the developing countries is unlikely within reasonable time and that the absolute amount of reserves at 80 per cent today will unchanged probably be only 40 per cent in a very few years especially if anything like the economic development envisaged is achieved. The probable balance of payments pressures during and after the plan period are optimistically assessed at a minimum; the fact that the latter in open economics tends to reflect

[1] Cp. p. 27 for fuller discussion.

all the many smaller but cumulative disequilibria of a high pressure economy is conveniently overlooked.

In fact there should not really be the need to use central bank credit. The fiduciary issue can be created by commercial bills, etc., while the central bank is free to acquire government bonds when the monetary situation warrants such a step. The smaller amounts of credit—mainly prefinancing needed for the development plan and compatible with the monetary equilibrium—can be obtained from the commercial banking system.[1] This is much less inflationary than central bank credit. The proviso is that the commercial banking system should not be swamped by government paper; it should still be in a position to advance credit freely to the private sector and semi-official institutions.

Moreover, the credits that could be advanced by a central bank are relatively small compared to the total size of the plans. The amounts foreseen are usually 2–8 per cent of the government part of the plan and are well within the probable shifts in both the phasing and the timing of the execution of the plan. Technical and other bottlenecks—especially in the new sectors being developed—are likely to retard the execution of most plans and their completion may easily take a couple of years longer than foreseen. This will ease the financing of the plan as the extra two years' worth of current income can then supply the missing millions. Therefore, recourse to central bank credit for financing the development plan should be the last type of financing used—and, in fact, it will probably be found that it is not necessary.

The continued availability at the central bank of the 2–8 per cent of the government part of the plan in foreign exchange would give an enviable measure of security and flexibility. Unforeseen developments reacting on the balance of trade and payments can be handled without them leading to a complicated situation. This small amount has at the central bank a utility out of all proportion to its size. It is a safety margin[2] which can obviate recourse to many difficult and unpleasant scrapings of the bottom of the purse while, when it is used internally, it is liable to be explosive.

The importance of the manner in which the domestic financing of the new plans is assured is perhaps only realized when their actual size is studied. As Table XVIII shows the newest plans foresee expenditure of 15–20 per cent of the GNP per annum, compared to

[1] Cp. p. 136.

[2] 'The larger the international reserves in relation to the domestic money supply the less the probability that the profit or utility-maximizing decisions of individuals to move out of cash into commodities or securities will have to be frustrated by the monetary authorities for fear of a balance-of-payments crisis.' Harry G. Johnson, 'Towards a General Theory of the Balance of Payments' in *International Trade and Economic Growth*, London, 1961, p. 157.

3–9 per cent previously.[1] The impact of such massive expenditure will be very far reaching. The former large foreign exchange reserves assured an easy financing of earlier plans with a minimum of disturbance. In spite of the then available resources, prices were rising slightly. With large scale financing now becoming a real problem maximum attention and care should be given so as to maintain the stability of the domestic price level and avoid unnecessary balance of payments disequilibria.

TABLE XVIII

Size of Development Plans

	Total Expenditure	Average Annual	% of GNP at outset of Plan
Ghana: £G million			
1951–57 . .	93·3	15·6	—
1957–59 . .	42·7	21·4	5·9
1959–64* . .	350·0‡	70·0	16·2
1963–68 . .	841·0‡	168·2	(*ca.* 34·0)
Morocco: FM milliard			
1949–53 . .	255·0	51·0	—
1954–57 . .	226·7‡	56·7	9·1
1958–59 . .	89·5‡	44·7	5·6
1960–64 . .	660·0‡	132·0	15·3
Nigeria: £N million			
1946–55 . .	56·0	5·6	—
1956–62 . .	146·3‡	24·4	2·7
1962–68 . .	676·5‡	56·4	(*ca.* 6·0)
Sudan: £S million			
1946–51 . .	14·6	2·9	—
1951–56 . .	45·5	9·1	—
1957–60 . .	41·9†	10·5	3·5§
1961–71 . .	565·4‡	56·5	16·7§

* Not completed.
† Includes expenditure on Managil extension.
‡ Planned expenditure.
§ Of GNP at constant prices.

SOURCES: Same as Tables XVI and XVII.

Successful efforts on the part of the monetary and financial authorities to assure a smooth domestic financing of the development plan will automatically increase the international credit standing of the country. Then more foreign capital is likely to be attracted

[1] It has only been possible to compare average annual expenditure with the GNP at the year of the start of the plan. Naturally, the proportions will vary through time, making actual expenditure probably slightly less than shown here.

than if the foreign creditors and donators, whether public or private, are not satisfied with the future financial stability of the country. Relatively easy access to foreign loans and grants means easier financing of the plan as well as foreign reserves sufficient to cover the requirements of the balance of payments.

FOREIGN BORROWING

The developing countries are nearly all dependent upon imports of foreign capital in order to be able to assure the full financing of the new and often ambitious development plans. The African countries hope for very important contributions and have allowed for these when making their plans.[1] However, they are finding it difficult to raise these amounts abroad. The main reason is that compared to the demand for it, foreign capital is a scarce commodity.

The latest plans foresee a very considerable amount of foreign financing. This is partly due to the fact that the plans have to be drawn up in order to secure the foreign financing while the size of the latter materially affects the plans. Naturally, the drafters often hoped for a maximum in each individual case.[2] The 1962–68 Nigerian plan foresees 'assumed' foreign capital aid at £N338·8 million calculated at 50 per cent of planned capital expenditure. The Sudanese plan 1961–62/1970–71 foresees total net foreign borrowing at £S143·5 million of which £S26·4 million is for the private sector and £S117·1 million for the public sector. The latter has foreign repayments of £S54·1 million to effect during the period, an amount which, it is hoped, can also be raised abroad which would raise foreign gross borrowing to £S197·6 million. Thus, foreign net borrowing would amount to 25 per cent and foreign gross borrowing to 35 per cent of total planned investment. The new plan in Ghana, still not finally approved, foresees foreign borrowing totalling £G370 million of which £G250 for the public sector and £G120 million for the private sector amounting to 44 per cent of total planned investment. The plans for the Rhodesias and Nyasaland have at least some £35 million or 25 per cent of the total still to be raised. While some part may be covered by the private domestic sector a larger part should be found abroad. Whether this will be possible in view of the country's political situation remains to be seen.

These four countries alone are thus hoping for disbursements of some £162 million annually in the years 1963–65. This amount of £162 million corresponds exactly to the total amount of aid given by

[1] *Economic Bulletin for Africa*, loc. cit., Vol. II No. 2 Chap. III, 'Economic Planning in Africa', Section V, Financing of Development Plans, pp. 39–43.

[2] No co-ordination of the amount of foreign capital becoming available and the expected demand for it exists.

Great Britain in 1961 to all developing countries. There are, moreover, many other African countries competing for foreign capital whether public or private. Further, £162 million is some 6 per cent of the total contributions by the OECD countries and Japan to underdeveloped countries and multilateral agencies in 1960[1] and Africa is not the only continent that needs foreign capital. It is thus extremely unlikely that these enormous sums can be made available even with the maximum goodwill and effort on the part of the rest of the world.

As these developing countries are thus competing for an extremely scarce commodity it is necessary for them to pay maximum attention to acquiring and maintaining the highest possible credit standing. This includes a large variety of factors, the main among them being:

(1) Domestic political stability.

(2) Legal systems which guarantee the right of ownership and free disposal of capital and income and fast redress in the courts if necessary.

(3) A monetary and financial policy that assures internal price stability, external equilibrium on the balance of payments and steady and fast economic growth.

(4) The exact fulfilment of international financial obligations.

(5) A minimum of administrative red tape; this applies both to the procedure of establishing a new plant or enterprise and to current operations after establishment.

(6) Pioneer status, etc., for new industries and enterprises. While these concessions are probably less important than normally believed they are universally in fashion and possibly affect a country's competitive position.

These points are all, except possibly number (6), of basic importance to the credit standing of the individual country. No amount of lip service can replace the actual existence of these conditions. Moreover, even the most sincere personal assurances of the Ministers of Finance or the most emphatic statements by Heads of State carry little weight when it is known that a section of the politicians of the country have other ideas. Even adherence to international agreements on the treatment of foreign capital—if they existed—would be of no assistance if a change of government in the country in question were likely to see their repudiation.

Evidently, the real factors such as the size of the population, its standard of education especially in technical spheres, diversified natural resources and exports, the speed of economic growth and the

[1] Organization for Economic Co-operation and Development, *The Flow of Financial Resources to Countries in the Course of Economic Development in* 1960, Paris 1962, p. 10.

potential growth of the domestic market are factors also taken into consideration when assessing a country's credit standing. These factors vary from country to country and place certain countries in a more favourable position. Good policies, however, can largely compensate for initial handicaps (e.g. the Sudan), while unsuccessful policies can jeopardize the most promising prospects.

Important also is the degree of economic growth already achieved. When basic infrastructure is available and manufacturing industries have a certain importance, sectorial self-sustaining growth appears to be possible, because these sectors become more attractive to private foreign capital. Before this stage is reached, countries are more dependent upon official foreign capital, whether loans or grants. Hitherto this has largely been the case in Africa and, except for certain individual countries and sectors, it will probably be some years before private capital is attracted in larger amounts to African countries.

If a developing country is considered creditworthy its opportunity of obtaining foreign financing is today considerably better than ever before. There has been a fundamental change in the approach to the financing of economic development and by the early 1960's not only had the amounts of aid become massive, but there had been a change in its type and form.[1] The terms on which development finance can be obtained have also been modified and, on the whole, rendered more favourable to the borrowing country.

There has generally been a lengthening of the repayment periods and loans can now often be given for twenty–thirty years by governments and up to fifty years by international institutions, notably the International Development Agency (IDA). Periods of grace before repayment starts vary but are often five–ten years. This new flexibility allows the structure of the loans taken up by any country to be adjusted in such a way that repayment is spread over many years, and that it is timed to coincide with the period when the country presumably has attained a certain degree of self-sustaining growth.

The variety of loans that can be obtained has also greatly increased. Numerous institutions and agencies for giving credits of all kinds have recently been established. Some are wholly official, some have been due to private efforts while many others are semi-official in that they receive assistance and support of some sort from the governments of their countries. They range from the financing (and sometimes administration) of technical aid,[2] through the insuring

[1] Antonin Basch, *The Future of Foreign Lending for Development*, Research Centre on Economic Development, University of Michigan, Ann Arbour, Michigan, March 1962, p. 44.

[2] For example, Switzerland opened a credit line in June 1961 of about $14 million for technical co-operation with developing countries.

and/or raising of short, medium and long term loans, to full-scale lending at official level by national institutions. Many of these latter are able to give grants as well as loans or loans on terms that are adjusted to the balance of payments problems of the developing countries.[1]

The most notable advance was the establishment in 1960 of IDA, a subsidiary of the World Bank. The IDA loan terms were tailored to meet the needs of 'countries whose balance of payments prospects would not justify their incurring, or continuing to incur, external debt entirely on conventional terms.'[2] The loans are made to governments for fifty years free of interest. Repayments start in the eleventh year at 1 per cent annually and increase in the twenty-first year to 3 per cent p.a. A service charge of three-quarters of 1 per cent per annum is made on amounts withdrawn and outstanding. The concessions are, however, only in respect of the balance of payments and do not affect requirement of high economic viability of the project for which finance is being supplied. These latter criteria are as strict as those of the World Bank.[3] These IDA-terms have become a pattern and have helped national institutions to be more liberal.

The efforts of governments and notably of the international institutions, headed by the International Bank for Reconstruction and Development, the Organization for Economic Co-operation and Development and, in some instances, of the United Nations, have led to a somewhat greater cohesion in the granting of long term loans. Especially the formation of consortia for the financing of certain countries and/or projects is one of the more promising. It has the outstanding advantage of assuring the collaboration of the commercial banks of the industrialized countries and thereby taps extra funds which might not otherwise be available for development aid. The private sector can contribute important amounts and, in fact, without its assistance, even the United States will be short of such capital. 'It is becoming clearer every day that there will not be enough capital for any substantial development whether in Latin America or elsewhere, unless private enterprise is given a chance to contribute all it can.'[4]

[1] For example, the US Agricultural Trade Development and Assistance Act, known as PL 480, under which surplus agricultural commodities are put at the disposal of the receiving country against repayment in local currencies. These counterpart funds are then used for US local disbursements including certain development expenditure especially for technical and educational purposes.

[2] International Development Association, *Annual Report* 1961–62, Washington 1962, p. 6.

[3] Thus the countries hoping to obtain financial assistance from IDA for non-profitable, non-strategic and/or not high priority projects will almost certainly be disappointed.

[4] 'Cleaning up the Foreign Aid Program', editorial, *Business Week*, New York, December 8, 1962, p. 140.

In order to encourage the flow of private capital, of the talents and energies of the private sectors towards the financing and development of the under-developed countries, the World Bank is going to establish a conciliation and arbitration centre. This is due to the belief that those countries 'who adopt as their national policy a welcome for international investment—and that means, to mince no words about it, giving foreign investors a fair opportunity to make attractive profits—will achieve their development objectives more rapidly than those who do not. For a country which is known to be hospitable to private investment will have access over the years to a much larger and more stable pool of capital than its neighbour which relies solely on government-to-government aid. It will have access, too, to a much larger pool of industrial personnel—managerial, administrative and technical—and to a much larger mass of scientific and technological information than it could possibly acquire in any other way. Most important of all, its economy will be stimulated and invigorated by the many different contacts, at many different levels, which a hospitable investment climate will make possible between enterprises and individuals within its own borders and those within the borders of the industrialized countries. None of these advantages is likely to be fully available to any nation whose government, however well motivated and however well administered, decides to relegate the private sector to a subordinate role.'[1]

The total of the efforts made have increased the disbursements of international finance for development purposes from the OECD countries and Japan from an average of \$3·500 million in the early 1950's to \$8·000 million in 1960;[2] of this total \$1·481 million or 18·5 per cent was in grants. That year the Eastern countries committed development aid to the amount of \$1·200 million. This total is committed, but disbursements, however, have lagged behind and were apparently only \$178 million in 1960.[3] Only 5 per cent of the total was given as grants. The normal terms for Russian loans are twelve years at 2½ per cent interest rate. Larger projects have had special terms. Interest rates are usually paid according to an export plan of the borrowing country at fixed prices. Sometimes, and especially in respect to the European Eastern block countries, the arrangements include commercial agreements. Though the Eastern countries earmark the capital they give for development aid according to a system other than the Western industrialized countries and

[1] George D. Woods, President of the World Bank, IFC and IDA, Address to the Boards, Washington, September 30, 1963, roneographed text pp. 10–11.

[2] OECD, loc. cit., p. 12.

[3] This includes the international institutions apart from the International Monetary Fund.

Japan, they appear to have serious difficulties in increasing the flow of actual disbursements.

The African countries have profited more than proportionately from the increase in aid. The USA increased its aid to Africa from $200 million in 1961–62 to $400 million in 1962–63, while Great Britain diverted thither in 1961 £87 million compared to £48 million the previous year. The Eastern block countries increased their aid to Africa from almost nil in 1958 to around $320 million commitments in 1961.[1] Of this amount $110 million went to Guinea and $120 million to Ethiopia (the UAR loans have been excluded). However, only a fraction has actually been disbursed.[2] France has always contributed the bulk of its finance for development to Africa and the total had increased again in 1960. Additionally, Africa has a source of finance of its own in the Kuwait Aid-Programme to Neighbouring Area.[3] One of the beneficiaries has been the Sudan, which obtained £7 million loan in 1962. The decision of 1963 to establish an African Development Bank should probably also lead, in the long run, to the supply of more funds for Africa.[4]

The major limiting factor on the terms of international lending is the increasing practice of only giving tied loans and grants, i.e. of stipulating that they must be spent in the lending country. Frequently, finance could only be obtained in a country where the price and cost level was higher than in other countries producing similar goods. There has been much dissatisfaction on this point because the higher costs often considerably reduce the value of the loan. However, two new trends are making the tying of loans less onerous. Firstly, the new upsurge in lending means that most industrial countries are prepared to give loans, especially for the purchase of commodities manufactured in their own country. Thus finance can be obtained in almost any of the countries from which the developing countries might want to buy. Secondly, the movement of prices and costs (especially wages) has been such that the important differentials formerly existing between the Western industrial

[1] G. V. Doxey, 'Economic Aid in Soviet Foreign Policy', *The Banker*, Vol. CXII, No. 440, October 1962, pp. 639–45. This is a well balanced and objective account of the various aspects of a difficult problem.

[2] Most African countries have obtained Eastern block financial aid. The larger loans have been restricted to certain set projects, e.g. Assuan Dam. However, smaller credits have been distributed throughout the continent, mostly cemented with trade agreements. The often surplus raw materials of the African countries are then used (at fixed prices) in payment for certain financial and technical help and assistance. Morocco, Tunisia, Ghana and the Sudan and Nigeria have all received such help. Especially in the case of the first four countries a 'balance' of some kind is sought in the sources of foreign aid.

[3] Release by Embassy of Kuwait, Washington.

[4] The World Bank alone had contributed around $885 million to Africa by June 1963. IFS.

countries have largely been attenuated. Thus, even when the tying of loans means having to buy in a more expensive market, the loss is much less than it was even three years ago.

However, the tying of loans is a practice that should not really be necessary as any lending country gains from the increase in international trade and activity thanks to the working of the multilateral trading system.[1]

The new terms, conditions and types of finance available for developing countries, have greatly mitigated one of the most serious problems, namely the weight of servicing debt taken on conventional terms.[2] By the end of the 1950's it was realized that at the rate at which loans were being taken up this burden was becoming too heavy, even when the projects being financed were fully economic.[3] It was suggested that not more than 10 per cent of the value of exports should have to be used for debt service and this has become a rule of thumb when drafting development plans.

The foreign indebtedness of the six African countries at the start of the latest plans was relatively small in comparison to other developing countries. Morocco and Tunisia have largely profited from the system of grants. The French contributed in the years 1954–58 95 per cent of total development expenditure as grants not only to these countries but to all French African Territories and Madagascar.[4] On these two countries' independence the Americans gave important contributions mainly on a grant basis. Ghana and Nigeria had used as development finance their own foreign reserves accumulated in the late 1940's and early 1950's. Their main source of external funds was Great Britain and these consisted mostly of grants and technical assistance and only in quite minor amounts of loans.[5] The Sudan had official commitments outstanding, £S19·7 million on December 31, 1961,[6] as well as certain debts on private account, but nothing that would impede borrowing on conventional

[1] See for instance, Wilfried Guth, *Capital Exports to Less Developed Countries*, Dordrecht 1963, pp. 46–52.

[2] International institutions normally lend at a minimum of 3½ per cent plus service charge. The rates of national official agencies are either according to their own market rate or around 4–7 per cent, with the exception of Italy (3–7 per cent) and France (0·5–5·8 per cent) where foreign lending is well below the market rates. OECD, loc. cit., p. 16.

[3] D. Avramovic and R. Gulhati (of the IBRD), *Debt Servicing Problems of Low Income Countries* 1956–58. Baltimore 1960, especially p. 59; and UN, *International Flow of Long Term Capital and Official Donations* 1951–59, New York 1961, p. 32; Net servicing and dividend payments in African countries as a percentage of exports was 9·9 in 1951–55 and 11·0 in 1956–59.

[4] UN, *Economic Survey of Africa since* 1950, New York 1959, p. 246.

[5] *Assistance from the United Kingdom for Overseas Development*, Cmnd. 974, March 1960.

[6] Bank of Sudan, *Annual Report* 1961, Khartoum, 1962, p. 36.

terms. Rhodesia and Nyasaland alone had a more important foreign debt; in 1962 it amounted on official account to £152·1 million,[1] while private enterprises also were indebted abroad.

It is the servicing of the borrowing for the new plans that will put a strain on the balances of payments. The Sudan probably has the most assured position. Loans from foreign governments and institutions in hand on December 31, 1962, amounted to £S34 million, while total debt was £S22·5 million. Unused American grants totalled £S16·9, while £S15 million had already been drawn.[2] Certain important private loans and credits had also been secured. Additional support was promised in 1963 including £S6 million (grant) from the USA under PL 480 and a loan of £5 million from Great Britain towards the development plan. Thus the Sudan has nearly half the foreign net funds it desired under its ten-year plan. The other countries have not succeeded in obtaining anything like the total of the loans they desired. However, foreign capital has become available for certain projects of high priority (e.g. the Volta Dam project in Ghana) or outstanding merit (e.g. the £4·2 million to the Nigerian Ports Authority raised on the London market) or for special needs (e.g. the IBRD and IFC loan of US $16·5 million to the Banque Nationale pour le Développement Economique of Morocco).

As the full amount of foreign finance needed for the development has not yet been obtained, it becomes very important that no project, which is wholly or partly to be financed by long term foreign capital, is started before this project's foreign capital really is available. Otherwise the foreign component (which almost invariably corresponds to offshore purchases) becomes financed at first by foreign short term credit which then must be met from the existing foreign reserves. These have usually been earmarked for specific purposes and are anyway on the low side in most countries, so that an 'unplanned' expenditure of them reduces the operational freedom of the country. Therefore, it is necessary to secure the foreign long and medium term loans and grants that are desired *ahead* of their expenditure. The tendency to disregard the basic difference between long term foreign borrowing for investment purposes and foreign short term credits for commercial purposes can have marked effects on both the balance of payments position and domestic monetary stability.

The domestic monetary disequilibrating effects are likely to arise in the demand for credit creation to make up the failing foreign funds. Evidently, a certain amount of prefinancing from the commercial banks can be justified. But anything that goes beyond the

[1] Central Statistical Office, *Monthly Digest of Statistics*, Salisbury.
[2] Bank of Sudan, *Annual Report* 1962, Khartoum 1963, pp. 40, 42.

bounds of the more immediate savings capacity of the country is likely to upset domestic equilibrium. This is especially the case if the credit has come from the central bank. The measures to re-establish balance will then have to verge on austerity.

When a country is unable to obtain the amount of foreign financing it desires and an increase in domestic financial resources does not compensate for this lack, the prolongation of the plan by a couple of years is the only solution. The additional current income should ease the financial problem. The fact, however, that financing is the reverse side of the same medal with real factors on the other, means that lack of finance will usually reflect lack of real resources. The latter are the basic reasons why the plan cannot be terminated in the time foreseen. As the new plans are mainly seen as target plans, subject to frequent revisions and with at least theoretical built-in flexibility a prolongation of the plan, the scrapping of marginal projects or, if the financial and technical position is good, the addition of desirable projects are all practical possibilities which have been envisaged from the start.

CHAPTER XXV

THE BALANCE OF PAYMENTS

The modern theory of international trade and payments establishes the balance of trade and payments of any country as the result of the sum total of all transactions between all residents and all non-residents. This approach, which is largely but not only based upon the work of the national accounting experts, has the outstanding advantage that it puts monetary and financial policy into the centre of the picture. The contrast is sharp to former approaches where the balance of trade and even payments were seen either as the result of the movement of real goods which could with impunity be limited at will or as the result of *net* domestic monetary transactions. In the first case monetary and financial considerations were mainly excluded, while in the second they were accorded by many an auxiliary role grafted on to the main body of theory by some of the more obvious links. The modern theory recognizes the great practical and policy making importance of money and finance.

The new global approach to the balance of payments reinstates in their central position such factors as the active volume of money and credit and the movements of prices and wages. Their analysis reaffirms the value of the parameters used in a 'net' approach, namely changes in the holding of liquid funds, i.e. velocity, and the creation of credit *provided* they are not compensated by changes in real factors. These latter are essentially the reserves that can be obtained from an economy below the full employment level, from inventories and from the leeway provided by an increase in productivity.[1]

These apparently simple theses translate into very complex actual situations, each country and each group of countries having its own peculiarities. The developing countries, and those of Africa in particular, have their own specific characteristics which, within the general framework, need special attention.

These African countries are all open economies, dependent—as was shown in Table II on p. 42—upon both exports and imports to an unusually high degree.

[1] Gottfried Bombach, 'Quantitative und monetäre Aspekte des Wirtschaftswachstums,' in *Finanz und währungspolitische Bedingungen stetigen Wirtschaftswachstums*, Schriften des Vereins für Socialpolitik, Neue Folge, Bd. 15. Duncker & Humblot, Berlin 1959, especially pp. 191–218. Also available in Basle Centre Series A. No 24.

With the exception of Nigeria, which has a differentiated structure of exports, half or more of the exports consist of one product, or one group of products. Typical for these countries is that there is almost no internal demand for the export products.[1] Short term increase in domestic demand is therefore not likely directly to decrease the quantity of goods available for export. Such a decrease is only likely if the propensity to work is decreased by greater prosperity. This is one of the major differences from industrialized countries and is only likely to disappear when the African countries export manufactures (or raw materials in short supply) which have both a domestic and a foreign market.

The exports are mainly raw materials which have seen falling world market prices from the Korea crisis to 1962 when prices stabilized and even rose slightly. The African countries have on the whole succeeded in maintaining their foreign income in spite of the fall in world market prices through an increase in the quantities sold.[2] Various attempts[3] have been made to discover the cause of the fluctuations of raw material prices and to attempt their stabilization, but without much success. All price stabilizing measures depend finally on a control of production. This is comparatively easy for extractive industries (e.g. tin in Nigeria), but almost impossible where weather, rainfall, pest, etc., cause fluctuations in the harvests. Evidently, if the world *per capita* consumption of raw materials were the same or even half that of the industrialized countries, there would be a very serious shortage of raw materials of all kinds. Thus economic growth and development will help the developing countries themselves.

The essence of the problem of the fluctuations of raw material prices is not really their price stability. The fluctuations in prices are often a useful indication of the world demand for the product and should induce corresponding changes in production so that an over-supply is avoided. The developing countries themselves can only gain by such an adjustment, which will prevent them from having increasingly unfavourable terms of trade. The developing countries have, however, a legitimate claim that they should be protected against sudden changes in world market prices. A first approach was the study of a complicated insurance scheme sponsored by the United Nations with the assistance of several technical experts.[4] The International Monetary Fund, which had been suggested as a suitable forum, was able, as it had the necessary resources,

[1] Major exception: vegetable and palm oil, as the standard of living rises.

[2] General Agreement on Tariffs and Trade, *Annual Report*.

[3] *Symposium über Rohstoffpreise*, Kyklos.

[4] United Nations, *International Compensation for Fluctuations in Commodity Trade*. Report by a Committee of Experts, E/CN. 13/40, New York 1961.

to enlarge without delay its former practices to include a scheme of Compensatory Financing for especially the developing countries. Under this scheme any country that can show cause of a 'temporary export shortfall' of foreign exchange due to 'circumstances largely beyond the control of the member', i.e. a fall in the world market price of its exports, 'can expect' that requests for drawing will be met.[1] The country has thus almost automatically the right to compensation through an addition to its foreign reserves. This drawing is supplementary to any drawings under the 125 per cent quota system, though the latter will be taken into consideration. The point of such assistance is that the individual country should not suffer for developments beyond its control and above all that its own economic development should not suffer a setback when the 'fundamental disequilibrium' is not domestic.

In 1963 the export prospects of these African developing countries were fairly good. Trade should be increasing under the influence of the booming economies in the industrialized countries with trade liberalization, especially of tropical products becoming a reality. Moreover, the economic growth being brought about in the developing countries themselves should be a long term support to demand while compensatory finance exists to cushion short term fluctuation. Additionally the developing countries are not merely free to attempt to differentiate their exports (by processing their raw materials or establishing new industries) but are receiving both financial help and technical assistance for this purpose. The formation of Customs Unions[2] among the developing countries themselves should give them larger markets for the manufacturing industries either just established or to be established. To the extent their agricultural production and raw materials are complementary an exchange already here should increase standards of living.

This brief survey of the export position shows what the monetary and financial authorities can do to enhance the export position. The financial authorities should supply the financial means needed for the production, establishment and modernization of export produce. The monetary authorities can see that the credit system supports the new activity. The limits are the issue of credit beyond normal needs so that the internal producer prices of exports—based possibly on an increase in wages—do not increase above those of the country's competitors on world markets.

[1] International Monetary Fund, *Compensatory Financing of Export Fluctuations*, Washington D.C., February 1963, especially pp. 24–5.

[2] The proposal by Pafmecsa to link the eighteen countries along the eastern seaboard of Africa into a Customs Union is an instance of these attempts. The West African countries should also gain by a Customs Union. A shortfall of government revenue—if any—due to such customs unions might be compensated by a turnover tax or more efficient direct personal taxation.

The import problem of the developing countries differs radically from that of the industrialized countries. This is due to the fact that the greater part of each increment in income, whether public or private, tends to be directed towards imported commodities (i.e. the foreign trade multiplier tends towards (1)). The less developed the country, the more this is usually the case. The reasons are several:

(1) Those who obtain higher incomes have a 'westernized' demand pattern acquired either through personal experience abroad or the 'demonstration' effect.

(2) The production of consumer goods for the domestic market is non-existent or insufficient in quantity and/or quality to meet new domestic demand.

(3) Though underemployment of both labour and sometimes raw materials exist, there is no possibility quickly of increasing domestic production. The developing countries have thus a short term problem similar to an industrialized country at a full (or over-full) employment level.

(4) Both capital goods, technical knowledge and sometimes raw materials have all to be imported.

(5) A very substantial part of the equipment needed for the development programmes has to be imported.

The efforts of the developing countries have all been directed towards decreasing the foreign trade multiplier, at least as far as it affects the private person—a necessary policy if there is to be room for substantial imports of capital equipment in the face of limited export possibilities. Two radically different, but complementary, policies are pursued. The attempt is made, on the one hand, to increase the domestic supply of goods demanded and, on the other, to contain domestic effective demand.

The increase of the domestic supply of demanded goods is to be achieved by the establishment, as quickly as possible, of domestic industries and services.[1] This policy has as subsidiary objects an increase in employment, the creation of a training ground for domestic entrepreneurs and technicians of various kinds, and the search for suitable export industries (e.g. the shoe industry in Tunisia). Even when such industry is established with assistance from foreign firms and technicians securing the quality of the goods

[1] As Albert O. Hirschman has pointed out in *The Strategy of Economic Development*, loc. cit., p. 120, the presence of imports is an excellent substitute for market research as they indicate existing demand. When calculating possible demand, the height of import duties has to be allowed for as potential demand at market prices may be considerably higher.

in question may be difficult. However, these quality differences are often grossly exaggerated as it is considered smart to buy foreign. Responsible ministers will, at least in public, make a point of demanding nationally produced consumer goods and also try to counteract the demonstration effect by living without some of the more expensive imported goods—air conditioners being a case in point.

Whatever the difficulties, the establishment of really profitable industries for the domestic market is a viable policy. Those who have become disenchanted have either seen a high cost, inefficient, badly selected and subsidized domestic industry created at all and any cost without any pressure being applied to increase efficiency; or they have witnessed the obvious, that, when one industry is established, the new demand engendered is immediately directed towards yet new imported goods.[1] Such an outcome can be partly avoided by a more balanced establishment of several well selected industries and by the control of effective demand.

One of the basic elements in the containment of effective demand is the maintenance of existing wage and salary scales unless a true increase in productivity comes about. The new employment of large numbers of persons, that should be the effect of the successful completion of the development plans, will already considerably increase the country's wage bill. So will the employment of increasing numbers of trained persons, persons who are still now acquiring specialized skills. This increase in the wage bill will, however, probably be less orientated towards imported goods, than would the same increase in the wage bill due to an increase in wages and salaries of already employed persons. In order to be able to maintain present wage and salary scales, the authorities have to maintain the stability of the domestic price level.

The other elements in the containment of effective demand have already been discussed and need be only mentioned. Suitable direct and indirect taxation and a wise handling of the credit system,with the use of all the tools necessary for the actual situation in a given country.

The African countries under discussion have supplemented these measures by both import controls and foreign exchange restrictions. Both are supposed to assist in the conservation of precious foreign exchange.[2] At best these controls are in force to 'have in reserve' if

[1] There are certainly some countries, but not under discussion, where comparative costs are such that they would probably do better to promote an export product (e.g. petrol) instead of diverting resources to the domestic production of commodities they can buy more cheaply on the world market.

[2] Both these controls are unfortunately sometimes used to serve specialized interests. Experience has shown that when such controls are administered by the central bank, abuses of all kinds are reduced to a minimum.

needed. Open general licences are then given freely for all normal trade. The countries which practise such a policy of free trade and payments have usually found that they really can control the demand for foreign goods by a combination of import duties and credit measures. Where this is not the case, there is usually undue secondary monetary demand in the country, emanating from overall budget deficits covered by credit creation either at commercial or central bank level. It is in such a situation that foreign exchange restrictions and import controls are thought to be 'needed'.

It is very doubtful if these controls accomplish their purpose. Their administration is difficult and their economic effects are far reaching. 'Any exchange control administration will, and does, find itself constantly bedevilled by the ingenuity of people in avoiding its administration.'[1] This leads to both favouritism (corruption) and to persons taking advantage of the premium price of restricted imports. To minimize frictions and bottlenecks, the exchange and import control authorities have to collaborate with other top-level officials who may not appreciate the situation of the country. The controls are hard to keep flexible because of lack of knowledge of the current situation. Though they can be altered by decree, the time taken for them to be effective is much longer than generally believed and they tend to build up commercial arrears, since previously assumed commitments exceeded the availability of foreign exchange.

The economic effects of controls almost invariably mean increased, not decreased, inflationary pressure.[2] This is due to the restrictions on especially consumer goods which are considered luxuries, in favour of 'essential' foodstuffs, raw materials and capital equipment. The price increasing effect of the (relative) void on the domestic markets becomes all the more marked the more severe the restrictions are. The resulting inflation, even a 'moderate' one, affects the distribution of income, decreases the propensity to save, alters the relative profitability of enterprises towards short term activity—thus decreasing potential economic growth—and generally tends to undermine the value—the internal and external value—of the currency. Over-valuation of a currency on international markets restricts export possibilities. This can lead to complicated systems of multiple exchange rates, which in reality are partial devaluations and normally lead to outright devaluation.

[1] Irving S. Friedman, Director, Exchange Restrictions Department, International Monetary Fund, *Foreign Exchange Control and the Evolution of the International Payments System.* Mimeographed English translation of Spanish text, August 1958, pp. 22–33.

[2] Foreign exchange restrictions designed to prevent the export of capital, which then lies fallow, will have a deflationary effect by merely increasing the liquidity in the country. A typical example was Morocco.

No such serious results of import control and foreign exchange restrictions have arisen in the countries under discussion. Most countries try to use as far as possible open general licences in combination with the control of credit. Slight inflationary pressures due to import restrictions are, however, ascertainable, but the fact that import prices of especially consumer goods have been stable or falling during the last two or three years has helped to minimize the pressures. On two occasions, however, the full gamut of exchange restrictions and import controls has been put into operation, namely in the Sudan 1957–59 and in Ghana 1961–62.

The full story of the Sudanese experience has still to be written. The essential facts were, however, described in the chapter on the Evolution of Monetary Policy.[1] The combination of all the corrective measures taken plus the luck of the movements in cotton prices[2] rapidly restored domestic equilibrium. Of strategic importance was the control of domestic demand, both private, through restrictions on credit, and public, by moderation in government finance. Thus the undue domestic monetary demand, which, having no other outlet, had spilled over onto the balance of trade, was eliminated. The growth of the national income was halted for one year, but the basis had been established for subsequent rapid growth.

It is still too early to know whether the introduction in Ghana in 1961–62 of import controls and foreign exchange restrictions will lead to similar gratifying results. It is evident that they have succeeded in reducing the deficit of the balance of trade from £G27·5 million in 1961 to £G2·1 million in 1962.[3] During the first six months of 1962 the retail price index for Accra rose from 125 to 130 (1954 = 100). The increase in prices is due to the increase in the money supply of 7 per cent. (The 'budgetary measures' of the previous year, 1961, had already had their effect in the autumn of 1961.) The latter increased both because of the 'new method' of financing the cocoa crop (i.e. internally) and because of government borrowing, especially through the sale of Treasury Bills, to the Bank of Ghana. 'Since the money was put back into the economy, the effect was also inflationary.'[4] The overall deficit on the budget was £G46·7 million in 1961–62. The deficit has been financed by the issue of Treasury Bills amounting to £G38·2 million by the end of 1962. The foreign exchange reserves had decreased by some £G50 million in two years, compared to £G28 million in the previous five

[1] Cp. p. 246.

[2] Since the introduction of compensatory financing the negative effects of this fortuitous element have been eliminated.

[3] Barclays Bank DCO, *Overseas Review*, 1963, p. 165.

[4] Bank of Ghana, *Quarterly Economic Bulletin*, June 1962, p. 20.

years, 1955–60. In August 1962, Ghana drew £G5 million ($14·2 million) from the International Monetary Fund corresponding to the gold tranche.[1]

The enlargement of the money supply cannot be effectively reduced but the economy of the country could be brought into balance in order to prevent a further deterioration of the internal value of the currency and a further loss of foreign exchange. The strategic factor is a balanced overall budget. Then no new creation for government account should be necessary and the funding of the Treasury Bill float would reduce the potentially dangerous liquidity. Such a policy seems to be necessary if the foreign capital component of the new and large development plan is to be secured.

* * *

These two African examples of balance of payments difficulties stress the central position of monetary and financial policy. In a situation where the supply of goods and services cannot quickly be increased and demand is brisk, the sum total of all transactions between residents and non-residents is the result of monetary and financial considerations.

The central position is undoubtedly that of the relationship between the central bank and the government. If the latter understands the points at issue it will not put the central bank under pressure to supply it with credit to permit a budget deficit. Should the government attempt the pressure, the central bank should ideally be in a strong enough position to refuse. Regulations concerning the amount of credit that can be advanced to the government and those pertaining to the creation of a fiduciary issue can here be of great moral support. A 'happy marriage' between the monetary and financial authorities, based on mutual consultation, should, however, eliminate the cause for discord.

The developing countries can, however, increase the goods and services at their disposal by securing foreign loans and grants whether public or private. By being the means of obtaining the desired capital goods and equipment, they leave the foreign reserves of the country free to assure the supply of consumer and other goods on the domestic market. Suitable taxation and credit measures will ensure that the demand does not become unlimited. Balance on the domestic market between effective demand and the supply of demanded goods and services will maintain the internal and external value of the currency. Obtaining foreign loans and grants should then not be too difficult.

[1] Such a drawing is almost automatic and does not commit the drawing country to internal measures.

The developing countries need not have balance of payments problems. They may, however, have balance of payments deficits. These are innocuous when they are covered ahead of time by foreign loans and grants. The foreign exchange effects of world market price falls of exports can be compensated. The monetary and financial authorities have the responsibility and the means for preventing domestic disequilibrium. Thereby they assure the solid foundation needed for growth and development.

APPENDIX I

MAIN CLAUSE OF THE STATUTORY OBLIGATIONS OF THE CENTRAL BANKS

Ghana: Ordinance No. 34 *of* 1957, *Art.* 5

The principal objects of the Bank shall be to issue and redeem bank notes and coin; to keep and use reserves and to influence the credit situations with a view to maintaining monetary stability in Ghana and the external value of the Ghana pound; and to act as banker and financial adviser to the Government.

Morocco: Dahir No. 1–59–233, *Art.* 5 *al.* 2 *of* 1959

1. La Banque du Maroc exerce le privilège d'émission de la monnaie.

2. Dans l'exercice de ce privilège, la banque s'efforce de contribuer, dans les limites de ses attributions et en accord avec la politique économique et financière arrêtée par le Gouvernement à:

—stabiliser la monnaie et assurer sa convertibilité;
—développer et régulariser le marché monétaire et le marché financier en relation avec les besoins de l'économie nationale;
—étendre les possibilités d'emploi et stimuler l'essor du revenu national.

Nigeria: Ordinance No. 24 *of* 1958, *Art.* 4

The principal objects of the Bank shall be to issue legal tender currency in Nigeria, to maintain external reserves in order to safeguard the international value of that currency, to promote monetary stability and a sound financial structure in Nigeria and to act as banker and financial adviser to the Federal Government.

Sudan: Act No. 60, 1959, *Art.* 5

The principal objects of the Bank shall be to regulate the issue of notes and coins, to assist in the development and maintenance of a sound monetary, credit and banking system in the Sudan, with a view to the orderly and balanced economic development of the country and the external stability of the currency, and to serve as banker and financial adviser to the government.

Tunisia: Loi No. 58–90, *Titre II, Art.* 34 *al* 3 (not as clearly as in the other Central Bank laws).

1. La Banque Centrale prête son appui à la politique économique de l'Etat.
2. Elle peut proposer au Gouvernement toute mesure qui, de l'avis du Gouverneur ou du Conseil, est de nature à exercer une action favorable sur la balance des comptes, le mouvement des prix, la situation des finances publiques et, d'une manière générale, le développement de l'économie nationale.
3. Elle informe le Président de la République de tout fait qui, de l'avis du Gouverneur ou du Conseil, peut porter atteinte à la stabilité monétaire.
4. Elle peut demander aux établissements bancaires de lui fournir toutes statistiques et informations qu'elle juge utiles pour connaître l'évolution du crédit et de la conjoncture économique. Elle est chargée notamment d'assurer à son siège la centralisation des risques bancaires.

APPENDIX II

AN AFRICAN VIEW ON COMMERCIAL BANKING

The following extracts from the *Official Report of Parliamentary Debates*, Ghana, Wednesday, August 24, 1960, give an African view of the problems that are encountered by modern commercial banking in Africa. While the complaints and criticisms made are found in a multitude of variants by persons of every type and kind, there is no other equally authoritative source. Conditions and practices are described which are found more or less marked throughout the continent and especially the ambivalent attitude towards banking (based on misunderstanding) and its relation to usury comes out clearly. Thus indirectly an explanation is given why not only sometimes the statutes but often also the policy of African commercial banks is far less liberal than in financially mature countries. Many of the conditions and attitudes are already out-dated in certain sectors of the communities, while individuals everywhere have a very nice appreciation of the possibilities and duties of borrower and lender within a modern banking community.

The original text has been edited; personalities and specific local references have been omitted so as to obtain as generally valid a picture as possible.

PRIVATE MEMBERS' MOTIONS

THE GHANA COMMERCIAL BANK

Mr C. C. K. Baah (*CPP—Eastern Gomoa*)*:* I beg to move, that the conditions upon which the Ghana Commercial Bank grants loans and overdrafts should be made less restrictive.

A commercial bank grants loans to and provides a means of payment by the transfer of deposits from one account to another by the people living in the same country. *Its most distinctive and significant feature is its power to create credit facilities by lending sums of money larger than those which have been deposited.* These functions are common to all fully developed commercial banks.

. . . The Ordinance under which they operate was indisputably prepared by British experts.

. . The result is that the loans and overdraft procedure of the Ghana Commercial Bank is so absolutely bad that it defeats the purpose and principle of international banking which, among other things, is the deposit of funds by the peoples of a country for the use and improvement of the economy of that country and its peoples. Instead of loans and overdraft facilities being decided upon by the Board of Directors on the recommendations after investigations or survey of the administrative officers, who know the value, turnover and a customer's ability to repay loans and overdrafts earlier granted him, this is not done. The Board of Directors refuse to grant these facilities when customers have been duly recommended; they rather approve of loans to people who do not even have a current account nor do they intend to operate any with the Bank.

As regards the Board of Directors, we all know that some of them are big business men as naturally they should be, and we do not envy them; we have no quarrel with them. But when they so perform or execute their duties as to show beyond all doubt that they intend to stifle the efforts of young businessmen and so avoid any competition with their businesses by flagrant refusal to renew overdraft and loan facilities with which these enterprising young businessmen run their promising businesses, then there is cause for alarm. . . .

The most alarming side of it all is that overdraft and loan facilities are denied to good customers of the Bank because these Managing Directors are themselves money lenders. Once they deny you and it is essential you must have money to run your business, you are compelled to go to them. The Mortgage and Loans scheme of the Bank has therefore suffered tremendously because of the inefficient way in which this vital *economic strategic* function of the Bank is operated. . . .

Not very long ago, a gold and ornaments loans scheme under which customers could be granted loans and overdraft facilities with gold ornaments as securities was instituted. But as a result of the restrictive policies of the Bank, this scheme has proved a complete failure. The Board of Directors, instead of the administrative officers of the Bank, have taken complete control over the grant of loans and overdraft facilities, which is contrary to the principles of international banking.

I have the true facts of certain things going on in the Ghana Commercial Bank which in the course of my speech I will reveal. How many Ghanaians have got enough buildings to guarantee every customer of the Bank who requires an overdraft or loan? Very few indeed! Yet the Board of Directors always insist on one getting an immovable property to secure a loan or overdraft irrespective of the amount involved, all because of the restrictions imposed by the Ordinance. When one goes abroad one can see that a daily-rated employee or salary earner who has got a bank account, *has only to get a guarantee from his employer*, and he is given a loan or overdraft. But in the Ghana Commercial Bank when a customer wants about £G20 loan or overdraft for a period of one month, the Bank will request him to bring not a gold ornament, but somebody who has a building to guarantee him.

I feel that this backward method of granting loans should not prevail in Ghana. I feel also that the procedure for granting loans and overdrafts is always determined by the confidence and trust placed in the clients in respect of their daily and monthly business turnover, but not by relationship as is at present the case in the Ghana Commercial Bank. . . .

The Bank is operated under such a restricted policy that within the last few years the complete failure of the loans and mortgages sections have been a total liability to the people of this country. Now, I think it will not sound strange to say that the Guarantee Corporation which our government, with their good intentions and good policies, established to help the people of this country to become richer and to strengthen our economy, has become a complete failure. Why should this be so? It is because loans granted to businessmen are required to be repaid within a very short period. I suggest therefore that they should be given longer periods in which to repay such loans.

If the Loans Section of the Ghana Commercial Bank grants a person a loan, say on the 10th of August they will require the first repayment instalment to be made on the 10th of the following month, and such deductions from his account are made accordingly. Even a moneylender who gives a loan to a poor man, will give him some time to repay. If the Bank gives a loan of £G2,000 to a businessman, an amount which is about one-fifth of the Bank's £G10,000 building, it will be expected of him to pay back over a period of three months. Now, suppose the businessman engages in a small scale industry which normally will take some time, say six months before yielding any profits, how can he be expected to meet the first instalment when it becomes due? This is highly impossible. The businessman will default and may ultimately go bankrupt. But whose fault is it that he defaults in the first place? It is not his fault; he defaults because of the principles of the Ordinance.

The Bank is more prepared to give loans to foreign firms than it is prepared to give loans to Ghanaians. How many Ghanaians have not lost their property through auction sales by the Ghana Commercial Bank? In fact, the Ghana Commercial Bank must change its attitude in granting loans to Ghanaians. Before the establishment of the Ghana Commercial Bank, Ghanaians had been taking loans from foreign banks such as the Barclays Bank and the Bank of West

Africa Ltd., and yet they had not lost their property as a result of these loans. But our Bank which should help us as far as loans are concerned, is now depriving people of their property. Whither are we drifting? Whenever one takes up a daily newspaper, 'sale of property by auction by the Ghana Commercial Bank' very often forms the leading article. Is the Ghana Commercial Bank out to help the people or to ruin them?

We all know that the Ghana Commercial Bank is not a charitable institution. But the conditions which this Bank attaches to the granting of loans constitute a hardship to the people and must be changed for the better. At present, when a man, desirous of establishing an industry or a business which may start production in five years' time mortgages his house for a loan or overdraft, the Ghana Commercial Bank requires him to start paying the loan just a month after the loan has been granted. If the man is given say £G3,000 he is asked to pay £G90 a month, and this should start from the month immediately after the grant of the loan; and when he fails to do so the Bank sells his house by auction. As it is, the Bank expects a person who is establishing an industry to build the necessary offices and workshops and have all necessary machinery assembled and start producing within a period of one month! . . . How can this be possible? Whilst the Ghana Commercial Bank expects the customers to start paying their loans almost immediately after the loan has been given, other banks in the country afford such facilities as enable the customers to pay their loans conveniently. In other countries customers start paying their loans only when their business starts full production. But our own Bank will not give such a facility to its customers. How many Members of Parliament have ever been granted say £G20 loan by the Ghana Commercial Bank to meet their rent if ever they have applied to the Bank? I am sure the Bank will not grant an MP even £G20 until and unless he mortgages his house to the Bank. But the expatriate Banks, such as the Barclays Bank, and Bank of West Africa Ltd., do give loans to Ghanaians on very easy terms and conditions. . . .

One other thing which I should like to bring to the notice of the people of this country is that we have got so many restrictions in our foreign policy. When one wants to transfer money to Russia one has got to fill in Form E.1—Exchange Control Form. But when one wants to transfer money to Great Britain no such restrictions are imposed. Can the Minister tell us how much money is transferred to Great Britain every year? If we do not take care we will be sitting in this House and one day this country will be declared bankrupt. All foreign firms have easy facilities for transferring money from this country, especially the Syrians and the Lebanese, and in my own personal opinion much money is going out of this country and it is high time our progressive government tightened the policy of transferring money out of this country.

We want money for our development. There was a hue and cry in this House when our progressive Minister of Finance brought in an amendment to introduce a Savings Bank in the Ghana Commercial Bank. There had been no Savings Bank in the Ghana Commercial Bank and it is only recently that one has been instituted, whereas other Banks have their Savings Departments. With the facilities which the Ghana Commercial Bank has got, the people of this country are saving their money in other Banks which transfer their money to other countries and they charge interest at the rate of 6 per cent whereas our own Bank gives out loans at the rate of 4 per cent or 3 per cent and then when we want money to put up industries ourselves we are told to go outside this country and borrow money.

Prince Yao Boateng (*CPP—Kpandu South*)*:* I beg to second the motion, that the conditions upon which the Ghana Commercial Bank grants loans and overdrafts should be made less restrictive. The Motion is very elastic and I am sure that all Members in this House will support it.

. . . I think there is one fact which should never be overlooked by Members of this House. That fact is that when Syrians and expatriates come to Ghana some of them come with less than £G50 but within a few months or years they are able to own big property here. Why? The reason is that the other banks give them overdrafts and other facilities which are never, never given to Ghanaians by the Ghana Commercial Bank. The aborigines, the people to whom this country belongs, are denied these facilities.

I now come to loans. When the Ghana Commercial Bank, the bank created and financed by Ghana, wants to give a loan to a businessman it does so on mortgage. If one owns a property which is worth about £10,000 one is given a loan on mortgage of that property to the tune of only £3,000, and one is required to repay this loan within a period of three years. But this is not so with the other Banks where a person is required to repay his loan, on mortgage of his property, within a period of seven years and he is given a six months' period of grace before starting to repay. It is therefore strange that in our own Ghana Bank we are denied this facility. . . .

I come to the Guarantee Corporation. This Corporation gives loans to Ghanaians, but if one has an amount of £200 one is given six shares and that means one will be given a loan to the amount of £600 to do business and one is required to repay this loan of £600 with interest within a period of six months. I ask, how on earth can one do business with £600 and make enough profit on it to enable one to pay back this loan to the Bank within this specified period of six months? The other Banks do not do that. In fact, this Guarantee Corporation has ruined a lot of Ghanaian businessmen and it is no wonder that we read in the newspapers nowadays that such and such property is to be sold by auction at Koforidua and so on and so forth. This is very bad and I say that our people are not being properly treated by our own Bank.

Let me turn to another point. A poor civil servant who earns about £680 per annum and, with apologies to you, Mr Speaker, even some of our Ministers who are supposed to be first-class gentlemen—everybody—are in one way or other in debt. The position is this. A civil servant who earns about £680 per annum, because of our family system, is burdened with many financial responsibilities. Sometimes a member of his family dies suddenly and he is asked to shoulder unforeseen financial responsibilities. Now this fellow instead of going to a moneylender—and Mr Speaker, you know how these moneylenders fleece their customers— . . .

I am merely proving my case, Sir. If for instance, a civil servant or any other person goes to a money lender to raise a loan of about £50 or £60, he will be asked to pay this amount, together with an interest of about £25 or £30 within three or four months. When this civil servant turns to our Ghana Commercial Bank for a loan or an overdraft of £G100, he will be given this amount to be paid in only six months. On the other hand, when this civil servant goes to the other Banks, namely, the Barclays Bank or Bank of West Africa, he is given wonderful facilities for repayment. He is given twelve months or twenty-four months within which the loan should be paid by monthly instalments. This affords him ample relief. But in our own Commercial Bank such facilities do not exist. Our Commercial Bank does not expand its activities. We therefore want it to expand its activities to places like Koforidua, Ho, Hohoe and others. In Swedru, for instance, we have the other Banks namely the Barclays Bank and the Bank of West Africa operating successfully. But one would ask: What is wrong with our own Commercial Bank? . . .

But, and a very big but it is, the way in which part of this Bank's work is carried on leaves much to be desired, especially when one is reminded that the aim of banking is primarily to provide means of encouraging the business of a country to be carried on satisfactorily. When we go to the Ghana Commercial Bank for an overdraft of between £G3,000 and £G5,000 to be repaid on or during completion of a contract, we are asked to repay such sums within six months. Sir, fancy the Bank asking a contractor who will take two years to complete some constructional work which he has undertaken on contract to repay a loan of one-third the contract price within six months when half of the work might not have been completed. Where is the contractor to get the money with which to repay such a loan within so short a time? This is rather difficult for the contractors and other businessmen, and I strongly appeal to the Minister responsible to recommend that the time limit for repayment of loans granted by the Ghana Commercial Bank be reasonably extended to enable hard working contractors and all who get loans to repay them conveniently.

Again, the system or procedure by which a person is asked to produce his income tax returns or repay what he already owes the Bank even though the grant of further loan or overdraft will enable such a person to get more valuable contract to enable him to repay everything he owes the Bank, must be changed. I say so because it often involves the contractors in preparation of turnover and income tax returns which take from three to four months and sometimes longer periods, during which part of the loan would have been repaid had it been granted earlier. . . .

Mr Ocansey: Thank you, Sir. The two British Banks—Bank of West Africa and Barclays Bank—have been in this country for well over thirty-five years, and they have helped African businessmen quite a lot in this country [Some hon. Members: 'Are you winding up?'] No, I am expressing my disagreement with some of the contributions made earlier. . . .

Mr C. E. Nimo (CPP—Akim Abuakwa North): In the colonial days the only Bank which was in existence was the Bank of West Africa and this was instituted in order to assist the Association of West African Merchants as well as European traders in this country. During those days there were few African traders and as the Africans began to realize the importance of banking they began to enjoy its facilities. . . . When the Africans found that they were not being treated fairly they approached the Colonial Bank, now Barclays Bank, to come to their aid. Today while I feel proud to say that Ghanaians have got their own national bank I regret to hear that the Bank is not offering the facilities we expected.

If in those days, the Barclays Bank helped Africans, why is it that our own national bank should not give facilities to African traders. We all support this Motion and we hope, if there have been some irregularities in this connection, that there will be a probe or enquiry into them so as to bring about fairness to traders and to all other people who enjoy banking facilities.

Mr S. G. Antor (UP—Kpandu North): . . . Although I am not endeavouring to hold brief for whoever the Acting Managing

Director of the Ghana Commercial Bank is, I wish to say briefly that before the Bank of Ghana or the Ghana Commercial Bank was established, the two Banks that have been mentioned—Bank of West Africa and Barclays Bank—had existed in this country and functioned to the benefit of the people for a very long time. Besides, since the Ghana Bank was established, and hon. Members will agree with me, we have never had a single Ghanaian to hold a responsible post in this new Bank. We went out of Ghana to bring in experts with experience to run our Bank for us. . . .

I think the actual problem is having more money in circulation in the country, more money for the workers, more money for the farmers and more money for the small businessmen. That is the problem and therefore what the mover of the Motion should concentrate on is probably to ask the Minister to request the Cabinet to make more money available to businessmen. The Government should also make use of money to import into the country machinery for our development work so that we may no more see what is going on on the Tema road where a thousand men are working on one water pipe. If there is sufficient machinery suitable for that job one machine could do it in less time than is taken by a thousand men. . . .

Minister of Works and Housing (*Mr E. K. Bensah*)*:* On a point of order. May I correct what the hon. Member just said, Sir. He said that on the Tema road a thousand men are working on one pipe. That is not correct. The Water Supply Division of my Ministry are now laying a pipe to connect Accra to Tema and the work is progressing so satisfactorily that they will complete it before the time scheduled. A thousand men are not working on the pipe as he says. He has not got the facts . . .

Mr Antor: . . . In any case, I am saying that the Motion now before the House, so far as the mover is concerned, demands . . . the expansion of the activities of the Bank, which is just one institution. Nobody prevents the Bank from opening more than one branch in Accra, or in the whole country if the Bank think it fit. If the Bank have enough money, if they know business and they want to compete with other Banks in the country, it is their duty—the duty of the management—to realize that in order to succeed they must open more branches in the country. If they think that by opening more branches they will incur a deficit and they therefore want to confine themselves to Accra, that is their own business. The other Banks which are really business-minded are opening branches all over the country, and as the mover says he is an executive member of the

Chamber of Commerce, he should use his executive position to induce the Bank to open more branches in Accra and in the country as a whole in order to increase the Bank's activities. If he does so the Bank will probably tell him the reasons why they have so far been unable to open more branches in Accra and in the country. They know their financial position; they have their experts whose extensive banking experience was known to the authorities before they brought them here to help us. If we have efficient men here to run . . .

Mr J. E. Appiah (*UP—Atwima-Amansie*): . . . I should like to start by saying, Sir, that I am quite satisfied, quite convinced, that the two so-called expatriate—word I hate—Banks like to see real competition in the banking world of Ghana. I am fortified in the belief by the simple knowledge that they believe in the capitalistic system and also the fact that they know, that under capitalism competition is the essence of life. And therefore when we make these suggestions, we make them because by getting the Ghana Commercial Bank to behave truthfully and properly as a fully-fledged Bank, they will give competition and thus lend flavour to the banking affairs of our country. It is in that spirit, that spirit of competition and free enterprise, that we offer such advice.

The first point is, it may be asked, why so many of us do not want to see the Ghana Commercial Bank at all; why so many Ghanaians do not even bother to pay their deposits into that Bank. The reasons are not far to find. The first one is this, that in any banking system, one of the things that a customer wants is the positive assurance that on no account and under no circumstances will his deposit be known to any outsider; and reasons for that, Sir, are not difficult to contemplate.

If Jack Johnson knows that Tom Brown has an account of £G20,000 or £G10,000 in the Bank and calls on him for financial assistance and he does not give it, he becomes an enemy; because he can no longer tell him, I am broke; for if he did, Jack would have found out before coming to him that he was not broke at all, but for reasons best known to himself he would not want to part with a penny to Jack Johnson. What is even more dangerous, is that we are in a country where inheritance is based on something very *huhudious*. The knowledge of one's accounts by one's nephew or relation may prompt a young man who is anxious to enjoy life to find means to bring one to one's untimely grave.

It is therefore most important that these things should be kept secret. I am not at all happy about the state of affairs of the Ghana Commercial Bank, because, Sir, it is unfortunately a well known fact now—and this must be said if it is to be rectified—that certain persons are in the habit of giving out these secrets to those who make enquiries, a thing which the two expatriate Banks will never do; and I can site the Barclays Bank particularly with whom I deal. The Manager of that Bank would have his head cut rather than to submit to any inquisitorial demand upon my financial position, as far as what is in the Bank is concerned, anyway. I think we can say the same thing for the Bank of West Africa Ltd. These Banks have enjoyed their position because in the course or the passage of the years Ghanaians and other Africans who have dealt with them have come to rely upon them in this matter of secrecy. And as I have said, in business one has to earn one's reputation and the Ghana Commercial Bank seems not to have learnt this.

Then there is the other thing. People who are supposed to be officers of the Bank sometimes enter into collusion with outsiders and make it possible for signatures to be forged and people's money extracted from the Bank when it should be clear as daylight to these officers that the signatures are fraudulent. I see some Members shaking their heads. [*Interruption*]—If the hon. Members will think seriously they will see what I mean. . . .

I will therefore suggest, in the first place, that a Staff Training School should be set up immediately. The Bank, I am sure, could ask the expatriate Banks to lend their lecturers in their Banks to advise and instruct the junior staff of the Ghana Commercial Bank who will be attending this junior staff school. It is important that this step be taken as quickly as possible if the Ghana Commercial Bank is to work on accepted principles.

. . Then, there is another little point. It has been complained to me, and that is why I make bold to say it. When people go to the Ghana Commercial Bank to ask for loans, sometimes instead of telling them whether they are prepared to give them the loans or not, the poor persons seeking the loans are called aside and told that they should go and see a Mr Jack Johnson who lives at Bukom Square or, in the case of Kumasi, Mr Jack Robinson who lives in Ashanti Newtown, whereas the Bank official who is giving this advice knows that this man is a moneylender who charges exorbitant rates of interest, sometimes 50 per cent or even 100 per cent and it seems that these bank officials are aiding and abetting usury, which is a thing that is not permitted by our laws. And if a person paid by the state uses his agents and his means of employment to aid crime then that is a sad state of affairs. . . .

There is the limit of £G5,000 overdraft for corporate bodies. That also I understand is a bye-law of the Ghana Commercial Bank. There is always some motive in making bye-laws, and I daresay that when that bye-law was made that was the time that by and large the average man in Ghana could not be expected to go to the

Bank and ask for a loan of more than £G5,000. But times have changed and people are becoming more and more enterprising, whether they be corporate bodies or not. Even individuals these days are so enterprising that an overdraft of £G10,000 or even £G20,000 is not too much to them. In the light of changing circumstances of our economic growth, the time has come when the Bank should do something about that also. In other words the £G5,000 maximum should be raised to the neighbourhood of £G10,000 or £G20,000. Because any man of little practical experience knows that in order to catch fish one needs fish, and the bigger the fish one puts on the bait the bigger the fish one catches.

It is no use at all trying to preach to the people of this country to help industrialize our country; to help themselves by coming together into corporate bodies; to undertake the number of things that hitherto had been undertaken by our friends from overseas when in truth and in fact those facilities do not exist for them to expand. And the sad thing is this. Again, I am told, reliably told, that while it is always very difficult for citizens of this country, whatever their political complexion, to get overdrafts or loans from the Ghana Commercial Bank, other persons find it very easy to get overdrafts or loans from the Bank which is supposed to belong to the people of this country. Therefore I think that the situation ought to be examined and rectified.

. . . The Ghana Commercial Bank is entirely our own and therefore as the Member for Kpandu North has said, all the cobwebs should be removed from within and without the Ghana Commercial Bank so as to give the young men in that Bank a chance and encouragement. I think some of them ought to be sent to Barclays Bank in England and Westminster Bank, where they have a school for training their staff, and I am sure that these two Banks will be only too delighted to have the opportunity of training our young men so that when they come back they can engage in healthy competition, which is the spice of economic life.

Minister Responsible for Finance (*Mr F. K. D. Goka*): In going through the Motion which reads that the conditions upon which the Ghana Commercial Bank grants loans and overdrafts should be made less restrictive, I have noticed with grave concern during the debate, that some serious allegations have been made against some employees of the Bank of Ghana or the Ghana Commercial Bank. And I must say right away that if it is true that these employees of the Bank have indulged in these practices, then they are very bad employees indeed. I say this because when Mr Eggleston was asked to establish this Bank, it was his aim and policy to establish this Bank on a very firm basis and to train Ghanaians to take over from him.

And if today after all his efforts he is to learn in England or wherever he may be, the good foundation he has laid is now in ruins, I think he will be very sorry indeed. Therefore if it is true that these employees have acted and are acting in this way, then they should be dealt with accordingly.

We all know the principles on which a Bank is run, and I am very grateful to the hon. Member for Atwima Amansie (Mr Appiah) for the tribute he has paid to the expatriate Banks which have served this country so nicely until recently when our own Bank was established, and still continue to serve us so well. I think we owe them a great debt of gratitude and we wish them to continue in that wise way.

Although the finance or capital used for the establishment of the Ghana Commercial Bank came from the government, we must know that the Bank is a trading concern which must look for profits, and therefore it must be guided by principles and policies laid down by the Board. I say this because in the course of his Motion, the hon. Member for Eastern Gomoa (Mr Baah) said that the Acting Managing Director of the Bank was operating to the letter of the Ordinance that established the Bank. If in fact, the Acting Managing Director is acting in consonance with and strictly to the letter of the Ordinance, I think he is doing his work properly. But on the other hand, if he is overstepping the bounds of the Ordinance then of course he is deviating.

If there is something wrong in that Ordinance, as pointed out by the hon. Member for Atwima Amansie (Mr Appiah) then there is room for an amendment. Therefore I for one will welcome the suggestion that it is high time that some of the clauses in the Ordinance are amended, and I can assure hon. Members that I will go through it and see that something is done in that direction.

While going into the principles of banking we must also think of the conditions imposed on the granting of overdrafts. In granting overdrafts the Bank should safeguard its financial stability; it should see that its money is not thrown away to people who are not creditworthy, so that in the long run the Bank goes bankrupt. I make mention of this point because the seconder of this Motion touched upon the Guarantee Corporation.

We all know that some of the conditions under which these loans were granted by this Corporation were really bad—they are not favourable. But on the other hand, we must think the other way round. Even if you are asked to pay back your loans within a period of six months, why can you not at least pay part of it, if you cannot repay the whole. Unfortunately, some of those people who were granted loans by the Ghana Commercial Bank refused to pay anything at all.

An hon. Member: Is that true?
Some hon. Members: It is true!

Mr Goka: The Commercial Bank, not being a charitable institution, should take appropriate measures to recover those amounts. And so we must rather advise those people that if they take loans from the Bank, they must go back and pay. That is one thing we have to note. I myself have secured some people in the Bank, and they refused to pay back the money, and therefore the Bank has had to deduct those amounts from my salary. So we must think of these anomalies and appreciate the fact that if the Bank refuses you such facilities, it is not the fault of the Bank. It is your duty, when you take these overdrafts to repay them; but it is rather unfortunate that this Bank, being a new institution, is not being treated fairly, because most of the amounts it gave out are now irrecoverable. So I am appealing to those who go in for loans and overdrafts to see to it that if they cannot pay the whole, they should at least pay part of it.

The hon. Member for Atwima Amansie (Mr J. E. Appiah) made a very serious allegation which I think should be probed because if it is true I do not think we are safe. If it is known that our secrets in the Bank are being sold out to people, then of course people will lose faith in the Bank. I would therefore assure the hon. Member that I will go into this matter personally and see that these wrongs are righted. [*Hear, hear.*]

Now back to the question about the staff school.

. . . It was only yesterday when I approved of the appointment of one Ghanaian as Deputy Director of the Bank; and it was only last week when the Osagyefo approved of the appointment of another Director in the Bank. I can assure hon. Members that the Africanization or the Ghanaianization of the Ghana Commercial Bank is receiving the attention of the government, and we shall see to it that everything is done as speedily as possible. Once again, I wish to assure hon. Members that the question of the Staff School will be looked into, and of course with the availability of funds, we are going to do our best, because only the best is good for Ghana, and in that light we shall see to it that the Ghana Commercial Bank is run to the advantage of the Ghanaian. [*Hear, hear.*]

Mr Baah: . . . I should like to remind the Minister that the Ghana Commercial Bank has never been lenient with customers who obtain loans from the Bank because when a customer is granted an overdraft spread over six months and he defaults in paying any instalment his property is sold readily. I am therefore appealing to the

Minister to consider extending the time of repayment of loans and overdrafts.

Question put and agreed to.

Resolved:

That the conditions upon which the Ghana Commercial Bank grants loans and overdrafts should be made less restrictive.

APPENDIX III

CONTRIBUTIONS BY MANAGEMENT TO LABOUR PRODUCTIVITY[1]

The contribution that can be made by management to labour productivity cannot be underestimated. This has been proved by comparisons between the industries and enterprises that have good, bad and indifferent labour policies.

The main problem that management has to contend with is that the labour force is usually not merely untrained but that it is largely composed of first generation industrial workers.[2] The individual worker is not only not integrated in the production process but has to become integrated into the whole context of a modern economy. He needs more help to overcome resistances and difficulties than does an unskilled worker in Europe and America. The African factory manager has thus not merely to increase the *capacity* of work of the individual worker but to face the greater problem of his adjustment to a changing society. He needs, however, to pay less attention, as yet, to incentives to increase the *willingness* to work—most workers are only too grateful to have a job.[3] (This does not mean that below standard treatment may not hamper productivity or lead to a large —and unprofitable—turnover in the labour force.) If attention is paid to these problems, not only is there usually a market short term improvement in productivity but the second and third generations show surprising adaptability.

The measures that have so far proved most efficient at increasing productivity per worker are the following:

[1] Part of the primary research for this note was done by Elyseo J. Taylor, then a staff member of the Basle Centre. It is based on investigations made in Ghana and Nigeria in the summer of 1960.

[2] This is confirmed by other observers. 'It is certainly true that an untrained labour force is likely to perform incomparably better in machine-paced operations, not so much because of a tendency towards slacking when the machine does not compel the work as because machine-paced operations provide for steadiness of pace and regular brief rest periods which the inexperienced self-paced worker has difficulty in observing.' A. O. Hirschmann, 'Investment Policy and Dualism in Underdeveloped Countries', *American Economic Review*, Vol. XLVII, September 1957, No. 3, p. 563.

[3] For definition of terminology and general evolution of productivity incentives see P. Florence Sargant, 'Past and Present Incentive Study' in *Productivity and Economic Incentives*, London, 1958, pp. 17–37.

(1) Special attention has been given to the training of individual workers and the man who does well is given a cash bonus usually paid out immediately.

(2) The health of the workers is given special attention in a variety of ways:[1]

(*a*) Routine medical checks and other measures of preventive medicine (inoculations, free distribution of anti-malaria pills, etc.).

(*b*) By making available a canteen where native food is served at reasonable prices, but where there is control on the nutritional value of the food, protein, vitamin, etc.

(*c*) In some few cases the enterprises have social workers, who check and control the health conditions of the workers' families and who give particular attention to adjustment problems of the family and especially of the women who have just come in from the bush.

(*d*) In at least one case an enterprise supplied skilled workers with motorized bicycles. The firm in question was really trying to get to the root of an evil. Public transport facilities are usually so deficient that workers may have to walk two to three hours to reach their place of work. Evidently with a four to six hours march a day their efficiency on the job is reduced.

(3) The way the management of an industry can greatly contribute to the productivity of the worker is *by placing the individual worker where he is most suited.* A first generation industrial worker can often learn one job and at the moving-band will keep up with its rhythm. His productivity will be satisfactory even in a non air-conditioned factory. But as soon as it comes to piece work this same man's productivity will decline. For instance, he cannot understand why a lorry should be loaded at a given rate. A third generation worker, however, would probably do the latter job extremely well because he is already adapted to the requirements of a modern factory.

There seems to be no reason to believe that the inhabitants of any of the developing countries are unable to meet the technical requirements of a modern economy. In spite of all the disappointments, a genial entrepreneur can always be found who has managed to adapt techniques in such a way that the first and second generation workers be educated so that by the time you come to the third generation many of these problems have been solved.

[1] In as much as these measures contribute directly to the productivity of the individual firm the relatively minor costs involved should be carried by the firm itself.

The fourth point on which an enterprise can contribute to increase its own productivity of labour is by trying to maintain a *stable corps of workmen* over time, if possible over the generations. This can be done by offering training and, in some cases, even scholarships to the sons of the workmen. Such an attitude to labour solves both a short and long term problem. The short term problem is that of migrating labour forces so common in practically all developing countries. The development of the industrial estate is a definite step forward, also from the point of view of the labour force.[1] The reasons for this stress on a permanent labour force are too many to go into here; but except in the case of plantation work of a strictly seasonal nature and with the same workers returning year after year, a migrant labour force requires continuous retraining. The social and other advantages of having learnt a skill are then sacrificed for a short term and costly cash income.[2]

The labour unions in developing countries unfortunately do not pay sufficient attention to the factors that will increase the productivity of labour. The reasons are numerous. Labour unions are young, they often think in terms of an ideal of socialism, of fair deals for everybody without realizing that these require an effort. The most serious effect of labour unions policy is, probably, their dislike of (important) wage differentials for skilled, semi-skilled and unskilled workers, whereas one of the most effective means of obtaining sufficient skilled workers is to allow a substantial differential in rates of pay for skilled as opposed to unskilled workers.

By and large it must be assumed that in practically all developing countries there is no 'reservoir' of skilled man power. This means that a new enterprise starting up must almost invariably envisage training its own workers. So great is the lack of skilled workers, foremen and the very large number of technologists of various kinds needed by a modern economy that this is the real bottleneck to all development plans.

In view of the lack of skilled workers it is not surprising that government after government has founded not merely technical high schools but technical training centres of various kinds, instituted apprenticeship training and on the job training. Progress is being made but it is a slow process and meets with a degree of, shall we call it, sociological resistance. The head of the technical college of Khartoum when asked how many of the students entering were prepared to take courses for electricians, plumbers, foremen, etc., admitted, with a wry smile, that he had no applicants for these

[1] UN, *Establishment of Industrial Estates in Underdeveloped Countries*, No. 60, II B. 4, New York, 1961.

[2] See also William J. Barber, loc. cit., p. 196.

courses; everybody wanted to be an engineer. And this is unfortunately typical.

This type of problem ought in time to be overcome as professions fill up; unemployment within the branch in question will rise and/or the economic return fall. Eventually this should encourage people to enter other professions and trades. However, thc sociological resistance is probably greater in the developing countries than it is in Europe or America because of the (imagined) loss of cast or face involved. And sociological valuations have not changed fast enough to adapt to the demands of a modern economy.[1]

Most new enterprises outside construction usually must count on training their own people. This not only applies to private enterprise but to the development plans of the governments themselves. The educational system should ideally produce the skilled workers, technicians, etc., that are needed and it is in fact possible to make reasonably accurate forecasts of the number and type of skilled personnel that will be needed five, seven or ten years hence. When an industry is planned the type of machinery is known ahead and the amount and type of labour can be estimated. These manpower requirements have been made for whole countries or for special branches. It has almost invariably been found that there is no prospect of being able to fill the ranks because on some or all points teachers and schooling facilities are in short supply, and overall requirements have to be scaled down either by decreasing the speed of development or by training senior men in personnel handling and in how to supervise and delegate. This can reduce by as much as a third the number of assistants he needs. This lower number of persons required compared to the number that the educational system could be expected to produce showed a much greater concordance between the number of persons who could be trained and those who were likely to be needed.

When considering the problems of skilled labour and its future formation, it must be hoped that the developing countries in general will succeed in keeping a balance between the formation of skilled workers and technicians and the formations of profitable industrial, agricultural and commercial enterprises, which give permanent jobs to their workers—a permanency that the erratic pattern of infrastructure cannot give. Only then can the social equilibrium be maintained which would assure that economic development can take place in a politically reasonably tranquil future—for it would be disastrous to have trained persons facing unnecessary unemployment.

[1] Peter F. M. McLoughlin, 'Economic Development and the Heritage of Slavery in the Sudan Republic', *Africa*, Vol. XXXII, No. 4, October, 1962, pp. 355–91. See especially pp. 376–83 on the cost increasing effect of the employment of labour by the Gezira tenant farmer.

APPENDIX IV

THE 'MONEY SUPPLY'[1]

The current definition of the money supply is that of the International Monetary Fund. It covers notes and coins in the hands of the public plus demand deposits of banks (less inter-bank deposits) and, where necessary, the assets of the postal checking system. It is thus designed to cover all the cash assets of the community while excluding the whole of the 'near money' assets. It is impossible in this article to survey the long discussion as to the appropriateness of this definition for any given country or certain particular groups of countries. It is the definition as it now stands which is under review.

The IMF money-supply definition has certain distinctive features, and chief among its advantages are the following five:

(1) It is conventional.
(2) It is easily assessed statistically.
(3) It corresponds to the money and credit actually used for transactions.
(4) It helps to form a measure for the velocity of circulation.
(5) It fits the Fisher formula.

One major advantage of this definition is the fact that it is conventional and its statistical counterpart can usually be supplied by any country today, and by the financially more mature countries for a considerable period. This makes possible both international and historical comparisons, however tricky and difficult they may be. Naturally, however accurately defined statistically, the 'money supply' may not have the same function in economies as different as those of the United States and Ireland, or of Nigeria and Great Britain. The variations in content are, however, certainly not greater and probably smaller than, say, those of the national income statistics. Moreover, the varying significance of the money supply in different countries should not be unknown to those who habitually use the term. Its relatively high degree of comparability has recently been seen in its unanimous acceptance as one of the items in the classification of financial assets and liabilities in the United Nations System of National Accounts.

The IMF definition has, moreover, the advantage of representing

[1] Erin E. Jucker-Fleetwood, 'The Money Supply . . .', loc. cit., pp. 16–18.

the money (cash and deposits) which is actually *used* for transactions of all kinds. If a bank grants a credit to a firm or individual—i.e. the item 'advances'—this credit is usually used immediately—or within a very short time—by the borrower and then is automatically turned into cash and/or deposits either in his own hands or in those of his former creditors.

The measures taken to control the money supply therefore should be able to regulate the volume of the transactions during any single period—apart from smaller variations caused by changes in the velocity of circulation of money. Thus *effective* demand can be controlled. Naturally if the monetary authorities have allowed large money claims to build up (for instance as a result of wartime liquidity) these can subsequently be drawn upon by the public at large without the sanction of the monetary authorities. Thus time (savings) deposits are often considered a dangerous 'near money' asset; but even when the public wants to mobilize its cash assets quickly (as it did during the Korean crisis) the savings banks can, if they wish, enforce their notification periods, whereas demand deposits, on the other hand, are effectively 'cash'. The argument extended to short term paper and investments will be examined below.

Once the money *actually used* for transactions has been identified, it is possible to use it as the basis for a calculation of the velocity of circulation. While the latter can never be more than a *symptom* of deeper forces at work (such as changes in expectations and behaviour) there is reason to believe that every economy has a 'normal' velocity for each given phase of its growth. Any deviation from this norm will act as a signal that greater changes are pending—just as a change in body temperature is a warning to a doctor without being a cause in itself. Changes in the velocity of circulation may have special relevance for analysis in financially less mature economies.

The money supply, as defined above, is the one which fits the celebrated Fisher formula and links up with the quantity theory of money. The Fisher formula is also known as the equation of exchange and is often written $MV = PT$ where M is the money supply, V the velocity of circulation, P the general level of prices and T the volume of transactions at their original prices.[1] The equation as such is a truism, i.e. it is always correct for any given moment in time. The essential difference between the equation of exchange and the quantity of money is that the latter explains a *causal* relation. For instance, an increase in the money supply through time will cause an increase in the general price level. This is not the place to enter into the involved discussion on the many

[1] The equation appears with many variations, some of which have considerable advantages over this, its simplest expression.

refinements of the quantity theory, or the niceties of its theoretical validity. The fact remains that, although the quantity theory of money may not be the refined analytical instrument many of its devotees have maintained, it has proved a surprisingly useful tool in the analysis of an ailing economy. The variables in the equation, especially money supply, velocity, and prices, are usually quickly available statistically, whereas more refined data are not. They also have the virtue of reflecting *current* behaviour of individuals, which is an important point of departure when seeking to assess their future behaviour.

These five important aspects of the money supply—viewed in accordance with the IMF definition (and its many precursors)—help to explain why it has long held a key position both in the theoretical discussion and in the monetary policy-making of the last fifty years. That its strategic position is now being questioned, especially for the financially more mature countries, is due to many factors, some valid, others based on misconception.

APPENDIX V

INFORMATION REQUIRED BY DEVELOPMENT BANKS

The following schedule is typical of the information required by development banks as the basis of their consideration of an application for financial assistance. It is reproduced here from *ICON—a Key to Development*, by kind permission.

The following are the headings under which the full description of the Project should be supplied.

1. NAME AND ADDRESS OF APPLICANT

Notes:

(*a*) If the contemplated business is to be conducted by a limited company or partnership, state also:—

(i) Name of company or partnership,
(ii) Full details of relationship of applicant to partnership or company (e.g. manager, secretary, partner, director etc.).
(iii) Other members of company or partnership, details of each one's capital participation and names and addresses of all directors (in case of a company).

(*b*) A copy of the Memorandum and Articles of Association should be supplied in the case of a company. If the individual, partnership or company concerned is already conducting a business, audited Balance Sheets and Profit and Loss Accounts of the last five financial years (if available) should be supplied.

2. PROJECT

State whether it is a new installation, or an expansion or improvement of an existing installation. Give a comprehensive description of the existing business (if any) and the business which the projected development is intended to create. Give also an outline of the manufacturing or other process to be carried out. (The form of this outline should be discussed with ICON before it is submitted.)

3. ESTIMATED CAPITAL COST OF PROJECT

This should be given in the form of a table, which should show the full cost of each of the categories mentioned below. If any items are to be purchased abroad, the cost should be divided into two columns, one showing the amount to be spent in Nigeria, the other showing the amount to be spent abroad.

(*a*) Land.

(*b*) Buildings and constructions of all kinds, referring separately to housing (if any), roads and services.

(*c*) Fixed plant and machinery, showing freight to site and cost of erection separately.

(*d*) Moveable plant, tools and equipment.

(*e*) Vehicles.

(*f*) Power plant, electrical installation, other services.

(*g*) Other items to be purchased.

(*h*) Amount required as working capital.

Note:

In appropriate cases, details of some or all of the above items will be needed, as also a plan of the buildings and factory lay-out.

4. PROPOSED CAPITAL STRUCTURE

Details of the way it is intended to obtain the capital (e.g. by issue of shares, loans, overdrafts, etc.), and amounts and sources of funds already promised or to be provided by the applicants.

5. REQUEST FOR ICON'S PARTICIPATION

The amount of finance requested from ICON and its proposed form (e.g. share capital, loan, etc.).

6. MANAGEMENT

Who will supervise the construction of the factory or other unit? Who will manage the business? Who will be in charge of the technical aspects of the business? Give brief details of the previous experience of all such persons.

7. RAW MATERIALS, ETC.

(*a*) List of main raw materials, quantity required per annum and source from which they will be secured. Any contracts made for their procurement should be referred to. State the number of weeks' supply of each material that will normally be held in stock.

(*b*) Fuel and power requirements, and how they will be obtained.

(*c*) Other services required, e.g. water, rail communications, waste disposal etc., and how they will be obtained.

8. LABOUR

Estimated labour requirements, detailing the skilled jobs; availability of the labour required.

9. ECONOMICS OF PROJECT

Describe the economic conditions which indicate the desirability and prospects of the project, e.g. the present Nigerian consumption of similar goods, or the evidence of an unsatisfied demand for them; the reason for believing that their manufacture in the locality chosen is practicable and will provide a satisfactory product at a competitive price; any benefits that the project will confer on the Nigerian economy; the applicant's view on future expansion or probable new lines of business; names and addresses of other firms supplying similar goods in the area of intended sales, with details of their sales, output and production capacity, manufacturers', wholesalers' and retailers' prices (if the goods are imported, the imported price should be given instead of the manufacturer's price).

10. ESTIMATED TRADING RESULTS

(*a*) What will be the daily output of the proposed plant? If the expansion of an existing plant is intended give the daily output at present and/or estimated after the expansion.

(*b*) Give the estimated turnover, operating costs and profits for the first three years of operation, showing depreciation, interest on loans and taxation. (ICON's staff will indicate the degree of detail required in relation to the various elements in the estimates.)

11. GENERAL

Any other relevant information, including degree of Government support for project, pioneer status, customs reliefs, etc.

12. REFERENCES

Names and addresses of persons who will provide references, including at least one Bank, and a firm of auditors.

APPENDIX VI

Table XIX

Total Money Supply and Gross National Product

	*Ghana**		*Morocco†*		*Nigeria‡*		*Rhodesia§*	
	TMS**	GNP	TMS	GNP	TMS	GNP	TMS	GNP
1950					44·8	521·0		
1951			146·7	450	57·6	582·5		
1952			164·8	546	72·5	627·8		
1953			191·2	592	75·9	679·7		
1954			209·2	619	92·4	793·4	98·2	338·3
1955	51·8	333	216·1	623	85·3	850·6	101·5	389·6
1956	54·1	344	176·4	675	93·7	900·9	108·3	435·5
1957	48·3	361	224·2	689	98·7	942·9	107·6	439·9
1958	50·6	383	258·4	851	98·0	971·4	99·2	447·4
1959	57·0	433	246·1	830	116·0	984·7	102·9	508·9
1960	67·1	465	287·0	926	127·9	1017·5	94·7	536·6
1961	91·3	491	306·7	898	128·6		109·1	546·8

SOURCES:

*Ghana:*** The figures of the Economic Survey 1961 (Accra, Ghana, 1962) do not correspond to those of the *International Financial Statistics*. The latter have been used here to obtain a continuous series.

Morocco: *Tableaux Economiques du Maroc*, 1915–59; *Service Centrale de Statistique*, till 1958 the Southern Region only.

Nigeria: P. N. C. Okigbo, *Nigerian National Accounts* 1950–57, Lagos 1962, p. 22 (GNP), and Federation of Nigeria, *Digest of Statistics*.

Rhodesia: *Economic Reports*, 1956–62, Federation of Rhodesia and Nyasaland.

* £G million. † Milliard de francs courants. ‡ £N million. § £R million.

BIBLIOGRAPHY

Achebe, Chinua, *No Longer at Ease*, London, 1960.

Adams, E. Sherman, 'The Problem of Economic Illiteracy', Address given by the Vice-President of The First National City Bank before The Annual Dinner of the Chamber of Commerce, New York, October 9, 1962.

Adomakoh, Albert, 'The Evolution of Currency and Banking in West African' Countries, in *Jahrbücher für Nationalökonomie und Statistik*, Vol. 174, No. 6, 1962, and Basle Centre Publication Series A, No. 42.

Aluko, S. A., 'Decimal Currency for Nigeria', *Morning Post*, January 17, 1962.

American Bankers Association, 'Crop Insurance is Growing Fast', *Banking Journal*, December 1962.

Amogu, Okwara O., *Savings in an African Economy*, University College of the West Indies, Social and Economic Studies, Vol. 5, No. 2, June 1956.

Aukrust, Odd, 'Investeringer og økonomisk vekst', *Forhandlingerne ved det nordiske nationaløkonomiske møde*, København, September 4–6, 1958, Copenhagen, 1959.

Avramovic, D. and Gulhati, R., 'Debt Servicing Problems of Low Income Countries, 1956–58', Baltimore, 1960.

Bagehot, Walter, *Lombard Street*, 14th Edition, London, 1915.

Baldwin, R. E., 'Having regard to the low money incomes of Africans and the scarcity of foreign capital for development purposes, what contribution financial and otherwise can Africans make towards the economic development of their countries?', *Nyasaland Economic Symposium*, July 18–28, 1962.

Balogh, Thomas, 'Structure économique africaine', *Revue Economique*, Vol. XIV, No. 2, March 1963.

Banton, Michael, *West African City*—A Study of Tribal Life in Freetown, Oxford, 1957.

Barber, William T., *The Economy of British Central Africa*, London, 1961.

Barclays Bank, 'New Bank for the Gold Coast', *Barclays Bank Review*, May 1953.

Barclays Bank, 'Central Banking in Africa', *Barclays Bank Review*, May 1958.

Basch, Antonin, *The Future of Foreign Lending for Development*, University of Michigan, 1962.

Bauer, P. T., *West African Trade*, A Study of Competition, Oligopoly and Monopoly in a Changing Economy, Cambridge (England), 1954.

Behrendt, Richard F., 'The Emergence of New Elites and New Political Integration Form and their Influence on Economic Development', *Transactions of the Fifth World Congress of Sociology*, Washington, 1962 (Vol. II).

Bertrand, Pierre, 'Dix années d'économie marocaine, 1945–55', *Insee*, Paris, 1957.

Black, Eugene R., 'Economic Development for the Peoples of Africa', Address delivered at Afrika Institut, The Hague, October 29, 1962.

Bombach, Gottfried, 'Quantitative und monetäre Aspekte des Wirtschaftswachstums', in *Finanz- und währungspolitische Bedingungen stetigen Wirtschaftswachstums*, Schriften des Vereins für Socialpolitik, Bd. 15, 1959, and Basle Centre Publication Series A, No. 24.

Bourguiba, Habib, 'Propos du Président Habib Bourguiba' in *La bataille économique*, April 17, 1956, to February 5, 1960, Tunis, August 1960.

Bovill, E. W., *The Golden Trade of the Moors*, London, 1958.

Brimmer, Andrew F., 'Banking and Finance in the Sudan', *South African Journal of Economics*, Vol. 28, No. 1, March 1960.

Brokensha, David W., *Christianity and Change*, Duquesne University, Pittsburgh, 1961.

Brown, Charles V. (Jr.), 'The Supply of Bank Money in Nigeria', *The Bankers' Magazine*, November/December 1960.

Buchanan, Norman S. and Ellis, H. S., *Approaches to Economic Development*, New York, 1955.

Burkhard-Wuhrmann, W., 'Vom Handel in Uebersee im Strom der Zeit', *Schweizerische Zeitschrift für kaufmännisches Bildungswesen*, Vol. 49, 1955.

Business Week Editorial, 'Cleaning up the Foreign Aid Program', *Business Week*, New York, December 8, 1962.

Cagan, P., 'The Monetary Dynamics of Hyperinflation', Ed. Milton Friedman, *Studies in the Quantity Theory of Money*, Chicago, 1956.

Cairncross, Alexander K., 'The Contribution of Foreign and Domestic Capital to Economic Development' in *Factors in Economic Development*, London, 1962.

Cairncross, Alexander K., 'Monetary Policy in a Mixed Economy', Wicksell Lectures, Stockholm, 1960.

Cameron, I. D. and Cooper, B. K., *The West African Councillor*, Oxford, 1961.

Chakravarty, S., *The Logic of Investment Planning*, Amsterdam, 1959.

Clauson, Sir G. L. M., 'The British Colonial Currency System', *Economic Journal*, 1944.

Cobbold (Lord), 'Some Thoughts on Central Banking', Stamp Memorial Lecture, London, 1962.

Crowder, Michael, *A Short History of Nigeria*, New York, 1962.

Cox-George, N. A., *Finance and Development in West Africa*, The Sierra Leone Experience, London, 1961.

Davey, P. L. P., 'Household Budgets in Rural Areas', *The Economic Bulletin (Ghana)*, Vol. VII, No. 1, 1963.

Davies, Reginald, *The Camel's Back*—Service in the Rural Sudan, London, 1957.

Diamond, William, *Development Banks*, The Economic Development Institute (IBRD), Baltimore, 1957.

Dorrance, Graeme S., 'The Effect of Inflation on Economic Development', *IMF Staff Papers*, Vol. X, No. 1, 1963.

Doxey, G. V., 'Economic Aid in Soviet Foreign Policy', *The Banker*, Vol. CXII, No. 440, October 1962.

Drakatos, C., 'Short Term Fluctuations in the Velocity of Circulation of Money in the UK, 1954–61', *Banker's Magazine*, December 1962.

Dupuy, P. M., 'Le Trésor et la monnaie au Maroc en 1918 et en 1962', *Bulletin Economique et Social du Maroc*, Vol. XXVL, No. 93, August 1962.

Friedman, Irving S., 'Foreign Exchange Control and the Evolution of the International Payments System', Mimeographed English Translation of Spanish Text, Washington, 1958.

Gaitskell, Arthur, *Gezira:* A Story of Development in the Sudan, London, 1959.

Gern, Jean-Pierre, 'Les voies ouvertes à la politique monétaire dans un pays d'Afrique', *Schweizerische Zeitschrift für Volkswirtschaft und Statistik*, No. 1, March 1963, and Basle Centre Publication Series A, No. 44.

Gern, Jean-Pierre, 'Morocco and Tunisia on the Threshold of Monetary Autonomy', *Zeitschrift des Instituts für Weltwirtschaft*, Vol. 90, No. 1, 1963, and Basle Centre Publication Series A, No. 39.

Gill, P. J., 'Future Taxation Policy in an Independent East Africa', *The East African Economics Review*, Vol. 9, No. 1, June 1962.

Golding, P. T. F., 'An Enquiry into Household Expenditure and Consumption and Sale of Household Produce in Ghana', *The Economic Bulletin (Ghana)*, Vol. VI, No. 4, 1962.

Greaves, Ida, 'Colonial Trade and Payments', *Economica*, February/March 1957.

Gregory, Sir Theodor, 'The Present Position of Central Banks', Stamp Memorial Lecture, London, 1955.

Griffith, V. L., *An Experiment in Education*, London, 1953.

Guillaume, Yves, 'Banques de développement', *Bulletin Economique et Social du Maroc*, Vol. XXII, No. 81, 1959.

Guth, Wilfried, *Capital Exports to Less Developed Countries*, Dordrecht, 1963.

Harris, Philip J., *Local Government in Southern Nigeria*, Cambridge (England), 1957.

Hawtrey, R. G., *A Century of Bank Rate*, London, 1938.

Hicks, Ursula, *Development from Below:* Local Government and Finance in Developing Countries of the Commonwealth, Oxford, 1961.

Hill, Polly, *The Gold Coast Farmer*, Oxford, 1956.

Hirschman, A. O., 'Investment Policy and Dualism in Underdeveloped Countries', *American Economic Review*, Vol. XLVII, September 1957.

Hirschman, Albert O., *The Strategy of Economic Development*, Yale, 1958.

Homer, Sidney, *A History of Interest Rates*, New Brunswick (N.J.), 1963.

Hunsworth, John, 'Decimalization for Britain? Case not Proven', *The Banker*, August 1961.

Institute of Social and Economic Research, 'Savings in an African Economy', University College of the West Indies, *Social and Economic Studies*, Vol. 5, No. 2, June 1956.

Jacobsson, Per, Opening Address—Presentation of 16th Annual Report of the International Monetary Fund, 16th Annual Meeting, Vienna, 1961, *Summary Proceedings*, Washington, 1962.

Jacobsson, Per, Opening Address—Presentation of 17th Annual Report of the International Monetary Fund, 17th Annual Meeting, Washington, 1962, *Summary Proceedings*, Washington, 1962.

Jacobsson, Per, *The Market Economy in the World of Today*, Jayne Lectures for 1961, American Philosophical Society, Philadelphia, 1961.

Johnson, Harry G., 'Towards a General Theory of the Balance of Payments' in *International Trade and Economic Growth*, London, 1961.

Jucker-Fleetwood, Erin E., Banks at Universities of Developing Countries, *Schweizerische Zeitschrift für Volkswirtschaft und Statistik*, Vol. 96, No. 2, 1960, and Basle Centre Publication Series A, No. 30.

Jucker-Fleetwood, Erin E., 'Economic and Financial Aspects of the Republic of the Sudan', Basle Centre Publication Series A, No. 35, Translation of articles published in *Neue Zürcher Zeitung*, April 21 and 24, 1961.

Jucker-Fleetwood, Erin E., 'Financial Position and Development Projects in Tunisia', Basle Centre Publication Series A, No. 31, Translation of articles published in *Neue Zürcher Zeitung*, October 22 and 24, 1960.

Jucker-Fleetwood, Erin E., 'Ghana's Budget for 1961–62', Basle Centre Publication Series A, No. 37, Translation of article published in *Neue Zürcher Zeitung*, August 13, 1961.

Jucker-Fleetwood, Erin E., 'Interest Rates, Prices and Relationship between Government Expenditure and Foreign Exchange Reserve', Address delivered before the Economic Society in Accra, June 25, 1961.

Jucker-Fleetwood, Erin E., *The Key Role of the Velocity of Circulation of Money and Credit*, Oxford Economic Papers, October 1958, and Basle Centre Publication Series A, No. 22.

Jucker-Fleetwood, Erin E., 'The Monetary and Financial Position of Ghana and Nigeria', Basle Centre Publication Series A, No. 29, Translation of articles published in *Neue Zürcher Zeitung*, June 27 and 28, 1960.

Jucker-Fleetwood, Erin E., 'The Money Supply in Mature and in Developing Countries', *The Irish Banking Review*, March 1961, and Basle Centre Publication Series A, No. 38.

Jucker-Fleetwood, Erin E., 'Nigeria's Six-year Development Plan', Basle Centre Publication Series A, No. 42, Translation of article published in *Neue Zürcher Zeitung*, August 14, 1962.

Jucker-Fleetwood, Erin E., *Der Radcliffe Report*, Zeitschrift für die gesamte Staatswissenschaft, 116, Bd., 3. Heft, 1960, and Basle Centre Publication Series A, No. 32.

Kaldor, Nicholas, 'Taxation for Economic Development', *The Journal of Modern African Studies*, January 1, 1963.

Kilby, P., 'African Labour Productivity Reconsidered', *Economic Journal*, June 1961.

Kitchen, Helen (Ed.), *The Educated African:* A Country-by-Country Survey of Educational Development in Africa, New York, 1962.

Klein, John J., 'German Money and Prices 1932–44', Ed. Milton Friedman, *Studies in thé Quantity Theory of Money*, Chicago, 1956.

Krotki, Karol, Jozef, *Twenty-one Facts about the Sudanese* (First Population Census of Sudan 1955–56), Salzburg, 1958.

Khruschchev, Nikita, Speech made before the Central Committee of the Communist Party, Moscow, November 24, 1962.

Kubinski, Z. M., *Public Finance for Stability and Growth in an Underdeveloped Export Economy*, Amsterdam, 1961.

Lahaye, Rémy, *Les entreprises publiques au Maroc*, Rabat, 1961.

Lerner, Eugene M., 'Inflation in the Confederacy', Ed. Milton Friedman, *Studies in the Quantity Theory of Money*, Chicago, 1956.

Lewis, William H., 'Islam and Nationalism in Africa', in *The Arab Middle East and Muslim Africa,* Ed. Tibor Kerekes, New York, 1961.

Lohrmann, Hajo, 'Local Finance in Africa', Internal Basle Centre Manuscript, Basle, 1962.

Loynes, J. B., 'Currency Board to Central Bank', *East African Economics Review*, December 1960.

Loynes, J. B., *The West African Currency Board,* 1912–62, London, 1962.

Lüke, Rolf E., *Von der Stabilisierung zur Krise*, Basle Centre Publication Series B, No. 3, Zürich, 1958.

Maddick, Henry, 'Decentralisation in the Sudan II and I', *Journal of Local Administration Overseas*, Vol. 1, No. 2, April 1962.

Marbach, Fritz, *Theorie des Mittelstandes*, Bern, 1942.

Marris, Peter, *Family and Social Change in an African City*, London, 1961.

Mars, J., 'Money, Public Finance and External Payments', in *Mining, Commerce and Finance in Nigeria*, Ed. Margery Perham, London, 1948.

Mars, J., 'The Monetary and Banking System and the Loan Market of Nigeria', in *Mining, Commerce and Finance in Nigeria*, Ed.Margery Perham, London, 1948.

Marshall, Alfred, *The Principles of Economics*, Book IV, 8th Edition, London, 1925.

Marty, André J., *Le Franc Marocain*—Monnaie satellite, Paris, 1957.

McLoughlin, Peter F. M., 'Economic Development and the Heritage of Slavery in the Sudan Republic', *Africa*, Vol. XXXII, No. 4, October 1962.

Miège, J. L., 'Origine et développement de la consommation du thé au Maroc', *Bulletin Economique et Social du Maroc*, Vol. XX, No. 71, January 1957.

Mommsen, E. W., 'Strukturwandlung der europäischen Rohstoffimporte', *Kyklos*, Internationale Zeitschrift für Sozialwissenschaften, Vol. XV, Fasc. 4, 1962.

Neumark, S. Daniel, 'Economic Development and Economic Incentives', *The South African Journal of Economics*, Vol. 26, No. 1, March 1958.

Nevin, Edward, *Capital Funds in Underdeveloped Countries*, London, 1961.

Newlyn, W. T. and Rowan, D. C., *Money and Banking in Colonial Africa*, Oxford, 1954.

Okigbo, P. N. C., *Nigerian National Accounts* 1950–57, Lagos, 1962.

Olakanpo, J. O. W., 'Monetary Management in Dependent Economies', *Economica*, November 1961.

Orewa, G. Oka, 'Taxation in Western Nigeria', *Nigerian Social and Economic Studies*, No. 4, Oxford, 1962.

Pigou, A. C., 'Types of War Inflation', *Economic Journal*, December 1941.

Probst, Frédéric G., 'La Planification au Maroc', Internal Basle Centre Manuscript, Basle, 1962.

Rhodesian Property and Finance, Banking Supplement, *Money Market and Banking in the Federation*, August 1959.

Rivkin, Arnold, 'The Politics of National Building: Problems and Preconditions', *The Journal of International Affairs*, Vol. XVI, No. 2, 1962.

Robertson, Sir Dennis H., *Essays in Monetary Theory*, London, 1940.

Romilly, V. P., 'The Money Market in the Federation of Rhodesia and Nyasaland', *The Bankers' Magazine*, December 1962.

Roosa, Robert, 'Reconciling Internal and External Policies', *Journal of Finance*, Vol. XVIII, March 1962.

Rosenberg, Nathan, 'Capital Formation in Underdeveloped Countries', *The American Economic Review*, Vol. L, No. 4, September 1960.

Salin, Edgar, 'Die neue Etappe der industriellen Revolution' in *Lynkeus*, Tübingen, 1963.

Sargant, Florence P., 'Past and Present Incentive Study', in *Productivity and Economic Incentives*, London, 1958.

Sayers, Richard S., *Central Banking after Bagehot*, Oxford, 1957.

Sayers, Richard S., *Modern Banking*, Oxford, 1951.

Smythe, Hugh H. and Smythe, Mabel M., *The New Nigerian Elite*, Standford, 1960.

Stolper, Wolfgang, 'Comprehensive Development Planning', Economic Commission for Africa Working Party, Addis Ababa, January 15–27, 1962.

Stolper, Wolfgang, *The Structure of the East German Economy*, Harvard, 1960.

Stucken, Rudolf, *Entwicklungsbedingungen und Entwicklungschancen der Republik Sudan*, Berlin, 1963.

Swiss Reinsurance Company, Swiss Insurance Training Centre, General Information and Program for the 1st Course in General Insurance, 1961–62, Zürich, 1961.

Taylor, Elyseo J., 'Entwicklungshilfe vom Standpunkt des Empfängers am Beispiel der Genossenschaften in der Wirtschaftsentwicklung Ghanas', *Schriftenreihe zum Handbuch der Entwicklungshilfe* (Entwicklungshilfe—einmal anders) Heft 10, Baden-Baden, 1963.

Taylor, Elyseo J., 'Les marchés en développement au Mali', *Revue économique et sociale*, No. 11, June 1963, and Basle Centre Publication Series A, No. 45.

Tawney, R. H., *Religion and the Rise of Capitalism*, London, 1926.

Terborgh, George, *The Bogey of Economic Maturity*, Chicago, 1945.

Tricart, Jean, 'Les échanges entre la zone forestière de la Côte d'Ivoire et les savannes soudanaises', *Les cahiers d'outre-mer*, No. 35, July–September 1956.

Trimingham, J. Spencer, *Islam in West Africa*, Oxford, 1959.
Tudeer, A. E., *The Bank of Finland*, 1912–36, Helsingfors, 1940.
Wai, U Tun, 'Taxation Problems and Policies of Underdeveloped Countries', *IMF Staff Papers*, Vol. IX, No. 3, November 1962.
Walker, D., 'In General Terms what is the Taxable Capacity in an Underdeveloped Country', *Nyasaland Economic Symposium*, July 18–28, 1962.
Wanner, Gustav, *Die Basler Handels-Gesellschaft A.G.* 1859–1959, Basel, 1959.
West Africa, 'They Prefer Soft Jobs', *West Africa*, No. 2406, July 13, 1963.
Woods, George D., *Address to the Boards of IFC and IDA*, Washington, September 30, 1963.
Youngson, A. J., *Possibilities of Economic Progress*, Cambridge, 1959.
Zolotas, Xenophon, 'Economic Development and Private Enterprise', *Bank of Greece Papers and Lectures*, No. 10, Athens, 1962.

OFFICIAL AND GOVERNMENT PUBLICATIONS

Ghana

Bank of Ghana, *Ordinance 1957.*
Bank of Ghana, *Act 1961 and Amendment.*
Bank of Ghana, *Quarterly Economic Bulletin.*
Central Bureau of Statistics, *Economic Survey*, Accra.
National Investment Bank of Ghana, *National Investment Bank Bill 1963 and Bye-Laws*, Accra.
Office of the Government Statistician, *Quarterly Digest of Statistics*, Accra.
The Government Printers, *Parliamentary Debate of August 24, 1960*, Accra, 1960.
The Government Printers, *Second Development Plan, 1959–64*, Accra.
Shephard, C. Y., *Report on the Economics of Peasant Agriculture in the Gold Coast*, Government Printer, Accra, 1936.

Morocco

Banque du Maroc, 'Etudes et Statistiques', *Bulletin Mensuel*, Rabat.
Banque du Maroc, *Rapport Annuel*, Rabat.
Banque du Maroc, *Réglementation et organisation de la profession bancaire*, Rabat.
Banque Marocaine du Commerce Extérieur, *Bulletin Mensuel*, Casablanca.
Banque Marocaine du Commerce Extérieur, *Rapport sur le premier exercice social*, Casablanca, 1961.
Banque Nationale pour le Développement Economique, *Statutes et Rapport Annuel*, Rabat.
Ministère de l'Economie Nationale, *Tableaux économiques du Maroc, 1915–59*, Rabat, 1960.

Nigeria

Central Bank of Nigeria, *Annual Report and Statement of Accounts*, Lagos.
Central Bank of Nigeria, *Ordinance and Amendment.*
Federal Government Printer, *Economic Survey*, Lagos.

Federal Office of Statistics, *Digest of Statistics*, Lagos.
Investment Company of Nigeria, *A Key to Development*, Lagos, 1960.
Okotie-Eboh, Chief Festus S., *The Mobilization Budget*, Budget Speech, 1962, Lagos, 1962.
Okotie-Eboh, Chief Festus S., *The Modernisation Budget*, Budget Speech, 1963, Lagos, 1963.

Rhodesia and Nyasaland

Bank of Rhodesia and Nyasaland, *Bank of Rhodesia and Nyasaland Act.*
Bank of Rhodesia and Nyasaland, *Annual Report*, Salisbury.
Central Statistical Office, *Monthly Digest of Statistics*, Salisbury.
Ministry of Economic Affairs, *Economic Report*, Salisbury.

Sudan

Agricultural Bank of Sudan, *A Short Note on the Agricultural Bank of Sudan*, Khartoum, 1960.
Bank of Sudan, *Annual Report*, Khartoum.
Bank of Sudan, *The Currency Act, 1956*, Khartoum.
Bank of Sudan, *Economic and Financial Bulletin*, Khartoum.
Bank of Sudan, Circular letter to banks containing conditions for the discount of bills of exchange or promissory notes and for loans against the collateral of such bills and notes, Khartoum, 1961.
Central Office of Information, *Sudan Almanac*, Khartoum.
Committee appointed by the Minister of Finance and Economics, *Final Report on cotton production costs in the private estates*, Khartoum, 1959.
Ministry of Finance and Economics, *Economic Survey*, Khartoum.
Siemienski, Z., *The Sudan Currency Board*, Ministry of Finance and Economics, Economic Section, Khartoum, 1957.
Sudan Currency Board, *Report*, Khartoum.

Tunisia

Banque Centrale de Tunisie, *Bulletin*, Tunis.
Banque Centrale de Tunisie, *Rapport Annuel*, Tunis.
Direction du Plan, *Bulletin de Statistique et d'Etudes Economiques*, Tunis.
Secrétariat d'Etat au Plan et aux Finances, *Annuaire Statistique*, Tunis.

OTHER COUNTRIES

Banque Centrale des Etats de l'Afrique de l'Ouest, *Rapport d'Activité*, Paris.
Cocoa White Papers, *Report on Cocoa Control in West Africa 1939–43 and Statement on Future Policy*, Cmd. 6554, 1944.
Statement on the Future Marketing of West African Cocoa, Cmd. 6950, 1946.
Comité Monétaire de la Zone Franc, *La Zone Franc*, Paris.
Commission of Inquiry into Banking, Currency and Credit, *Reports*, Stationery Office, Dublin (Ireland), 1938 .
Committee on the Working of the Monetary System, '*Radcliffe*' *Report*, H.M. Stationery Office, London, 1959.

Federal Reserve Bank of New York, 'Creeping Inflation', *Monthly Review*, Vol. 41, No. 6, 1959.

Federal Reserve Bank of New York, 'Inflation and Economic Development', *Monthly Review*, Vol. 41, No. 8, 1959.

Federal Reserve Bank of New York, 'International Development: The New Central Banks', *Monthly Review*, Vol. 42, No. 10, 1960.

Loynes, J. B., Report on the Future of the Currencies of Sierra Leone and the Gambia, The Government Printer, Sierra Leone, 1961.

REPORTS AND PUBLICATIONS OF INTERNATIONAL ORGANIZATIONS

Bank for International Settlements, *Annual Report*, Basle.

F.A.O., *Projet F.A.O. de Développement Méditerranéen*, Rome, 1959.

F.A.O., *Agricultural Credit in Economically Underdeveloped Countries*, Rome, 1959.

F.A.O., *Report of the Working Party on Crop and Livestock Insurance*, Bankok, Tailand, August 27 to September 7, 1956, Rome, 1957.

GATT, *Annual Report*, Geneva.

I.D.A., *Annual Report*, Washington.

International Institute of Differing Civilizations, *Development of a Middle Class in Tropical and Subtropical Countries*, Brussels, 1956.

I.L.O., *African Labour Survey*, Geneva, 1958.

I.L.O., *Expanded Programme of Technical Assistance*, Report to the Government of the Republic of Sudan on a Productivity Mission (January–April 1959), Geneva, 1960.

International Monetary Fund, 'The Adequacy of Monetary Reserves', *Staff Papers*, Vol. III, No. 2, October 1953.

International Monetary Fund, *Compensatory Financing of Export Fluctuations*, Washington, 1963.

International Monetary Fund, *International Financial Statistics*, Washington.

O.E.C.D., *The Flow of Financial Resources to Countries in the Course of Economic Development in 1960*, Paris, 1962.

United Nations, *Demographic Yearbook*, New York.

United Nations, *Economic Bulletin for Africa*, Addis Ababa.

United Nations, *Economic Survey of Africa since 1950*, New York, 1959.

United Nations, *Enlargement of the Exchange Economy in Tropical Africa*, New York, 1954.

United Nations, *Establishment of Industrial Estates in Underdeveloped Countries*, New York, 1961.

United Nations, *International Compensation for Fluctuations in Commodity Trade* (Report by a Committee of Experts), New York, 1961.

United Nations, *International Flow of Long Term Capital and Official Donations*, 1951–59, New York, 1961.

United Nations, *Statistical Yearbook*, New York.

United Nations, *Structure and Growth of Selected African Economies*, New York, 1958.

INDEX

For Product Safety Concerns and Information please contact our EU
representative GPSR@taylorandfrancis.com
Taylor & Francis Verlag GmbH, Kaufingerstraße 24, 80331 München, Germany

www.ingramcontent.com/pod-product-compliance
Ingram Content Group UK Ltd.
Pitfield, Milton Keynes, MK11 3LW, UK
UKHW022009180926
475701UK00003B/282

* 9 7 8 0 4 1 5 8 4 9 6 1 6 *